PLACING FACES

MANCHESTER
1824
Manchester University Press

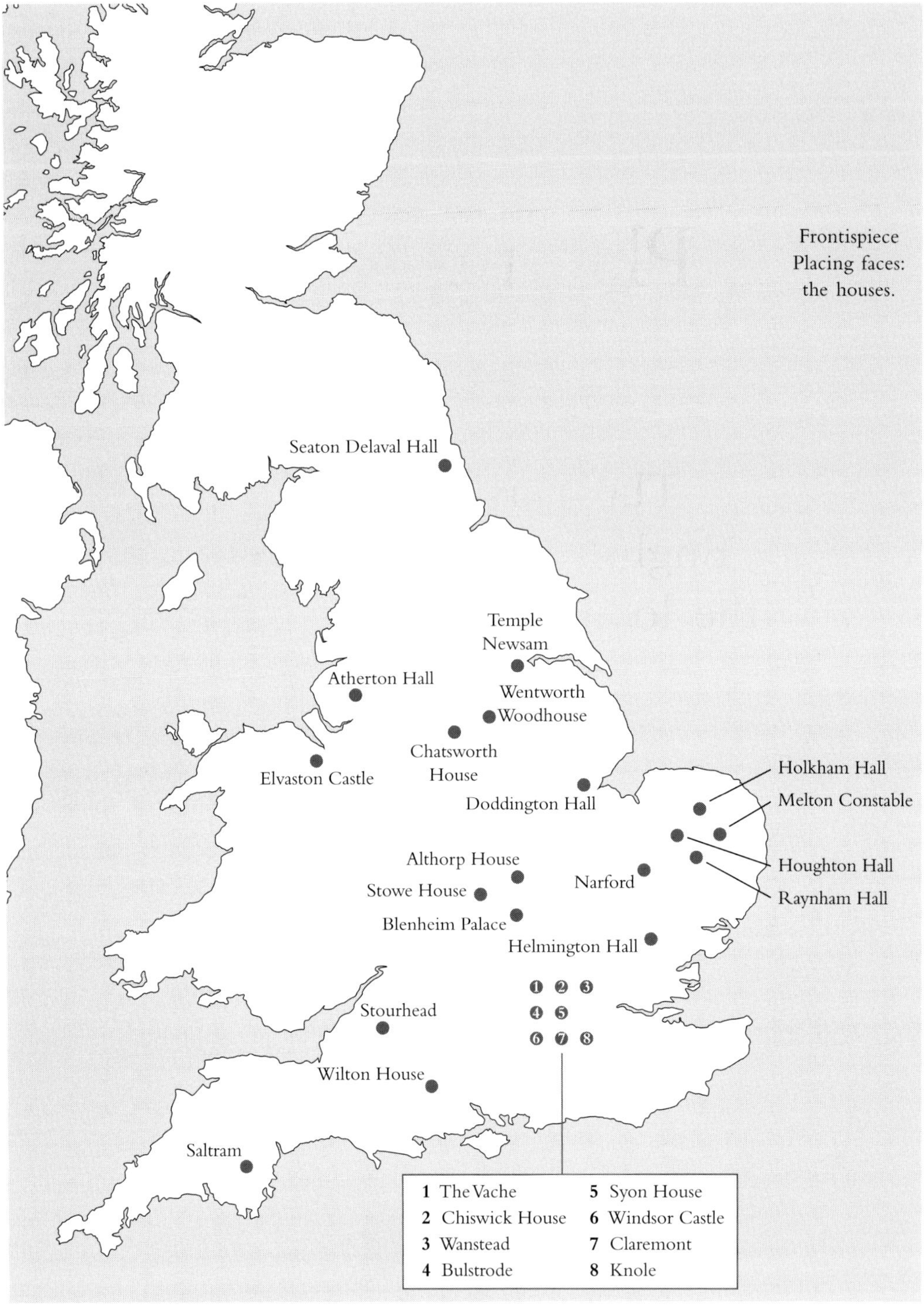

Frontispiece
Placing faces:
the houses.

Placing faces

The portrait and the English country house in the long eighteenth century

EDITED BY GILL PERRY,
KATE RETFORD
AND JORDAN VIBERT,
WITH HANNAH LYONS

Manchester University Press
Manchester and New York

distributed in the USA exclusively by Palgrave Macmillan

Published by Manchester University Press
Oxford Road, Manchester M13 9NR, UK
and Room 400, 175 Fifth Avenue, New York, NY 10010, USA
www.manchesteruniversitypress.co.uk

Distributed in the United States exclusively by
Palgrave Macmillan, 175 Fifth Avenue, New York,
NY 10010, USA

Distributed in Canada exclusively by
UBC Press, University of British Columbia, 2029 West Mall,
Vancouver, BC, Canada V6T 1Z2

British Library Cataloguing-in-Publication Data
A catalogue record for this book is available from the British Library

Library of Congress Cataloging-in-Publication Data applied for

ISBN 978 07190 9039 4 hardback

First published 2013

Typeset in Monotype Bembo
by Carnegie Book Production, Lancaster
Printed in Great Britain
by TJ International Ltd, Padstow

Contents

III Imperial designs

Plates

Plates appear between *pp.* 142 and 143.

Figures

Contributors

Emma Barker is Senior Lecturer in Art History at the Open University. She is the author of *Greuze and the Painting of Sentiment*, 2005, and the editor of *Contemporary Cultures of Display*, 1999, and *Art and Visual Culture 1600–1850*, 2012.

Harriet Guest is Director of the Centre for Eighteenth Century Studies, University of York. Her books include *Empire, Barbarism and Civilisation*, 2007, and forthcoming (2013): *Unbounded Attachment: Sentimental Revolution and Women's Writing from Wollstonecraft to Austen*.

Ruth Kenny is Assistant Curator 1750–1830 at Tate Britain. She completed her PhD on the Irish artist Hugh Douglas Hamilton and is currently undertaking research into the rise of the pastel medium in eighteenth-century England and Ireland.

Hannah Lyons has just completed an MA in Eighteenth Century Studies at York. She has curated her first exhibition, *Views in the Himalayas: The Adventures of James Baillie Fraser*, at the Victoria Gallery & Museum, Liverpool. She currently works at Tate Modern and Tate Britain.

Gill Perry is Professor of Art History at the Open University. She has published widely on eighteenth-century and modern art. Her books include *Femininity and Masculinity in Eighteenth Century Art and Culture* (ed.), 1994; *Gender and Art* (ed.) 1999; *Spectacular Flirtations*, 2007; *The First Actresses*, 2011.

Kate Retford is Senior Lecturer in History of Art at Birkbeck College, University of London. She has published widely on eighteenth-century portraiture and her books include *The Art of Domestic Life*, 2006. She is currently writing a book on the conversation piece.

Desmond Shawe-Taylor has published widely on eighteenth-century portraiture, including his book *The Georgians: Eighteenth-Century Portraiture and Society*, 1990. He was Director of Dulwich Picture Gallery from 1996 until 2005, when he was appointed Surveyor of The Queen's Pictures.

Jordan Vibert has recently completed a PhD at the University of York's Centre for Eighteenth Century Studies. She currently works at Bristol Museum and Art Gallery and M Shed.

Susie West is Lecturer in Art History and Heritage Studies at the Open University. She researches UK heritage practices and the English country house, with particular attention to the history of the private library. Her forthcoming book is titled: *The Country House Library 1660–1830*.

Alison Yarrington is Professor of Art History and Dean of the Faculty of Arts and Social Scences at the University of Hull. She has published widely on the history of sculpture, collecting and collections. She is academic adviser to the Chatsworth Sculpture Gallery redisplay.

Acknowledgements

THE idea for this collection arose from an international conference on the theme of the portrait and the country house organised by Hannah Lyons and Jordan Vibert at the Centre for Eighteenth Century Studies, the University of York. The conference generated a rich cross-disciplinary discussion between academics, researchers, curators and members of the public. Two of the speakers, Gill Perry and Kate Retford, welcomed the opportunity to be part of an editorial board leading on-going conversations and helping to develop the project into this edited collection. The editors sought to expand the research involved, inviting contributors with interests and specialisms across a range of media including painting, sculpture and architecture. *Placing faces* is the outcome of a truly collaborative process of shared research and ideas. The editors would like to thank all the authors for their stimulating and original contributions to this collection.

Many colleagues, archivists, librarians, researchers and institutions have supported, encouraged and enabled the production of this collection. We are indebted to the Centre for Eighteenth Century Studies at York for providing funding and support for the original conference and for encouraging the development of a related publication. There are many individuals who have supported the project and offered advice and research leads. These include: Mark Hallett, John Barrell, Marcia Pointon, Harriet Guest, Alistair Laing, Susan Siegfried, Leslie Johansen and Ruth Larsen. Many other individuals have provided help and information and are acknowledged in endnotes throughout the collection. We are immensely grateful to our two anonymous readers whose insightful and constructive criticism helped to improve our final draft. We would also like to thank the many museum and country house collections, especially the National Trust, and private owners who have kindly supplied images and information.

We could not have produced this illustrated book without generous financial support from the Open University research fund. Special thanks also to the Paul Mellon Centre for Studies in British Art for their generous contribution towards the costs of the colour illustrations. Finally, this publication has benefited hugely from the enthusiasm and support of Emma Brennan, our commissioning editor at Manchester University Press. Her advice and patience have been invaluable.

Spencer family tree, showing their connections with the Churchill and Poyntz families

See Chapter 6

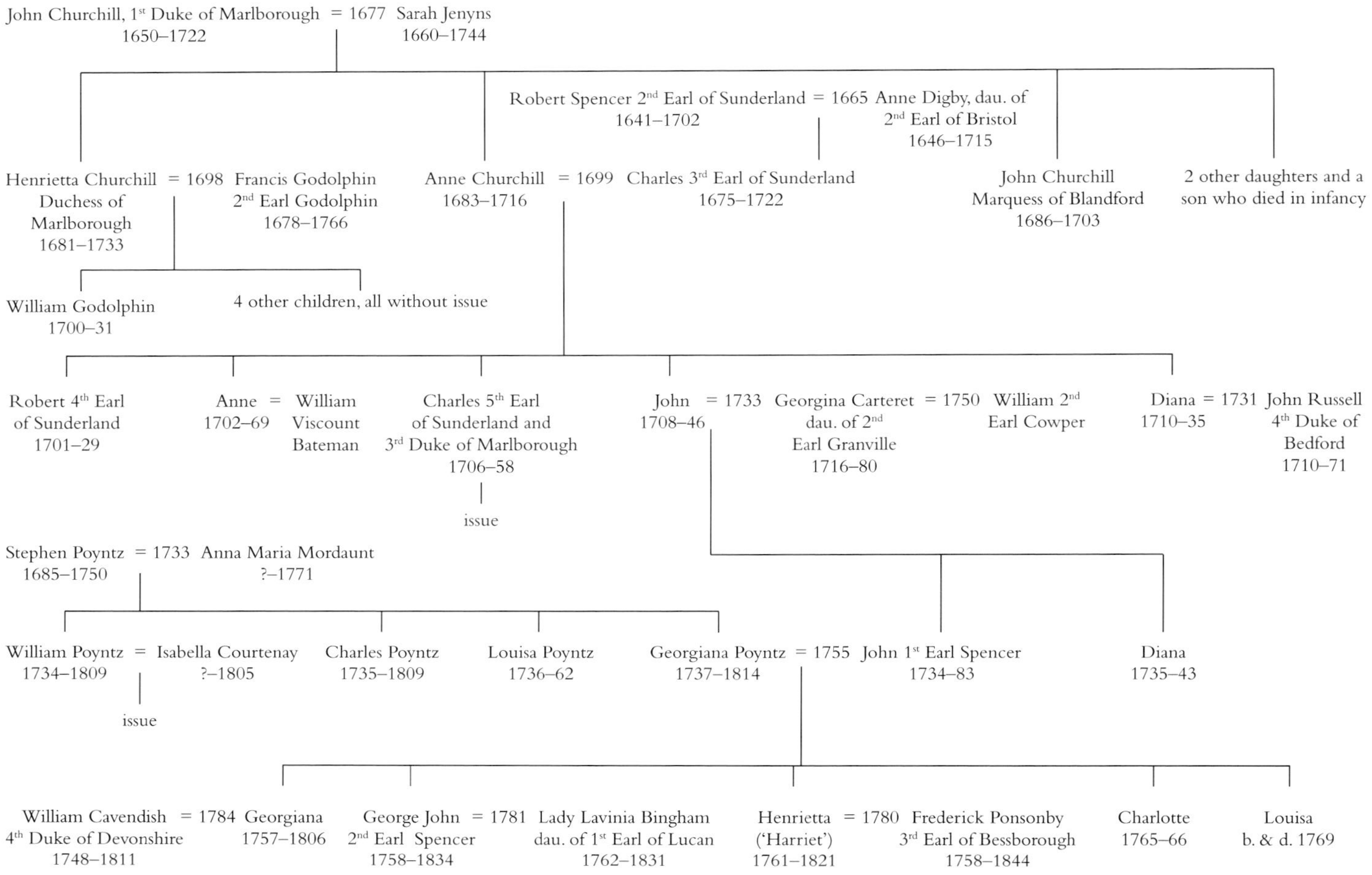

Introduction: placing faces in the country house

Kate Retford, Gill Perry and Jordan Vibert

Placing faces

On 24th September 1776, Samuel Curwen, once a Salem merchant but at this date a loyalist exile in England, arrived at the seat of Henry Hoare (1705–85, usually referred to as Henry II) at Stourhead in Wiltshire. After he and his two companions had refreshed themselves at the inn with 'a cold Collation' and 'a bottle of most excellent cyder', they set off to view the house:

> one passes on a flight of noble steps to the center door letting into the hall, by appearance the common sitting room of the owner, when he makes this house his residence; in this hall hangs a full length picture of Mr. Hoare on horseback drawn in younger days, the face, the drapery and the Horse executed by different hands, as the Housekeeper told yet the lines of different pencils are not to be discerned.[1]

Hoare was, by this date, in his early seventies, but the portrait by Michael Dahl, horse by John Wootton, shows him as a young man just after his father had died (plate 1). At the time of its execution, the sitter had not only just inherited the lucrative family business, Hoare's Bank, but had also recently married Ann, the daughter of Lord Masham.[2] The picture was clearly intended to mark his newfound status. It is a strikingly assertive image, not least in its vast size as the canvas measures roughly three metres square. In his vibrant red waistcoat and blue coat, Hoare appears calm and in control (perhaps to a degree of boredom), even though his large grey-white stallion rears up onto its hind legs. An expanse of landscape illuminated by the glow of a sunset suggests an ample estate, whilst the column to the left conveys a typical hint of status and the country seat. It was quite an image to be greeted with immediately on walking into the house, and Horace Walpole the decade before had been similarly struck: '*In the Hall;* Mr Henry Hoare on a white horse; the horse by Wootton, large as life & good'.[3]

'Mr Henry Hoare' has to be seen 'In the Hall' at Stourhead: face and place are indelibly linked (figure 1). The messages conveyed by a portrait, indeed any image, are clearly affected by (and affect) the location in which it is displayed: by architecture and adjacent décor; by other pictures and surrounding objects. In recent years, a number of historians of eighteenth-century art have explored such issues of context, but predominantly in relation to the public exhibitions which began in London in the 1760s. The seminal show, *Art on the Line*, held at Somerset House in 2001–2, unpicked the viewing conditions experienced in spaces such as the Royal Academy Great Room, and the ways in which exhibits were presented, experienced and received. In the accompanying volume of essays, scholars such as David Solkin, Marcia Pointon and Gill Perry, amongst others, explored the ramifications of this environment for portraiture, viewers participating in a 'convivial activity of identification, recognition, self-recognition, emulation and self-projection': 'Visitors … would have viewed images of public and private figures interactively, matching existing knowledge and hearsay to what they saw on view, speculating about personal histories, and sharing anecdotes.'[4] Portraitists with business sense tapped into this, painting the celebrities of the day. Joshua Reynolds, for example, was quick off the mark when Lawrence Sterne arrived in London in March 1760, flush with the resounding success of the first two volumes of *The Life and Opinions of Tristram Shandy*. Reynolds worked quickly enough not only to bring his portrait of the author in front of a curious public at the Society of Artists' exhibition the following year, but also to ensure that the mezzotint by Edward Fisher could be shown in the same display.[5]

But exhibited portraits were then delivered or restored to their owners, packaged up and sent off to the residence which was to be their ultimate destination.[6] And, crucially, much eighteenth-century portraiture either antedated the advent of exhibitions, or was transferred straight from the studio to the house. In the case of family portraits painted for the gentry and aristocracy, this was almost always the

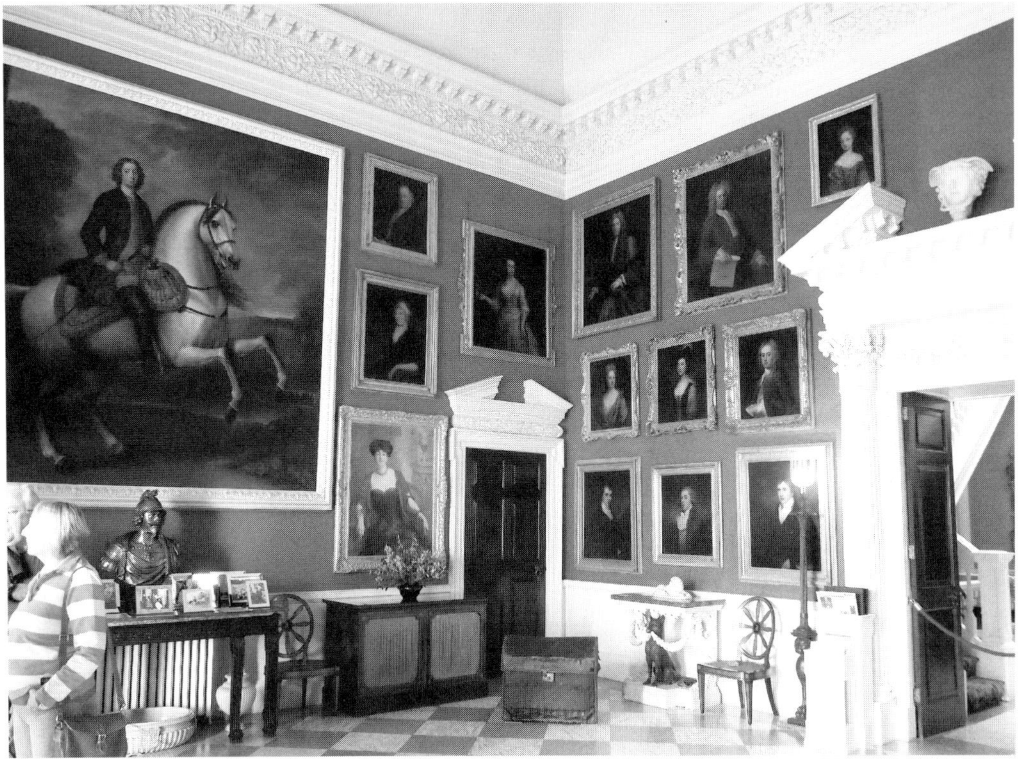

Figure 1 The entrance hall at Stourhead.

country house. You may have displayed your finest old masters in London, but your ancestors were always in the country. As Giles Waterfield has noted: 'The galleries filled with family portraits which Walpole so frequently encountered during his visits to country seats were not found in the capital.'[7] This was partly a matter of pragmatism. A family portrait collection did not have to get very large before it simply wouldn't fit in a town house. But, much more significantly, as is shown again and again in this collection of essays, it was the country house that lay at the heart of an elite family's identity. However much time they spent in London, they would always be 'the Spencers of Althorp' or 'the Herberts of Wilton'. Town houses were often leased, whilst country houses were expressive of permanence, status and inheritance. They were associated with the founders of a family's fortune and status; they were linked to the land and estate which still underpinned economic and political power; and it was there that lineage and succession were most clearly expressed.[8] Arthur Devis's

Robert Gwillym of Atherton and his Family (c.1745–47), on the front cover of this book, shows an owner embedded at the heart of his country estate. Gwillym's directive gesture may be restrained and polite, but it proprietorially takes in his wife and children, his household family as represented by his steward, approaching across the lawn, and, crucially, Atherton Hall in the background.

The country house was not quite a rural equivalent to the exhibitions of the Society of Artists or the Royal Academy, but it is important to note at the outset that, as many of the essays show, these were scarcely 'private' homes. In addition to the presence of extended family members, friends, acquaintances, tenants, business and political associates and the like, there was a fair amount of tourism. Samuel Curwen's perambulation in Wiltshire, trooping around the houses of the great and good, was a pretty characteristic activity for a member of the middling or upper classes at this date.[9] John Britton in 1801 was overdoing it when he claimed that 'People of all ranks visited Stourhead', but such trips were certainly a staple of 'polite' leisure time.[10] Furthermore, whilst the eighteenth century by no means saw the scale of country house visiting to be seen in the Victorian era, there was clearly already an imperative felt by all parties concerned that owners should make their properties and their possessions accessible.[11] The ways and degree to which they did that varied greatly. Letters of introduction were sometimes required, sometimes not (Curwen considers it worth noting that, on reaching the house at Stourhead, his party 'gained an easy admittance'[12]). The largest properties and most important collections had accompanying published catalogues, other houses had a certain amount of information available on site. Many (like Stourhead at the time of Curwen's visit) relied on the knowledge of the housekeeper or other servant who could escort the curious tourist around. Some owners were even considerate enough to ensure that accommodation was available in the vicinity. A nearby inn facilitated visitors to Kedleston Hall in Derbyshire, whilst the Golden Eagle at the entrance to Stourhead's gardens was, as Mrs Lybbe Powys observed; 'built by Mr. Hoare for the company that comes to see his place'.[13]

This, then, is the environment to be explored by the essays in *Placing faces*, concerned with how our understanding of a portrait such as that of Henry Hoare II deepens and changes when we study it within the country house for which it was intended, and in which it was displayed.[14] This volume examines how such an image could contribute to a carefully choreographed display of wealth, power, lineage and/

or political affiliation; how it could function as part of a positioned performance on the part of the owners. We have to take into account the location in which such a portrait was displayed. The function of a room within the overall plan of the house, its relative importance, the degree to which it was accessible to visitors, its décor – all affects the portrait's signification. It might be hung in a grand gallery, one component of a traditional sequence of household heads – or a commemorative eulogy to military heroes, as explored in Desmond Shawe-Taylor's essay 'The Waterloo Chamber before the Battle of Waterloo'. It might take its place in a row above a series of bookcases, as in the library at Narford, the subject of Susie West's chapter, 'Life in the Library', absorbing and feeding into that room's associations with history, scholarship and shared learning. It is highly significant that Hoare's portrait was hung in the entrance hall of his country property, at the very threshold, rather than encountered later on in the house. It was shown in a room intended for the purpose of reception, and was immediately visible to every person who entered. There, it made a bold statement of the family's recently acquired wealth, status and power. The Hoares, significantly, were 'nouveau riche'.[15] Henry's grandfather, Richard, had been the son of a horse-dealer and a goldsmith's apprentice, but he secured the Hoares' subsequent name and fortune when he founded the family business in 1672. Henry's father, Henry I, had used some of their newly acquired wealth to purchase the manor of Stourton, pulling down the extant house and constructing one of the first country villas in the new Palladian style, designed by Colen Campbell. This was just finished by the time of his death, but Henry himself didn't move in until after the death of his mother in 1741. By the time Walpole and Curwen came to peruse the family home, he had added to what was previously a fairly paltry collection to create an impressive display of works of art and, most significantly, had created the famous landscape gardens which still draw thousands of visitors today.

Shearer West has proposed that the country house acts as a frame for the portraits within it, and we also have to consider a portrait alongside the other portraits which accompany it.[16] As is shown so clearly in Susie West's chapter and Alison Yarrington's essay, 'Marble, Memory and Theatre', likenesses were engaged in 'conversations', their various meanings and their significance amplified by and even dependent upon their mutual relationships. Today, Hoare's picture can be seen embedded in a vast display of family portraits which fills the entrance hall at Stourhead, so that one is rather overwhelmed by faces on arriving at the house. Dahl and Wootton's huge canvas dominates the south wall of the room, but it is part of a display hung, in many places, three pictures deep. On the west wall, a portrait by Jonathan Richardson of Richard Hoare as Lord Mayor (1712) begins the visual family tree. The 'founder' is effectively seated back to back with his heir, Henry I, who grasps a paper showing the elevation of the house (Michael Dahl; c.1722). The two wives of Henry II are also present: Susanna Colt, painted by Hans Hysing, at one end of the south wall (1733); Ann Masham by Dahl at the other (c.1726). *Henry Hoare II* needs to be seen in the context of the sitter's linear and nuclear families. In many cases, that is also true of the sitter's extended family. The web of connections visually evident in such a display often extends outwards, as the constant process of intermarriage and complex arrangements of inheritance continually bound families together. A visitor to Blenheim Palace, for example, can see the same Reynolds portrait of George, 4th Duke of Marlborough (1764) as can be viewed in the colonnade room at Wilton, the doubling of the painted likeness expressive of the link between the two families and houses formed by the crucial marriage of the Duke's sister to the 10th Earl of Pembroke. Portrait, house, estate and family work together as a potent entity, and in the case of great houses such as Blenheim and Wilton, as will be discussed in more detail below, their cumulative meaning further extends outside the history of the families concerned to that of the nation. A visitor faced with the likeness of a great military or naval figure would be encouraged to reflect on battles won and lost, whilst the family portraits in the house of a major political dynasty prompted reflection on the sitters' various actions and allegiances.

However, seeing the portrait collection as a complex entity, emphasising the place of Hoare's portrait in that entrance hall display at Stourhead, immediately raises practical issues which have challenged the contributors to this volume. Henry's equestrian portrait may have already functioned as an elaborate nameplate to the house by the time Walpole and Curwen entered the front door, but it was not surrounded by all the family portraits we see today. Inevitably, country house tourists such as these rarely give us complete accounts of what they saw, but the first published catalogue to the house of 1800 tells us that it was, at that date, mostly surrounded by classical landscapes. The only portrait to have joined it was another large canvas depicting Henry's successor and grandson, Sir Richard Colt Hoare, with his own prospective heir.[17] It was Colt Hoare who soon afterwards made the decision to cluster the Hoares' portraits around these two large paintings, which effectively structure the display. He had certainly undertaken his remarkably systematic reorganisation of the pictures in the house by the date of the next edition of the catalogue, 1818, and he explained his rationale in his *History of Modern Wiltshire* of 1822:

> family portraits [are] a very appropriate decoration for the first entrance into a house, as well as for the pannels of a dining-room. They remind us of the genealogy of our families, and recall to our minds the hospitality, & c. of its former inhabits, and on the first entrance of the friend, or stranger, seem to greet them with a SALVE, or welcome.[18]

Colt Hoare makes, here, a number of crucial points. The family portrait collection is a visual family tree, and, indeed, in some houses the visitor would actually be presented with a diagrammatic version in order that each individual likeness might be mentally positioned in his or her correct place in the line. In his account, he regrets that the various sizes of the pictures mean they 'cannot be conveniently placed in chronological order', but rectifies that in his text by structuring the discussion around a clear progression through the generations. He begins with the portrait of Richard Hoare as the 'personage … to whom the present family owes its chief opulence', and then moves on to Henry I and Henry II, noting the presence of the portraits of the latter's wives.[19] Colt Hoare also clearly builds on the external orientation of Henry's grand equestrian portrait, but tempers its rather strident and bombastic message. Multiplying the likenesses, adding quantities of smaller portraits, he creates a sense of sociability and offers a rather friendlier gesture of greeting to the newly arrived visitor.

But Colt Hoare changes the original display. *Henry Hoare II* has to be seen in the context of the portrait collection, of the house and the estate, but, as is shown in many of these essays, those are constantly evolving and developing phenomena. In 'Dirty Dancing at Knole', Gill Perry notes how the new wife of the 3rd Duke of Dorset (understandably) moved the nude statue of his former mistress, the dancer Giovanna Baccelli, by Locatelli out of its prime position at the foot of the Great Staircase at Knole House. Yarrington unpicks the 6th Duke of Devonshire's many rearrangements of his sculpture gallery at Chatsworth, whilst Shawe-Taylor explores the ramifications of various and changing displays of military portraits in the Royal Collection in the early nineteenth century. A visitor to Stourhead today ascends one of two staircases to a freestanding portico constructed in 1838, and not the single large flight to the engaged frontispiece which Curwen would have encountered in the 1770s. The visitor today experiences the portrait in the context of a hang organised by the sitter's grandson, and not that conceived by the sitter himself. Portraits are always being acquired, reorganised within the house – and even reorganised between different houses belonging to a family. Sometimes, they are sold or given away – as in the case of Wanstead, the subject of Kate Retford's essay, 'The Topography of the Conversation Piece', along with the entire collection prior to the house's destruction in 1823. It is only on occasion that a particular hang of interest survives intact, and something of its attendant spatial dynamics and visual effect are fully appreciable. Portraits set in overmantels, or shown in fixed schemes within plaster frames, have often been more resistant to the whims of subsequent owners. This is true of the family portraits by John Verelst at Beningbrough Hall, set into overdoors; the plasterwork frames installed in the parlour at Rousham in the 1760s, to house new and reworked portraits; and the extraordinary series of historical portraits manufactured by Biagio Rebecca for Audley End, incorporated into arched frames within a new decorative scheme the following decade. In such cases, the portraits become part of the very fabric of the house, literally united with the building in conveying the family's history and identity.[20] In such cases, the desire for permanence was fulfilled. In so many other examples, however, extant hangs have to be put next to visitor accounts, catalogues, inventories, sketched records of displays and any other available scraps of material in order to recover any single scheme.

Fixed displays may have been intended as a bulwark against the vagaries of history, and scholars may engage in re-creative research in order to negotiate sales, rehangs, fires and so on, but those processes can sit in tension with the country house's crucial nature as a palimpsest. Both the story of a family and the story of a country house inexorably evolve with the passage of time. That important sense of progress would be evident even in one lifetime, as the portrait of a young boy at the knee of his mother was joined by a Grand Tour portrait of that same sitter, now in his early twenties. Another likeness might be produced, linked to a further key life stage such as inheritance, the building of a new family seat, or the substantial redecoration of an extant property. After all, a portrait has to have somewhere to hang, and the substantial building and rebuilding of houses in the English countryside in this period provides an important backdrop to the essays presented here.[21] A marriage portrait and/or a family group showing the next generation might be further additions.[22] Jonathan Richardson claimed in 1715 that 'In Picture[s] we never … grow older', but the picture *collection* always emphasised the successive life events and stages which rendered that process more than apparent.[23] Interestingly, Colt Hoare's reorganisation of his family portraits at Stourhead was not a solely backward-looking enterprise. He notes in his 1822 account that 'space [in the hall] is left for the *nati natorum*, and for the future possessors of this mansion', and, in the process of excusing the length of his narrative, he evokes his descendants who, he hopes, will benefit from the recorded information: 'We ought to consider ourselves as existing not solely for ourselves, and to bear in mind the *non sibi sed posteris*.'[24]

Any descendant's new addition to a portrait collection would have to take into account that setting and its current occupants.[25] An artist might actually represent that environment within the picture, as in the case of Joseph Nollekens's portrait of the Tylney family at Wanstead (1740). As Retford explores, this shows the sitters within the saloon at Richard Child's palace, and is relatively unusual within the genre of the conversation piece for a detailed accuracy of setting which enables a strong, significant relationship with the fabric and flow of the house and estate. Or, a portrait might have to be painted on a particular scale, as in the case of Reynolds's portrait of Theresa Parker at Saltram House, Devon (1770–72), intended to hang as a pendant to a full length of one of her husband's ancestors. A compositional reference might be made to an earlier work, a motif might be adopted from an important extant portrait in the collection, or an heirloom might be included which had passed though and been pictured by various generations. The same artist might be used: Dahl significantly not only painted Henry Hoare II, but also his father and one of his wives. The sitter might be garbed in Van Dyckian dress, as in the case of the 11th and 12th Dukes of Norfolk painted by Thomas Gainsborough (1783 and c.1788 respectively). The vogue for early seventeenth-century costume in portraiture at this date was to do with a fashionable nostalgia for the Caroline court and its modishness at masquerades, but it also suggested lineage – and here the passage of time between these Dukes of Norfolk and their predecessors at Arundel Castle, painted by the likes of Van Dyck and Mytens, is ellipsed in a vision of continuity.[26] The classical drapery in which so many of Reynolds's female sitters are swathed was about lifting portraiture closer to the hallowed status of history painting, and bestowing an air of dignity and grandeur. But it was also about circumnavigating fashion and custom, again allowing some sense of permanence. Combining this with other techniques, such as use of bitumen to give a warm old masterly glow, Reynolds hoped his portraits would have an effect praised by Fanny Burney at Knole; 'they are so bewitching, and finished in a style of taste, colouring, and expression, so like their companions, that it is not, at first view, easy to distinguish the new from the old'.[27]

Houses, homes and 'mistresses'

Through the combination of imposing architectural context and strategically positioned portraits, country houses could 'bewitch', inform and enthral the visitor, whether an eminent invited guest or an eighteenth-century 'tourist'. These decorated spaces offered up narratives of dynasty, family history and political endeavour that this collection seeks critically to examine. However, the extent to which such houses or so-called 'stately homes' were in fact 'homes' in the modern sense is a question that has informed this study, especially in relation to gender. Evolving definitions of the 'home' – the idea of 'dwelling' and its relationship with the structure of the house – have enriched recent debates within the spheres of cultural geography, architectural and design history, history, literature, anthropology, sociology and philosophy, among others.[28] As a fertile research area that straddles disciplines, the historical idea of the 'home' is of special interest to this collection, contributing to our understanding of the social significance of these imposing country houses and their contents. Influential cultural historians Philippe Ariès and Witold Rybczynski have both charted the evolving concept of the 'home' in Europe from the medieval period to the twentieth century, suggesting that the term was increasingly separated from the word 'house'.[29] While Ariès viewed the home as the setting for an emerging concept of 'privacy' in his ground-breaking (yet controversial) exploration of family life in the eighteenth century, Rybczynski charted the evolution of the idea of 'home' that is (as he argues) enmeshed with developing, and culturally specific, notions of 'comfort', 'domesticity', 'intimacy' and family privacy.[30] He argues for the evolution of an idea of 'comfort' in the 'European consciousness', which in eighteenth-century France revealed the 'extent of the influence of bourgeois values on court life'.[31] But he also suggests that the preference for country houses within upper-class and bourgeois English society resulted in a style of living that was more relaxed than its French counterpart, and that 'eventually produced a different domestic ideal'.[32] These are bold generalisations, drawn from observations about the nature of the British court and aristocracy, and the proliferation of country seats, especially in Georgian England. He argues that, during this period, the English aristocracy were more powerful and more independent from a centralised court than their French counterparts:

> They were landed gentry whose wealth, and whose pride, were their rural properties. There was, then, no equivalent in England to the French courtly style; instead the countryside was held in high regard, and it was not considered provincial to live there. Out of this state of affairs emerged a singular phenomenon, the English country house, which supplemented, if it did not replace, the city as the locus for social life. This prompted the American ambassador to remark: "Scarcely any persons who hold a leading place in the circles of their society live in London. They have *houses* in London in which they stay when Parliament sits, and occasionally visit at other seasons; but their *homes* are in the country."[33]

Such general observations need some critical unpacking, especially in relation to Rybczynski's ideas of increasing domestic intimacy, not to mention the on-going scholarship on the relative importance of 'town houses'.[34] For many scholars of the period, the development of the eighteenth-century 'home' is inseparable from an emerging notion of domesticity, especially within the middle classes.[35] That said, this collection is concerned with the various ways in which the nobility and the upper classes negotiated evolving ideas of domesticity in the organisation, management and decoration of their large country estates. In an attempt to explore and redefine an eighteenth-century concept of 'home' for the elite, some recent research has considered issues of *how*, *when*, and *for whom* such grand houses might have constituted 'homes', and the picture that emerges is inevitably complex and variable. For example, Dana Arnold and Judith S. Lewis have considered the gendered implications of the idea of the 'home' in relation to these country estates and their relationship with the 'town house'.[36] They have both addressed the question of how aristocratic women might have experienced country houses that they first inhabited after marriage, and were often encouraged to leave after the accession of the eldest son. Some recent scholarship has also explored patterns of consumption among upper-class women, revealing a complex picture of women's relationships to the building, design and furnishing of some of these large country houses.[37]

The OED offers a definition of the home dating back to 1460 as 'a place of one's dwelling and nurturing'.[38] More modern notions, like those developed by Rybcznski, have emphasised notions of comfort, privacy and intimacy, that sometimes sit uneasily in relation to eighteenth-century houses in which divisions between public and private spaces are often difficult precisely to identify, not to mention the burgeoning academic discourse on the shifting relationship between the public/private spheres during the period.[39] Amanda Vickery has argued that, despite the claims of writers such as Ariès, 'the elite hostess' of the landed gentry would have engaged in an 'open-handed hospitality [that] was still crucial to the maintenance of social credit and political power'. Such convivial liberality might be seen to be at odds with the theory that the country house became an increasingly inward-looking, private space. She writes, 'the idea that the home was a refuge insulated from the social world is one that would have perplexed the rural gentry in this period'.[40]

The eighteenth-century country house then offers us a rather more complex notion of 'home' or the supposedly 'private' inhabited domain than does the modern middle-class house with its well-established associations with feminine domesticity. Moreover, as we have seen, the 'homes' encompassed within these grand buildings were often culturally and politically enmeshed with their family histories. They were conceived of primarily as 'family homes', as spaces that nurtured dynasties, handed down over generations. Hence, the metonymic concept of the 'family seat'. Chapters in this book reveal how the strategic display of family portraits helped to narrate such dynastic histories. And, as noted above, family portraits were most often displayed in the country home, rather than the town house.[41] In fact one of the definitions of 'home' offered by the OED, dating from 1595, embraces a nationalistic sense of family history: 'One's own country, one's native land: the place where one's ancestors dwelt'.[42] The eighteenth-century notion of 'family' could carry several associations for an aristocrat. As Naomi Tadmor has shown, it could involve both historical and national lineage, and (more modern) kinship.[43] This collection explores the diverse ways in which ideas of lineage, kinship, power and gender relations might be represented through the content and positioning of portraits in the country house.

But lineage was determined, of course, by the male line. Women only rarely inherited the houses in which they were born, and after marriage would usually move to their husband's house or estate. Moreover, the problem of primogeniture and the patriarchal system of inheritance concerned several eighteenth-century writers, among them Fanny Burney. Her novel *Cecilia, or Memoirs of an Heiress*, first published in 1782, presents her eponymous heroine as a kind of pseudo-male; after the deaths of her parents the will according to which she inherits the family estate stipulates that her husband must take her name on marriage.[44] If she, or her husband, refuses these conditions, then she loses her estate. As ancestral achievements and status were associated with the male lineage and title, she is compelled to keep the masculine part of her name. As a woman who inherits – or an heiress, 'she is not seen as an independent person but as a conduit for conveying money from one man's family to another'.[45] Elizabeth Atherton, the wife and mother in Devis's *Robert Gwillym of Atherton and his Family*, was just such a conduit. The clear narrative of patrilineal descent and heritage embedded in the composition of the painting, indicating that Atherton Hall is to pass to the small boy to the right of the image, belies the fact that it was she, a wealthy heiress, who had brought the house and estate into the Gwillym family. Such broken lines and indirect descent did not tend to feature in advertised stories of elite dynasties and their country houses.[46]

Notwithstanding such intractable social conventions and constraints, there is increasing evidence that many upper-class women valued and helped to develop and decorate their country houses, and even formed emotional attachments to them. Enabled by an education in drawing and mathematics, some elite women became involved in the design of their houses.[47] And women's roles as 'mistress' of house and home, and both patron and subject of family portraits, have increasingly intrigued studies of the period.[48] The decorating, planning and collecting skills of elite women such as Louise de Keroualle, Caroline Lennox, Baroness Holland or Theresa Parker are now well documented.[49] Parker, for example, took a leading role in extending the art collection at Saltram; she and her husband John commissioned several family portraits by Reynolds, intended for display in the house.[50] Theresa also bought four works on classical themes by Angelica Kauffman that now hang on the main staircase, but may have originally been intended for the Great Room at Saltram, a relatively 'public' position in the house that would have helped to convey the educated, classical credentials of the family collection. That same acquisition of cultural capital was affirmed through the display of art works collected on the Grand Tour.[51] In 1771 Theresa appealed to her brother Lord Grantham to: 'remember if you meet with anything abroad, of pictures bronzes etc. that is valuable in itself, beautiful and proper for any part of Saltram we depend so much upon your taste and judgement that you must not lose an opportunity of procuring it for us'.[52] Theresa Parker, then, was both the subject of and an active agent in the development of the collection at Saltram. The visibility and tastes of such 'mistresses of the house' offer rich and varied material for further research, as is demonstrated in essays in this collection by Emma Barker, Ruth Kenny, Gill Perry and Jordan Vibert.

While Vickery has questioned the eighteenth-century notion of 'home' as an increasingly private and inward-looking space, Judith S. Lewis has posited the possibility of a nuanced definition of 'home' for aristocratic women in her study of the domestic lives of Sarah Duchess of Marlborough at Blenheim, Frances Viscountess Irwin at Temple Newsam, and Frances, Viscountess Boringdon at Saltram House. Although each of these women formed different relationships with the spaces of their country estates during different historical periods (across the eighteenth century), Lewis argues that there is evidence in each case of 'a spirit of domesticity' and attempts to incorporate into these buildings *both* grand display and sites of family intimacy.[53] The history of Sarah Duchess of Marlborough is, perhaps, among the best documented of these aristocratic lives, especially after she married John Churchill in 1678, and helped to oversee (and often to challenge) Sir John Vanbrugh's plans for a grandiose, baroque monument to the Duke of Marlborough, largely bank-rolled by Queen Anne.[54] Blenheim Palace was begun in 1705 and completion continued after the Duke's death in 1722, under Sarah's management (figure 2). In fact after the Duke had suffered a stroke in 1716, she had already taken control of the project, fallen out with Vanbrugh and fired him. According to reports, she was in constant dispute with the architect, as 'where he wanted to create a national monument, she wanted a grand but comfortable home'.[55] The Duchess of Marlborough was famously ambivalent about Blenheim, and although she played a key role in the decoration, furnishing and selection of art works for the palace, she also directed the building of two other, less grandiose homes for the Marlborough family. Firstly, she managed the building of Marlborough House in Pall Mall, commenced in 1709, and her home when she died in 1744. In 1732–33 she also directed the building of her own country villa at

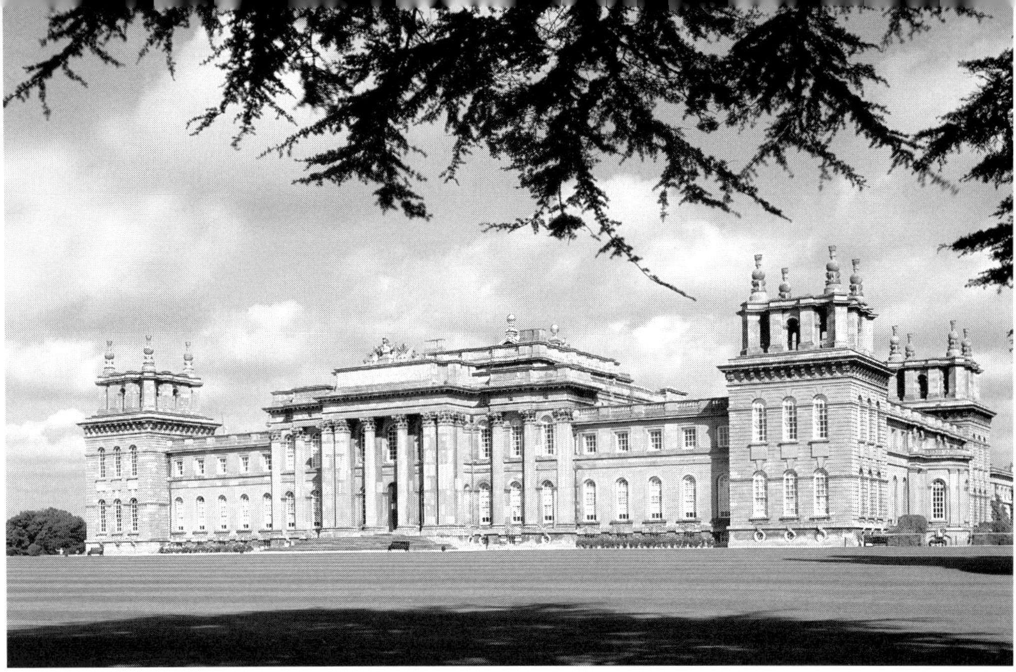

Figure 2
The south front of Blenheim Palace, Oxfordshire.

Wimbledon, designed by Robert Morris and Henry Herbert, 9th Earl of Pembroke. Here she commissioned a simple, neoclassical design that according to Frances Harris was 'plain and clean' and easily accessible on one floor.[56] For Sarah Duchess of Marlborough, then, different houses suggested different definitions of 'home'. While the stately Blenheim Palace was the ancestral home that spoke of lineage, power and military achievements, Wimbledon represented her own preferences and housed many of her own possessions, suggesting a more modern, personalised notion of home that evoked comfort and her own identity.[57]

However, there were many other eighteenth-century elite women who managed to integrate a more modern notion of home into the imposing ancestral spaces that they took on after marriage. Lewis has cited the example of Frances, Viscountess Irwin who moved into her marital home, Temple Newsam in Yorkshire in 1758 (figure 3). Known as the 'Hampton Court of the North', Temple Newsam was distinguished by its Tudor and Jacobean history and was renovated rather than rebuilt in the eighteenth century, a plan of works that included landscaping by Capability Brown. Significantly in the context of this book, the house's enormous Jacobean Gallery was transformed into a Picture Gallery and Library, affirming the important role of such public spaces for the display of family portraits and art acquisitions. Lady Irwin's letters are full of expressions of pleasure in her country house, and demonstrate a consistent linkage of the house with her immediate family and the

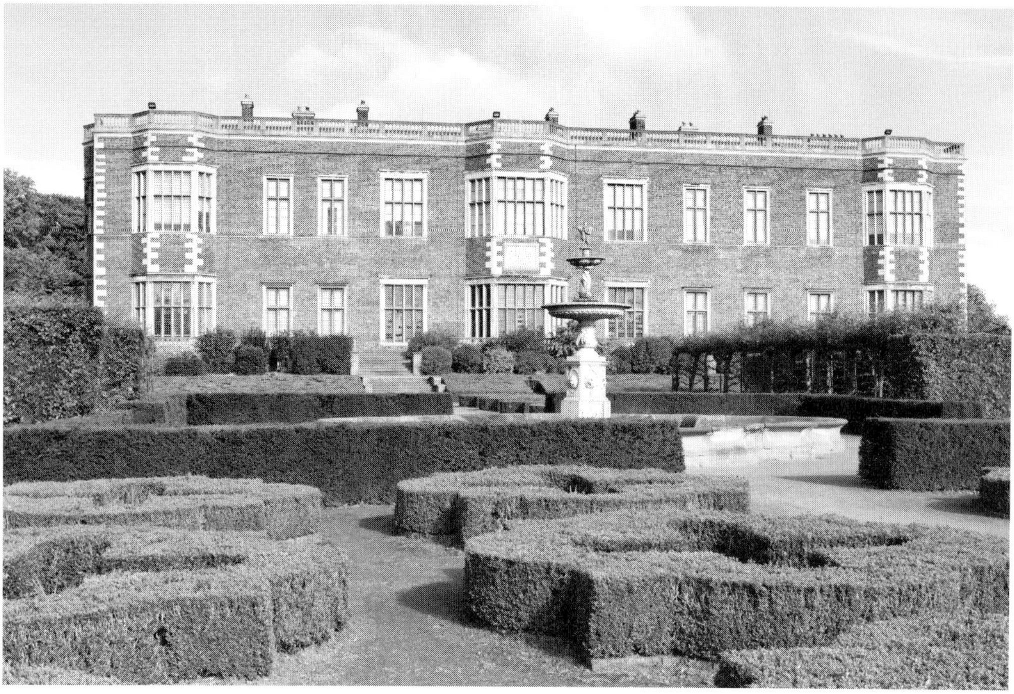

Figure 3
External view of
Temple Newsam,
Leeds.

intimate activities of kinship. They reveal Lady Irwin's association of country life with domesticity and sincerity; according to Lewis, she chose 'to cultivate a rural, domestic self'.[58] Temple Newsam was very much her 'home', in all the senses of that term explored thus far.

These multivalent notions of 'home' within the long eighteenth century are, of course, closely related to other social, cultural and architectural shifts. Following the two revolutions between 1650 and 1714, a republic and a change of dynasty, the landowning class became increasingly powerful, and property and land became a vital measure of status. As Mark Girouard has described it: 'the polite world saw themselves as an elite, whose claim to run the country was based on having a stake as property owners, and was reinforced by the culture, education and *savoir faire* of which its country houses were an advertisement … The members of the property owning elite moved among themselves with relative equality. They no longer found the rigid hierarchies of a formal house a sympathetic setting.'[59] Girouard posits the notion of 'a social house' that enabled more mobility between – and more social mixing within – the houses of the nobility and the gentry. In formal houses of the sixteenth and seventeenth centuries the state apartments were usually found in a line following the main axis of the house, often between a large hall and saloon. These were replaced in some early eighteenth-century houses by long enfilade suites of rooms that could be used for communal activities and that followed a social hierarchy, leading to the private apartments, as, for example, at Blenheim. These shifts both enabled the development of the 'social house' but also allowed more privacy in the separate apartments. As we have seen and as contributors to this collection reveal, the positioning of portraits within different spaces of this social hierarchy of rooms could affect the meanings that the works conveyed to a contemporary audience. These portraits and their positioning played crucial roles in fashioning the reputations of their sitters. They could also help to define and redefine spaces, contributing to a complex interplay between gendered boundaries of 'public' and 'private'. A portrait that was displayed in a private bedchamber, dressing room or closet would have been viewed by fewer people than one displayed in a grand hall or gallery, or on the main staircase, and might be seen to signify a more intimate or personal relationship with the viewer. For example, Kenny's essay, '"Apartments that are not too large"', explores the functions of pastel portraits in women's dressing rooms, arguing that such spaces acted as a locus for a wide range of feminine domestic activities – a kind of 'stage set' for the acting out of femininity. In contrast, Perry suggests that the strategic positioning of a life-size sculpture by Locatelli of Baccelli by the main staircase at Knole House encouraged a more public and male-dominated discourse on her (unmarried) social status, her sexuality and mythological precedents. If the portrait subject was a woman, her status as legally married wife – or mistress – could be implicated in her positioning. If the latter, her sexuality would frequently be the object of concerned debate, and any claims to make the country house her 'home' would inevitably be fraught with cultural, moral and even political problems.

Portraits of power

We have seen how Lady Irwin sought 'a rural, domestic self' at Temple Newsam, and, from the early eighteenth century, retirement to the country was frequently conjured in the popular imagination of the cultured elite as a retreat from the concerns of public life. Through classical conceptions of the pastoral handed down in Virgil's *Eclogues* and Horace's *Epodes*, the country was imagined as an idealised space set apart from the vice and folly of the city and removed from the worlds of political ambition at home and bloody warfare abroad.[60] In the course of the eighteenth century, this mode became increasingly gendered as feminine, and came to dominate in women's poetry.[61] Portraits of the period, and particularly portraits of women, contributed to this fantasy of rural retirement in relation to the country house in several ways. The kind of portraits created by Reynolds and others in the 1760s and 1770s, depicting women seemingly at leisure in country estates, offered viewers precisely this idealised fantasy of pastoral life, as Jordan Vibert discusses in her essay, 'Framing Sir Francis'. While many of these portraits were exhibited in London and circulated as prints, such as those sold as a series of engravings under the general title of *The Beauties of the Present Age*, they were more often than not ultimately destined to hang in those very country houses where the leisured retirement they depicted was supposedly taking place.[62] Reynolds's portrait of Georgiana Cavendish, Duchess of Devonshire, painted in 1776 and engraved as one of the *Beauties* in 1780 (figure 4), for instance, hung in her mother's bedroom at Althorp in Northamptonshire, and was probably originally intended for more public display within the house as a companion piece to a contemporaneous image of the Duchess's brother, George, Lord Althorp, similarly suggestive of rural retirement.[63] As much as the country house provided a frame for such a portrait, serving to anchor its vision of pastoral retirement to a specific place, such portraits also provided a frame for the house, helping to link it to idealised notions of country retirement set apart from public concerns. As Mark Hallett has suggested, *The Beauties of the Present Age*, painted during the American War, may be read as pictorial versions of the kind of poetry of the period which 'promoted the fictions of the pastoral and the environs of the country estate as representational alternatives to the narratives and imagery of a troubled military conflict'. They could thus serve to establish the estates in which they hung as offering retreats from the more public, masculine concerns of nation and empire, played out in the bloody battlefields of North America and the fraught political arena of London.[64]

This would have been particularly apparent, as Vibert reveals, in paired portraits of men and women, either consciously painted as companion pieces, or brought together in their display within the country house so as to engender comparisons or parallels between them. Desmond Shawe-Taylor suggests, for instance, that Reynolds's

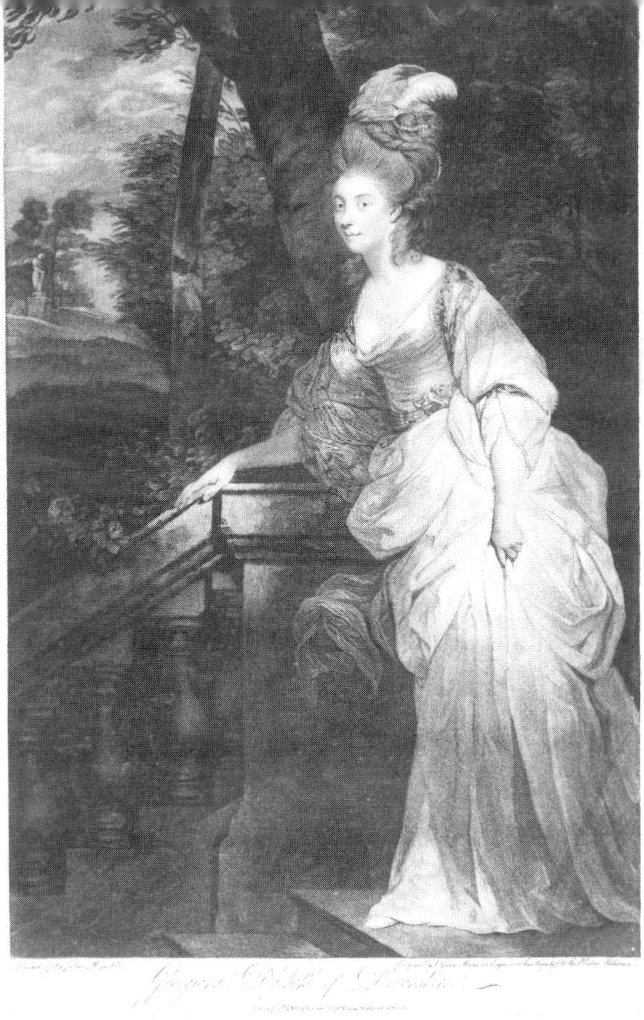

Figure 4
Valentine Green after Joshua Reynolds, *Georgiana, Duchess of Devonshire*, 1780, mezzotint, 63.3 × 38.5 cm.

portrait of Jane Fleming, later Countess of Harrington (1778), standing in a windswept rural landscape, was displayed as a pair, probably at the family's country seat of Elvaston Castle in Derbyshire, with a slightly later military portrait of the sitter's husband, a famed military hero of the American War. Her gesture left thus served to direct the viewer's attention towards her spouse.[65] Through this hang, war – and the American War, in particular – is set against a contrasting scene of pastoral peace and feminine retirement. Reynolds's portrait of Ann, Viscountess Townshend (1779–80), issued as an engraving in 1780 as one of the *Beauties of the Present Age*, worked in a similar way.[66] This was painted as a companion piece to Reynolds's portrait of Lady Ann's husband, Viscount George Townshend (1778–79), dressed in full armour, contrasting her apparently peaceful rural retirement at Raynham Hall, the Townshend family's ancestral home, with his engagement in the work of war as Master-General of the Ordnance.[67] Significantly, Lord Townshend was himself engaging in fantasies of idyllic retirement in his letters to Lady Ann at the time, positioning Raynham as a retreat from fashionable London life. 'Do me ye justice Ann to believe', Lord Townshend wrote to his wife in April 1773, shortly before their marriage, 'I had rather feed your horses at Rainham than be at ye Masquerade.'[68] In other, later letters, Townshend's longing for the peaceable retirement of Raynham stands in stark contrast to his marked despair at the world of war and politics as the American War reached its bloody climax. 'Ye character of ye Country is lost and the national strength and abilities are crumbling into ruin', he lamented to Lady Ann in December 1778, placing the situation in an all too jarring contrast with 'our clemency and our retirement' at Raynham.[69] While it's unclear where Reynolds's portraits of Lord and Lady Townshend were ultimately displayed – little evidence, in this case, survives of the final hang – their most obvious intended home would have been Raynham. Townshend's portrait, at least, was recorded in the state dressing room there in 1811.[70] Displayed together at Raynham Hall, the portraits would have acted as a cue for reading the house as the site of peaceable rural retirement, gendered as feminine, far removed from the more public masculine concerns of nation and empire.

However much the country house was associated with retirement from the masculine world of war and politics in this period, though, it was undoubtedly the site and symbol of just such kinds of civic activity and power. The boom in house building in this period can be attributed to the crucial role country houses played in establishing the wealth, power and status of their owners. Around one hundred and fifty houses were built in Britain in the first half of the eighteenth century alone, often at great expense. Blenheim Palace, for example, cost £260,000 in 1716, the equivalent of over thirty million pounds today. At the end of the century, Fonthill Abbey in Wiltshire cost William Beckford no less than £400,000, a cool twenty-five million in today's money.[71] Houses could also change hands for vast sums. A few years after his ascension to the peerage of Ireland in 1762, for example, Lord Robert Clive – Clive of India – bought Claremont Hall in Derbyshire for £30,000 from the recently widowed Duchess of Newcastle.[72] Whether inherited, built or bought with 'new' money amassed through commerce or industry, the country house and its estate was, as Dana Arnold writes, 'a symbol of the power and wealth of the landowner and more broadly the social, political and cultural hegemony of the ruling classes', functioning as 'a place of business, whether political or estate', a cultural repository of artistic productions and a space in which the 'social rituals' of the elite took place.[73]

For those with 'new' money, such as the Hoares or the Childs, building or buying a house could enhance their social status. The country house and estate also crucially legitimised its male owner in the political sphere, with such property securing his right to vote and to sit in parliament.[74] If in possession of an aristocratic title along with this land, he was further guaranteed a seat in the House of Lords.[75] For Whig grandees of the period, brought up on classical republican ideals of landed virtue, inherited property developed more particular political associations, signifying the financial independence and freedom from Crown influence that guaranteed political independence.[76] And country houses could act, of course, as symbols of military power. Blenheim Palace was a great and lasting monument to Marlborough's status as a fêted military hero, decorated with carved stone symbols of his heroic deeds, which cost over £4,000.[77] A hundred years later, in 1817, the Duke of Wellington was gifted Stratsfield Estate in Hampshire by the nation, and plans were made to replace the old house with a new one, to be named Waterloo Palace in commemoration of his great triumph.[78] Though never realised, the planned house clearly suggests the capacity of the country house to communicate strong military as well as political narratives.

Portraits could play a significant part in defining and making visible these narratives of political and military power which clustered round the country house. As this collection shows, the use of the family portrait as a visual marker of ancestry and lineage served to underscore the owner's political as well as social legitimacy, vested in the estate and the title so often handed down with it. Images of ancestors and other prominent political figures could communicate specific political messages. At Kedleston Hall in Derbyshire, the ancestral home of the Tory Curzon family, for example, portraits deliberately bought for and displayed in the state apartments over the course of the eighteenth century – including a portrait of Mary Curzon, Countess of Dorset, who was governess of Charles I's children – strongly suggested the family's Jacobite sympathies.[79] In the mausoleum at Wentworth Woodhouse in Yorkshire, commissioned in 1783 and completed in 1788 (figure 5), on the other hand, a series of portrait busts of prominent Whigs such as Edmund Burke, surrounding a statue of Whig prime minister Charles

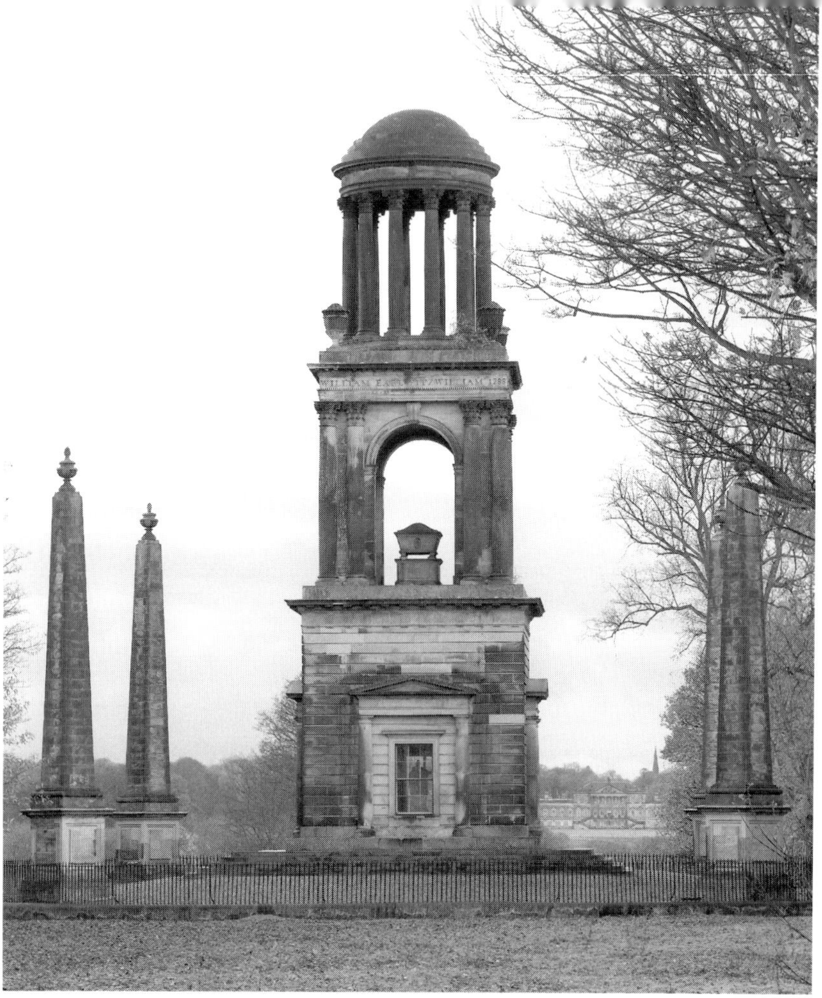

Figure 5
Mausoleum at Wentworth Woodhouse, Yorkshire, commissioned 1783, completed 1788.

Watson-Wentworth, 2nd Marquess of Rockingham in the stance of a Roman orator, was an overt display of the family's involvement in Whig politics and of their adherence to the classical republican ideals that underlay it.[80] These political meanings were also enhanced by structures in the wider landscape. On the neighbouring estate of prominent Rockingham Whig, Thomas Howard, 3rd Earl of Effingham, a hunting lodge built for and named in memory of the Boston Tea Party in 1774 faced and overlooked the Wentworth estates, drawing the shared landscape into a complex metaphor of Whig affiliation, landed virtue and the associated defence of liberty locally and in relation to North America.[81] Set in this wider landscape, the Rockingham mausoleum and the portraits it contained would have also accrued associations with and memories of the family's leading involvement in the defence of liberty during the American War.

The portraits of family which lined the walls of so many rooms in the country house could also communicate aggrandising narratives of military power by representing men in military attire, often alluding to specific battles. Such portraits were highly conventional and came to define, as Shawe-Taylor illustrates in his essay, a particular kind of heroic ideal. Within the country house, these portraits could provide models for the men of the family to imitate. As Richardson commented, in his influential *Essay on the Theory of Painting*, looking at the kind of portrait that offered 'an Abstract of one's life', a male viewer might be 'excited to imitate the Good Actions, and persuaded to shun the Vices of those whose examples are thus set before them'.[82] The replication of poses or gestures across portraits could serve to suggest just this process of imitation across the generations, indicating a continuing ancestral narrative of military endeavour spanning the centuries. Reynolds's portrait of Lord Townshend in full armour, posed with one hand on a table and the other on his hip, would have resonated with a series of seventeenth-century portraits installed in the saloon at Raynham Hall in the 1620s, depicting a band of volunteers raised by the sitter's ancestor, Horace Vere, Baron Vere of Tilbury, to defend the Palatinate of Frederick V, the propagator of the House of Hanover, against the Spanish.[83] According to surviving descriptions of the portraits, dating from the time of their removal and sale, many of the men stand in the same pose that Lord Townshend adopts in Reynolds's portrait.[84] Working in dialogue with these older portraits at Raynham, the portrait of Lord Townshend would have positioned him as following the example of this great ancestor, suggesting a continuing ancestral legacy of martial activity in defence of the nation, and specifically in defence of the Protestant succession (particularly since both Lord Townshend and Horace Vere held the role of Master-General of the Ordnance).

Apart from their political and military messages, portraits could also draw attention to and make explicit broader narratives of imperial expansion and dominion which underlay the English country house. Since Raymond Williams so succinctly exposed the economic relationship between the country estate and slavery, it has been impossible to ignore the extent to which the country house was embedded in Britain's imperial project.[85] A huge number of the nation's country houses were built, bought or improved from fortunes made in Britain's colonial possessions: Beckford's Fonthill was funded by a family fortune made from slave plantations in the West Indies, while Lord Clive's purchase and improvement of Claremont was funded through the vast personal fortune he had amassed expanding the British empire through his involvement with the East India Company.[86] The many black servants who appeared in portraits of the period draw sharp attention to the origins of the money by which the country estate was bankrolled.[87] In the collections of Seaton Delaval Hall, for instance, a portrait of Sir John Hussey Delaval's eldest son, John Delaval, painted by William Bell in 1770, depicts him with bow in hand, alongside a black servant carrying a set of arrows. John and this servant are positioned in a landscape which recalls that around Ford Castle in Northumberland, a house and estate in the family's possession which John's father had spent considerable sums rebuilding and improving in the 1760s. That newly rebuilt property can be seen in the background of a companion portrait of John's mother, Susannah Hussey Delaval, painted by Bell the same year.[88] Bell's portrait of John is evidently a showy display of landownership, with the young Delaval's status as heir to the estate before him encoded in his right to hunt within it. The inclusion of a black servant alongside John also draws attention to the colonial landownership and slavery by which these estates and improvements were funded. The Delavals had financial interests in North Carolina and, in the later 1760s, John's father had sought advice from a Liverpool slave trader on how to run a plantation in East Florida.[89]

Portraits could also work with the interiors of houses to establish bombastic narratives of imperial conquest and containment. As Hermione De Almeida and George H. Gilpin note, a portrait of Lord Clive of India commissioned from Benjamin West, which shows him receiving revenues from the Moghul of Bengal, was displayed in his dining room at Claremont among 'plaster reliefs of elephants, camels and other exotic motifs' symbolic of India.[90] Here, the use of exotic animals speaks directly to the kind of colonial improvement and containment in which Clive was involved through his work for the East India Company. As de Almedia and Gilpin suggest, 'elephants were a distinct symbol of British possessions in India', not least because they were thought to be 'easily tamed'.[91] These symbolically 'tamed' elephants are contained and improved through their representation within the architectural and decorative modes of the English country house, and would have worked in dialogue with portraits depicting Clive's involvement in Britain's imperial expansion into India, creating a grand narrative of imperial conquest. In this room, Clive and his guests would have been faced with a constant reminder that they were dining – perhaps quite literally – off the fruits of Britain's Indian empire.

However, the ways in which portraits created or contributed to more public masculine narratives within the country house were not always easily readable, as many essays in this collection reveal. Portraits could often interact with their surroundings to create more complex and sometimes unstable narratives about the very people and events they purported to celebrate. For example, while the mausoleum at Wentworth Woodhouse seems to celebrate Whig allegiance, the positioning of those sculptural portraits in a space that is fundamentally about loss and mourning engenders a curious coincidence. Associated with loss, these portraits may inadvertently resonate with wider narratives about the splits among the Whigs that ensued after Rockingham's death and the creation of the Fox-North coalition, which was followed by the opposing Foxite and Pittite parties.[92] No longer was there a united Whig party or Whig interest as in Rockingham's day: the Earl of Effingham, for example, whose neighbouring hunting lodge stood as a visible symbol of such political strength and unity, had seceded at the point of the Fox-North coalition and became a firm follower of Pitt.[93] Is the Rockingham mausoleum to be read as a confident celebration of continuing Whig affiliation – or as a more troubled and melancholy memorial to a political golden age now past? How do individuals who lurk on the outside of the mausoleum within the surrounding landscape, such as the Earl of Effingham, but who are not represented within it, shape or contribute to its meanings? Uncertainties and hesitations over the meanings of memorials also cluster around monuments to Captain James Cook, as Harriet Guest reveals in her essay 'Commemorating Captain Cook in the Country Estate'. Comparatively small and modest monuments to Cook at Stowe House and The Vache in Buckinghamshire, Guest argues, may reflect the unease and uncertainties surrounding Cook's involvement in imperial expansion against the backdrop of the fraught American War. Here, mourning Cook may also become a way of mourning a particular vision or ideal of empire which has been lost. More broadly, the memorials to the dead heroes at Stowe, who had been so central to the bloody fight for empire, also bring notions of imperial landownership to the estate; the local landscape becomes an imperial landscape, a space in which the tensions and uncertainties of imperial power abroad might be articulated and negotiated. Alison Yarrington identifies a similarly complex topographical conflation in her essay, revealing how a portrait of Napoleon in a barren landscape suggestive of his political exile, and two portrait busts suggestive of Russian imperial rule, came to be associated with the gardens at Chatsworth through reflections caught in a looking glass, producing a melancholy and meditative narrative of empires won and lost grafted onto an English estate.

Portraits of women could also cause all sorts of problems or difficulties for bombastic and celebratory narratives of political activity and military conquest, even when those portraits seemed so fundamentally distanced from more masculine concerns of nation and empire. Perry illustrates, for instance, how images of the dancer Baccelli crossed and complicated the boundaries between the public and private and domestic at Knole in relation to feminine identity and celebrity culture. She also underscores how such complications surface in terms of the political connotations and functions of Knole, as representations of Baccelli became almost unavoidably embedded in the political history and identity of the house. Pairings of men and women of the kind Vibert explores also reveal how female portraits could complicate and undermine apparently confident displays of martial heroism within the house. Acting as representational 'stand-ins' for men engaged in the work of war, women depicted in portraits could, rather than adding a complimentary gloss, suggest the kind of blurring of gendered boundaries and resulting effeminacy that characterised narratives of national impotency and emasculation during the Seven Years War and the American War.[94] Reynolds's companion pieces of Lady Mary Worsley and Sir Richard Worsley (c.1776), at leisure in rural settings probably intended to indicate their family estate, provide a good example. Lady Worsley is garbed in a riding habit fashioned from the regimental uniform of the South Hampshire Militia, worn by her husband.[95] On the one hand, Lady Worsley becomes an apt analogy for her husband's anticipated participation in the defence of the nation. On the other, her cross-dressing could come to undermine her husband by making him appear less masculine. Such a reading could have resonated with uncertainties or anxieties about Worsley's involvement in the war as a military man seemingly content to stay within the English militia, where he would have avoided seeing any direct action, rather than volunteering for action in North America, for example.[96] Even portraits of women that seem far removed from the more masculine, public concerns of nation and empire may, it seems, when framed in certain ways within the country house, turn tail and present a far more troubling vision of political power and military heroism than may have been intended by those who hung them on their walls.

This introduction has explored some of the multivalent ways in which portraits engaged with their country house settings. When we view Wootton and Dahl's portrait of Henry Hoare II in the entrance hall at Stourhead, we can understand its declaration of the family's newfound wealth, power and privilege. When we consider the particularities of Blenheim Palace, a vast, expensive monument to the Duke of Marlborough's military triumphs; of Saltram House, with its careful evocation of the Parker family's classical, educated credentials; of Raynham Hall, representing a peaceful rural retreat for its owners – then we can start to understand the various meanings of the portraits displayed within those spaces. The individual likeness provides us with characterisation, dress, attributes, composition, and so on, with which to work. The likeness within the broader context of the portrait collection reveals much more: complex networks of linear, nuclear, extended and household family ties; male, female and heterosocial friendship circles; political affiliations of varying persuasions and types. Within a carefully coordinated display, within the country house and its estate, the portrait pulls in external narratives of war and empire, attempting to work those narratives to the owners' advantage, but sometimes instead creating something altogether more ambiguous or even negative.

The essays in *Placing faces* explore these themes in detail, and are arranged into three, overlapping sections. 'A Walk around the House' focuses on some discrete locations within the country house, and the ways in which portraits interacted with those spaces: the saloon and the ballroom at Wanstead; the library at Narford; the Sculpture Gallery at Chatsworth. The processes and meanings of display are at the forefront of these essays by Kate Retford, Susie West and Alison Yarrington, together with the interactions between pictures, objects, people (resident, visiting and represented/referenced) and designed environments. The next section, entitled 'Women's Space?', is, above all, concerned with the complex relationships between different types of femininity and private and public spaces within the country house. Whilst Ruth Kenny and Emma Barker explore narratives of family and kinship, Gill Perry's essay unpicks how the representation of a mistress, and a mistress with a visible public profile at that, could work within the long established walls of Knole. Indeed, this raises a key theme of *Placing faces*. Although portraits of family members, living and deceased, were certainly at the heart of the eighteenth-century country house collection, these were far from the only faces to be found there. As well as mistresses, there were friends, there were kings and queens, and there were historical figures of note alongside contemporary worthies. This latter group included great military heroes, past and present, who feature in the final section of this volume: 'Imperial Designs'. Here, Desmond Shawe-Taylor, Jordan Vibert and Harriet Guest explore the significance of likenesses of such figures as Captain Cook and the Duke of Wellington within collections, working through the complex ties between families, their houses and imperial conflicts including the Seven Years War, the American War of Independence and the Napoleonic campaigns.

These thematically arranged essays range back and forth across the long eighteenth century, taking us from Sir Richard Child in the 1720s through to the 6th Duke of Devonshire in the 1840s. We move from full-length, even outsized oil portraits through sculpted busts and monuments to modestly proportioned pastels. We encompass 'amateur' works by Mrs Grenville and Lady Burlington as well as renowned performances by the foremost portraitists of the day: Thomas Gainsborough, Joshua Reynolds, Thomas Lawrence, Antonio Canova. The houses considered span relatively modest dwellings such as The Vache, great houses such as Wanstead, Chatsworth and Knole, and the royal residence of Windsor Castle. And the chapters take us around those houses, from entrance halls to saloons and staircases, from the intimacy of the dressing room to the grandeur of the gallery. They employ a range of methodological approaches, marrying exploration of complex questions about such matters as space, power and gender with in-depth research into collections and their display. Yet, there remains so much more work to do. Our knowledge of these houses and their collections is constantly deepening, as tools to assist research (such as the work of the Public Catalogue Foundation) develop and become ever more sophisticated. And the country house portrait collection provides an ideal forum in which to continue to nuance our understanding of the complex nature of 'home' and 'family', and the fluid boundaries between such categories as public and private; masculine and feminine; domestic, national and imperial.

Notes

1 A. Oliver (ed.), *The Journal of Samuel Curwen, Loyalist*, 2 vols. (Cambridge, MA: Harvard University Press, 1972), I, p. 229.

2 For the Hoares, Stourhead and the collection, see the guidebook, *Stourhead, Wiltshire* (London: National Trust, 1997); Alistair Laing, *Stourhead: Illustrated List of Pictures and Sculptures* (published online, 2010); Alistair Laing, *In Trust for the Nation: Paintings from National Trust Houses* (London: The National Trust in association with National Gallery Publications, 1995), pp. 237–8. See also Christopher Hussey, 'Stourhead, Wiltshire', *Country Life*, 83 (18 June 1938), 638–42; St John Gore, 'Prince of Georgian Collectors: The Hoares of Stourhead – I', *Country Life*, 135 (30 January 1964), pp. 210–12 and 'A Worthy Heir to Greatness: The Hoares of Stourhead – II', *Country Life*, 136 (6 February 1964), 278–80; John Cornforth, 'Stourhead, Wiltshire', *Country Life*, 188 (8 September 1994), 64–7.

3 Paget Toynbee (ed.), 'Horace Walpole's Journals of Visits to Country Seats', *Walpole Society*, 16 (1927–28), 41. Mrs Lybbe Powys visited Stourhead the month before Curwen, and also noted Hoare's portrait – although she was more taken with Carlo Maratti's *Marchese Niccolò Maria Pallavicini Guided to the Temple of Virtue by Apollo, with a Self Portrait of the Artist*, 1705, then also in the hall. Emily J. Climenson (ed.), *Passages from the Diaries of Mrs Philip Lybbe Powys of Hardwick House, Oxon 1756–1808* (London, New York and Bombay: Longmans, Green and Co., 1899), p. 171.

4 Marcia Pointon, 'Portrait! Portrait!! Portrait!!!', in David Solkin (ed.), *Art on The Line: The Royal Academy Exhibitions at Somerset House, 1780–1836* (New Haven and London: Yale University Press for the Paul Mellon Centre for Studies in British Art and the Courtauld Institute Gallery, 2001), pp. 95, 96; Gill Perry, 'The Spectacle of the Muse: Exhibiting the Actress at the Royal Academy', in Solkin, *Art on The Line*, pp. 111–26. See also Mark Hallett, 'Reading the Walls: Pictorial Dialogue at the British Royal Academy', *Eighteenth-Century Studies*, 37:4 (Summer 2004), 581–604.

5 Martin Postle (ed.), *Joshua Reynolds: The Creation of Celebrity* (London: Tate Publishing, 2005), cat. 33, p. 144.

6 Kate Retford, 'Reynolds's Portrait of Mrs Theresa Parker: A Case Study in Context', *British Art Journal*, 4:3 (2003), 80–6.

7 Giles Waterfield, 'The Town House as Gallery of Art', *London Journal*, 20:1 (1995), 51. See also M.H. Port, 'Town House and Country House: Their Interaction' in Dana Arnold (ed.), *The Georgian Country House: Architecture, Landscape and Society* (Stroud: Sutton, 1998), pp. 117–38; M.H. Port, 'West End Palaces: The Aristocratic Town House in London, 1730–1830', *London Journal*, 20:1 (1995), 17–46; Francis Haskell, 'The British as Collectors', in Gervase Jackson-Stops (ed.), *The Treasure Houses of Britain: Five Hundred Years of Private Patronage and Art Collecting* (New Haven and London: Yale University Press, 1985), pp. 50–9.

8 J.M. Robinson, 'Ancestral Piety', in Donald Garstang (ed.), *The British Face: A View of Portraiture 1625–1850* (London: P. & D. Colnaghi, 1986), pp. 11–13.

9 Adrian Tinniswood, *A History of Country House Visiting: Five Centuries of*

Tourism and Taste (Oxford: Basil Blackwell in association with The National Trust, 1989); Esther Moir, *The Discovery of Britain: The English Tourists, 1540–1840* (London: Routledge and Kegan Paul, 1964), chapter 6; Ian Ousby, *The Englishman's England: Taste, Travel and the Rise of Tourism* (Cambridge and New York: Cambridge University Press, 1990).

10 John Britton, *The Beauties of Wiltshire*, 2 vols (London: Vernor and Hood, 1801), II, p. 3.

11 Peter Mandler, *The Fall and Rise of the Stately Home* (New Haven and London: Yale University Press, 1997), prelude and chapter 2

12 Oliver, *Journal of Samuel Curwen*, I, p. 229.

13 Climenson, *Diaries of Mrs Philip Lybbe Powys*, p. 168.

14 For previous scholarship which has informed the discussion in this introduction, see, in particular, Marcia Pointon, *Hanging the Head: Portraiture and Social Formation in Eighteenth-Century England* (New Haven and London: Yale University Press for the Paul Mellon Centre for Studies in British Art, 1993), section I, part I; Oliver Millar, 'Portraiture and the Country House', in Jackson-Stops, *Treasure Houses of Britain*, pp. 28–39; Francis Russell, 'The Hanging and Display of Pictures, 1700–1850', in Gervase Jackson-Stops, et al., *The Fashioning and Functioning of the British Country House* (Washington DC: National Gallery of Art, 1989), pp. 133–53.

15 Hussey, 'Stourhead', 639 made an interesting suggestion that Hoare may have been emulating the similarly 'nouveau riche' Child family at Wanstead (discussed in Kate Retford's essay) in employing Campbell as their architect.

16 Shearer West, 'Framing Hegemony: Economics, Luxury and Family Continuity in the Country House Portrait', in Paul Duro (ed.), *The Rhetoric of the Frame: Essays on the Boundaries of the Artwork* (Cambridge: Cambridge University Press, 1996), p. 71. For work on the portrait hangs at Narford Hall, Raynham Hall and Wolterton Hall, see Andrew Moore, 'Hanging the Family Portraits', in Andrew Moore and Charlotte Crawley, *Family and Friends: A Regional Survey of British Portraiture* (London: Her Majesty's Stationery Office, 1992), pp. 31–8. For work on that at Clandon Park, see Karen Stanworth, 'Picturing a Personal History: The Case of Edward Onslow', *Art History*, 16:3 (1993), 408–23. For the portraits at Blenheim, see Mark Hallett, 'A Monument to Intimacy: Joshua Reynolds's *The Marlborough Family*', *Art History*, 31:5 (2008), 691–720. For Kedleston, see Kate Retford, 'Sensibility and Genealogy in the Eighteenth-Century Family Portrait: The Collection at Kedleston Hall', *Historical Journal*, 46:3 (2003), 533–60. For Radburne Hall, see Martin Myrone, *Bodybuilding: Reforming Masculinities in British Art 1750–1810* (New Haven and London: Yale University Press, 2005), pp. 123–7.

17 *A Description of the House and Gardens at Stourhead, in the County of Wilts, …* (Salisbury and London: J. Easton, 1800), pp. 7–10.

18 *A Description of the House and Gardens at Stourhead* (Bath: Messrs. Barratt and Son, 1818), p. 6; Richard Colt Hoare, *The History of Modern Wiltshire*, 6 vols (London: J. Nichols & Son [etc.], 1822–44), I, p. 70.

19 Hoare, *History of Modern Wiltshire*, I, pp. 70–1.

20 West, 'Framing Hegemony', pp. 70ff.

21 Christopher Christie, *The British Country House in the Eighteenth Century*

(Manchester: Manchester University Press, 2000); R. Wilson and A. Mackley, *Creating Paradise: The Building of the English Country House, 1660–1880* (London: Hambledon and London, 2000); Arnold, *The Georgian Country House, passim.*

22 Shearer West, 'Patronage and Power: The Role of the Portrait in Eighteenth-Century England', in Jeremy Black and Jeremy Gregory (eds), *Culture, Politics and Society in Britain, 1660–1800* (Manchester: Manchester University Press, 1991), pp. 136–42.

23 Jonathan Richardson, *An Essay on the Theory of Painting*, 2nd edn (London: A. Bettesworth, 1725), p. 7.

24 Hoare, *History of Modern Wiltshire*, I, p. 85.

25 Kate Retford, *The Art of Domestic Life: Family Portraiture in Eighteenth-Century England* (New Haven and London: Yale University Press for the Paul Mellon Centre for Studies in British Art, 2006), chapter 5 and conclusion.

26 Deborah Cherry and Jennifer Harris, 'Eighteenth-Century Portraiture and the Seventeenth-Century Past: Gainsborough and van Dyck', *Art History*, 5:3 (1982), 287–309.

27 Charlotte Barrett (ed.), *The Diary and Letters of Madame d'Arblay*, 6 vols (London: Macmillan & Co., 1904), I, p. 272.

28 The literature on this theme across disciplines is exhaustive. Apart from the work of Ariès and Rybczynski discussed below, perhaps one of the most influential twentieth-century studies of the 'home' is Gaston Bachelard's *The Poetics of Space: The Classic Look at How We Experience Intimate Places* (New York: Beacon Press, 1994; first published 1958, trans. 1964). The book reveals the author's background in psychoanalysis and phenomenology, and offers poetic and imaginative exploration of the meanings of the house and home within modern culture. More recently, the disciplines of Cultural and Human Geography have made significant contributions to modern debates on spaces of the home, including the work of Alison Blunt and Robyn Dowling in their collection *Home* (London: Routledge, 2006) and Doreen Massey's influential writings on space. Beatriz Colomina's edited collection, *Sexuality and Space* (New York: Princeton Architectural Press, 1992) has also helped to place gender issues firmly on the map in the analysis of domestic space within Design History. Within eighteenth-century studies the idea of the 'home' has been interrogated (directly or indirectly) through studies focused on different areas, including architectural history, and/or issues of gender, class and the family. Mark Girouard's *Life in the English Country House: A Social and Architectural History* (New Haven and London: Yale University Press, 1978) and Christie's *British Country House* have been influential in their explorations of the social and spatial meanings of eighteenth-century country houses. For literature on gender and the family see endnotes 35, 36, 37 and 43 below.

29 It should be noted here that the English language is rare in having the term 'home', although the latin *domus* has multiple usages. In many modern languages to say one is 'at home' often requires the use of several other words, using the 'house' as a metonym. Thus one is à *la maison* in French, *zu Hause* in German, *en casa* in Spanish or *ba bayit* in Hebrew. For a fuller discussion of these issues see K.H. Adler, 'Gendering Histories of Home and Homecoming', in K.H. Adler and Carrie Hamilton, *Homes and Homecomings:*

Gendered Histories of Domesticity and Return (Chichester: Wiley-Blackwell, 2010), p. 4.

30 Philippe Ariès, *Centuries of Childhood: Social History of Family Life* (New York: Vintage, 1962); Witold Rybczynski, *Home: A Short History of an Idea* (London: Penguin Books, 1986)

31 Rybczynski, *Home*, p. 88.

32 *Ibid.*, p. 106.

33 *Ibid.*, p. 105.

34 See, for example, Port, 'Town House and Country House', pp. 117–38; Rachel Stewart, *The Town House in Georgian London* (New Haven and London: Yale University Press, 2009). Joseph Friedman is also currently undertaking important work on the town house.

35 Domesticity has been seen to have a close relationship with new concepts of sociability and women and/or femininity. See Leonore Davidoff and Catherine Hall, *Family Fortunes: Men and Women of the English Middle Class 1780–1850* (London: Routledge, 1992). However, the roles of eighteenth-century middle-class men in the domestication of the eighteenth-century home have also recently come under scrutiny. See Karen Harvey, 'Men Making Home in Eighteenth-Century Britain, in Adler and Hamilton, *Homes and Homecomings*, pp. 66–86.

36 Dana Arnold, 'Defining Femininity: Women and the Country House', in Arnold, *The Georgian Country House*, pp. 79–99; Judith S. Lewis, 'When a House is Not a Home: Elite English Women and the Eighteenth-Century Country House', *Journal of British Studies*, 48:2 (April 2009), 336–63.

37 See Judith S. Lewis, *Sacred to Female Patriotism: Gender, Class and Politics in Late Georgian Britain* (New York and London: Routledge, 2003); Helen Berry, 'Women, Consumption and Taste', in Hannah Barker and Elaine Chalus (eds), *Women's History: Britain, 1700–1850, an Introduction* (London: Routledge, 2005), pp. 197–9; John Styles and Amanda Vickery (eds), *Gender, Taste, and Material Culture in Britain and North America, 1700–1830* (New Haven and London: Yale Center for British Art and the Paul Mellon Centre for Studies in British Art, 2006). Amanda Vickery has also published widely on the subject of the culture of 'gentlewomen' and the permeable boundaries between public and private lives, including her *The Gentleman's Daughter: Women's lives in Georgian England* (New Haven and London: Yale University Press, 2003; first published 1998).

38 *Oxford English Dictionary*, vol. I (Oxford: Clarendon Press, 1973), p. 976.

39 Jürgen Habermas, *The Structural Transformation of the Public Sphere: An Inquiry in a Category of Bourgeois Society*, trans. T. Burger and F. Lawrence (Cambridge: Polity Press, 1992).

40 Vickery, *The Gentleman's Daughter*, p. 196.

41 See above, and endnote 7.

42 *Oxford English Dictionary*, p. 976.

43 Naomi Tadmor, *Family and Friends in Eighteenth Century England: Household, Kinship, and Patronage* (Cambridge: Cambridge University Press, 2001). Tadmor argues convincingly for multiple notions of the family co-existing within eighteenth-century social discourse. She also posits the notion of the

'household family' that were not defined by blood or marriage, but held together by a system of 'household management' (see pp. 18–42).

44 Fanny Burney, *Cecilia, or Memoirs of an Heiress*, ed. Margaret Ann Doody (Oxford: Oxford University Press, 1999).

45 Margaret Anne Doody, 'Introduction to *Fanny Burney*', *ibid.*, p. xvi.

46 Kate Retford, 'Patrilineal Portraiture? Gender and Genealogy in the Eighteenth-Century Country House', in Styles and Vickery, *Gender, Taste, and Material Culture*, pp. 315–17.

47 Women's roles in the planning of eighteenth-century houses is discussed by Dana Arnold in 'Defining Femininity: Women and the Country House', in Arnold, *The Georgian Country House*, pp. 85ff.

48 Rosemary Baird has explored the varied roles of aristocratic women who upon marriage became mistresses of large country houses in *Mistress of the House: Great Ladies and Grand Houses 1670–1830* (London: Weidenfeld and Nicolson, 2003).

49 *Ibid.*, chapters 5, 7 and 12 and see endnote 50 below.

50 Including a full length of John Parker (RA, 1773) and a portrait of *Theresa Parker with her son John* of 1772–75. Reynolds was a regular visitor to Saltram, and ten of his works are currently in the collection. For Saltram, see Richard Stephens's essay in Sam Smiles (ed.), *Sir Joshua Reynolds: The Acquisition of Genius* (Bristol: Sansom, 2009); Retford, 'Reynolds's Portrait of Mrs Theresa Parker', 80–6 and Baird, *Mistress of the House*, chapter 12.

51 Dana Arnold has explored the importance of foreign tourism and the Grand Tour in her chapter 'The Illusion of Grandeur? Antiquity, Grand Tourism and the Country House', in Arnold, *The Georgian Country House*, pp. 100–16.

52 Letter of 23 August 1771, cited in Baird, *Mistress of the House*, p. 204.

53 Lewis, 'When a House is Not a Home', 355.

54 Apart from Judith S. Lewis's study, see for example, Frances Harris, *A Passion for Government: The Life of Sarah, Duchess of Marlborough* (Oxford: Clarendon Press, 1991). She also features prominently in Baird, *Mistress of the House*.

55 Baird, *Mistress of the House*, p. 42.

56 Harris, *A Passion for Government*, p. 304.

57 As Lewis has argued 'Multiple houses served different functions.' ('When a House is Not a Home', 350).

58 *Ibid.*, 352.

59 Girouard, *Life in the English Country House*, pp. 189–90.

60 For discussions of the classical pastoral and eighteenth-century pastoral poetry, see M. Mack the elder, *The Garden and the City: Retirement and Politics in the Later Poetry of Pope* (Toronto and London: University of Toronto Press, 1969); M.S. Røstvig, *The Happy Man: Studies in the Metamorphoses of a Classical Ideal*, 2 vols (Oslo: Norwegian Universities Press, 1954).

61 For a useful overview of female poets and the pastoral genre, see Paula R. Backscheider, *Eighteenth-Century Women Poets and Their Poetry: Inventing Agency, Inventing Genre* (Baltimore: Johns Hopkins University Press, 2005), pp. 233–57. For some specific examples of this type of poetry, see Mary Darwall, 'Rural Happinss. To a Friend' and 'Elegy on Leaving' in *Original Poems on Several Occasions. By Miss Whateley* (London: R. and J. Dodsley,

1764), pp. 29–33, 34–5; J. Griffiths, 'Anacreontic, Inscrib'd to Mr. P …., Upon asking the Author, why she did not Treat upon War' and 'A Pastoral' in *A Collection of Juvenile Poems, on Various Subjects* (Warwick: J. Sharp, 1784), pp. 9–11, 11–13.

62 For the most comprehensive and illuminating discussion of these portraits, particularly in relation to notions of pastoral retirement, see Mark Hallett, 'Pall-Mall Pastoral: Sir Joshua Reynolds, Celebrity and Sensibility', paper presented at the Centre for Eighteenth Century Studies Research Seminar, York (4 December 2007). Thanks to Mark Hallett for very kindly providing Jordan Vibert with a copy of this paper. A version of the paper is forthcoming in Hallett, *Joshua Reynolds: Portraiture in Action* (Paul Mellon Centre for Yale University Press, forthcoming 2013).

63 See also David Mannings, *Sir Joshua Reynolds: A Complete Catalogue of His Paintings*, 2 vols (New Haven and London: Yale University Press for the Paul Mellon Centre for Studies in British Art, 2000), II, pp. 124, 427; Hallett, 'Pall-Mall Pastoral', pp. 17–18.

64 Hallett, 'Pall-Mall Pastoral', p. 19.

65 Desmond Shawe-Taylor, *The Georgians: Eighteenth-Century Portraiture and Society* (London: Barrie & Jenkins, 1990), p. 156.

66 Mannings, *Reynolds*, II, p. 445.

67 *Ibid.*, II, p. 447. For a more comprehensive account of these portraits, in relation to each other and the country house, see Jordan Vibert, 'Women, Portraiture and Political Representation, 1765–1787' (PhD dissertation, University of York, 2011), pp. 118–70.

68 George Townshend, 4th Viscount Townshend, Portman Square, London, to Lady Ann Townshend, [Raynham Hall, Norfolk], 26 April 1773, British Library, London, MS Letters (typescript Correspondence) of Ann, Lady Townshend, Blakeney Collection, Add. 63110, fo. 67.

69 George Townshend, 4th Viscount Townshend, Portman Square, London, to Lady Ann Townshend, [Raynham Hall, Norfolk], December 1778, BL, Letters of Ann, Lady Townshend, Add. 63110, fo. 102.

70 Mannings, *Reynolds*, II, p. 447.

71 Christie, *British Country House*, pp. 4, 15–16. All figures have been calculated using the retail price index according to 'Measuring Worth', www.measuringworth.com/.

72 Christie, *British Country House*, p. 10.

73 Dana Arnold, 'The Country House: Form, Function and Meaning', in Arnold, *The Georgian Country House*, p. 16.

74 For some clear overviews of the relationship between property and political power in this period, see Richard Price, *British Society 1680–1880: Dynamism, Containment and Change* (Cambridge: Cambridge University Press, 1999), pp. 242–4; W.A. Speck, *Stability and Strife: England, 1714–1760* (London: Edward Arnold, 1977), pp. 143–6.

75 Speck, *Stability and Strife*, pp. 35–6; Christie, *British Country House*, pp. 4, 98–9.

76 For a useful summary of this 'country party' ideology in relation to landownership see John Barrell, 'The Public Prospect and the Private View: the

Politics of Taste in Eighteenth-Century Britain', in Simon Pugh (ed.), *Reading Landscape: Country-City-Capital* (Manchester: Manchester University Press, 1990), pp. 28–9.

77 Christie, *British Country House*, pp. 38–9.

78 *Ibid.*, pp. 44–5.

79 *Ibid.*, p. 197. See also Retford, 'Sensibility and Genealogy', 533–60.

80 See M.J. Charlesworth, 'The Wentworths: Family and Political Rivalry in the English Landscape Garden', *Garden History*, 14:2 (Autumn, 1986), 134–5.

81 For a fuller discussion of Boston Castle and its political resonances and meanings, see Vibert, 'Women, Portraiture and Political Representation', pp. 192–7.

82 Richardson, *Essay on the Theory of Painting*, p. 14.

83 Victoria Townshend Durham, *Short Guide Historical and Descriptive to Raynham Hall* (Fakenham, Norfolk: The Lancaster Press, 1951), p. 9; D.J.B. Trim, 'Vere, Horace [Horatio], Baron Vere of Tilbury (1565–1635)', in *Oxford Dictionary of National Biography*, Oxford University Press, 2004, www.oxforddnb.com/view/article/28211, accessed 22 July 2012.

84 James Durham, *The Collection of Pictures at Raynham Hall, being 3 Annotated Catalogues* (Raynham, Norfolk: James A.C. Durham, 1926), pp. 11–13. See, also, the reproduction of one of these portraits in Quincy Lee, 'A Catalogue of British Old Master Paintings in the Collection of the Louisiana State University Museum of Art' (MA thesis, Louisiana State University, 2009), pp. 11–12, Louisiana State University Electronic Thesis and Dissertation Collection, accessed 5 June 2011, http://etd.lsu.edu/docs/available/etd-04152009-092929/.

85 Raymond Williams, *The Country and the City* (New York: Oxford University Press, 1973), pp. 279–80. For a more recent and extensive discussion of the relationship between the country house and the British empire, see Stephanie Barczewski, *British Country Houses and Empire, 1700–1945* (Manchester University Press, forthcoming 2014).

86 Christie, *British Country House*, pp. 10–11.

87 For the most comprehensive account of colonial subjects in eighteenth-century portraiture, see Beth Fowkes Tobin, *Picturing Imperial Power: Colonial Subjects in Eighteenth-century British Painting* (Durham, NC and London: Duke University Press, 1999), pp. 27–55.

88 Stafford M. Linsley, 'Delaval, John Hussey, Baron Delaval (1728–1808)', *Oxford Dictionary of National Biography*, Oxford University Press, 2004, www.oxforddnb.com/view/article/39337, accessed 22 July 2012.

89 John Charlton, *Hidden Chains: The Slavery Business and North East England* (Newcastle: Tyne Bridge Publishing, 2008), pp. 127–8.

90 Hermione de Almeida and George H. Gilpin, *Indian Renaissance: British Romantic Art and the Prospect of India* (Aldershot and Burlington, VT: Ashgate, 2006), p. 104.

91 *Ibid.*, p. 295.

92 For a useful overview of these splits and their causes see Ian R. Christie, *Wars and Revolutions: Britain, 1760–1815* (London: Edward Arden, 1982), pp. 146–57.

93 George Thomas Keppel, 6th Earl of Albemarle, *Memoirs of the Marquis of*

Rockingham and His Contemporaries, 2 vols (London: Richard Bentley, 1852), II, p. 408.

94 See Kathleen Wilson, *The Sense of the People: Politics, Culture and Imperialism in England, 1715–1785* (Cambridge: Cambridge University Press, 1998), pp. 185–92, 202–3, 219–27, 253–4; Robert Jones, *Literature, Gender and Politics in Britain during the War for America* (Cambridge: Cambridge University Press, 2011), pp. 34–5, 124–7, 237.

95 Mannings, *Reynolds*, II, pp. 483, 482.

96 Jordan Vibert is grateful to Robert Jones and Mark Hallett for an enlightening discussion about these two portraits, which has significantly contributed to her readings of them in this introductory essay.

I

A walk around the house

1

The topography of the conversation piece: a walk around Wanstead[1]

Kate Retford

BEFORE the 'faces' in any portrait can be 'placed', they have, of course, to be identified. Biography is paramount in connecting the portrait and the house which can draw out its full meaning and significance. This is perhaps nowhere more apparent than in the case of a painting by Joseph Francis Nollekens, now owned by Fairfax House (plate 2). For a long time, uncertainty obscured the identities of the sitters in this image. This was not overly of concern for Fairfax House, a Georgian townhouse in York which showcases a notable collection of eighteenth-century furniture. For this museum, at the time of acquisition, the predominant appeal of the Nollekens portrait was much less the sitters than the beautifully rendered Palladian interior in which they are posed, with its marble fireplace, gilt architectural details and grisaille overdoors. Similarly, when the painting was included in two important exhibitions in the 1980s (*Rococo* at the V&A in 1984, and *Manners and Morals* at Tate in 1987), it was as a fine example of a 'conversation piece', as one of the best extant paintings by Nollekens, displaying the artist's debt to both his native Flemish origins and French traditions, and, again, as a meticulous description of Georgian interior décor.[2] A long-standing association with the Tylney-Long family and Wanstead House in Essex was discussed but refuted in the catalogues to both shows, principally because Wanstead 'had no Venetian windows such as the one shown here'.[3] However, it has recently been demonstrated, primarily by Peter Brown (lately Director at Fairfax House), that the opening to the left of the portrait is not the central section of a Venetian window as previously believed. Rather, it is a tall, arched door, visible in eighteenth-century views of the east front of Wanstead (figure 6).[4] The clarification of this point has led the way to acknowledging the painting both as, indeed, a representation of Lord Tylney with his family – and, most significantly, as a strikingly accurate depiction of an interior at Wanstead House.

'One of the finest houses in the kingdom'

Wanstead was a great Italianate mansion created by Colen Campbell, and pivotal in the early eighteenth-century Palladian revival.[5] Considerable funds were at Campbell's disposal as his patron, Richard Child, Viscount Castlemaine and later Earl Tylney, was the son and heir of the immensely wealthy Sir Josiah Child, merchant and most famously Governor of the East India Company. Josiah had converted most of his fortune into property, buying up a Jacobean house and about 300 acres of land at Wanstead in 1673, and concentrating his efforts on

Figure 6 Anon., *Wanstead House from the East*, 1730s?, oil on canvas, 99 × 124.5 cm.

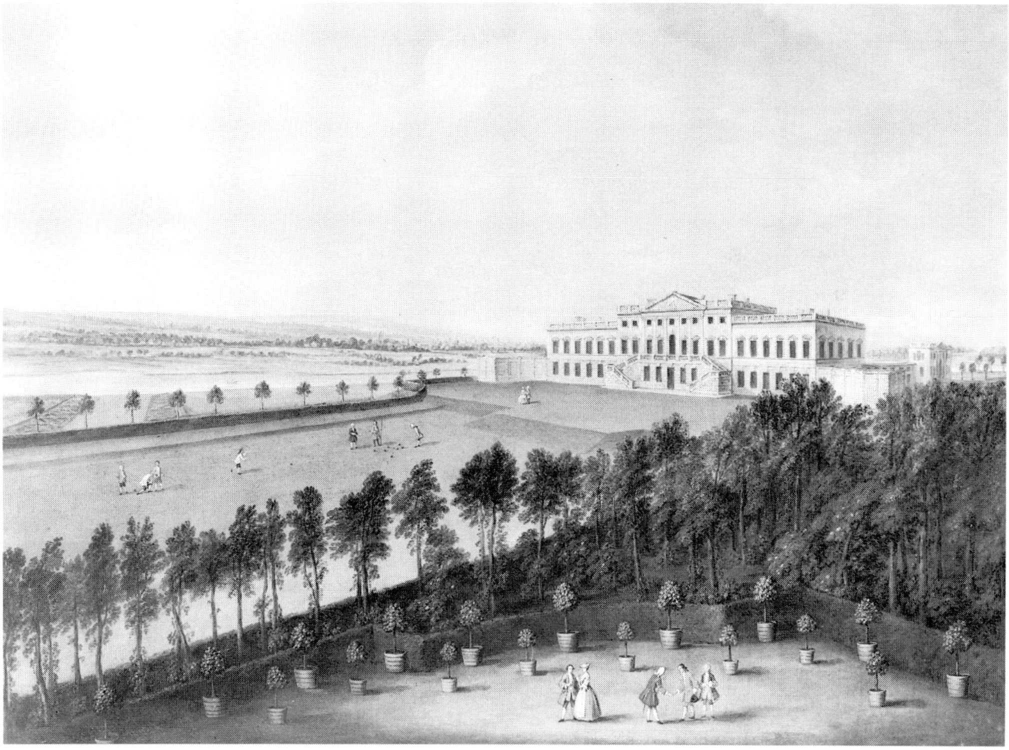

developing the gardens. Richard inherited in 1704, but it was not until a decade later, prompted by a change in his political fortunes, that he decided to demolish the old building and to construct what was to be called by contemporary commentators: 'a very magnificent palace'; 'one of the noblest houses in *England*'; 'one of the finest houses in the kingdom'.[6] Wanstead was a large and lavishly ornate house, featuring interior decoration by William Kent. It was routinely acknowledged to be one of a 'big five' of country houses, along with Blenheim, Wilton, Houghton and Holkham.[7] However, the glory and opulence of Child's Palladian palace was, in contrast to that of its peers, shortlived. Whether due to bad debts, bad management, or bad lifestyle (it depends on the historian), the entire contents of Wanstead was offered in a thirty-two day sale by Robins in 1822.[8] The very fabric of the house was pulled apart and sold off as building materials the following year.[9] All that remains today is a large, grassy hollow on the first hole of an east London golf course.

The Fairfax House portrait was lot number 318 in that 1822 sale: 'NOLLIKINS – Interior of the Saloon of Wanstead House, with an Assemblage of Ladies and Gentleman – *A Conversazione*'. And it

Figure 7 Joseph Francis Nollekens, study for *The Tylney Family in the Saloon at Wanstead House*, c.1740, red chalk, with grey and brown wash, over graphite, 22.1 × 33.4 cm.

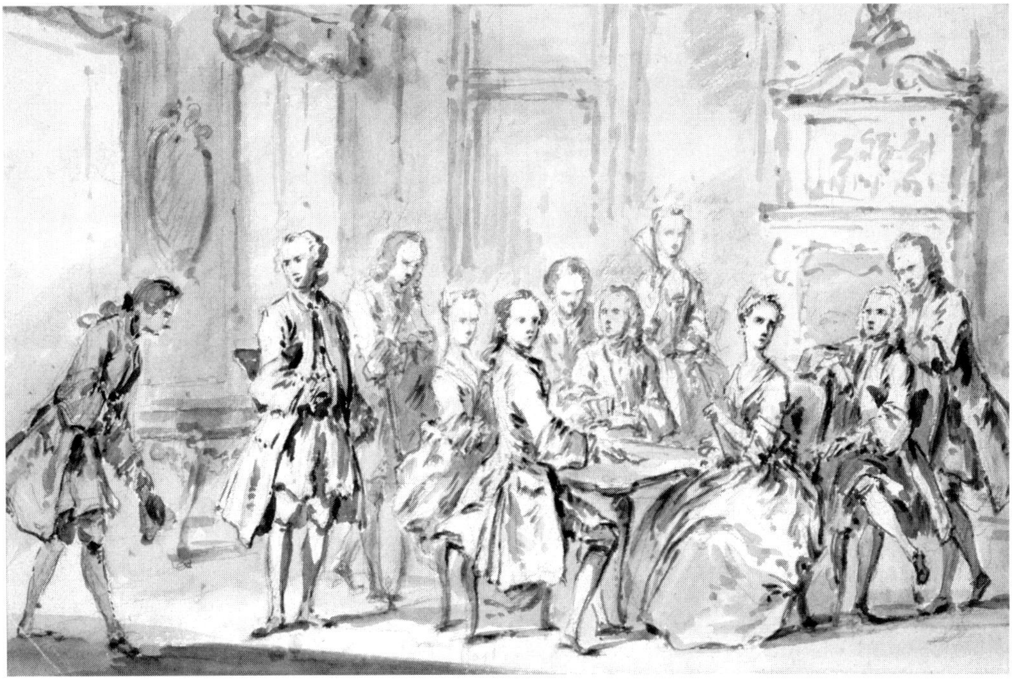

records, in precise detail, this impressive space located at the heart of Child's palace.[10] Interestingly, in a preparatory drawing, Nollekens paid attention to working out the placement and interaction of the sitters, but not to capturing the setting described in the finished work (figure 7). Despite a few minor alterations – principally the addition of an extra male sitter, third from the right, and the replacement of the bowing gentleman on the left with little James, Sir Richard's grandson, attended by his nurse – Nollekens broadly maintained the dispersal of figures he had worked out in red chalk and wash.[11] However, the interior in the final portrait is notably different to that in the drawing – at some point, the specific supplanted the generic. Whether the decision to locate the card party in the saloon was a belated one, or whether Nollekens was only trying to work out poses and groups in the sketch, unconcerned with the setting at that point in the process, he subsequently put considerable effort into making a highly accurate record of this thirty foot square space.

Evidence which has emerged over the last few years has revealed this painted interior's extraordinary degree of veracity. The elaborate fireplace, around which the thirteen sitters are grouped, was one of the pieces of the fabric of Wanstead to be sold in 1823, and it has since been located, along with a doorcase, a wrought iron stair balustrade and items of panelling, at a house in Cambridge. It still has its overmantel frame, but it is now entirely white and has lost its pediment and reclining female figures.[12] The mythological canvas set into that frame – which seems rather strangely to suggest an undressed representation of Sir Richard's daughter, Emma, posed below, through proximity and physical similarity – is clearly that sold as lot 194 in 1822: 'CASALI – Pandora. The artist has chosen the moment when Mercury is presenting Pandora to Prometheus, whose experience taught him to refuse the dangerous gift of Jupiter; Epimetheus, his brother, less wary and prudent, fell violently in love and married her, and received the fatal box, whose contents diffused misery through the world.'[13] The list goes on. The décor of the room matches contemporary descriptions of its 'richly gilt and embossed' decoration.[14] The red and gilt chairs were purchased at the Robins sale on behalf of the Earl of Pembroke, and can currently be seen at Wilton.[15]

The verisimilitude of this setting is striking not least because it is relatively rarely demonstrably the case. 'Conversation piece' portraits – depicting groups engaged in sociable and leisured activities on modestly proportioned canvases – were a new thing in early eighteenth-century

England, and one of the form's most significant innovations was an emphasis on setting.[16] As the sitters shrank in scale and were pushed back into the picture, so there was all the more room for minutely detailed exterior and interior spaces. The conversation piece was not just a sub-genre of portraiture, it was also an art intimately intertwined with the 'things' of Georgian Britain: with rococo overmantels and Chippendale commodes; with classical garden pavilions and balustraded terraces. Indeed, the engagement of this sub-genre of portraiture with the material culture of the times has long been its main source of interest. When it was effectively rediscovered in the 1930s, thanks to a seminal exhibition organised by the politician, social host and art collector, Sir Philip Sassoon, many of the rave reviews focused on the delights offered by the meticulously detailed renderings of Georgian homes and gardens.[17] Christopher Hussey's lyrical account is typical:

> Not the Van Eycks nor the Italian primitives were more open-handed in filling their pictures with barely relevant but wholly enchanting miscellaneous objects for the sheer joy of painting them. This endearing trait is most apparent in the work of [Johan] Zoffany ... how laboriously and lovingly he drew the teapots and chimney-pieces and pictures on the wall![18]

Those teapots and chimneypieces have remained at the heart of the conversation piece's appeal – evident in its treatment in 1954 by Ralph Edwards, predominantly a historian of English furniture, and in Mario Praz's *Conversation Pieces* of 1971, a book rooted in its author's fascination with interior design and the decorative arts.[19]

There has thus been a persistent temptation to see these little portraits as almost proto-photographic snapshots of eighteenth-century homes. The dangers of this temptation have been pointed out on many occasions, and scholars have rightly highlighted examples in which the setting in a conversation piece has clearly been invented. The oeuvre of Arthur Devis is richest in this regard, providing cases of almost complete duplication of location which render fabrication undeniable.[20] In portraits such as *Mr and Mrs Bull* (1747) and *Mr and Mrs Dashwood* (1750), we find the same attributes, the same landscape over the fireplace, the same busts and the same overdoor featured in images of different sitters from different parts of the country.[21] Less attention has been paid to what is actually a wide spectrum of possibilities embedded in the production of the conversation piece, from such cases of falsification through to instances of careful transcription. Whilst we have pure invention in Devis's portrait of *Mr and Mrs Bull of* (but not 'in') *Ongar*, in other examples, notably in a number of works by Johan Zoffany, we rather find 'tweaking'.[22] The apparent verisimilitude of Zoffany's highly finished paintings was particularly alluring to those early twentieth-century commentators:

> It is this sort of little historical touch – the fact that a family is drinking tea with a silver set still in existence, perfectly recognisably depicted on the table, or the accurate representation of the exterior or interior of a definite house – that adds so enormously to the interest of a picture by Zoffany.[23]

However, Zoffany frequently tempered accuracy with artistic licence, in order to maximise his picture's aesthetic and iconographic potential. Certainly, in his portrayal of *Queen Charlotte and her two eldest Sons* of 1764–65, we find a faithful rendering of a French clock still to be found in the Royal Collection, and scrupulous painterly description of the lace cover on the Queen's dressing table. However, these were the King's rather than the Queen's private rooms in Buckingham House, and that dressing table has been placed in a highly unlikely position, right in front of the central door on the garden façade.[24]

Examples where evidence points to an accurate transcription of an actual space – particularly an actual *interior* space – are few and far between. The Nollekens at Fairfax House is thus a relatively rare, and intriguing case. Perhaps the most crucial factor in this painting's distinctiveness is Child's close relationship with the artist. Nollekens was working for an extremely wealthy man who was able and wanted to provide him with something approaching traditional-style patronage. George Vertue noted this closeness in the account of Nollekens's art and life he penned following the painter's death in 1748: '[Nollekens] had some reputation & meritt. was employd by people of Fashion. Mostly. & particularly by Ld Castlemain, Earl of Findly [Tylney] & – that Lord was very kind to him'.[25] Significantly, no fewer than seventeen pictures by this artist are listed in the Wanstead sale.[26] Child was clearly an important enough patron to go the extra mile for. This sustained relationship also makes Nollekens's familiarity with Wanstead, and with its interiors and contents, a logical conclusion. The artist must have spent a considerable amount of time at Child's home and, indeed, the Fairfax House painting was not the only one he executed which recorded the house. Lot 311 in 1822, now untraceable, was 'NOLLIKINS – *Females Bathing, in a Landscape, with a distant View of Wanstead House*'.[27]

The fact that Child was so immensely wealthy and powerful meant that his house was filled with the kinds of 'things' worth recording. A prominent member of the 'nouveau riche', he largely acquired bespoke 'things', anticipated rather than established heirlooms, to be passed down through subsequent generations.[28] They were also 'things', crucially, which could be seen by hosts of visitors. As we saw in the Introduction to this volume, it was deemed virtually incumbent on the elite to allow some level of access to their country houses and their collections in this period, and Wanstead appears to have welcomed considerable numbers through its gates from the outset.[29] The span of tourists 'from the Pallace to the Cott ... from Proud Quality, to humble Swains' described in a 1712 poem about the gardens, or Daniel Defoe's account of '[great] Crowds' in 1724, is no doubt overstated.[30] The copper plates with engraved borders 'for visiting tickets to view Wanstead House' described in the 1822 catalogue probably dated from later than the period under scrutiny.[31] However, there is enough evidence to show that Wanstead was already a popular place of resort in the early eighteenth century. Child's lavish interiors and impressive possessions clearly attracted a level of public notice which must have encouraged their commemoration.

A trip to the ballroom

Were we to walk through the invitingly opened door on the left of the back wall in Nollekens's portrait and proceed down the enfilade, we would ultimately find ourselves at approximately the position in the ballroom at Wanstead occupied pictorially only a decade before by William Hogarth (plate 3).[32] Sir Richard Child clearly had a penchant for the conversation piece idiom as, when he came to commission Nollekens to paint himself and his wife entertaining guests in 1740, he had already requested much the same sort of image from Hogarth in 1728.[33] This picture was described in the Wanstead sale catalogue as 'A View of the Interior of the Ball Room of Wanstead House, with a Numerous Assemblage of Ladies and Gentlemen. *A highly curious and interesting Picture by this inimitable and immortal Artist.*'[34] Now more succinctly entitled *An Assembly at Wanstead House* by the Philadelphia Museum of Art, it clearly provided a model for Nollekens's later work as a certain amount of cross-referencing has taken place.

The fact that each portrait features a card party could simply be explained by the popularity of that narrative device in conversation pieces.[35] However, Nollekens refers to and plays on that depicted in the Hogarth, notably in his positioning of Sir Richard and his wife, Lady Dorothy. In both portraits, Dorothy is seated to the right of the card table, leaning back towards her husband behind her. Her pictured engagement in the play may have declined in the intervening ten year period, from proudly displaying her winning card to her spouse to apparently ignoring the card just dealt to her in order to take a pinch of snuff, but the resonance is clear. Hogarth's painting also provided a precedent for Nollekens in its clear engagement with the specific spaces created for Child at Wanstead. Whilst his extraordinary image (cramming no fewer than twenty-five figures into a space around thirty inches wide) has been at the centre of the same toing and froing over the question of accuracy as the Nollekens, much of the depicted interior has similarly been verified.[36] Visitors commonly remarked on the glut of gilt in the ballroom, carefully depicted by Hogarth.[37] The pictured settees have been identified and located, and the (unusually framed) tapestries on the right-hand wall, depicting 'Alexander at the Battle of Granicus' and 'Telemachus detained by Calypso', were certainly in the depicted location.[38] An account of the ballroom penned in 1788 by the Reverend Stebbing Shaw tells us that the picture over the fireplace is 'an admirable painting of Portia, the wife of Brutus, by Schalken, who has given the finest effect of light from a lamp'.[39] The sculpted head below is probably the 'elegant bust of Julia', sold as lot 82 by Robins.[40]

However, the 'matching' exercise is rather more complicated with the Hogarth than with the Nollekens. The theme that emerges from the pictured objects has significance for what has convincingly been suggested as the occasion for the painting: Richard and Dorothy's twenty-fifth wedding anniversary.[41] Julia was renowned as the faithful wife of Pompey, whilst Portia was so devoted to her spouse, Brutus, that she killed herself by swallowing live coals following his death. Both could be seen as providing suitable – if extreme – models for Dorothy, seated in the exact centre of the canvas with her winning card. The marital theme is further emphasised in the motif of the two mutually absorbed dogs positioned between the couple. On the one hand, the thematic resonance suggests artistic creativity and licence. On the other, the wealth of documentation available points to another transcription of another luxuriant interior at the house. Perhaps the presence of representations of Portia and Julia in the ballroom was purely fortuitous? Or, perhaps this setting was deliberately selected for the portrait courtesy of its iconographic potential? The painting and the bust could have been elsewhere in the house when Child commissioned Hogarth in 1728, artistically relocated by the artist to enrich his portrait's meaning.[42] It is even just about possible that the set-up of the room described by Shaw in the 1780s was a later arrangement *inspired* by this image. Ultimately, the precise nature of this complex interplay between tangible, provable fact and the artist's characteristic narrative creativity has to remain a matter for conjecture.

Before returning up the east side of the house to the saloon, it is worth paying some attention to the Telemachus tapestry which hangs on the wall above Sir Richard. Hogarth's selection of viewpoint resulted in the inclusion of only the far left-hand section, but the consequent isolation of the figures of the music makers, excising the main protagonists completely, was suitable, conventionally and appropriately enough providing a link with the artistic traditions of the garden of love and the *fête galante*.[43] However, whilst the limitations of space necessitated a certain compression of the figures, it cannot explain the repositioning of a rather large, upturned silver urn, so that it sits, prominently, directly above Sir Richard's head. Perhaps some Hogarthian subversion creeps into the picture here – easing for us the incongruity of the commission. It was one of Hogarth's first forays into the realms of painting and portraiture, and the fact that he worked for Child for three years, spending time at Wanstead, sits rather uncomfortably with his professed and highly evident distaste for the artistic values of Italianate art and Palladianism, and the artistic figure of William Kent.[44] The substantial, ornate vessel about to roll on to Child's head could have been a dig from an artist opposed to everything his patron represented.

Back to the saloon

I'd now like to turn us to the right, and head back up the enfilade which opened to the side of the Telemachus tapestry – to head north towards the saloon again, and ahead to 1740 and Nollekens's portrait. This journey up and down the east side of the house allows for a very different perception of and relationship with the space depicted in the Fairfax House painting to that gained from an initial viewing. Taken in isolation, this conversation piece conveys an impression of stasis characteristic of the genre. We see such box-like spaces time and time again. Many of these paintings wear their single-point perspectival constructions on their sleeves, the vanishing point emphasised through the delineation of receding floorboards, carefully positioned carpets, and precisely drawn architraves. As is common, our first impression on encountering this painting is of a stage set; a rather artificial, 'set up' performance of sociability. Words frequently applied to the conversation piece include 'static', 'frozen', 'immobile' and 'iconic', and it's easy to see why.[45] There's something distinctly schematic about the nominal activities used to link the stiff little figures in these portraits, connected through motions and gestures, but mostly intent on avoiding each other's gazes. Certainly, we seem sometimes to have interrupted the party. Several of the sitters here catch our eye, and the figure of the Captain is positively animated for this mode of portraiture, twisting round to look at us as he lays the next card, one foot lifting off the floor.[46] However, as is typical, there is a dominant sense of posing, of a *tableau* lacking much *vivant*.

This sense of posing and the regard of the sitters gives us a strong presence as the viewer, and we are clearly located in space by the single-point perspective. Indeed, as Matthew Craske has recently shown, such images appear to express and extend hospitality.[47] This is the idea at the heart of a painting such as Devis's *Mr and Mrs Hill* of c.1750–51 (figure 8). Whilst Mrs Hill is paused in the act of needlework, she looks

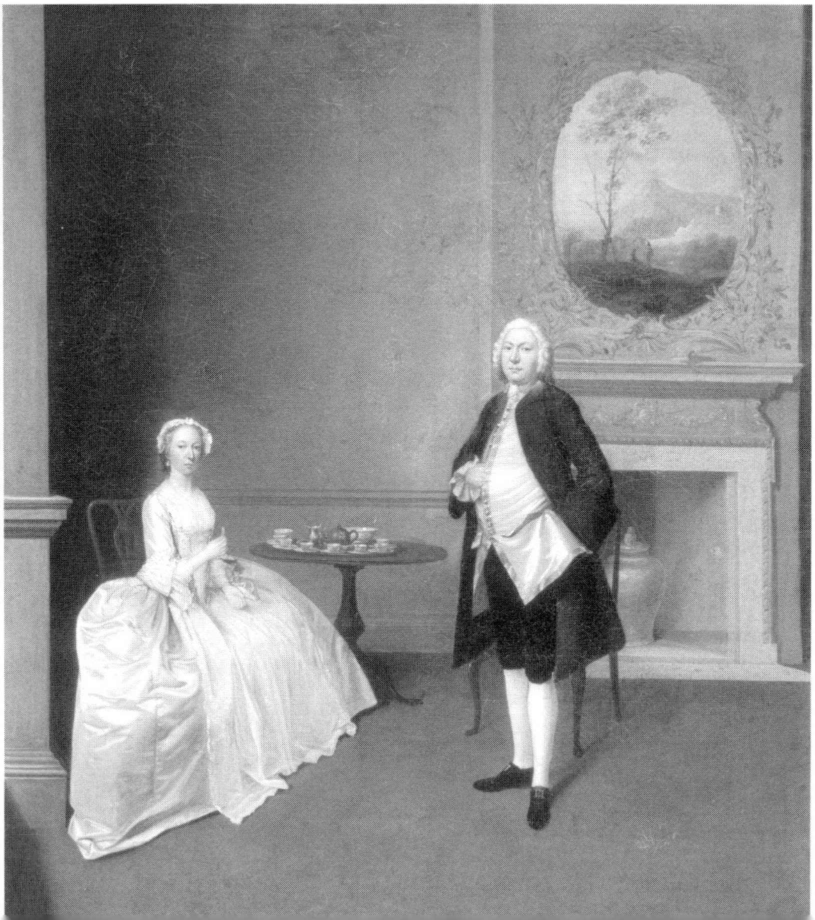

Figure 8 Arthur Devis, *Mr and Mrs Hill*, c.1750–51, oil on canvas, 76 × 63.5 cm.

up to meet our eye, echoing the direct gaze of her husband. It seems we are expected, as the tea table is not laid just for two, but carries seven cups along with a sugar bowl, milk jug and teapot. The fireplace behind Mr Hill is also resonant in this implication of imminent hospitality, as becomes particularly evident from reading William Chambers's *Treatise on Civil Architecture*, published a few years later. This states that the main door of any reception chamber should be positioned opposite the chimneypiece, thereby allowing a host to greet his or her guest from directly before the fire.[48] The externally oriented performance we have here is one of politeness, of sociability, of a *complaisant* welcome.

However, as is to be expected, the interior in the portrait of the Hills is fictitious. It appears in numerous portraits by Devis with only minor variations, and is quite possibly based on a corner of his studio.[49] Mr Hill's fireplace is schematic – it's a motif, a device to assist the correct impression of hospitality. The fireplace in Nollekens's portrait, in contrast, can now be seen in a house on the Hills Road in Cambridge. In this painting, once we know and explore the specificity and accuracy of the painted environment, we encounter a rather

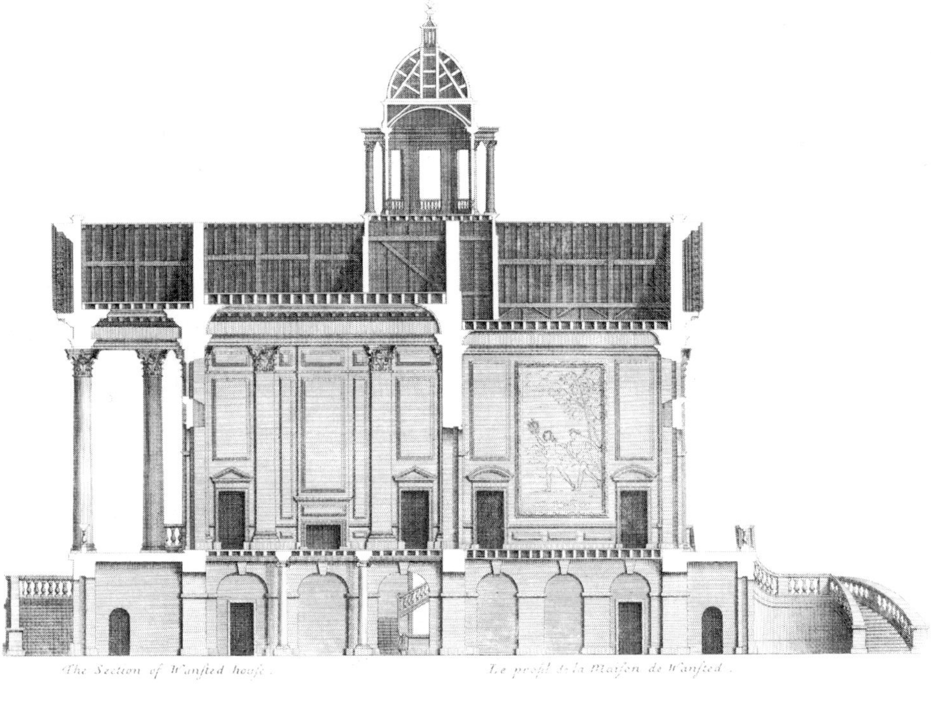

Figure 9 Colen Campbell, *Vitruvius Britannicus*, 3 vols (London, 1717), I, plate 26: 'The Section of Wansted house'.

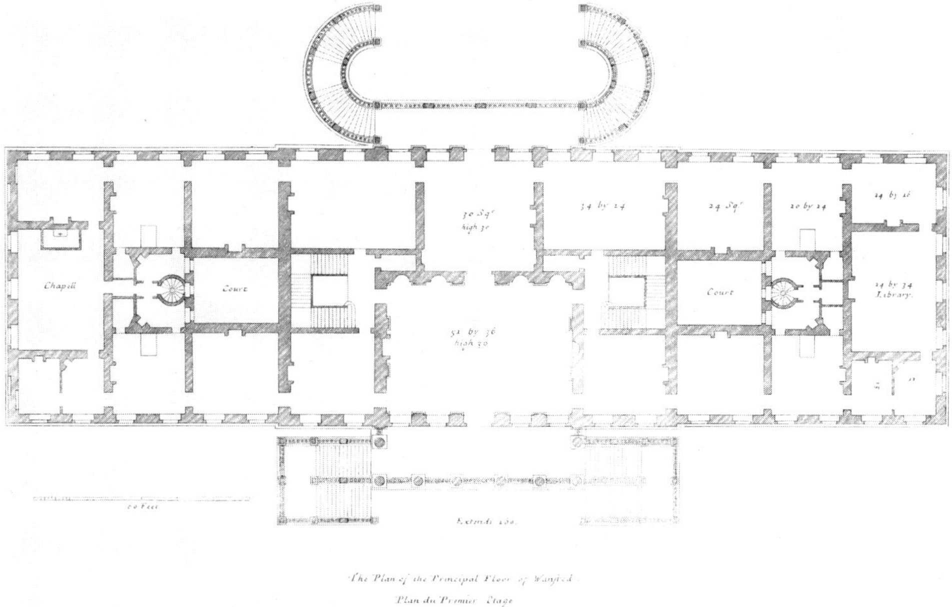

Figure 10 Colen Campbell, *Vitruvius Britannicus*, 3 vols (London, 1717), I, plate 23: 'The Plan of the Principal Floor of Wansted'.

different viewing experience and our sense of presence is heightened. Every contemporary viewer of the Nollekens would have been familiar with the house, as the portrait was part of its collection. The house now lost to us, we can recapture a more historically acute experience by viewing the portrait alongside the cross-section of the house published in Campbell's *Vitruvius Britannicus* (figure 9).[50] Although it wasn't built quite as here represented, we broadly see the view towards which Child and his family are staring. Our enhanced knowledge and physical sense of the saloon completes the box-like space depicted by Nollekens, enclosing us within it. The invisible fourth wall becomes a real wall behind us. Studying Campbell's plan of the house, the predominant impression of a stage set breaks down still further, and the open door now leads – not behind a two dimensional backdrop – but into a succession of state rooms (figure 10).[51] It serves to evoke the complete view through the house described by Mrs Powys in 1781: 'To look through the suite of apartments has a fine effect, 360 [*sic*] feet, the length of the house.'[52] We now have an awareness of the hall and the front façade of the house lying to our right, whilst we sense the gardens opening out to our left.

A walk around the house

Nollekens's painting derives a sense of space and movement from this close relationship with the fabric of Wanstead, acquiring a dynamism arguably lacking in the representation itself. The image must have gained considerable kinetic resonance when contained within the house it so carefully depicted. Our immediate sense of a highly ocularcentric experience of space – the upright observer, gazing directly ahead – gives way to a much more complex, somatic experience.[53] The contemporary spectator could imagine the possibility of movement, based on previous experience of the pictured room and prior perambulation around the house. Great mansions such as Wanstead had a definite 'flow', an 'ideal' order in which the house and its rooms would be seen and experienced. Whilst that 'flow' would have been something of an underlying idea for those living in the house, moving around its rooms as need, daily routine and ritual required, it structures every catalogue and every visitor's account. A view of the west of the house, a pendant to the illustrated view of the east, shows one's approach, perhaps riding or travelling in a carriage around the huge octagon basin which lay before its main façade.[54] The sightseer would then commence his or her 'Wanstead experience' in the hall, visit the ballroom, and view the saloon, before exiting through that arched door which proved so troublesome in the identification of the picture, stepping out onto the terrace beyond and descending the staircase into the garden.[55] No self-respecting tourist would miss the exterior aspect of Wanstead, as the grounds, established by Josiah and developed by Richard, were renowned.[56] The 'Heroick Poem', *Flora Triumphans*, was published in 1712, and John Macky dubbed them 'the finest Gardens in the World' in a 1722 guidebook.[57] The import of the landscape was such that Campbell deliberately designed Sir Richard's house to give good views over the surrounding area. In *Vitruvius Britannicus*, he describes; 'the principal Story ... raised from the Court by a large Rustick Basement 15 foot in Height: The Situation requiring this Height, to afford the State-Apartments a Prospect to these excellent Gardens'.[58] And every account of the saloon noted that it 'front[ed] the Garden' as a matter of course.[59]

Out into the garden

All elements in Nollekens's careful delineation of the saloon no longer appear equal. The door on the left becomes a much more powerful presence, thanks to the view we now know it frames and the access to the gardens we now know it provides. The artist's slight skewing of the space, so that we see more of the left than the right, becomes significant. We imagine taking the next step on the tour – the 'easy descent' from the saloon described by Peter Muilman – and walking out into the garden.[60] We now move away from Campbell's plans of the house and into the domain of John Rocque's maps of the estate (figure 11). Continuing our stroll, we might progress across the expanse of grass outside, navigating the drop in the lawn, and move into the space depicted in that view of the east front (see figure 6). We might become one of the figures bowling on the green (only if we're male), or we might join the individuals promenading in and enjoying the orange tree garden in the foreground.[61]

This might seem a little whimsical. But the juxtaposition of the Nollekens with these other images which document the layout and spatial experience of the house and grounds at Wanstead enables an amplified understanding of the portrait. It allows us to recapture something of the initial viewing experience of the painting: an awareness of its acute sense of place; a comprehension of the relative importance of elements in the room; a sense of the connectedness of the depicted space with other spaces within and without the house. It also highlights the intimate connection between the conversation piece and estate painting. A medley of prototypes are available when attempting to unpick the emergence of this new sub-genre of portraiture – a whole host of models can, and have been identified. Indeed, scrutinising Joseph Francis Nollekens's biography, it seems he had exposure to almost all of them.[62] Like a significant number of conversation piece artists, he hailed from Antwerp, home to detailed, small group portraits by artists such as Gonzales Coques, the intricately described interiors of the *kunstkammers*, the conviviality of the 'merry company' paintings and the *Gardens of Love* of Rubens and his contemporaries – all likely candidates. He had spent some time in France, and can be perhaps best be characterised as a pasticher of Antoine Watteau. Indeed, J.T. Smith claimed Nollekens had actually studied under Watteau, arguing 'his pictures, in point of subject and scenery, were somewhat similar to those of his master, though in other respects they were far short of that tasteful artist's feeling'.[63] The 1822 sale catalogue, conversely, proudly claimed several of Nollekens's paintings from the house to be 'painted with *all* the taste and elegance of Watteau'.[64] A Nollekens *Music Party* – traditionally associated with the Wanstead collection and perhaps one of a pair of *fête champêtres* by the artist sold in the Robins sale – clearly flags up his debt.[65]

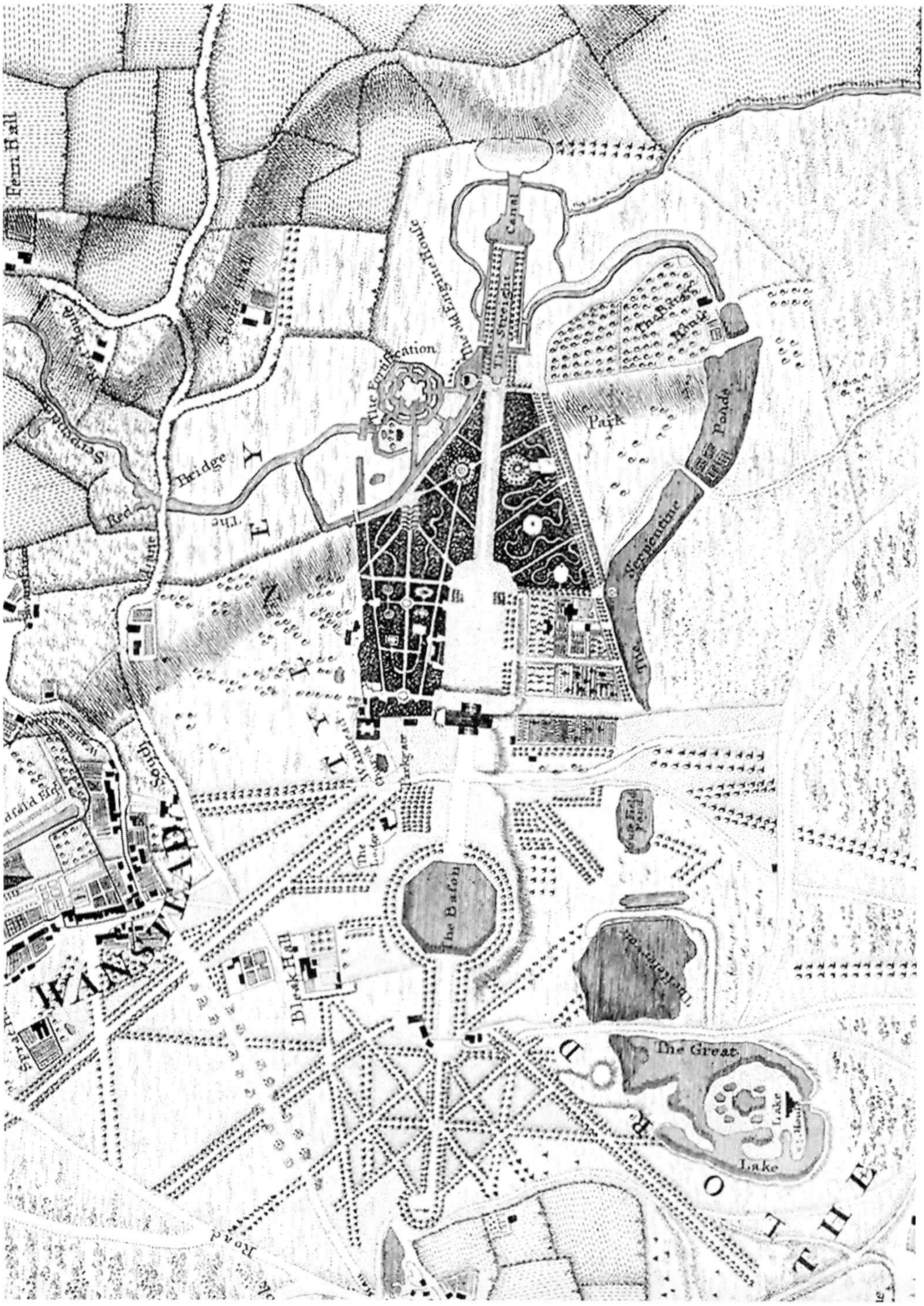
The Fortification
Canal
The old Engine House
Park
Ponds
The Serpentine
Red
Bridge
The Bason
Black Hall
The Great
Lake
Fern Hall
Road

However, the estate portrait, another important prototype for the conversation piece, also has a presence in Nollekens's biography. From Vertue, we learn that he had 'been under Mr Tillemans the painter', likewise an artist from Antwerp.[66] It seems, from piecing together various accounts, that Nollekens had come to England with his father as a boy, moved to France with his family, and then returned to this country in 1733 – the date usually given for his arrival. It must have been during his first stay in this country that, like Devis, Nollekens worked with the painter dubbed by John Harris 'the doyen of the country house portrait'.[67] It seems likely that the Nollekens 'Females Bathing, in a Landscape, with a distant View of Wanstead House', identified in the 1822 sale, owed much to his tutor. One of Tillemans's key contributions to the evolution of country house portraiture was a new emphasis on the Foreground Gathering, such as the one which presumably occupied the lower portion of Nollekens's lost landscape.[68] These figures in topographical paintings are sometimes generic, sometimes specific: sometimes a 'staffage of strollers' to coin Richard Quaintance's phrase, sometimes portraits to parallel the portrait of the house.[69] Estate paintings featuring particular individuals provide an explicit link between such scenes and the conversation piece – most clearly the exterior conversation piece.[70] The only real difference between a Prospect such as Tillemans's *Thoresby Hall* of 1725, with the 1st Duke of Kingston-upon-Hull enjoying a hunt in the foreground, and Devis's Okeover portrait, now at the Yale Center for British Art, is a lowering of the gaze, as we move closer to the assembled figures and experience a relative shift in the emphasis between house and sitters.[71] It is hard firmly to draw the line between such images and, indeed, some considerable ink has been spilt in the attempt to separate out (artificially, I would argue) sporting pictures, estate portraits and conversation pieces.

The importance of estate painting for conversation pieces runs deeper than this, however. These landscapes fed into a contemporary emphasis on surveying and documenting, a 'Modern' interest in empirical observation, which informed the conversation piece more broadly. The view of the east front of Wanstead does not portray individuals, but it shares something of the Nollekens portrait's approach to and engagement with the material world: the tightly described detail; the tangibility of physical space and objects; the picturing of various usages of the environment; the itemising of interactions between figures. If topographical landscapists such as Tillemans specialised in what Harris called 'activity views', then surely the Nollekens is also an

(*opposite*) Figure 11 From John Rocque, *An Exact Survey of the City's of London, Westminster ye Borough of Southwark and the Country near ten miles round ...*, 1744–46.

'activity view'.[72] The portraits of the house and gardens at Wanstead and the portrait of the family in the saloon served to record the Place: the Place as geographical reality and the Place as socially experienced and constructed; the Place as the abode of Child and his family and the Place as tourist attraction. The view of the east front with its generic figures documents leisured use of the grounds, and is situated at the more public end of the 'Wanstead experience'. This is the realm of John Macky's guidebook and Mrs Powys's diary account of her stay with a cousin in nearby Leytonstone.[73] The Nollekens lies at the more private end of the spectrum. After all, it shows members of the Child family and their social circle. Its 'activity view' is of Sir Richard himself, proprietor of the estate, overseeing a card game, embedded in a group dominated by members of his nuclear family. And, although we can't pinpoint exactly where at Wanstead the Nollekens portrait was displayed, our best guess is that it wasn't in one of the most public rooms of the house. It could perhaps be the 'Family Conversation Piece' identified hanging in a closet on the main floor in a 1795 inventory.[74] It could be one of '2 Conversation Pieces' located in a bedroom.[75] But it does not seem to have been a feature on the tour.

However, as demonstrated in the Introduction to this collection of essays, too much fruitful scholarship has explored the complexities of 'public' and 'private', particularly in work on the country house, for it to be as straightforward as this. Places such as Wanstead were homes *and* monuments.[76] They were houses in which people lived *and* stopping points on tours of England. One might argue that the two facets were presumably discrete. Child's saloon could, at one point in the day, be a place for someone like Mrs Powys to pause in their traipse around the official circuit to admire the gilt, the 'pretty' fireplace, the mythological painting in the overmantel. At another time, perhaps later in the day, it could be inhabited by the family for leisured and sociable activities, using and experiencing the layout of the house in very different ways. Certainly, there is an impression that sometimes two worlds collided. For example, when Samuel Curwen visited Kedleston Hall in 1777, he managed to get a peek into the domestic existence of the Curzons: 'The eldest daughter of the Family going in a loose country dress to take a ramble over the lawn, on discovering us hastily retreated back, and disappeared.'[77] Seven years earlier, an employee of the Duke of Marlborough had to write to a close friend of the family, urging him to stop telling people it would be fine to see Blenheim before the official opening time of three o'clock. He pointed out that this not only contradicted the specific orders of the Duke, but 'the little Ladys are Continually in the Appartments, except the hours that the house may be show'd'.[78] One imagines the children being whooshed into the private quarters as The Public approached.

But such accounts also show up connections. Visitors could, if lucky, get a glimpse of the family. The family, as Judith Lewis has explored in recent work, could experience less privacy and less comfort as a result of their house's orientation towards that public.[79] The nameless tourist could imagine domestic use of the rooms being toured. The family member would be aware of the public orientation and ideal spatial dynamic of those same rooms, even as they lived in and used them on a daily basis. And there were plenty of grey areas between the poles of the 'family' and the 'tourist', evident, for example, in newspaper reports from the period spanning the Hogarth and Nollekens portraits. On 30 December 1731, the *London Evening Post* reported that Child 'Last Tuesday … gave a grand Entertainment at his fine seat at Wanstead, to his Tenants and all the Parish of Wanstead, of both Sexes, which were about 100 in number, and in the Evening was a Ball, which continued till two the next morning.' The same year, he threw a dinner for 'several of the Foreign Ministers and Persons of Distinction'.[80] When his daughter Emma married Sir Robert Long, Child kept 'open house for ten days' in celebration.[81] When his eldest son returned home from the Continent, yet another 'grand entertainment' was held, featuring 'Two large oxen … roasted whole', and 'several hogsheads of beer' dispersed 'to the populace'.[82] Such occasions highlight the slippages between Public and Private in a great house like Wanstead. 'Wanstead' was the family home, it was a mansion enjoyed by privileged guests, it was a demesne with events hosted by the landowner and attended by tenants, and it was a palace intended to instil awe in anonymous tourists. These were not discrete, but overlapping realms, and something of this multi-faceted nature, the complex meanings of the spaces of such a major country seat, is captured in the juxtaposition of Nollekens's portrait, Campbell's plans, the topographical landscapes and John Rocque's maps.

Conclusion

In a Devis portrait such as *Mr and Mrs Hill*, the contemporary setting, dress and objects are generic. We are concerned here with the delicate appeal of the rococo style, the lustre of silk, the sheen of ceramic, the polish of mahogany – but not with the things the Hills actually owned.

The sitters participate in and demonstrate the codes of approved conduct of the day; the rituals of politeness, of welcome and hospitality. In Nollekens's portrait of the Tylney-Long family at Wanstead, the same tangibility, the same sense of the materiality of objects is now linked to their specificity. The room ceases to be a schematic space intended to prompt certain reactions dependent on common contemporary understanding of architectural elements such as the hearth. That hearth now occupies a particular position on a particular wall. It orients us and helps to evoke a nuanced sense and understanding of space in one of the most important and visited mansions of its day. If the conversation piece was an art concerned with (to employ George Vertue's phrase) the 'mode & manner of the time & habits', the mode and manner here is that connected with the great country house, and our understanding of its encapsulation in the Nollekens is not complete until one views it alongside other representations of Wanstead.[83] What initially seemed a stage set becomes a highly specific space – here occupied by the family and select associates enjoying a card game, at other times admired by the sightseer, recently entered through the door on the far wall and about to descend to the gardens. The portrait contributes to a broader project to describe and document the Wanstead experience: one which encompassed the appearance and 'flow' of its interior and exterior spaces – and which included its roles as a family home, as a site for the socialising of the great and the good, as a major house dispersing its beneficence over the local community, and as a tourist attraction.

Notes

1 This essay is part of a larger book project on the eighteenth-century conversation piece. I am most grateful to participants at the *Placing Faces* conference at York, 11 June 2011, and those at the History of Art department research seminar, University of Oxford, 25 October 2011, for comments on earlier versions of this work.

2 Michael Snodin (ed.), *Rococo: Art and Design in Hogarth's England* (London: Trefoil Books, 1984), p. 35; Elizabeth Einberg (ed.), *Manners and Morals: Hogarth and British Painting 1700–1760* (London: Tate Gallery Publishing, 1987), pp. 122–3. For Nollekens, see M.H. Liversidge, 'An Elusive Minor Master: J.F. Nollekens and the Conversation Piece', *Apollo*, 95:119 (January 1972), 34–41.

3 Einberg, *Manners and Morals*, p. 122.

4 I am grateful to Peter for conversation and help on this and other issues. I am also indebted to his paper, 'Wanstead: A Fall from Grace', presented at the Wanstead symposium at the Georgian Group, 2 December 2008. George Robertson and William Lowry's *A view of Wanstead House in the County of*

Middlesex with a group of people on the lawn, pen and black ink, grey and brown washes, sold Sothebys, 20 July 1978, lot 39 gives another view of the East front.

5 For the house, see H.E. Stutchbury, *Architecture of Colen Campbell* (Cambridge, MA: Harvard University Press, 1967), pp. 27–30. See also Fiske Kimball, 'Wanstead House, Essex', *Country Life*, 74 (2 December 1933), 605–7; Winifred V. Phillips, *Wanstead through the Ages*, 2nd edn (London: Vawser & Wiles, 1949); Geoffrey Atwell, 'Wanstead House', *Essex Review*, 63 (April 1954), 67–82.

6 Arthur Young, *A Six Weeks Tour, through the Southern Counties of England and Wales*, 2nd edn (London: W.Strahan, W. Nicoll, 1769), pp. 242–6; Peter Muilman, *A New and Complete History of Essex*, 6 vols (Chelmsford: M. Hassall,1769–72), IV, p. 229; *The Ambulator, or A Pocket Companion in a Tour Round London* (London: Scatcherd and Whitaker, 1794), p. 288; Emily J. Climenson (ed.), *Passages from the Diaries of Mrs Philip Lybbe Powys of Hardwick House, Oxon 1756–1808* (London, New York and Bombay: Longman, Green and Co., 1899), p. 205.

7 Young, *Six Weeks Tour*, p. 246; Muilman, *New and Complete History of Essex*, IV, p. 229.

8 *Wanstead House, Essex. Magnificent Furniture, Collection of Fine Paintings and Sculpture, Massive Silver and Gilt Plate, Splendid Library of Choice Books, The Valuable Cellars of Fine-Flavoured Old Wines, Ales, &c., &c.* (London: J. Brettell, 1822), hereafter *Wanstead Sale*. The variety of interpretations available was explored at the Wanstead symposium in 2008.

9 *The Times*, 14 May 1823.

10 *Wanstead Sale*, 10th day, lot 318.

11 Martin Eidelberg, 'More about Old Nollekens', *Apollo*, 157:493 (March 2003), 24. Eidelberg recognised this as a sketch related to the Nollekens portrait, although he denied the link with Wanstead. I am grateful to Tim Couzens for information relating to the identification of James, from Wiltshire and Swindon Archives, Longs of Draycot Cerne papers.

12 A.P. Baggs, 'The After-Life of Wanstead', *Georgian Group Journal*, 6 (1996), 131–3.

13 *Wanstead Sale*, 9th day, lot 194. There has been some confusion over the attribution of this painting. It was purchased in 1822 by Colonel Hugh Duncan Baillie, for £40, and he sold it on in March 1824, as 'Casali, Mercury and Pandora, a group of four beautiful figures elegantly designed and pleasingly finished (painted for Wanstead House)', for £10 10*s*. I am indebted to Tim Couzens for this information, and for so generously sharing his extensive work on the Wanstead sale catalogue. Comparison with other paintings by Casali support this attribution, and the 1822 catalogue lists a number of works by that artist in the collection. However, the picture has sometimes been attributed to Nollekens himself. The *Ambulator*, pp. 289–90 describes a picture 'of Pandora, by Nollikens, father of the present sculptor of that name' over the fireplace in the saloon, and William Tegg in *A Sketch of Wanstead Park, and of the House which Formerly Stood there* (London: Tegg, [c.1882]), giving an account of the interior of the house from a work dated

1809, refers, p. 23, similarly to 'a picture of Pandora, by Nollekens the elder' in that location. Atwell, 'Wanstead House', 70 draws on these sources. It seems likely that confusion arose between the Nollekens conversation piece and the picture it reproduced. There is further error in Kimball's 'Wanstead House', which makes, p. 606, reference to a *statue* of Pandora by 'Nollekens' in the room.

14 Stebbing Shaw, 'A Tour to the West of England, in 1788' (London, 1789) in John Pinkerton, *A General Collection of the best and most interesting Voyages and Travels in all Parts of the World*, 17 vols (London: Longman, Hurst, Rees, and Orme, 1808–14), II, p. 179.

15 Thanks to Peter Brown for this information. For items which ended up at Chatsworth, see Denis F. Keeling, *Wanstead and Chatsworth: Treasures from Wanstead House Acquired by the 6th Duke of Devonshire* (Wanstead: Tylney Press in association with The Wanstead Historical Society, 1997).

16 The following summary is based on Kate Retford, 'The Evidence of the Conversation Piece: Thomas Bardwell's *The Broke and Bowes Families* (1740)', *Cultural and Social History*, 7:4 (December 2010), 493–510 and 'From the Interior to Interiority: The Conversation Piece in Georgian England', *Journal of Design History*, 20:4 (2007), 291–307. For an introduction to the eighteenth-century conversation piece, see Ellen G. D'Oench, *The Conversation Piece: Arthur Devis and his Contemporaries* (New Haven: Yale Center for British Art, 1980). The most recent text on the subject is Desmond Shawe-Taylor, *The Conversation Piece: Scenes from Fashionable Life* (London: The Royal Collection, 2009).

17 *Loan Exhibition of English Conversation Pieces in aid of the Royal Northern Hospital at 25 Park Lane, March 4th to 30th (inclusive) 1930* (London: Battley Brothers, 1930).

18 Christopher Hussey, 'Conversation Pieces: Sir Philip Sassoon's Exhibition, March 4th – 30th', *Country Life*, 67 (15 February 1930), 263.

19 Ralph Edwards, *Early Conversation Pictures from the Middle Ages to about 1730: A Study in Origins* (London: Country Life, 1954); Mario Praz, *Conversation Pieces: A Survey of the Informal Group Portrait in Europe and America* (London: Methuen, 1971).

20 D'Oench, *Conversation Piece, passim.*; Stephen Sartin, 'Arthur Devis: His Life and Art', in John Hayes and Stephen Sartin (eds), *Polite Society by Arthur Devis, 1712–1787* (Preston and London: Harris Museum and Art Gallery, 1983), pp. 22–8.

21 The Bull portrait is currently on loan to the Metropolitan Museum of Art from the NYU Conservation Center. That of the Dashwoods is in a private collection. These portraits are reproduced in Retford, 'From the Interior to Interiority', 292, 295.

22 For Zoffany see Mary Webster, *Johan Zoffany RA, 1733–1810* (New Haven and London: Yale University Press, 2011); Martin Postle (ed.), *Johan Zoffany RA: Society Observed* (New Haven and London: Yale University Press, 2011).

23 Mary Chamot, 'English Conversation Pieces', *Country Life*, 67 (8 March 1930), 345.

24 For this painting, see, in particular, Shawe-Taylor, *Conversation Piece*, cat. 20,

pp. 110–13.

25 George Vertue, 'Notebooks', *Walpole Society*, 22 (1933–34), 137.

26 *Wanstead Sale*, 8th day, lots 10, 16; 9th day, lots 138, 225; 10th day, lots 307, 308, 311, 314, 316, 317, 318, 320, 321. The list of Nollekens works is included in Liversidge, 'An Elusive Minor Master', 41.

27 *Wanstead Sale*, 10th day, lot 311.

28 William Gilpin, *Observations on several parts of the counties of Cambridge, Norfolk, Suffolk and Essex. Also on several parts of North Wales; relative chiefly to Picturesque Beauty* (London: T. Cadell and W. Davies, 1809), p. 5, was damning about the status of the Childs as 'an upstart race' in a tour of 1769.

29 See Sally Jeffery, 'The Gardens of Wanstead House', in Katherine Myers (ed.), 'The Gardens of Wanstead: Proceedings of a Study Day held at the Temple, Wanstead Park, Greater London' (25 September 1999), p. 18 (Ilford Record Office, ref. YW 301).

30 *Flora Triumphans: Wanstead Garden An Heroick Poem most humbly addrest to the Honourable Sir Richard Child* (London: William Redmayne, 1712), p. 5; Daniel Defoe, *Tour thro' the Whole Island of Great Britain*, 3 vols (London: G. Strahan, 1724–27), I, p. 137.

31 *Wanstead Sale*, 3rd day, lot 31.

32 For this painting, see Arthur S. Marks, '*Assembly at Wanstead House* by William Hogarth', *Philadelphia Museum of Art Bulletin*, 77:332 (Spring 1981), 3–16; Richard Dorment, *British Painting in the Philadelphia Museum of Art from the Seventeenth through the Nineteenth Century* (Philadelphia: Philadelphia Museum of Art, 1986), pp. 157–62.

33 John Ireland, *A Supplement to Hogarth Illustrated*, 2nd edn (London: G. and W. Nichol, 1804), p. 21, reproduces Hogarth's 'Account taken January 1, 1731, of all the pictures that remain unfinished. – Half payment received.' This includes 'An assembly of twenty-five figures, for Lord Castelmain, August 28, 1729.'

34 *Wanstead Sale*, 9th day, lot 171.

35 For card parties in conversation pieces, see David Solkin's discussion of Hogarth's *Wollaston Family*, 1730, in *Painting for Money: The Visual Arts and the Public Sphere in Eighteenth-Century England* (New Haven and London: Yale University Press for the Paul Mellon Centre for Studies in British Art, 1992), pp. 84–90.

36 Marks in '*Assembly at Wanstead House*', 3, 8–13, stated that the painting showed the ballroom, and identified the Schalken, the statue of Julia and the tapestries, but said that Hogarth had invented the furniture, overblowing the style to criticise Kent. He also suggested, pp. 10–11, that the head on the fireplace might represent Kent. Richard Dorment in *British Painting in the Philadelphia Museum*, pp. 159–62, also identified the space, whilst denying the veracity of the furniture. He discussed the possible meaning of the painting of Portia and the sculpture of Julia within the portrait, whilst rather sidestepping the questions around their actual existence in the Wanstead collection.

37 See, for example, Young, *Six Weeks Tour*, p. 244; Muilman, *New and Complete History of Essex*, IV, p. 229; *Ambulator*, p. 289.

38 Information on the settees from Peter Brown, included in 'Wanstead: A Fall

from Grace'. I am grateful to Peter for comments on the tapestry frames. The tapestries were sold in the *Wanstead Sale*, 10th day, lot 6, '*A splendid Panel of Tapestry,* REPRESENTING Alexander's Passage of the Granicus of the finest Workmanship, and in the highest Preservation, and may be truly called a *Chef-d'oeuvre*, with a carved and gilt open Flower Work Border, 22–Feet-6 wide – 11–Feet-6 high' and lot 7, 'A Ditto, Calypso receiving Telemachus at the Island of Crete, surrounded by her numerous Attendants, with carved and gilt open Flower Work Border, 22–Feet-6 wide – 11–Feet-6 high'. See Marks, '*Assembly at Wanstead House*', 12–13. See also Tegg, *Sketch of Wanstead Park*, p. 23 and the *Ambulator*, p. 289.

39 Shaw, 'Tour to the West of England', p. 179. See also Tegg, *Sketch of Wanstead Park*, p. 23 and the *Ambulator*, p. 289. *Wanstead Sale*, 9th day, lot 167, 'Schalken – Portia destroying herself by eating fire. A very exquisitely high finished picture of great beauty and powerful effect'.

40 *Wanstead Sale*, 8th day, lot 82.

41 This proposal was made by Dorment in *British Painting in the Philadelphia Museum*, pp. 159–60. It was followed by Ronald Paulson in *Hogarth*, 3 vols. (New Brunswick: Rutgers University Press, 1993), I, pp. 206–7 and the catalogue entry in Mark Hallett and Christine Riding, *Hogarth* (London: Tate Publishing, 2006), cat. no. 48, p. 98.

42 Paulson, *Hogarth*, I, p. 207.

43 Marks, '*Assembly at Wanstead House*', 13; Dorment, *British Painting in the Philadelphia Museum*, p. 160.

44 Discussed by Marks, '*Assembly at Wanstead House*', 9–11; Dorment, *British Painting in the Philadelphia Museum*, p. 158.

45 See, for example, Peter de Bolla's analysis of the conversation piece in *The Education of the Eye: Painting, Landscape, and Architecture in Eighteenth-Century Britain* (Stanford, CA: Stanford University Press, 2003), chapter 2.

46 This figure is identified as 'Capt' in the British Museum sketch.

47 Unpublished paper by Matthew Craske, 'Conversations and Chimneypieces: The Eighteenth-Century English Conversation Portrait as a Conventionalised Representation of an Act of Hospitality', 2010. I am most grateful to Matthew for allowing me to see an early draft of this work.

48 William Chambers, *A Treatise on Civil Architecture* (London: J. Haberkorn, 1759), p. 78.

49 D'Oench, *Conversation Piece*, pp. 49–50.

50 See Colen Campbell, *Vitruvius Britannicus*, 3 vols (London: Colen Campbell and Joseph Smith, 1717–25), I, plates 21–7 for Wanstead.

51 Campbell's plan was not entirely as built. The curving steps, for example, on the garden façade, were apparently changed in execution to resemble those at the front. Furthermore, the ballroom was remodelled out of the library suite at the south end of the house within Campbell's lifetime.

52 Climenson, *Diaries of Mrs Philip Lybbe Powys*, pp. 205–6.

53 See, for example, Christopher Tilley, *A Phenomenonology of Landscape: Places, Paths and Monuments* (Oxford: Berg, 1994), chapter 1; Juhani Pallasmaa, *The Eyes of the Skin: Architecture and the Senses*, pref. Steven Holl, 2nd edn (Chichester: Wiley, 2005).

54 There exists a third related topographical view of Wanstead, taking a bird's eye view from the east and showing the ring of water running around the grounds, owned by Newham Museum Services. For information on these paintings, I am indebted to Sally Jeffery's work on the gardens of Wanstead – her paper at the 2008 Georgian Group symposium, 'An Overview of the Landscape from Child to Kennedy'; and 'Gardens of Wanstead House', pp. 22–3. Many thanks to Sally for providing me with copies of these papers. See also John Harris, *The Artist and the Country House: A History of Country House and Garden View Painting in Britain, 1540–1870* (London: Sotheby Parke Bernet, 1979), p. 323. A traditional attribution to Charles Catton the Elder must be rejected, as Catton was born in 1728 and the most likely dating for the views is the 1730s. This is because they include wings which were planned, but never executed. There seems to have still been an intention to construct them in the 1730s. They appear, for example, in John Rocque's map of Wanstead of 1735: *Plan of the House, Gardens, Park and Plantations of Wanstead in the County of Essex*. However, by the mid-1740s, it seems to have been accepted that they would never be built. They do not appear on Rocque's view of Wanstead in his 1744–46 *An Exact Survey of the City's of London, Westminster ye Borough of Southwark and the Country near ten miles round* ... for example. I am grateful to the discussion between Sally Jeffery and John Harris at the Georgian Group symposium on this point. It was quite common for images such as these to show features planned but not yet constructed.

55 For this order, see, for example, Muilman, *New and Complete History of Essex*, IV, pp. 228–31; Young, *Six Weeks Tour*, p. 244; Shaw, 'Tour to the West of England', p. 179.

56 For the gardens, see Jeffery, 'Gardens of Wanstead House', *passim*. See also Fiske Kimball and Ian Dunlop, 'The Gardens of Wanstead House, Essex', *Country Life*, 108 (28 July 1950), 294–8; 'Wanstead Park: A Survey of the Landscape', Debois Landscape Survey Group, June 1990.

57 *Flora Triumphans, passim.*; John Macky, *A Journey through England, in Familiar Letters from a Gentleman Here, to his Friend Abroad*, 2nd edn (London, 1722), p. 19.

58 Campbell, *Vitruvius Britannicus*, I, p. 4.

59 *Ibid.*, I, p. 4; Macky, *Journey through England*, p. 23.

60 Muilman, *New and Complete History of Essex*, IV, p. 231. See also Macky, *Journey through England*, p. 23.

61 There had been a dedicated bowling green at Wanstead, shown in Leonard Kip and Johannes Knyff's views of Wanstead in their *Supplément du Nouveau Théâtre de la Grand Bretagne* of 1728. This had been dismantled by the time Rocque produced his 1735 *Plan of the House, Gardens, Park and Plantations of Wanstead*. See Jeffery, 'Gardens of Wanstead House', pp. 14, 16. For bowling see Anne Laurence, 'Space, Status and Gender in English Topographical Paintings, c.1660–c.1740', *Architectural History*, 46 (2003), 88.

62 Liversidge, 'An Elusive Minor Master', *passim*.

63 J.T. Smith, *Nollekens and His Times* (London: Century, 1986), p. 3

64 *Wanstead Sale*, 9th day, lot 225. See also 10th day, lots 308, 316.

65 Oil on copper, 36.8 × 45.7 cm, sold in the Spencer-Churchill sale of 1965. See Liversidge, 'An Elusive Minor Master', 38. I am grateful to Tim Couzens for information on this picture.

66 Vertue, 'Notebooks', 137.

67 Liversidge, 'An Elusive Minor Master', 35–6; Eidelberg, 'More about Old Nollekens', 23. John Harris, *The Artist and the Country House from the Fifteenth Century to the Present Day* (London: Sothebys, 1995), p. 15. For Tillemans, see Robert Raines, 'Peter Tillemans, Life and Work, with a List of Representative Paintings', *Walpole Society*, 47 (1978–80), 21–59.

68 Harris, *Artist and the Country House* (1995), p. 15.

69 Richard Quaintance, 'Who's Making the Scene? Real People in Eighteenth-Century Topographical Prints', in Gerald Maclean, Donna Landry and Joseph P. Ward (eds), *The Country and the City Revisited: England and the Politics of Culture, 1550–1850* (Cambridge: Cambridge University Press, 1999), p. 135.

70 For a discussion of the link, see John Hayes, 'Introduction' in Hayes and Sartin, *Polite Society*, pp. 12–13.

71 The Tillemans is in a private collection. Arthur Devis, *Leak Okeover, Rev. John Allen and Captain Chester at Okeover Hall, Staffordshire*, 1745–47.

72 Harris, *Artist and the Country House* (1995), p. 8.

73 Macky, *Journey through England*, pp. 19–24; Climenson, *Diaries of Mrs Philip Lybbe Powys*, pp. 205–6.

74 'Long vs Phipps: An Inventory of the Household Furniture, Linen, China, Glass, Books, Wines and Effects of the late Sir James Tylney Long Bart deceased at Wanstead House in the County of Essex. Febry 1795', National Archives C111/215, fo. 21.

75 *Ibid.*, fo. 43.

76 See, for example, Judith L. Lewis, 'When a House is Not a Home: Elite English Women and the Eighteenth-Century Country House', *Journal of British Studies*, 48:2 (2009), 336–63; Mark Girouard, *Life in the English Country House: A Social and Architectural History* (New Haven and London: Yale University Press, 1978).

77 A. Oliver (ed.), *The Journal of Samuel Curwen, Loyalist*, 2 vols. (Cambridge, MA: Harvard University Press, 1972), I, p. 353, 27 May 1777.

78 Anon. from Blenheim to John Moore, 25 June 1770, British Library Additional MS 61,672, fo. 127.

79 Lewis, 'When a House is Not a Home', *passim*.

80 *London Evening Post*, 8 November 1731.

81 *Daily Journal*, 2 June 1735.

82 *Grub Street Journal*, 12 April 1733.

83 Vertue, 'Notebooks', 71.

2

Life in the library

Susie West

THIS CHAPTER explores portraiture in a particular space, that of the private library in the English country house. Through a discussion of a group of portraits positioned within that space, I examine some of the possible social and cultural meanings of this display, rather than follow a detailed analysis of individual images.[1] The country house library emerges as a key site for discourses around knowledge and identity for the English elite, from the seventeenth century onwards.[2] Although libraries within English country houses are familiar to heritage house visitors, as part of a standard tour around the reception rooms, there is an important caveat to this familiarity. As the first part of my discussion demonstrates, the library has a historical trajectory of moving around in the country house plan, as that plan itself responds to and shapes the social uses of the great house. Our 'heritage' encounters with libraries are usually in the context of a later nineteenth-century remodelling of routes around the house, often placing the library in a historically specific relationship to rooms such as dining and withdrawing rooms. It follows that such routes are not representative of earlier phases of these spatial relationships. I stress this spatial contingency as an essential preamble to considering how portraiture is deployed around the house.

The country house library in the long eighteenth century was an important resource for the creation and maintenance of cultural life, through the medium of print, both textual and graphic. Exchanges and debates between city and country, male and female personas, could be assembled on the shelves, representing the landed estate's version of the coffee house.[3] The library room became increasingly prominent within the country house, as the organisation of space within the house evolved to produce the suite of reception rooms that by the end of the period consistently linked the library to the drawing room as a public space.[4]

Libraries have been noted for their non-book collections, particularly assemblages of antiquarian curiosities and fine art groups of coins, medals and small bronzes. Little attention has been paid to portraiture within the library, beyond the antique tradition of author portraits above the bookcases.[5] While this tradition was taken up in the eighteenth century through busts of classical authors (the lost interior scheme at Blickling Hall, Norfolk, is an excellent example), portraits tended not to infiltrate the library, at least partly as a result of the available space for display above the bookcases. Family portraits were least likely to be hung in the library, but portrait series of public figures are known and emerge as a distinctive category within the uses of portraiture in the country house.

My discussion focuses on the surviving library room at Narford Hall, Norfolk, as the vehicle for an exploration of how the portraiture, in a series of paintings hung above the bookcases and in busts and miniatures positioned on furniture, contributes to the interior scheme. The room was commissioned by Sir Andrew Fountaine (1676–1753), who was probably his own architect, and who was a well-known virtuoso. I argue for the presence of a complex scheme of interactions between the portraits, based on the associations and oppositions contained in the biographies of the depicted 'great men'. I suggest that there is an emerging theme of English cultural achievements represented within the portraiture, and a highly personal theme of friendship specific to Fountaine. This was not a room open to all visitors, but one that was open to those who could understand and make use of the specialist collections, of books, coins and medals, within.

The library within the house plan

The uses of portraiture within this distinctive space relate closely to the design scheme for the room, and its evolving place within the country house plan.[6] Libraries in English country houses become more visible, at least in the archives, during the seventeenth century. Typically, a small study was adjacent to the owner's bedchamber, on the upper floor of the house. It was segregated from the public rooms, or state apartments, which spread over the ground and first floors, linked by the great stairs. By the early eighteenth century, state rooms were laid out across one floor only, on the first floor or *piano nobile* of newly built houses. Libraries were still planned to relate to the owner's apartment (bedchamber, dressing rooms) and were not integrated into the new state room layout. A prime example of this arrangement is Houghton Hall, Norfolk. Houghton was built from 1720–29 for the most powerful politician of the time, Sir Robert Walpole, First Minister. The formal entrance to the house was up external stairs to the first floor Stone Hall, from which guests would be admitted to the state rooms on the right-hand side of the house. Walpole's bedchamber apartment was on the left-hand side, separated from the hall by a family parlour. His dressing room and library were next to his bedchamber, all luxuriously fitted out but not on the state rooms route.[7] The sole portrait in Walpole's library at Houghton Hall was that of George I, a royal gift, placed over the chimneypiece. The library room was otherwise entirely given over to books, in a fully architectural scheme of mahogany panelling, completed by 1729. This type of wood panelled interior for libraries, with only overdoor and overmantel spaces for paintings, is typical of late seventeenth and early eighteenth-century libraries.

The architectural history of the private library within the country house took a new direction in the early decades of the eighteenth century, leaving the example at the newly fitted out Houghton Hall as a rather conservative nod to the past. Instead, newly built libraries began to encroach on the public side of the house plan, becoming more accessible from the state apartments: a decisive step on the long arc of the trajectory from family to reception room. This next phase is gloriously represented by the long library at Narford Hall, Norfolk, created from 1718, which forms the main subject of this discussion.[8] Although libraries did not become fully integrated into the public rooms until at least the 1740s, they did lose their association with the owner's apartment. Bedchambers tended to be relocated to the second floor, away from the state room floor, while libraries remained on the principal floor. They were still not visible on the principal axis through the state rooms. At Holkham Hall, Norfolk, a palatial Palladian revival house for the Earl of Leicester, the long library was kept in a separate wing with the owner's apartments, away from the monumental state rooms and sculpture gallery of the main block of the house.

After the 1740s, the country house plan evolved into a circuit plan, in which the principal reception rooms opened in to each other, allowing guests to circulate, via the hall. The circuit plan, and the newly visible library within this plan, can be demonstrated in the houses of Robert Adam. He remodelled the Jacobean Syon House, Middlesex, for the Duke of Northumberland into this plan. The Syon library is a true room of parade, the final public room in the circuit, designed to equal the preceding dining and drawing rooms. Here, past and present portraits gazed down on the fashionable world. Adam's 1762 scheme for Syon House remodelled the Jacobean long gallery as a neoclassical library. Syon was not the principal venue for the display of Northumberland portraits, and the library scheme instead displays a series of portrait medallions integrated into the wall surface, contrasting with sculpture and the books. By the 1760s, the library carried equal social status and visibility with the great hall, and dining and withdrawing rooms.

This mobility of the library within the house plan affected how the library was intended to be presented within a sequence of rooms, family or state. The increasing visibility and accessibility of the library therefore affected the intended uses and appropriate design schemes. With this contingent planning in mind, the Narford Hall library can be understood in the context of the spatial relations of its creation date, 1718. It was not intended to be an addition to the state rooms of the older house, but it was distinct from the owner's bedchamber apartment within the house.

Narford Hall was built 1702–4, in the established form of the later seventeenth-century country house: a stripped down classicism, emphasising length over height, and easily adaptable to the funds available. The 1702 house took the form of a rectangle, two rooms deep, with a central hall and great stairs, and symmetrical rooms to either side (figure 12). Narford's owner was the younger son of an old Norfolk family, who had returned to the county to establish his own landed estate. Andrew Fountaine (1632–1706) moved with his second wife, Sarah Chicheley, at a time when their children were adults; Andrew Fountaine had benefited from the patronage of his father-in-law Sir Thomas Chicheley of Wimpole Hall, Cambridgeshire, and his metropolitan presence helped his son, also named Andrew, establish his own early introduction into Court circles. In order to assess the younger Fountaine's creation of the new library room and its interior scheme, I am going to use a brief biographical discussion of his cultural interests and connections, which will be shown to be strong influences on the portraiture within the library.

Sir Andrew Fountaine: collecting and networks

Marcia Pointon reminds us that the uses of portraiture, by patrons and other viewers, can invoke assumptions about the competences required to access a range of meanings ascribed to these images. The

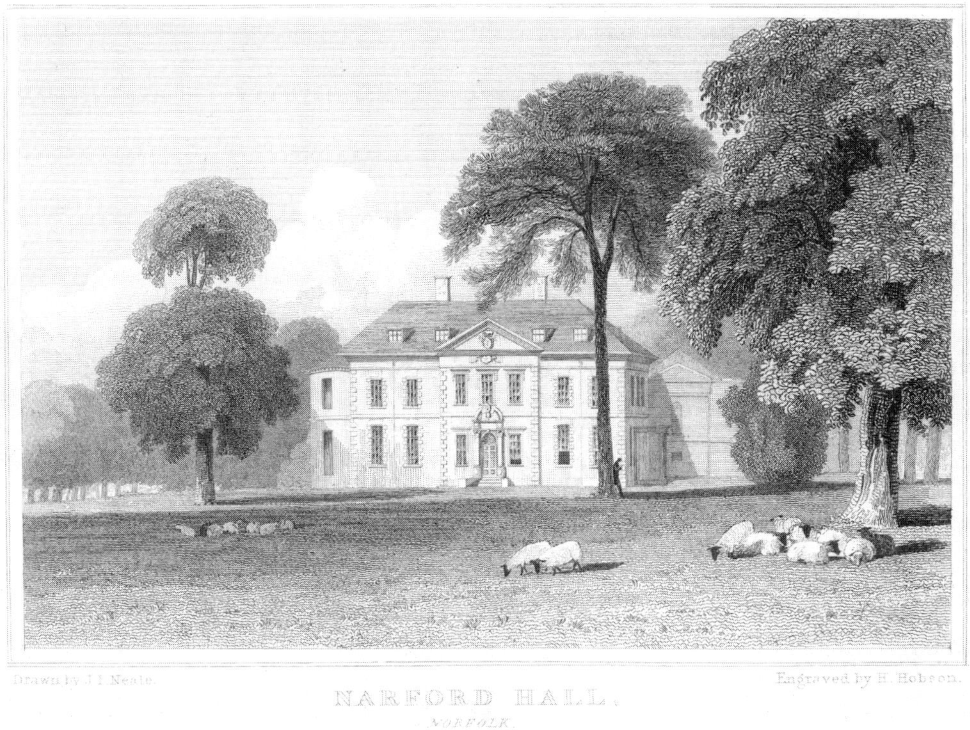

Figure 12 Narford Hall, Norfolk, engraved in 1819, showing the 1702 house with the 1718 library wing to the rear and right of the house. Narford Hall, Norfolk, from J.P. Neale, *Views of the seats of noblemen and gentlemen, in England, Ireland, Scotland and Wales* (London: Sherwood, Neely and Jones, 1819).

means of decoding portraiture arise from the cultural milieu and experiences of the viewer, the accumulated education and aspirations that facilitate the viewer's understanding of the image-specific codes and the wider social contexts of the encounter.[9] In working with the gallery of portraits assembled and displayed within the Narford library, I am drawing attention to the competences primarily of the patron, the younger Andrew Fountaine (1676–1753). The son of a relatively obscure landed gentry father, albeit one who seems to have had some virtuoso interests, the younger Fountaine was celebrated during his lifetime for his virtuoso achievements and social connections, and his reputation endured through the nineteenth century. More recently, scholarship on the Palladian revival of the early eighteenth century and on the cultural significance of county networks has further informed our historical appreciation of both Sir Andrew Fountaine and Narford Hall.[10]

While his father was building the house on the new estate, the younger Fountaine was away on his first Grand Tour from 1701–4.

He was already knighted, as a result of his Oxford career at Christ Church College. Here he had been chosen to make the Latin oration to William III on his visit to Oxford in 1698, and as custom dictated, William knighted him. As a student, he had already made something of a name for himself as a virtuoso, 'one that has spent much of his time upon coyn's & Pictures and understand's them well. And has a good collection of both, especcially of Italian prints', as he was described in 1699 by Edward Thwaites, Dean of Queen's College, Oxford.[11] Thwaites recommended Fountaine to the cleric and scholar George Hickes. Hickes needed help finishing his major publication on the early Germanic cultures, and Fountaine contributed an essay on Saxon coins which seems to have been innovative in linking linguistic and historical questions to the inscriptions found on the coins, 'in the new spirit of historical investigation'.[12] However he had acquired this precociously advanced interest in numismatics, it is clear that he had a strong visual sense of coins as material objects, a sense also found in his interest in the visual arts.

Fountaine's charm is a characteristic quality of contemporary accounts, and it must have been evident for his inclusion on the diplomatic mission to take the Act of Settlement, concerning the succession of the English crown, to the dowager electress Sophia (1630–1714) in Hanover in 1701. This was a highly politically charged mission, designed to ensure the peaceful succession of the crown to a legitimate Protestant, after the death of the obvious heir, Queen Anne's son William, Duke of Gloucester, in 1700. Sophia was a granddaughter of James I; it would be her son George who succeeded after Anne died in 1714. The significance for Fountaine was cultural, rather than political, as he stayed on in Europe, a success at the Hanoverian court. Hanover was emerging as a centre of the Palladian revival, an architectural turn away from the Baroque towards new interpretations of Andrea Palladio's sixteenth-century classicism.[13] Fountaine would adopt this new direction in architecture at his own house. He was already well enough versed in the arts and sciences to maintain a correspondence with the great German philosopher and mathematician, Gottfried Wilhelm Leibnitz (1646–1716), then librarian in the ducal library at Hanover. Leibnitz supported his admission to the Royal Society of Berlin (Leibnitz was a corresponding Fellow of the Royal Society, London). In Italy, he established a friendship with Cosimo III de Medici, Grand Duke of Tuscany. Fountaine's character is caught in a letter from a fellow traveller, Robert Nelson, to his mother, reassuring her of his Grand Tour progress and mentioning that ''tis well Sir Andrew has in the sweetness of his conversation so strong a remedy against those prejudices that might arise from his great Erudition'.[14] Fountaine's happy combination of an evidently charming personality and deep knowledge of matters close to all virtuosi's hearts, especially of coins and medals, made him a sought-after acquaintance. He was also useful to his friends back in England, commissioning works of art and exporting them on their behalf, as he did for Thomas Herbert, 8th Earl of Pembroke (1656/7–1733).[15]

Sir Andrew Fountaine gained further experience of European culture when he travelled to Holland in 1705, on another diplomatic mission, with the Earl of Pembroke. Here he made further purchases of books and coins, to be displayed at his London home.[16] In 1706 he inherited the Narford estate, aged thirty. His London life continued, enlivened by an official visit to Ireland where he befriended Jonathan Swift, with summer visits to Narford, until he undertook a second Grand Tour from 1713. He was away for four years, in Paris, Turin, Florence, Rome and Venice, returning through Germany.[17] Still a keen collector, searching out coins and medals, he was said to have 'out-Italianed the Italians themselves' in his success.[18] On his return to England in 1717, he began to alter Narford Hall, adding the library wing.

Fountaine never married, and the fragmentary records of his life, chiefly the vivid appearances he makes in Swift's letters up to 1713, do not suggest any particular attachments.[19] His remained close to his sister Elizabeth (m. Edward Clent) and his brother Brigg, although both predeceased him; his sister's grandson Brigg Price Fountaine continued the family line. His social persona as a single man, active at Court and welcome at the greatest aristocratic houses, prompts the question of who was the intended audience for his refashioning of his father's house, architecturally and through the collections? Whose gaze traversed the library portraits? The challenge here is to recover the meanings and associations that would have been shared by Fountaine and his milieu.[20] Any biographical approach needs to be supported and extended by a consideration of the significance of the portraits as a group and in their setting.

The interior scheme of the library

Fountaine's architectural work at his house was in advance of the 1720s movement towards the Palladian revival in England, although he would become a member of the inner circle of patrons and designers associated with Richard Boyle, 3rd Earl of Burlington (1694–1753) and his protégée William Kent (1686–1748), who supported the style.[21] Kent met Lord Burlington making his Grand Tour in 1719 and accompanied him back to England later that year.[22] There is no direct evidence that Fountaine and Kent knew each other in Rome, although it is hard to credit that the two Englishmen would not have been introduced by mutual friends.[23] However, by 1718, Fountaine was back at Narford finishing his rapidly constructed library wing, and Kent was yet to start his English career.

Current scholarship suggests that Sir Andrew Fountaine was his own architect, and that he went on to design at least one other room (for his friend Sir Matthew Decker's house in Richmond, Surrey) as well as being treated as an essential adviser for building projects in the 1720s elsewhere in Norfolk. The house at Narford was built against an older service courtyard; Sir Andrew used the projection of a rear wing of this yard to create a new wing for his library (see figure 12). He followed the most recent examples of English architecture published in Colen Campbell's *Vitruvius Britannicus* of 1715, treating the library exterior as a first floor *piano nobile* in a demonstration of 'advanced Palladian taste'.[24]

The interior remains as 'an outstanding example of an early eighteenth-century interior' (figure 13). The long room (40 by 16 feet) is entered from the south, with four sash windows along the west wall. The north door exits to a later print closet, added in the 1730s. The fireplace on the east wall makes a sculptural contribution to the interior scheme through its swags, rams heads and satyr's face, in a 'forceful, Antique manner'.[25] Three walls are lined with bookshelves, to two-thirds of their height. The joinery of the shelving is simple, with divisions between cases marked by slim minimalist pilasters.[26]

Above the shelves, the sequence of portraits attracts the eye, before the full splendour of the painted ceiling is perceived. There are 31 portraits, presented as three paired heads at each end of the room and as single heads along the east wall, though above the fireplace, in separate frames, is a further paired couple. The west wall is hung with three three-quarter length portraits, one each between the windows, and with single heads at each end. The portraits have black frames, with gilded corner decorations, and are hung against a monochrome painted surface, greyish in tone. The frames of the double portraits are set between decorative panels that mark the vertical accents rising from the door architraves, the chimneypiece and the corners of the room. The deep

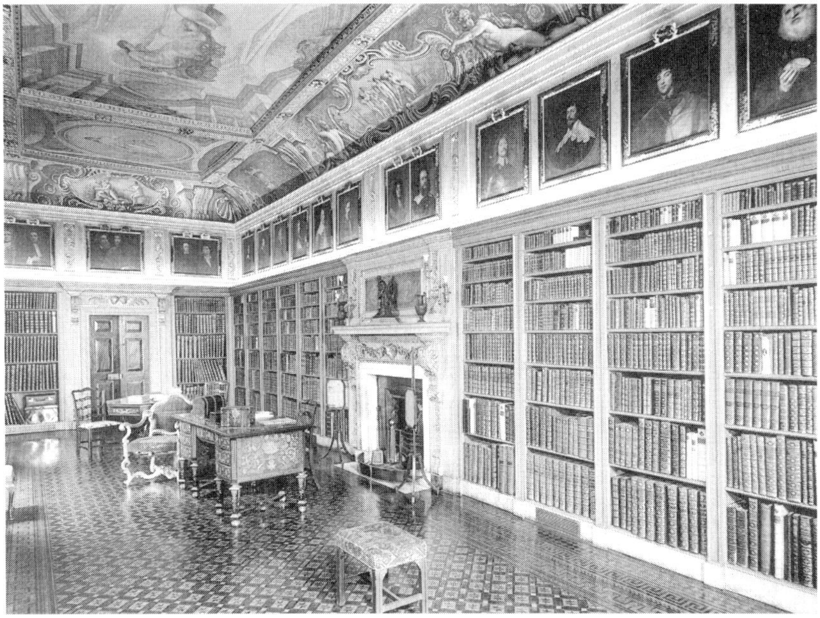

Figure 13 Interior of the Narford Hall library, photographed c.1992.

coving is painted with classical grisaille figures with gilt highlights. The flat ceiling is given an illusionistic architectural treatment, with painted divisions containing allegorical scenes of Morning, Noon (Apollo driving his chariot) and Night.

The portraits are copies, the work of a single painter, using a variety of sources to create this unified sequence of heads. Andrew Moore suggests that the latest date for an original portrait source, that of Dr Richard Mead, is 1725, which may indicate a possible completion date for the sequence for Narford.[27] Some or all were set up by 1728, when Fountaine's friend Sir Matthew Decker and his family came to stay at Narford. Decker called the library 'prodigeously [*sic*] handsome', noting that 'above the bookcases are several pictures of great men, with the names upon them'.[28] Given the careful attention to detailing the proportions of the plaster work above the bookcases (above), it is difficult to imagine this interior scheme without the rhythm of the visual relationship between the bays of the bookcases and the frames of the portraits above them. I suggest that if Fountaine initiated the construction of the library wing in 1718 he was also planning ahead for the completion of the portrait sequence, assembled over the ensuing seven or so years.

The library ceiling work is undated and unattributed and opinions diverge about the relationship between the style of the coving painting and the Morning, Noon and Night pieces: two hands and thus two dates? If so, in which order? The Georgian Group visit in 1991 identified a baroque ceiling and a later, classical coving, but more investigation is needed.[29] The *quadratura* effects in both coving and ceiling, of fictive brackets and an illusionary architectural frame for the view of Apollo, draw on established painting traditions from the seventeenth century; in early eighteenth-century England, such painterly effects would mimic, or challenge, the success of Italian *stuccadores* working during the 1720s.[30] It is worth noting that the fictive cartouches of the coving each appear to stand away from an apse, whose interior surface is punctuated by gilt coffering, in the manner of William Kent's early painted ceiling for the new Cupola Room at Kensington Palace (1722). This illusionary coffering was not unique to Kent, but it is a visual trick he used extensively.[31]

This is not to propose an attribution, but to note that Kent's training in Italy as a painter resulted in painted schemes that were thoroughly Roman. Kent's first known commission on his return to England was to paint the coving and ceiling of the saloon at Burlington House, Piccadilly, London, for his patron the Earl of Burlington; he began the sketches in January 1720.[32] Fountaine was fully involved in London life on his return to England, appointed Vice-Chamberlain to Caroline, Princess of Wales, and allegedly also tutor to her son Prince William.[33] There is no direct evidence for the origins of Fountaine's friendship with Lord Burlington, although a letter of 1717 from Burlington to Fountaine survives.[34] A significant indication of their friendship survives at Narford, in the form of the large mythical canvases by Antonio Pellegrini (1675–1741) installed in the central hall.

Pellegrini first worked in England from 1708 to 1713. The canvases at Narford are said by family tradition to have been a gift from Burlington, possibly in 1720 when Burlington House was being remodelled.[35] The canvases were certainly installed by 1728, when they were viewed by Sir Matthew Decker, who noted 'a handsome hall, painted in panels, with History pieces; the carved work gilt'.[36] A family tradition at Narford records the creation of a painted ceiling in the hall, whitewashed in the nineteenth century, and Knox attributes two of the hall overdoors to Pellegrini.[37] The putative painted ceiling commission for the hall (apparently too scandalously sexual, however mythological, for nineteenth-century viewers) does put the library scheme into a wider context for Fountaine's presentation of his interiors. In this continued Italian dominance, the presence of the Pellegrini canvases and the library ceiling at Narford remained at the forefront of taste.

In the library there is a distinct contrast between the ebullient effects of the coving and ceiling and the very restrained cornice that separates them from the wall treatment. This cornice is in harmony with the shallow relief of the cornice to the bookcases, both alluding to the Doric order in their simplicity. The choice of frame style for the portrait sequence is similarly sober, taking a later seventeenth-century style at a time when the new preference for completely gilt frames was beginning to dominate.[38] The dark frames complement the dark backgrounds surrounding the heads, allowing the flesh tones and highlights from white linen or satin textiles to take prominence.

There was an early model for this use of portraits elsewhere in Norfolk, at Melton Constable, the house built by Sir Jacob Astley (1639–1729) between 1664 and 1687 (figure 14). Here Astley framed

Figure 14 Interior of the ground floor library, Melton Constable Hall, Norfolk, showing the portrait series rehung from the seventeenth-century first floor library.

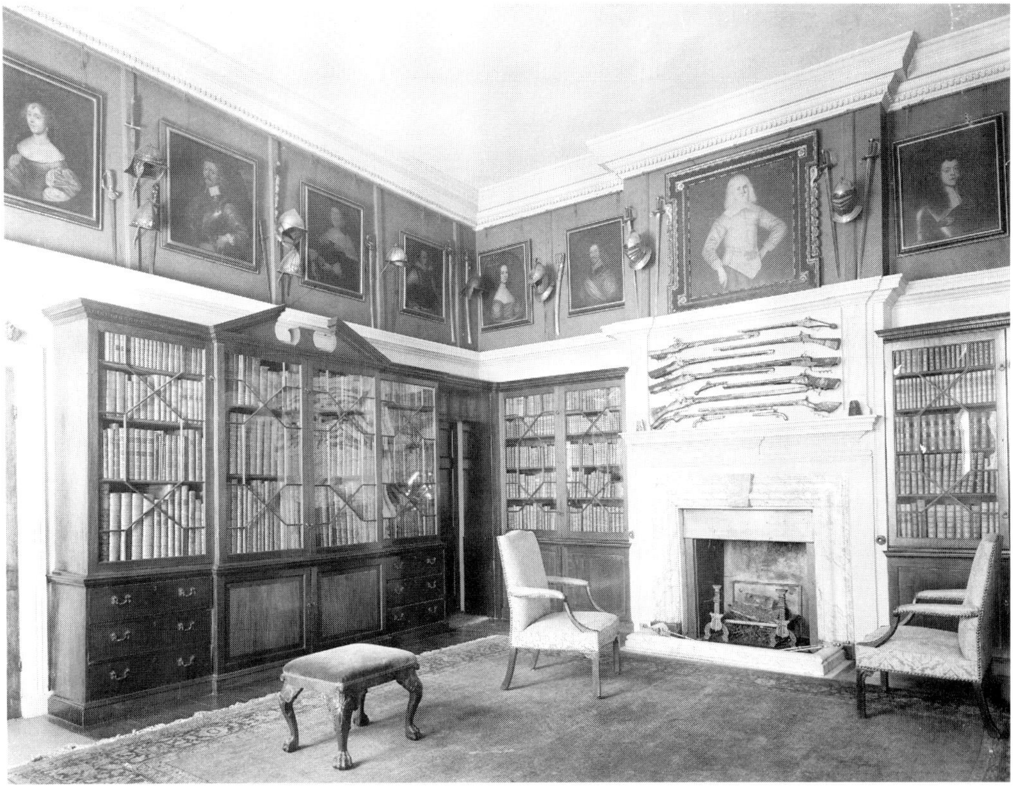

his seventeenth-century family portraits in uniform dark frames, with gilt borders on the mouldings. The exception, hung over the fireplace, was the portrait of Sir John Astley (d. 1639), Master of the Revels to James I, who (later) received a Kentian lugged frame with oakleaf pendants, also painted black. Sir Jacob inherited a group of ancestral portraits in 1694, which suggests the *terminus post quem* for setting them up in this manner in the Melton Constable library.[39] Sir Jacob Astley was of Fountaine's father's generation, both Royalists from old minor gentry Norfolk families. The Narford portraits are not family, but friends and great figures from the past; they are not old artefacts, but new versions. I suggest that the choice of frame style deliberately ages the Narford portrait sequence, emulating the 'authentic' accumulation of generations of images represented in the Melton Constable library. The imposition of a frame style imposes a systematisation that enhances visual similarities, and masks differences, between the images so treated.[40] For the Narford library portraits, then, in contrast to the contemporary impact of the painted ceiling, some historicising effects are deliberately produced through the choice of frame style.

Faces and spaces

The men (there are no women) represented range from Titian (b. 1488) to contemporaries of Fountaine; despite this chronological expanse, there is a biographical logic in the way in which portraits are positioned in relation to others in the series. Given that this series was created from prints or accessible originals, by a single artist, I suggest that this deliberate assembly carries meanings that are recoverable. The portrait series carries iconographic weight, although a single scheme (such as political contemporaries or Fountaine ancestors) is not immediately discernible. The sitters' names are derived from the cartouches on each frame (see list below). The same names were documented in the first publication discussing Narford Hall, the entry for Narford in the county history of Norfolk written during Sir Andrew's lifetime (the topographical project benefited from his scholarly assistance).[41]

The Narford heads, as copies, betray no value particularly assigned to the display of an original master's work; the painter is not a primary figure. Instead, I am adopting Harry Berger's notion of the 'fiction of objectivity'.[42] The act of portrayal, where a sitter adopts a pose in a studio in consultation with the artist, is smoothed away, unacknowledged by either party in the creation of the image. The sitter is portrayed as if unaware of, or unengaged by, the artificiality of sitting for a formal image. The resulting image makes an appeal to the viewer's desire for an accurate and objective insight into the sitter's personality, revealed by the privileged access to the 'unaware' facial characteristics of the sitter. This latter access is of course the fiction. As a result, the image is used to supposedly 'reveal' the character.

Berger prioritises a discussion of the meaning of the gaze to make the bridge between the formal properties of such portraits and the meanings that viewers, as socially and visually literate members of a group, bring to the images. He suggests that the gaze is the visual 'dimension of the dominant discourses by which a culture constructs its subjects to imagine and represent themselves'.[43] Such dominant discourses carry the normative values of dominant groups. In the Narford portraits, these are the discourses of the early eighteenth-century English elite, particularly the emerging ideas about relationships between artistic taste, social leadership and national identity. As David Solkin expresses it, early eighteenth-century masculine portraits displayed the mask of politeness, the successor to the moral virtues of Renaissance civic humanism, as a visual expression of society's norms.[44] These are historically and geographically specific discourses, played out in literary forms such as the new magazines (*The Spectator*, *The Tatler*), in the wider visual culture of landscape design (the shifts towards programmatic garden content and an identifiably English style) and increasingly in the English country house as the locus of cultural and political expression. This latter shift is exemplified by the deliberate presentation of aristocratic houses as forums for and spaces of personal power, away from Court, and the rise of representations of interiors, seen in England after 1700.[45]

I wish to argue that the Narford library portrait sequence is an expression of Fountaine's relationship to contemporary discourses about political power and aspects of English identity. As can be seen from the list below, these are the 'famous men' or 'great men' acknowledged as such by visitors and inventory takers. The portrait series thus fits in to the established genre of portraits of historical notables, and to the Renaissance practice of collecting and displaying groups of such portraits.[46] The Narford series is not a collection that looks back to the antique — there are no ancient Greeks or Romans — but to creators of Renaissance and early modern European culture, with England at its centre.

The paired portraits are usually of historical contemporaries. Dr Richard Mead and Dr John Radcliffe are paired as friends, royal doctors and antiquaries. Titian and Aretino are both early sixteenth-century

Italian cultural figures, Inigo Jones is the English apostle of Palladio. Over the fireplace, Prince Rupert, soldier and first cousin to Charles II, is with Sir Kenelm Digby, another seventeenth-century figure of chivalric achievements. Ben Jonson and William Shakespeare were friends, Jonson's role in the posthumous publication of Shakespeare ensured his reputation, echoing the relationship between Palladio and Jones. Cardinal Mazarin is paired with the Vicomte de Turenne, contemporaries under Louis XIV, and Samuel Butler and Charles Cotton are contemporary seventeenth-century poets.

I have produced the following list, detailing the identifications of the Narford library portraits:

1 Dr Richard Mead, 1673–1754, physician, Whig virtuoso
2 Dr John Radcliffe, 1650–1714, physician, patron
3 Titian (Tiziano Vecellio), c.1488–1576, Venetian painter, close friend of Aretino
4 Pietro Aretino, 1492–1557, Italian poet and prose writer, journalist
5 Inigo Jones, 1573–1652, English architect and scenographer to the Stuart courts
6 Andrea Palladio, 1508–80, Italian architect
7 Nicholas Lanière, 1588–1665, composer, painter, engraver
8 Sir Peter Paul Rubens, 1577–1640, Flemish painter and designer
9 Dean Henry Aldrich, 1647–1710, Dean of Christ Church, Oxford, divine, scholar
10 Sir John Maynard, 1602–90, judge, Whig constitutional lawyer
11 Gustavus Adolphus, 1594–1632, King of Sweden 1611–32, expansionist
12 Pope Alexander VII, 1599–1667, pope 1655–67, patron of arts in Rome
13 Prince Rupert, 1619–82, nephew to Charles I, soldier and linguist
14 Sir Kenelm Digby, 1603–65, author, naval commander, diplomatist, virtuoso
15 James Graham, 5th Earl of Montrose, 1612–50, Royalist military commander
16 Admiral Robert Blake, 1599–1657, Commonwealth naval hero

17 Thomas Wharton, 1st Marquis of Wharton, 1648–1715, Whig politician
18 Cornelius Janssen, 1593–1664, Stuart portrait painter
19 Edmund Waller, 1606–87, poet, royalist MP
20 Edward Pococke, 1604–91, Christ Church orientalist
21 Ben Jonson, 1572–1637, poet and playwright
22 William Shakespeare, 1564–1616, poet and playwright
23 Cardinal Jules Mazarin, 1602–61, Cardinal and Chief Minster of France, patron
24 Henri de la Tour d'Auvergne, Vicomte de Turenne, 1610–75, Commander French army
25 Samuel Butler, 1612–80, satirical poet
26 Charles Cotton, 1630–87, poet and linguist
27 Dr Humphrey Prideaux, 1648–1724, Dean of Norwich, orientalist and divine
28 William Cavendish, 2nd Duke of Devonshire, 1673–1729, Whig leader
29 Dr John Tillotson, 1630–94, Archbishop of Canterbury, celebrated preacher
30 Thomas Herbert, 8th Earl of Pembroke, 1656–1733, President of the Royal Society
31 Dr John Wallis, 1616–1703, mathematician

Some of the sitters such as Dean Aldrich were known to Sir Andrew, indeed as Dean of Christ Church College, Aldrich selected the young Andrew for the oration to William III, resulting in his knighthood. By 1725 only three friends were alive, Dr Mead, the 2nd Duke of Devonshire, and the 8th Earl of Pembroke. Others are seventeenth-century British figures whose gentlemanly achievements transcended political divisions, such as Admiral Robert Blake and Sir Kenelm Digby. Several of them acted in the service of two contrasting regimes, like Dr John Wallis, chaplain to Charles II and codebreaker for William III, and Dr John Tillotson, chaplain to Charles II and Archbishop of Canterbury for William III. Both these men successfully negotiated the transition from Stuart to Orange royal rule, in support of a continued Protestant succession. International statesmen and patrons of the arts, such as Pope Alexander VII and Cardinal Mazarin, represent nationalist interests in their investment in the creation of Italian and French culture, but also participated in international dialogues around contemporary approaches to a classical inheritance. Despite Sir Andrew's travels around the

German courts and his warm reception there, the German states are not represented. Hanoverian royals are represented elsewhere in the house, in the group of royal portraits hung on the great stairs, but in the library there was no room, for example, for Leibnitz. This portrait scheme looks away from the new constitutional fact of a German-born monarch, back to the older triangular relationship of English, French and Italian culture, a relationship that has shaped English identity through conflict and adoption.

If the suggested cultural relationships are historically nuanced by political tension and increasingly by English cultural discourses about national style, the preceding linear analysis of the paired portraits is rather safe. The portraits are, after all, in three-dimensional space, set around the walls of the room. The portrait scheme can be analysed for visual inter-relationships between sitters, suggesting a dynamic to the hang that utilises the great space of the library room. I have argued above that the paired portraits demonstrate biographical logic, not unexpectedly. But a wider view of how these faces interact with each

Figure 15 Schematic plan of the Narford library portraits, showing inter-relationships between the sitters.

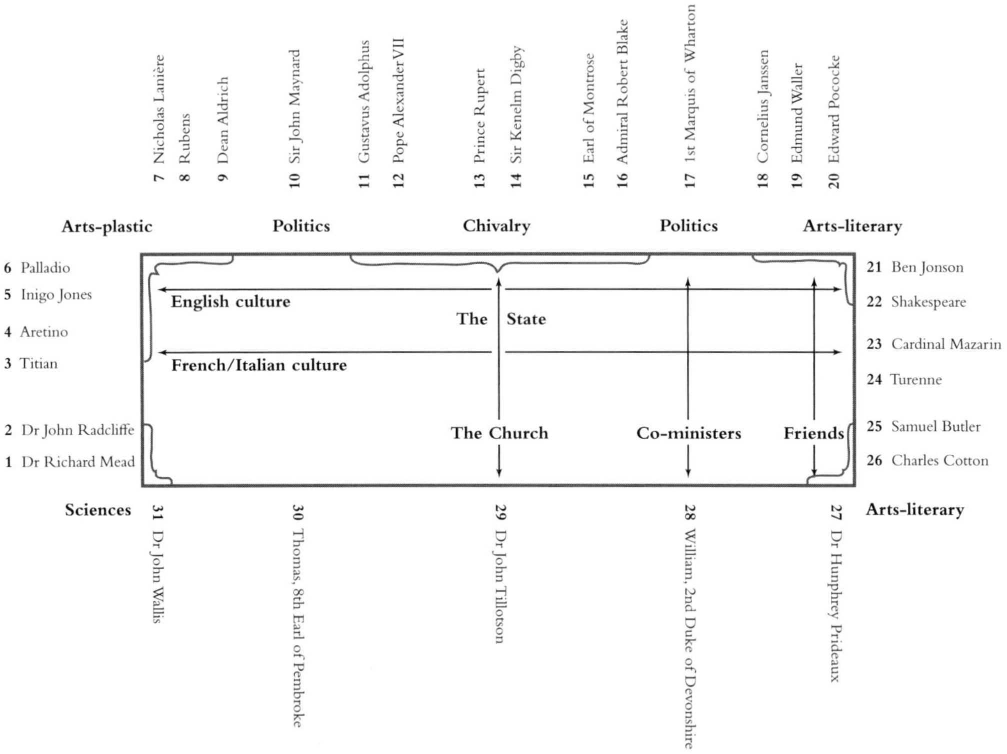

other reveals a balanced and systematic arrangement, with portraits in groups representing sciences, the plastic arts, the art of chivalry and literary arts. These groups are given greater force of meaning by cross-cutting oppositions, shown schematically in figure 15. Mighty French figures stare the length of the library at great Italians; the church (Archbishop Tillotson) faces the state (or the embodiment of divine rule through the house of Stuart, in the person of Prince Rupert). Complementary sightlines include two iconic figures of early Stuart culture in the plastic and literary arts facing each other down the length of the library. Friends Edward Pococke and Humphrey Prideaux look across the width of the room to each other, as do political co-ministers the 1st Marquis of Wharton and the 2nd Duke of Devonshire. The painted gazes interact with each other across the space of the room, and their placing must also draw the viewer into a more complex sequence of looking than simply following a circuit. The gaze is male and the little world created within the library is also male.

Further spatial complexity is suggested when the furnishings of the library are considered, adding layers of visual and material richness to the interior. Later in the eighteenth century, that great experimenter with historical styles, Horace Walpole, created his own historicising portrait scheme for the gothic library at Strawberry Hill, in which roundels of copies from seventeenth-century portraits sit within an architectural setting of heraldry and High Gothic. For Pointon, this scheme 'inscribes Walpole into the past'.[47] Aspects of the Narford furnishings also contribute to the sense of the past within the library; I want to go on to suggest that one piece of furniture set the tone for much of this scheme, including the historicising frames. This piece is the Mazarin cabinet.

'The whole furniture and ornaments herein'

The Norfolk antiquary Francis Blomefield declared of Narford Hall that 'the whole Furniture and Ornaments herein are sufficient to excite the Curiosity of the Learned, and preserve the Memory of their judicious Owner'.[48] Furnishings in the library are listed in the 1753 post-mortem inventory.[49] The collections in the room included sculpture, antiquities and specialist furniture such as coin cabinets. Fountaine had been a noted coin and medal collector since he was a student. The presence of these cabinets in the library, rather than in another room, suggests associations between the historical value of the coins and medals, and the histories retained on the bookshelves. Such intended associations became a feature of collections during the seventeenth century, in European private and institutional libraries. Collectors' coin cabinets could be invested with considerable design significance, signalling the rarity and historical value of the pieces they housed. For example, Horace Walpole commissioned a specialist cabinet on his return from his Grand Tour, in order to house and display a collection of ivory miniatures, both mounted on the outside of the cabinet doors and stored within.[50] When Sir Matthew Decker viewed the Narford room in 1728, he recorded that 'Two fine cabinets stand on one side, and two flat cabinets or book cases in the middle.'[51] By the time of the 1753 inventory, there were three cabinets, two matching (for medals) and one in ebony 'with brass ornaments and 21 miniature Pictures upon it'. The ebony cabinet, which is said to have belonged to Cardinal Mazarin, contained a collection of wax casts of intaglios, numbering 1,430. Cardinal Jules Mazarin (1602–61) assembled extensive collections, displayed in the Palais Mazarin, Paris, and dispersed after his death. I suggest here that the Narford cabinet is indeed from the Mazarin collection.

The cabinet in Narford, recorded as having '21 miniature Pictures upon it' in the 1753 inventory, appears to be a match for the description given in an inventory of Mazarin's furniture, made during his lifetime.[52] The cabinet is the upper chest of drawers, resting on a later base (figure 16). The description in the Mazarin inventory is further confirmed by the presence of the portrait miniatures, in round and oval frames, set on the base, frieze and upper pediment of the cabinet. Sir John Cullum saw 'miniatures of French Persons, well done in oil-colours' on the cabinet, when he visited in 1767.[53] There are two outstanding differences between the Mazarin inventory description and the surviving cabinet at Narford. First, the number of miniatures: 48 in 1653, 21 in the 1753 Narford inventory. Second, the cabinet is on a later stand, which takes the form of a kneehole desk of shallow drawers, designed as a monumental archway and ornamented with a Vitruvian scroll motif. This later stand must have been commissioned by Sir Andrew and again, it bears the stylistic influence of William Kent's designs for library furniture (as that for Chiswick House, Burlington's villa).

If, as seems likely from its correlation with the Mazarin inventory description, this is indeed a cabinet from the Cardinal's collection, there is a further association in Fountaine's circle to explain its arrival. The bulk of the Mazarin sculpture collection was acquired by Fountaine's close friend, Thomas, Earl of Pembroke, for display at Wilton House,

Wiltshire. Pembroke's purchase is not closely dated, but broadly assigned to the 1720s. The Mazarin cabinet seems to set a keynote for the decorative scheme. In its historical association with the outstanding cultural collections of a famous French statesman, partially on display in the Louvre and the Bibliothèque Mazarin and familiar to Fountaine through his visits to Paris, it adds material depth to the visual associations contained within the portrait scheme (which includes Mazarin's image) in the library. The visual richness of the black shades of the ebony and the gilt highlights from the ormolu fittings are exactly carried through in the portrait frames. It is no coincidence that the cabinet is displayed in the centre bay of the window wall, beneath the half-length portrait of Dr John Tillotson. This central position accords with the 1753 inventory's record of the three cabinets between the four windows. The portrait above is emphasised by reliefs immediately below the frame, modelled as an archbishop's mitre flanked by palms. This relief decoration finished exactly above the top of the Mazarin cabinet. Without the date of acquisition, it is speculation, but one supported by the associations noted here, to suggest that the Mazarin cabinet was owned by Fountaine by the time he returned from his second European tour and began planning his new library.

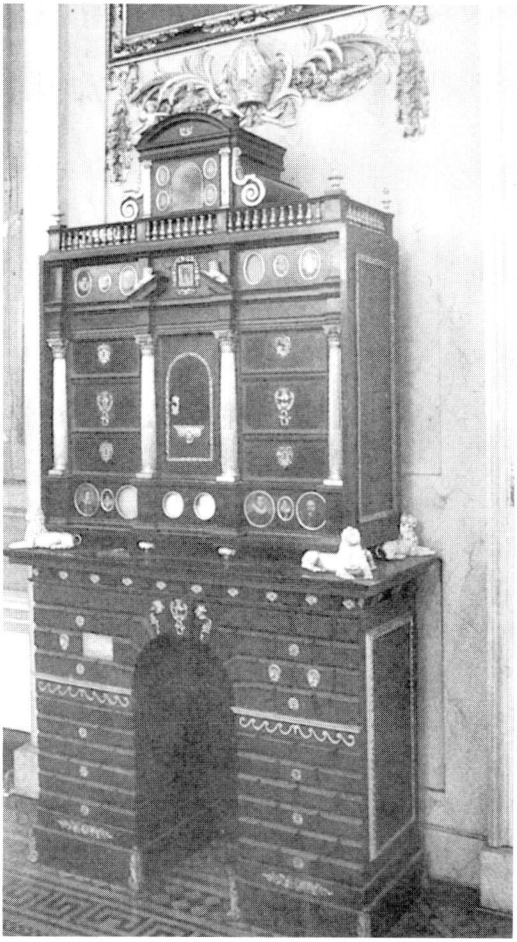

Figure 16 The Mazarin cabinet, Narford Hall library, sitting on the later, Kent-influenced, base. Photographed in 1988.

The function of the Mazarin cabinet as a receptacle for a large collection of wax casts of intaglios (engraved semi-precious stones referred to by Fountaine's contemporaries as 'gems'), is also significant not just for the scale of the collection but for the nature of the objects. Fountaine was a serious collector of these small bearers of images, along with the 2nd and 3rd Dukes of Devonshire and the 8th Earl of Pembroke.[54] The tradition of engraving gems in relief (cameos) or incising them (intaglios) came from ancient Greece and Rome, and ancient specimens were particularly prized by collectors. The first publications of engraved images of these stones appeared by the early eighteenth century. Aside from the methodological problems in dating the gems and identifying their subjects, such collections and publications contributed to the tradition of using these stones for their portraiture and iconography. The Mazarin cabinet is therefore shot through with representations of the human face, mythic, heroic and famous: in teeming multitude within its drawers, and in select miniatures on its exterior. It contributes to the extended scale and range of portraits within the Narford library, adding a micro level to the life-size heads above it.

The three cabinets made a greater visual impact through the additional collections that were displayed on and below each, as recorded in 1753. The Mazarin cabinet, with a decorative top unsuitable for supporting objects, was garnished below with 'a broken antique statue', presumably placed within the arch of the later base. It was flanked by 'ancient earthen tubs' which I am tempted to identify as locally sourced funerary urns (a class of archaeological object discussed by Norfolk's great seventeenth-century antiquary, Sir Thomas Browne[55]). One of the pair of cabinets of medals supported a plaster bust of Raphael on it along with more antique urns, cups and covers; below were a large green terracotta vase and two gilt busts. The other cabinet of medals supported a Roubiliac clay bust of Fountaine and a selection of vases in marble, 'Egyptian' alabaster and terracotta (with antique painted figures); underneath were the pairs to the objects under the first cabinet (a vase and two gilded busts).

The antiquities added a greater historical dimension to the collections, reaching back in to British prehistory, and reaching outwards to the Old Testament civilisation of Ancient Egypt. The ancient objects take their place in the repertoire of virtuoso collections, the museum-like representation of a selection of cultures beyond those who produced coins. They contribute additional forms and materials to the library interior, but do not disturb the dominance of the human figure represented in paint and by sculpture.

The remainder of the inventoried contents included the display on the mantelpiece: Shakespeare's monument, flanked by vases and bronze sphinxes (figure 17). The monument is a small-scale bronzed plaster cast of the *modello* for Shakespeare's monument in Westminster Abbey, by William Kent, executed by Peter Scheemakers in 1740 and installed in 1741. Shakespeare's burial monument was erected in St Mary's church, Stratford-upon-Avon, Warwickshire, before 1623. The

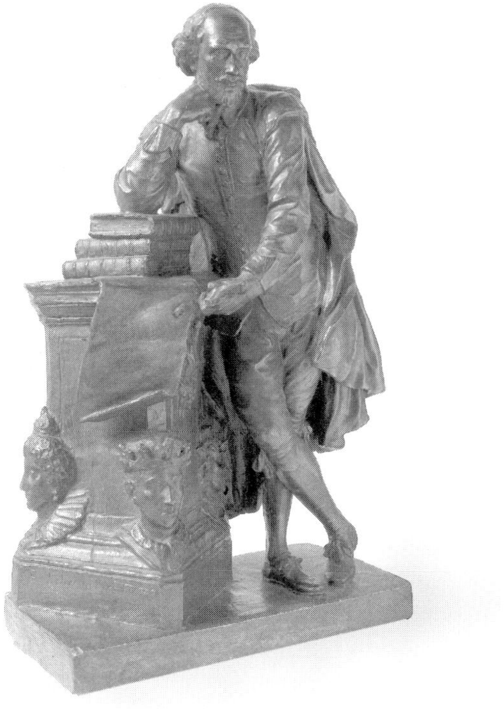

Figure 17 Bronzed plaster cast of the modello for the Shakespeare Westminster Abbey monument, by Peter Scheemakers, 1740.

sculpted half-length of Shakespeare in the act of writing was engraved for reproduction in Dugdale's *Antiquities of Warwickshire*, a widely disseminated county history published in 1656 and again in 1730.[56] As a graphic image, Shakespeare's first monument was well known to readers with antiquarian interests. The presence of a souvenir, or memorial of Shakespeare, in the material form of the model for the Westminster monument is notable for its early date: the cult of the author, or Bardolatry as literary critics have dubbed the discourses around Shakespeare, grew no earlier than from the 1730s, leading up to the tragedian Garrick's jubilee in Stratford in 1769. There is an important point to note here for the significance of Shakespeare in the Narford library, that an eighteenth-century understanding of the Shakespeare plays appropriated them as 'celebrations of British monarchy and British power', as Robert Hume summarises arguments made by literary historians Michael Dobson and Gary Taylor.[57] Shakespeare, already represented in the framed portrait series, was awarded the prime position on the mantelpiece beneath representatives of English chivalry; I suggest that his presence was less for his artistic merits as a poet and playwright (merits only later explored) than for his emerging role as chronicler of the nation through the history plays. The artistic qualities of the cast of the *modello* are somewhat greater than the 1623 wall monument: other examples may have circulated in the Kent/ Burlington circle but they remain to be identified.[58]

Shakespeare's statue joined the named portrait busts, and the anonymous gilded busts. Busts in the early modern library are a well-known visual trope, and Malcolm Baker has led recent scholarship in exploring the relationship between the sculpted image and the book collections they adorn, particularly for the series of busts acquired by college libraries in Oxford, Cambridge and Dublin. Contemporaries treated series of portrait busts as equivalents to painted portraits, in calling on the 'famous men' trope; Baker has shown that portrait busts were readily reproduced, and that verisimilitude in facial features was more important to contemporaries than 'individualistic' treatment of drapery. On these terms, portrait sculpture was judged for the quality of representation of the face, more than for its adoption of visual codes for drapery or pose.[59] In the Narford library, its creator was represented in clay by a contemporary artist, Roubiliac, who had also modelled the 8th Earl of Pembroke (for the library of Trinity College, Dublin).[60] The marble head of Fountaine by Roubiliac is still at Wilton House, and it is tempting to speculate on whether Sir Andrew Fountaine or Lord Pembroke was the patron, and which version was the gift. The bust of Raphael introduced the most famous artist of the High Renaissance to the room, one even more highly regarded than Titian, whose portrait is included in the painted series. The busts and statuary add further layers of scale and texture to the complex assemblage of portraiture within the room.

'Great men': friends in the library

This then is the library room as it survives, as it was inventoried in 1753 on the death of its creator, and as I reconstruct some aspects of its creation. I do not wish to claim that this is a complete reconstruction; like the room itself, this representation is a palimpsest with some obscured features. The surviving decorative scheme, together with a large part of the historic book collection, despite the loss of the extra layering created by time and the portable objects, is a rare example of early eighteenth-century taste. I have argued that this is a historicising taste. But how was the viewer intended to perceive this gallery of images as a group?

Historical comments on the portrait sequence used already in this discussion demonstrate that the viewers easily identified the subjects as 'great men' or 'famous men'. The competences called on from the viewer to make this identification were relatively simple: aided by the textual identification on the frame of each sitter, contemporary viewers understood the whole (made up of the parts of each portrait) to represent those men who had entered the history books. Each sitter could be viewed as fulfilling the norms of 'being great', in the terms that my biographical list of identifications suggests for each individual, and as the dominant discourses of fame and greatness created a canon of exclusively masculine historical persons. Rather than emphasise the biographical correlations that could be made between Fountaine's political and cultural allegiances and his choice of sitters, I prefer now to turn towards the uses of this particular group of portraits in this particular setting: the 'purposes of display' that Patrick Maynard reminds us are intended in pictures 'made for use'.[61]

Narford Hall, in its compact original form of 1702, does not appear to have had a picture gallery. A Norfolk neighbour, the architect and virtuoso Sir Roger North, remodelled his purchase of an old manor house at Rougham Hall from 1690, to house his collections on retiring to the country from London. As well as creating a suite of rooms for his own use (library and study, away from his lively family), Sir Roger created a first floor picture gallery. Such galleries were not the prerogative of the aristocratically wealthy, and I think the emphasis on display that this term 'gallery' carries is a useful one to bear in mind for Narford. Galleries, with or without pictures, were frequently occurring spaces in sixteenth-century great houses, used for indoor walking and associated with opportunities for private conversations, away from formally conducted social exchanges in state rooms.[62] Their lengths of wall became a site of display for pictures; by the time Sir Andrew was touring Europe, he could encounter picture galleries in any royal or elite house that he gained access to.

Practices of viewing picture galleries have been investigated recently by Frances Gage, in a discussion of the relationship between picture galleries, medical theories concerning exercise and health in the late Renaissance, and the uses of princely collections in Italy in the seventeenth century. Gage is particularly interested in the uses of landscape paintings, viewed within the more public galleries and open loggias, but she makes a useful distinction between genres and appropriate levels of public access within palaces. The enormous households of family, officials and lower status servants in Italian palaces had segregated and hierarchical access to spaces within the palace, and would view pictures distributed accordingly. In her review of treatises on health, Gage also reminds us of the English author Robert Burton's views on the beneficial effects of art works and antiquities of all types for the mental and physical health of the viewer, as expressed in *Anatomy of Melancholy* (1621). The viewer is expected to use a combination of close looking and gentle walking to achieve the ideal balance.[63]

This combination (Burton included reading as a beneficial practice) is possible in the Narford library, as the preceding discussion of the furnishings has shown. The genre of paintings on display is that of portraiture, and it is one that requires the competences of informed understanding to retrieve the exemplary qualities of the sitters. The Narford library was not filled with quantities of furniture to impede the walking viewer during Sir Andrew's lifetime, and we should not conflate its early eighteenth-century appearance with later presentations of country house libraries set up for Victorian house party entertaining. The length of the room and the interplay between the sitters in the painted portraits encourages the viewer to perambulate, pause and reflect. The viewer's gaze must also shift in focal length, from upwards and outwards to the portraits above the bookcases, to downwards and inwards to contemplate the micro scale of the portrait miniatures and the 'hidden faces' within the coins, medals and intaglio collections. This is not a disembodied gaze, then, but one that must be mobilised through an active body.

I opened this discussion with an insistence that the country house library has had a changing position with the house plan over time, and that each example needs to be understood within historically specific spatial relations, that may have been erased in later manifestations of libraries within the same house. This spatial distinctiveness is particularly relevant to the related issue of access: who in the household and as a visitor might be expected to enter the room and use it for its social purpose (rather than simply to service it). Who, then, might the active viewers, seeking recreation and solace within the gallery-like library at Narford, have been?

Fountaine, particularly through his London life, was a sociable man, moving within Court circles and also linked, through personal contact and the exchange of letters, to wider European circles of learning, discussed earlier. He was an active figure in a series of male networks, formed through shared interests in collecting; his life spanned the emergence of formal institutions centred on collecting practices from the early years of the Royal Society (founded 1660), through the refounding of the Society of Antiquaries of London in 1707, to the foundation of the British Museum in 1753.[64] Informal networks also flourished, such as the Kit Kat Club, founded at an unknown date in the 1690s by the publisher (and Shakespeare enthusiast) Jacob Tonson for the promotion of the arts.[65] Tonson insisted that members had their portraits painted by Sir Godfrey Kneller, later displayed in Tonson's newly built gallery to his outer London house; Burlington was a member.[66] Less structured still, but important meeting places for like-minded men, were the new urban coffee houses, multi-purpose sites of display and talking shops for virtuosi; a familiar milieu for Fountaine.[67] The range of public meeting spaces (nodal points in these social networks) available to men of the correct social status complemented and reinforced the private practices of collecting possible in domestic settings.

Away from the London networks, Fountaine appears to have sustained a local network based on his virtuoso interests. Norfolk antiquaries and book collectors certainly knew of Fountaine's interests and Blomefield thanked him for help with materials for the county history of Norfolk. Fountaine also welcomed house guests such as Decker and his family, and I presume that his strong friendships with other Norfolk landowners such as Thomas Coke of Holkham and Charles Townshend of Raynham (who remodelled the Raynham library), and the marriage of Lord Burlington's sister Elizabeth to Henry Bedingfeld of Oxburgh, meant that each would have had regular access to the other libraries.[68] However, at home, the unmarried Sir Andrew had no other family members to make claims on the library's space, beyond visits from his sister and brother. The contents of the library represent a set of personal connections that extended across Europe, but which were primarily enacted away from Narford.

Friendship figures in the way in which Fountaine settled his affairs, making particular provision for the care of the library collections. Sir Andrew's will left the enjoyment of the house to his brother-in-law before his nephew came of age, and appointed James Thom, 'clerk', to act as librarian until that time. Thom also received the medal collection, which is a strong hint that this was more than a straightforward custodial position.[69] Thom is otherwise unknown as a member of the household; the surname may be Scottish. A Revd James Thom, visible in archive collections from the 1750s to 1803, was vicar of Castle Acre, Norfolk, from 1750 until 1756 and subsequently rector of nearby Southacre and Bridgham, Norfolk.[70] I think it is reasonable to identify the temporary librarian of Narford with the Revd Thom of Castle Acre, a neighbouring parish to that of Narford. Interestingly, Sir Andrew had the gift of the living for Narford (he could appoint the vicar to the parish), but the Revd Thom, in Castle Acre, was appointed by a different patron, the Earl of Leicester, as Thomas Coke had become in 1744. Thom, then, was in the circle of the Burlington friends, and perhaps something of an antiquary himself, as he left some notes on the history of Castle Rising, the Norman seat of the Dukes of Norfolk.[71] I suggest that the gift of the medals, housed within the library, and the honorary appointment of librarian, shows a close friendship based on trust and shared interests, between the young clergyman (who must have been in his first appointment) and Fountaine.

It is fitting that the chronology for Fountaine's use of his library ends with an act of friendship, because the portraits include two of his closest friends, the Earl of Pembroke and the Duke of Devonshire. Lord Burlington's portrait was hung in the hall, surrounded by his generous gift of the Pellegrini canvases. Naomi Tadmor's recent work on the roles of friendship in eighteenth-century England has noted the intersecting relationships between friendship and patronage. The language of friendship was used to mediate patronage relationships; those in relations of power need not have excluded friendship from their account of how that power was exercised.[72] Tadmor is less interested in male friendships, although there is a body of research that does explore historically situated male friendships.[73] The eighteenth century has been identified as a period in which gender relations, the socially codified norms for male and female personas, shifted from an older, more loosely defined set of acceptable interactions between and within different genders, towards more rigorously policed behaviours suitable for appearing masculine or feminine. Members of society biologically defined as male or female were increasingly expected to behave as overtly masculine or feminine, and not to transgress behavioural boundaries – for men, into non-masculine effeminacy.

I have been exploring the cultural milieu of a man born towards the end of the seventeenth century, a period when the language of male friendships clearly extended comfortably into the realms of affection and erotic love, a discourse written in to play texts so thoroughly as to produce 'its own seeming normativity'.[74] Literary historians have pursued these discourses in texts, whereas at Narford we are viewing the visual signs of friendship, but I do not wish to ignore the persuasive conclusion advanced by George Haggerty, for example, that male romantic friendships were unexceptional well into the eighteenth century.

Haggerty insists that we do not import the gender codes of our own time into these friendships, particularly over the question of sexual activity between men. Instead, he argues for a culture in which male affection and desire could be expressed in public discourses, drawing on the classical concepts of the value of male friendships. This is not to exclude women, particularly as marriageable commodities, although individual female characters are hard to identify in the fragmentary records of Fountaine's social interactions. His success in his life is marked by older, more powerful men selecting him for friendship and the advantages flowing from that connection, from Dean Aldrich at Christ Church, to the Grand Duke of Tuscany. These friendships, broadly constructed around esteem and affection, are on display in the Narford library.

Of course, the visual display of friendship carries with it aspects of personal memory, the evocation of past experiences, just as the visual display of the remaining 'great men' more generically prompts the act of recollection of their achievements.[75] Memory is intimately connected to history, both personal and also the practice of history that Sir Andrew himself contributed to, through his numismatic work and antiquarian interests. As a gallery, the library room functioned to display the tools for recollection, in the forms of the 'great men' portraits at micro and macro scales and the books on the shelves. As a personal assemblage, the library room reflected Sir Andrew's enduring friendships in the form of a material biography of his own life and times. This material environment is overseen by the ceiling depiction of Apollo, the omniscient Roman god, under whose gaze all of these lives were played out.

Conclusion

Fountaine was a gentleman scholar of the Palladian revival, an associate of Lord Burlington and his aristocratic circle, and his library represents a new direction in the presentation of book rooms. In the context of Palladian libraries, the Narford room is exceptional in its iconographic complexity, mixing restraint in the form and detailing of the wall shelves and the historicising portrait frames, and brio in the allegorical painted schemes. Throughout this discussion, I have insisted that the historical significance of this room must be derived from a reading of both the creator's biography and the contexts of the scheme within the house and wider currents. As a result, several readings are possible, carried by the portraits. The predominant one is that the interior scheme displays messages about English national identity, based on a proud history of cultural achievements (rather than conquest or mercantile success, which are also possible narratives for English history). England takes her place alongside the Renaissance figures of Italy and France, a scheme enhanced by the later acquisition of the Shakespeare cast.

As I suggest, its meanings are informed by reflections on the circumstances of Fountaine's life. The library portrait series contrasts with Sir Andrew's use of portraits elsewhere at Narford, including a set of royal portraits which reference his service to the court of the Princess of Wales. The library portraits also commemorated personal friendships, and I have suggested that male friendships, across a spectrum of emotional bonds, took the place of kin relationships in Sir Andrew's life. This is a highly personal presentation of works that, in the case of the portrait series, were carefully programmed and positioned with acquired pieces, such as the Mazarin cabinet. The portraits on the walls interacted with each other, through their paired associations and their own gazes across the space of the room; and with the presence of the sculptural faces below them, in the busts and the hidden faces on the coins, medals and intaglios secreted away in the cabinets. This layering of portrait genres suggests the visual richness that once filled Sir Andrew's library, a room that retains considerable impact as an emblematic expression of its virtuoso owner.

Notes

1 In this respect I follow Marcia Pointon's distinction between the individual image and the social constructions around the practices of viewing portraiture. Marcia Pointon, *Hanging the Head: Portraiture and Social Formation in Eighteenth-Century England* (New Haven and London: Yale University Press for the Paul Mellon Centre for Studies in British Art, 1993), p. 1.

2 G. Jackson-Stops and J. Pipkin, *The English Country House: A Grand Tour* (London: The National Trust and Weidenfeld and Nicolson, 1984); John Brewer, *The Pleasures of the Imagination* (London: HarperCollins, 1997); S. Jervis, 'The English Country House Library', in N. Barker (ed.), *Treasures from the Libraries of National Trust Country Houses* (New York: The Royal Oak Foundation and The Grolier Club, 1999), p. 114; James Raven, 'The Representation of Philanthropy and Reading in the Eighteenth-century Library', *Libraries and Culture*, 31:2 (1996), 492–510; Susie West, 'Studies and Status: Spaces for Books in Seventeenth-century Penshurst Place, Kent', *Transactions of the Cambridge Bibliographical Society*, 22 (2002), 266–92.

3 R. Myers and M. Harris (eds), *Property of a Gentleman: The Formation, Organisation and Dispersal of the Private Library* (Winchester: St Paul's Bibliographies, 1991); I. Jackson, 'Approaches to the History of Readers and Reading in Eighteenth-century Britain', *Historical Journal*, 47:4 (2004),1,041–54.
4 Mark Girouard, *Life in the English Country House: A Social and Architectural History* (New Haven and London: Yale University Press, 1978); this chapter draws on research in Susie West, 'The Development of the Library in Norfolk Country Houses, 1660–1830' (PhD dissertation, University of East Anglia, 2001) and my forthcoming monograph on the architecture and design of the English private library, University of Toronto Press.
5 André Masson, *The Pictorial Catalogue, Mural Decoration in Libraries*, trans. D. Gerard (Oxford: Clarendon, 1981); Colin Tite, *The Manuscript Library of Sir Robert Cotton* (London: British Library, 1994).
6 The pattern of how the library moves around the house plan is discussed within my thesis and forthcoming book, where the following houses are discussed in greater detail.
7 J. Harris, 'The Architecture of the House', in Andrew Moore (ed.), *Houghton Hall, The Prime Minister, the Empress and the Heritage* (London: Philip Wilson, 1996), pp. 20–4.
8 Pointon, *Hanging*, p. 9.
9 *Ibid.*, p. 9.
10 Narford collections are discussed in Andrew Moore, *Norfolk and the Grand Tour* (Norwich: Norfolk Museums Service, 1985); Andrew Moore, *Dutch and Flemish Painting in Norfolk* (London: Her Majesty's Stationery Office, 1988); Andrew Moore and Charlotte Crawley, *Family and Friends: A Regional Survey of British Portraiture* (London: Her Majesty's Stationery Office, 1992); English Palladianism in J. Bold and J. Reeves, *Wilton House and English Palladianism: Some Wiltshire Houses* (London: Her Majesty's Stationary Office, 1988); J. Harris, *The Palladian Revival: Lord Burlington, His Villa and Garden at Chiswick* (New Haven and London: Yale University Press, 1994).
11 R. Harris, *A Chorus of Grammars: The Correspondence of George Hickes and His Collaborators on the Thesaurus Linguarum Septentrionalium* (Toronto: Pontifical Institute of Mediaeval Studies, 1992), p. 273.
12 *Ibid.*, p. 51.
13 B. Arciszewska, *The Hanoverian Court and the Triumph of Palladio: The Palladian Revival in Hanover and England c. 1700* (Warsaw: Wydawnictwo Dig, 2002).
14 Narford Library MSS, quoted in Moore, *Grand Tour*, p. 28; H. Pagan, 'Andreas Fountaine Eques Auratus A.A.A.F. III Vir', *British Numismatic Journal*, 63 (1993), 120; Moore, *Dutch and Flemish*, p. 12..
15 F. Russell, 'A Collection Transformed', *Apollo*, 169:567 (21 June 2009), 48–55; Moore, *Grand Tour*, p. 94.
16 Pagan, 'Andreas Fountaine', 117.
17 Brinsley Ford, 'Sir Andrew Fountaine, One of the Keenest Virtuosi of His Age', *Apollo*, 122:285 (November 1985), 355–7.
18 Jonathan Richardson, *Richardsoniana: or, Occasional reflections on the Moral Nature of Man* (London: J. Dodsley,1776), pp. 331–2, in Richard Dorment, *British Painting in the Philadelphia Museum of Art from the Seventeenth through*

the Nineteenth Century (Philadelphia: Philadelphia Museum of Art, 1986), p. 166.

19 H. Williams (ed.), *The Correspondence of Jonathan Swift*, 5 vols (Oxford: Clarendon Press, 1963); H. Williams (ed.), *Jonathan Swift, Journal to Stella*, 2 vols (Oxford: Blackwell, 1974).

20 Marcia Pointon has described the 'field of the portrait and its connotations', *Hanging*, p. 1.

21 It is worth clarifying that the man most strongly identified as the designer of the English Palladian revival, William Kent, was not at this date (1717) associated with many of the English patrons of the 1720s. Kent was working in Italy from 1710, based in Rome, where he met the young Thomas Coke, Lord Lovel (the future Earl of Leicester), in 1714, who had as developed cultural tastes as Fountaine. Coke used Kent to assist him in purchasing books and works of art and to make commissions in Italy; years later, in the 1730s, Coke was able to rebuild his manor house at Holkham, Norfolk, into the Palladian palace that is Holkham Hall, assisted by Kent, Burlington and Fountaine.

22 John Cornforth, *Early Georgian Interiors* (New Haven and London: Yale University Press for the Paul Mellon Centre for Studies in British Art, 2004), p. 138.

23 Kent may have been aware of his presence in Rome in 1716, Kent letters MSS (14 January 1716) cited in *The Grand Tour, Dictionary and Archive of Travellers*, 'Arundell, Hon. Richard', www.grandtour.amdigital.co.uk.libezproxy.open.ac.uk/Dictionary/TravellerDetails.aspx?documentid=58119&prevPos=58119&let=a&vpath=TravellerBrowseonline edition, accessed 24 June 2012.

24 S. Parissien, J. Harris and H. Colvin, 'Narford Hall, Norfolk', *Georgian Group Report and Journal* (1987), 49–61.

25 *Ibid.*, 53.

26 The bookcases are currently painted in a light oak graining, but this may not be the original treatment (the delicate parquet floor was installed in 1860, a possible date for refreshing any paint schemes).

27 Andrew Moore's long engagement with the art works in Norfolk country houses is unequalled, and I am extremely grateful to him for access to his unpublished work on the Narford library portraits, also discussed in Moore, *Family and Friends*.

28 Sir Matthew Decker's diary of a tour, 21 June to 12 July 1728, Wiltshire Record Office, Wilton Papers, 2057, F 5/2.

29 Parissien, Harris and Colvin, 'Narford Hall', 57. I responded on my visit to a Kentian coving and a possibly later ceiling on my encounter with the room.

30 Cornforth, *Early Georgian*, pp. 31–6.

31 *Ibid.*, p. 141.

32 *Ibid.*, p. 139.

33 Narford Library MSS; Moore, *Family and Friends*, p. 31.

34 Moore, *Grand Tour*, p. 38.

35 George Knox has discussed the Burlington/Narford Pellegrini works in detail, and suggests that there are in fact two possible dates for their installation at Narford; the first being the gift of the large Burlington canvases,

created 1708–13, which were altered to fit the Narford Hall, and the second being the occasion of Pellegrini's return to England in 1719 (for six months, a period Knox acknowledges is brief) to add to the scheme. George Knox, 'Antonio Pellegrini and Marco Ricci at Burlington House and Narford Hall', *Burlington Magazine*, 130:1,028 (November 1988), 846–53.

36 Sir Matthew Decker's diary of a tour, 21 June to 12 July 1728, Wiltshire Record Office, Wilton Papers, 2057, F 5/2.

37 Knox, 'Antonio Pellegrini', 846–53.

38 Jacob Simon, *The Art of the Picture Frame: Artists, Patrons and the Framing of Portraits in Britain* (London: National Portrait Gallery, 1996), pp. 50–1.

39 Melton Constable library interior, in its 1687 location, is discussed in West, 'Development of the Library', chapter 3; Christopher Hussey, 'Melton Constable, Norfolk, the Seat of Lord Hastings – I', *Country Life*, 64 (15 September 1928), 364–70 and 'Melton Constable, Norfolk, the Seat of Lord Hastings – II', *Country Life*, 64 (22 September 1928), 402–9. Some of the library portraits are displayed at Seaton Delaval Hall, Northumberland, there by descent.

40 Pointon, *Hanging*, p. 34.

41 F. Blomefield, *An Essay towards a topographical history of the county of Norfolk*, vol. III (Lynn and London: W. Whittingham and R. Baldwin, 1769), p. 521.

42 Harry Berger, 'Fictions of the Pose: Facing the Gaze of Early Modern Portraiture', *Representations*, 46 (Spring, 1994), 103.

43 *Ibid.*, 94.

44 D.H. Solkin, 'Great Pictures of Great Men? Reynolds, Male Portraiture, and the Power of Art', *Oxford Art Journal*, 9:2 (1986), 42–9.

45 The key discussion of early eighteenth-century politeness is supplied by L. Klein, *Shaftesbury and the Culture of Politeness: Moral Discourse and Cultural Politeness in Early Eighteenth-century England* (Cambridge: Cambridge University Press, 1994); H. Jacobsen, *Luxury and Power: The Material World of the Stuart Diplomat, 1660–1714* (Oxford: Oxford University Press, 2011), particularly pp. 103–36; H. Greig, 'Eighteenth-century English Interiors in Image and Text', in Jeremy Aynsley and Charlotte Grant (eds), *Imagined Interiors: Representing the Domestic Interior since the Renaissance* (London: V&A Publications, 2006), pp. 102–27.

46 Summarised briefly in Pointon, *Hanging*, p. 62; Eugene Dwyer, 'André Thevet and Fulvio Orsini: The Beginnings of the Modern Tradition of Classical Portrait Iconography in France', *Art Bulletin*, 75:3 (September 1993), 467–80.

47 Pointon, *Hanging*, p. 14.

48 Blomefield, *Norfolk*, III, p. 521.

49 'An inventory of the goods and effects of the late Sir Andrew Fountaine knight deceased at his late house at Narford', 1753, National Art Library, London, Memorandum book, 86.22.160.

50 The Walpole Cabinet, 1743, Victoria and Albert Museum: W.52-1925.

51 Sir Matthew Decker's diary of a tour, 21 June to 12 July 1728, Wiltshire Record Office, Wilton Papers, 2057, F 5/2.

52 H. d'Orléans Aumale, *Inventaire de tous les meubles du Cardinal Mazarin.*

Dressé en 1653, et. publié. d'après l'original, conservé dans les Archives de Condé (London: Whittingham and Wilkins, 1861), pp. 251–2. This describes a cabinet ornamented with four gilded lions, four gilded Corinthian columns, architectural frontispiece and gilded balustrade, an upper storey in the form of a segmental pediment supported by pilasters flanked by scrolls, as found on the Norfolk cabinet.

53 Journal of a Tour Through Part of Norfolk, 1767, Rev. Sir John Cullum, Suffolk Record Office, Bury St Edmunds, E2/44/3. With thanks to Owen Thompson for supplying the reference and extract.

54 Diana Scarisbrick, 'Gem Connoisseurship: The 4th Earl of Carlisle's Correspondence with Francesco de Ficoroni and Antonio Maria Zanetti', *Burlington Magazine*, 129:1,007 (February 1987), 90–104; collecting practices for classical sculpture by English virtuosi, including coins and gems, are surveyed in Jonathan Scott, *The Pleasures of Antiquity: British Collectors of Greece and Rome* (New Haven and London: Yale University Press for the Paul Mellon Centre for Studies in British Art, 2003).

55 Thomas Browne, *Hydriotaphia, Urn-Burial, or, A Discourse of the Sepulchral Urns Lately Found in Norfolk (London: Edward Dod, 1658).*

56 Diana Price, 'Reconsidering Shakespeare's Monument', *Review of English Studies*, New Series, 48:190 (May, 1997), 168–82.

57 Robert D. Hume, 'Before the Bard: "Shakespeare" in Early Eighteenth-Century London', *English Literary History*, 64:1 (Spring, 1997), 67.

58 I am grateful to Laura Turner, York Museums Trust, for information about the only known example in a public collection, with provenance from the Turner family of Kirkleatham, noted in a wider discussion of the pose by Terry Friedman, 'Scheemakers's Monument to the Best of Sons', *Burlington Magazine*, 122:922, Special Issue Devoted to Sculpture (January 1980), 61–7.

59 M. Baker, 'The Making of Portrait Busts in the Mid-Eighteenth Century: Roubiliac, Scheemakers and Trinity College, Dublin', *Burlington Magazine*, 137:1,113 (December 1995), 821–31; M. Baker, 'Public Images for Private Spaces? The Place of Sculpture in the Georgian Domestic Interior', *Journal of Design History*, 20:4 (2007), 309–23.

60 The Roubiliac clay bust is now in the Norwich Castle Museum & Art Gallery.

61 Patrick Maynard, 'Portraits as Displays', *Philosophical Studies: An International Journal for Philosophy in the Analytic Tradition,* 135:1 (2007), 111–21.

62 Rosalys Coope, 'The "Long Gallery": Its Origins, Development, Use and Decoration', *Architectural History*, 29 (1986), 43–84.

63 Frances Gage, 'Exercise for Mind and Body: Giulio Mancini, Collecting, and the Beholding of Landscape Painting in the Seventeenth Century', *Renaissance Quarterly*, 61:4 (2008), 1,167–207.

64 R. Sweet, *Antiquaries: The Discovery of the Past in Eighteenth-century Britain* (London: Continuum, 2004).

65 O. Field, *The Kit Kat Club: Friends Who Imagined a Nation* (London: Harper Press, 2008).

66 John Ingamells, *Later Stuart Portraits, 1685–1714* (London: National Portrait Gallery, 2009), p. 376; portraits displayed in the National Portrait Gallery, London, and Beningbrough Hall, Yorkshire (National Trust).

67 The roles of coffee houses in the formation of public discourse have recently been explored at length by B. Cowan, *The Social Life of Coffee: The Emergence of the British Coffee House* (New Haven and London: Yale University Press, 2005) and M. Ellis (ed.), *Eighteenth-century Coffee House Culture*, 4 vols (London: Chatto and Pickering, 2006).

68 For Holkham, Raynham and Oxburgh Halls and their owners see West, 'The Development of the Library', p. 257.

69 The National Archives, PROB 11/184, 268.

70 James Thome [*sic*] is listed as vicar by Blomefield, 'Freebridge Hundred and Half: Castleacre', in *Norfolk*, VIII, pp. 356–77; Label of three brace of partridges sent from Sir Harry Fetherston and B. Lethieullier to Revd James Thom, vicar of Castle Acre, 1750–56, Norfolk Record Office, MC 240/4, 678X6; 'Indenture: Lease for 7 years. John Knight of Langold (Notts) and Revd James Thom, clerk, rector of Bridgham, executors and trustees of Richard Croftes of West Harling, esq., decd, to John Smith of Bridgham, farmer. 30 Jan 1788', NRO, MS 6461, 6C4.

71 Historical notes on Castle Rising by Revd Thom, eighteenth century, Norfolk Record Office, HOW 836, 350X1.

72 Naomi Tadmor, *Family and Friends in Eighteenth-Century England: Household, Kinship, and Patronage* (Cambridge: Cambridge University Press, 2001).

73 See most recently the literature on aspects of masculinity reviewed in K. Harvey, *The Little Republic: Masculinity and Domestic Authority in Eighteenth-century Britain* (Oxford: Oxford University Press, 2012), pp. 2–23.

74 George Haggerty, *Men in Love: Masculinity and Sexuality in the Eighteenth Century* (New York and Chichester: Columbia University Press, 1999), p. 26.

75 A distinction pursued by P. Ricoeur, *Memory, History, Forgetting*, trans. K. Blamey and D. Pellauer (Chicago and London: University of Chicago Press, 2004), pp. 1–55.

3

Marble, memory and theatre: portraiture and the Sculpture Gallery at Chatsworth

Alison Yarrington

Furnishing 'a great house'

In his *Handbook to Chatsworth and Hardwick*, written during 1844, William Cavendish, 6th Duke of Devonshire (1790–1858) provided a personal guide to his ancestral Derbyshire home.[1] Privately printed in the following year and composed as a series of letters to his elder sister Harriet, Countess Granville (1785–1862), this was not meant to be a general guide for eager tourists who, on the days that Chatsworth was on view to the public, would wait 'anxiously' for the gates to open at eleven o'clock.[2] It was instead 'to be considered as private as a letter', according to the inscription in the Duke's hand on the copy presented to his other sister, Georgiana, Countess of Carlisle (1783–1858). Acting as 'showman'[3] to his siblings this account of these familiar spaces and the objects they contained at this time are intimate, full of familial fondness and recollection, revealing close friendships and long-standing allegiances as well as those material changes to the fabric of the building that he had made over the years. Anecdotes of personalities and small incidents are included alongside details of the changes he had wrought on this 'Palace of the Peak',[4] the consequence of a sustained programme of renovation and new accommodation that had commenced in 1818 with the assistance of his architect Sir Jeffry Wyatville. The main feature of these 'improvements' was a new north wing, facilitating his many interests and pleasures, including a library, a dining room, a top-lit sculpture gallery, an orangery, a plunge pool, and a banqueting and charade room, that later became a theatre. It was in the Sculpture Gallery and the adjoining Orangery however that the Duke's role as showman was wrought in reflexive ways that, as expressed in the *Handbook*, operated on different levels, simultaneously intensely private and public facing. Here the 'speaking likenesses' of those whom he admired and revered were displayed with sculptures of mythical, divine and semi-divine subjects in a setting that evoked both the dramatic and poetic (plate 4).[5]

Whilst admitting that 'he who has to furnish a great house is embarked in a sea of trouble'[6] the *Handbook* provides evidence of the enduring pleasure that Chatsworth also induced in the Duke. It was a place that encapsulated memories of his youth – 'life's golden time' – and those from the intervening years, many of these being prompted by his possessions as much as the spaces in which they were contained.[7] Chatsworth, as its heritage demanded and when required could become a grand theatre of display. For example it was orchestrated to great effect when the young Queen Victoria visited in 1843: 'all that unbounded wealth could procure, and all that refined taste could effect, was brought to bear, to beautify and adorn Chatsworth on this auspicious occasion [...] Thousands of the choicest plants, magnificent candelabra, sculptures, rich and elegant furniture and a thousand other beautiful things'.[8] One of these 'beautiful things' was Lorenzo Bartolini's copy of the Medici Vase commissioned in 1819 and in situ by 1822, the year in which the Duke purchased some of the few antiquities in his sculpture collection at the Wanstead sale.[9] This magnificent object, during one of its owner's many rearrangements of the Sculpture Gallery, had come to rest in the Orangery on its way to the 'pleasure ground', which the Duke was then bedecking 'with white marble'. This instance of the ways in which chance could play a part in the arrangement of the sculpture collection is recounted in one of the anecdotes in the *Handbook*: 'being wheeled thus far on its way, the effect was so beautiful under orange and araucaria, that it stopped short, and here remains'.[10] In this setting, between the Sculpture Gallery and the gardens, this finely wrought marble was often illuminated: 'of a night it holds powerful lamps, that send up such a magical light on the branches of the Altingia, that people cry out Fairy land'. This was one of those elaborate special effects that made the young Queen's visit so memorable.[11] But Chatsworth was more than a stage for ritual and grand display; for the 6th Duke it was at the same time home, a refuge and a place of intense personal intellectual and artistic pleasures as the acquisition and arrangement of his sculpture collection demonstrates.

The transformational effect of the 6th Duke's 'love of marble' upon Chatsworth is indicated by Rhodes's comment in the 1824 edition of his *Peak Scenery: or Excursions in Derbyshire* that 'Chatsworth is not rich in sculpture', noting that on 'passing through the different apartments, a few busts were seen', the majority of which were 'modern'.[12] But in a footnote to this statement Rhodes commented upon the ways in which this bleak sculptural terrain was now undergoing significant change as the result of a sustained programme of improvement that included new and plentiful purchases.[13] *Peak Scenery*, dedicated to the 6th Duke, was illustrated by Francis Chantrey, one of the few London-based sculptors that he favoured. By 1824 the sculptor, who was born nearby in Hallamshire, had become a renowned Royal Academician and arguably the leading fashionable portraitist in Britain. He advised the 6th Duke on the early furnishing of the Sculpture Gallery, obtaining columns of precious marble as well as ensuring that the much-coveted *Hebe* by Canova was transported safely from Lord Cawdor's collection to Chatsworth in 1822.[14] Although this activity and the amicable relations between the two men would seem likely to presage commissions, little portrait sculpture by him was made for Chatsworth. An exception is his portrait of King George IV that initially was located in the Sculpture Gallery, according to the evidence of guidebooks and an early inventory of the sculpture by Richard Westmacott.[15] But according to the *Handbook* the bust, which 'electrified the King's friends whilst he lived' had become less popular by 1844, 'now it is not so easy', noted the 6th Duke, 'to make them perceive its merits' (figure 18).[16]

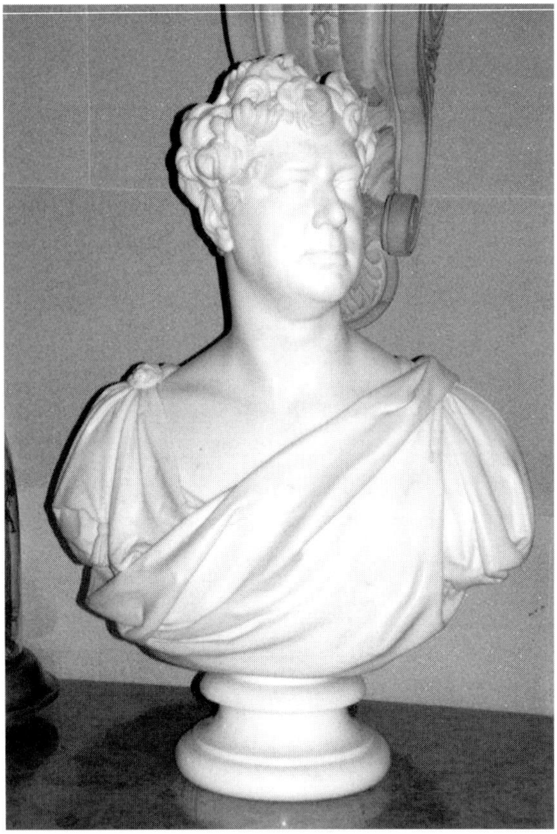

Figure 18 Francis Chantrey, *King George IV*, 1822.

At this date the bust of King George IV was housed in the Second State Drawing Room, a room with hangings of green velvet 'and eight not very prepossessing full lengths hung upon them'.[17] It took its place alongside more marble portraits of royal and imperial persons and historic pieces of furniture, the latter including the chairs of King William IV and Queen Adelaide used at the coronation in Westminster Abbey when the 6th Duke was Lord Chamberlain. The 6th Duke's commentary upon the busts in this setting indicates what he demanded from this form of contemporary portraiture. For example, that of the 6th Duke's friend and youthful travelling companion, Emperor Nicolas I of Russia, a commission from the Prussian sculptor Christian Daniel Rauch (1777–1857) provided what he considered to be a passable portrait of the Tsar; 'it would be difficult to fail in copying those regular features of the finest head in the world'. It was clear that he had greater admiration for Rauch's 'unrivalled' tomb sculpture of Queen Louise at Charlottenberg, but deemed the sculptor's bust of the Queen's daughter Charlotte, Empress Alexandra Feodorovna (of Prussia), too 'unlike' the sitter to purchase. In order to provide a closer match to this remembered likeness he chose to order a bust from 'a lesser artist', Carl Friedrich Wichmann (1775–1836), one that was in his view more 'like' the sitter.[18] These enduring portraits of noble friends now far away, mementos of happy times, were placed upon half columns of dark yellow marble, a colourful setting that brought into play his love of marble and mineralogy that was so clearly articulated in the Sculpture Gallery. Gifts of malachite furniture and objects[19] received from the imperial Russian family punctuated Chatsworth, material evidence of a close and blossoming relationship. The Duke records the placing of the gifts with obvious pleasure: in the State Dining Room a symbol of Tsarist rule and dominion, 'Peter the Great on horseback [...] a present from Maria Feodorowna, the mother of the Emperor. It is very good and like the statue [...] The beloved and respected Empress sent it to me after the Coronation at Moscow';[20] in the First State Drawing Room, a gift from the Grand Duke Michel Pavlovitch, 'the completest model of a Russian peasant's house [...] a chef d'oeuvre of execution and complete finish of all the details';[21] in the Sculpture Gallery, a vase of rare Siberian marble on a jasper pedestal, alongside the extraordinary light-reflective table top formed from a chance find of a slab of 'brilliant crystals of Labrador' in the Nevsky Prospekt during a visit to St Petersburg.[22] This chance 'find' also provided a decorative panel in the pedestal of Bartolini's *Bacchante*, an ambivalent sculptural work that could signify both pleasure and loss. In the west garden were two 'imperial' trees planted by the 'brothers Nicolas and Michel Paulowitcsh' that, like the friendship between the 6th Duke and Prince Nicolas, had naturally grown and flourished.[23] These heartfelt connections with the Russian imperial family that punctuate the *Handbook*, emphasise an emotional synergy and the enduring place of the Cavendish family within this international European ruling elite. At the same time there is also a sense of inevitable transience of such relationships and power. This is apparent in the 6th Duke's arrangement and description of the Drawing Room at Chatsworth, formerly the 1st Duke's Dining Room, and the memories that it prompted: 'Here we acted numerous charades: sometimes their theatrical curtain remained suspended over the table at which we dined. Here dined with me the Grand Duke Nicolas. The Princess Victoria's charade of Kenilworth happened after the books had been replaced in the library, but before the other changes: the date of that was 1832, her first visit'.[24] In this same room he introduced – supposedly to make up for 'the want of decoration' and to create regularity in the asymmetric interior – full-length portraits that emphasised his family's long-standing relationship with Britain's monarchical history. This was again presented as a *mise-en-scène* with portraits of 'Mary Queen of Scots, and Charles I., from Chiswick; Henry VIII., and Philip II., General Monk [an architect of Charles II's restoration], and two Tintorets from Devonshire House'.[25]

Accompanying the imperial Russian portrait busts in the Second State Drawing Room was that of Louis XIV, 'brought at the Duchesse de Berri's sale at the same time as Granet's picture', which according to its owner 'could find no other place' at Chatsworth.[26] Almost without exception these busts, commissioned or acquired by the 6th Duke were, as Rhodes had noticed, contemporary works by living sculptors. This was almost invariably the case with the 6th Duke's purchases, even when the busts were of ancient heroes, for example the bust of *Achilles* by Rennie. The fine head of Alexander, repaired by Thomas Campbell and a head of Faustina that belonged to Canova, were among the few busts of antiquity in the collection. In comparison to full-scale marble statues where the weight, scale and vulnerability of the material made changes of site difficult, busts were more easily and often moved. Rhodes's footnote about the sculptural changes being wrought at Chatsworth came at the time when many of those works destined for the Sculpture Gallery were underway in the Roman studios of the 6th Duke's chosen sculptors, with some already resting in the wings, awaiting the building's completion. This strong current of activity contrasted with the 5th Duke's earlier scant interest in sculpture. Despite sitting for his portrait to the Irish sculptor Christopher Hewetson whilst in Rome in the company of Sir Watkin Williams Wynn during their Grand Tour, he acquired relatively few sculptures,[27] and the only mention in the *Handbook* of a work belonging to the author's mother, the Duchess Georgiana, was 'the little bust of a laughing Faun' described as 'a great favourite' of hers that her son remembered 'was always on the chimney-piece of her dressing-room in London'.[28] Later their heir would effect a significant marmoreal change upon Chatsworth, so much so that, by the Duke's death, marble worked into exquisite forms and decoration was firmly embedded in the house's interior.

The Sculpture Gallery

Nowhere was the 6th Duke's self-proclaimed love of marble more pronounced than in the Sculpture Gallery. The role of the sculpted portrait in this dedicated space was more fixed, although not permanently so, than in the other rooms. Just like the ebb and flow of conversations those between these 'speaking likenesses' within the gallery changed as works were introduced and rearrangements took place.[29] Research towards the redisplay of the Chatsworth gallery that was realised in 2009 revealed several of the changes put in place by the 6th Duke: from the gallery's inception in the 1820s to its completion in 1834, and then over the twenty-four years before his death.[30] Although there can be no complete record of the evolution of this display, nevertheless, rather like the natural light that still moves across the space from day through to night, there are moments of illumination. What is evident is that when new works were brought into the room they changed its appearance and evoked new narratives, often theatrical and sometimes abstruse, which, for the period up to 1844, the *Handbook* does much to capture. What is also clear is how the arrangements in this space were not fixed but part of the owner's continuing enthusiastic engagement with his collection that continued beyond the *Handbook*'s publication. For example, in November 1846 the 6th Duke met the American sculptor Hiram Powers in Florence and 'saw and liked him'.[31] He admired the 'lovely' *Greek Slave* but surprisingly, given his enthusiasm for contemporary 'poetic' sculpture so clearly articulated in his collection, it was a copy of a bust of a missed friend, Edward Everett (1794–1865), who had until the previous year been American Ambassador in London, that he chose to order for the Sculpture Gallery.[32] Another later prize was purchased from the Royal Academy Exhibition in 1854, the oval portrait medallion of Lady Alwyne Compton by Alexander Monroe, which he set into a pier of the wall of his gallery.[33]

These purchases and other later acquisitions that included the bronze busts by Charles Cordier purchased from the Great Exhibition of 1851, show the 6th Duke's interest in contemporary portrait sculpture was constantly evolving.[34] But in the early years of his collecting career, the epitome of sculptural perfection for him was always Antonio Canova, an aesthetic obsession that remained constant throughout his life. The sculptor's death in October 1822 was of great significance for the Duke personally and in terms of the future shape of his collection, as it cut short both a developing friendship and made the impulse to acquire more of the now finite number of his works ever more urgent. Thus a patron-sculptor relationship that had seemed set fair to produce a collection that would rival other admired collections, for example that of Count Sommariva at the Villa Carlotta and in Paris, was radically altered. Before this devastating event he acquired *Hebe* (1808–14), moved to Chatsworth in 1822 by Chantrey; the head of Petrach's *Laura* (1818) obtained through the intervention of the Duchess Elizabeth; and also placed a commission for a statue of the sculptor's choice of subject which resulted in the *Endymion* (1819–22). His earliest purchase of Canova's work was made in Paris when in 1818 he acquired the seated portrait statue of Letizia Ramolino Bonaparte, Madame Mère (1804–7). He would admire the 'exquisite' finish of this marble by torchlight both before and after it was placed in its final resting place in the Sculpture Gallery at Chatsworth. Immediately after Canova's death he acquired his portrait bust of Madame Mère that he considered particularly fine. It was also at this time that he acquired (through his friend and fellow Canovite the Marchioness of Abercorn, who had bought it from Sartori) his colossal portrait head of Napoleon (1803–22), the last portrait of the Emperor by Canova, which he was to give pride of place to in the central west bay of the gallery. Then in 1824 in order to complete this Bonaparte family group, he commissioned a seated portrait statue of Napoleon's sister Paolina Borghese from Thomas Campbell, a decision that was to become a source of frustration for the Duke as the sculptor's 'habitual procrastination' meant it could not be in place until 1840.[35]

Alongside these major sculptural items was the Duke's collection of smaller Canovian souvenirs, fragments of marble, prints, portraits and other memorabilia. These included the sculptor's modelling tools which he placed in the Sculpture Gallery originally in a tazza behind the head of Napoleon, later embedding them in a case in the wall. He continued to make Canova's presence felt at Chatsworth with the purchase of bronze and zinc copies of the *Magdalene*, *Venus Italica* and *Endymion*, as well as marble copies from Bienaimé of Carrara to people the gardens.[36] The preference for works by those Rome-based sculptors who emulated Canova, including his pupils Gibson and Finelli, is apparent in the commissions made by him or through his Roman agent, Gaspare Gabrielli, until the latter's death in 1828. It is therefore unsurprising that the permanent keynotes of the gallery, providing its dominant conversation, were the outsize busts of the 6th Duke by Campbell and of Canova by Rinaldo Rinaldi, the sculptor who operated the master's studio workshop after his death, commissioned in 1823. These imposing portrait heads, firmly ensconced in the walls of the gallery, provide a permanent dialogue between patron and sculptor that permeates the arrangement of the space. The 6th Duke had the two portraits placed in niches above and to either side of the doors leading from the Sculpture Gallery to the Orangery, guarded below by the copies after Canova's lions for the papal tomb of Clement XIII Rezzonico, commissioned by the 6th Duke from Benaglia and Rinaldi. The resulting silent interchange between patron and sculptor is one that could only have voice in memory, or more precisely 'in memoriam'. It has been argued elsewhere that the death of Canova in 1822 was the orchestrating principle in the 6th Duke's acquisition of works in advance of the building's completion.[37] The arrangement of this wall was viewed by those who entered from the Dining Room en route to pleasure and entertainment in the rooms beyond, encountering these mortals in the company of immortals and other semi-divines in marble form.

The architecture of the 6th Duke's gallery paid tribute to the recently opened Braccio Nuovo in Rome, where Canova and Cardinal Consalvi had played such significant roles in its successful inauguration.[38] Prompted by his stepmother the Duchess Elizabeth, a resident in Rome, he had visited and admired this state-of-the-art sculpture gallery that had opened in 1822, recording in his diary his wish to emulate certain features in his own sculpture gallery. The Chatsworth room and its contents reveal the 6th Duke's love of Italy as well as his specific interest in contemporary sculpture and mineralogy. The portrait sculpture that he would place in the Sculpture Gallery also made direct reference to post-Napoleonic Rome, and included those for whom he had particular admiration and fondness: Consalvi, Canova, the Duchess

Elizabeth, Napoleon's sister Paolina Borghese and their mother, Letizia Bonaparte. The arrangement of their portraits in the new gallery was carefully articulated, creating complex and shifting narratives that, like the textual patterning of the *Handbook*, were arranged according to personal affiliations, affections and emotional allegiances and often with touches of humour or reflective melancholy.[39]

The transience of the temporal is a strong presence in the gallery both directly in the portraits and in the statues of poetic and mythological subjects. The vulnerability of strength and beauty in the face of fate and time is a recurring narrative; for example Albacini's statue of the wounded *Achilles* commissioned by the Duke as a pendant statue to the arrested moonlit perfection of Canova's *Endymion*, plucks the fatal arrow from his heel. Further into the body of the gallery, Rennie's colossal portrait head of the Homeric hero turns as though disturbed by those who enter from the south doors to watch their approach. The purchases of works made during the intervening decade between Canova's death and the gallery's completion in 1834, were made at a time when death was a dominant factor for the 6th Duke. If the tortured landscapes scarred by Napoleonic conflict made an indelible impression on the young Duke travelling for much of the time in the company of the Crown Prince Nicolas of Russia, across Germany, the Nordic countries and Russia in the years after Waterloo, the loss of family and friends in the 1820s was both personal and directly affecting. In Rome the Duke witnessed his stepmother the Duchess Elizabeth's death on 30 March 1824 and then organised for the body's embalmment before accompanying the lead-lined coffin home to Devonshire House, a journey that ended on 19 May. The coincidence of the death of the Duchess Elizabeth and his own mother Duchess Georgiana on the same day eighteen years apart was a dreadful and deeply felt event as his diary entries show.[40]

On the day after the Duchess Elizabeth's death he had cause to be concerned about another Roman resident whom he held in great affection, Napoleon's sister 'poor Pauline' who 'was very ill last night and this morning. She has been bled and blistered. Is she too to die?'[41] She would survive but died the following year. Her marble portrait at Chatsworth eternalises her mature beauty, showing no indication of mortal attrition, and it is interesting to notice that the 6th Duke also owned an early painted portrait of her which he describes in the *Handbook*, 'when she was the wife of General Leclerc, and as she must have looked when she left her idolizers at Paris, to follow him to St. Domingo; and very young she was then, by her own account'.[42] The 6th Duke's placing of this youthful portrait is of interest as part of a recurring theme of transience and loss at Chatsworth during his lifetime.

In memoriam: narratives of exile and loss

The Duke's initial plans for his gallery, both in prospect and then during its construction, were inevitably modified by subsequent events and acquisitions. The eventual placing of Campbell's portrait of Paolina as pendant to the statue of her mother who died soon after the gallery was completed[43] with the portrait head of the son and brother between is another example of an in memoriam narrative of exile and loss. Campbell's statue includes a large portrait medallion of Napoleon which Paolina holds and appears to study, comparing it with Canova's portrait bust of her brother that her statue is facing (figure 19). Further allusions

Figure 19 Thomas Campbell, *Paolina Borghese*, 1824–40.

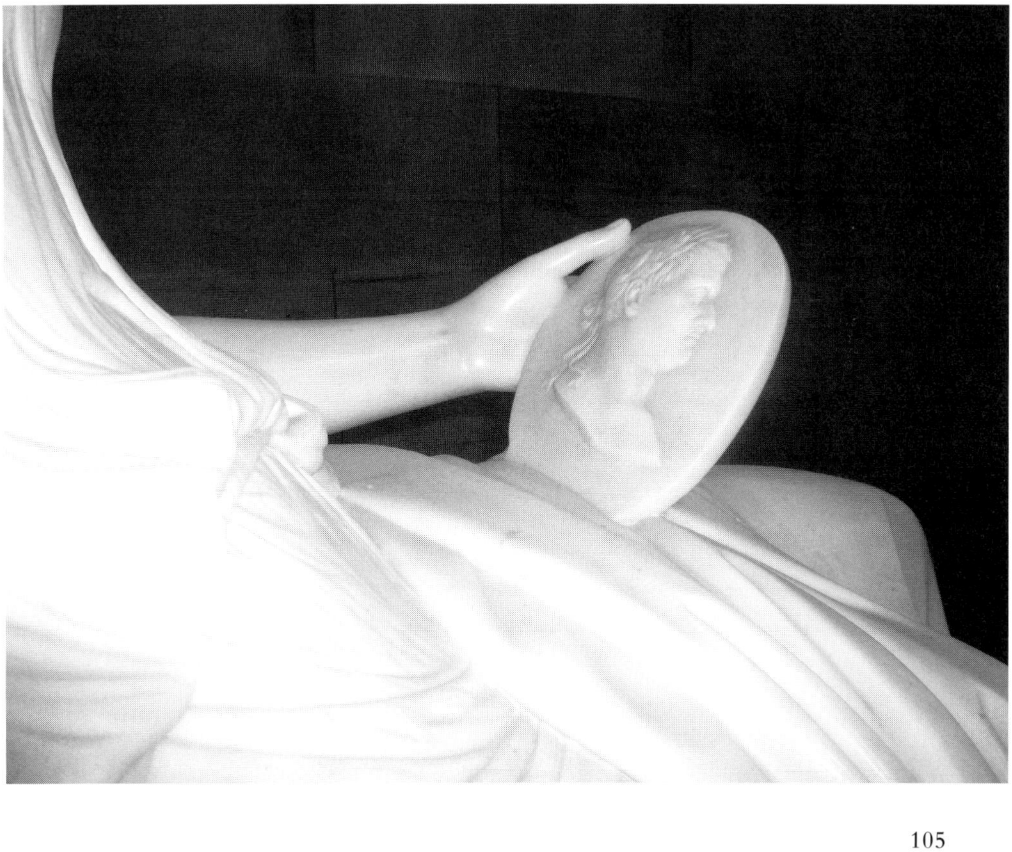

to exile were also materially present in the Napoleonic medals made of Elba iron set into the statue's pedestal, another gift from Paolina to the 6th Duke, and which appeared elsewhere in the house. Whilst writing the *Handbook* the 6th Duke had purchased from Benjamin Robert Haydon two 'window panels', *Napoleon in Exile* and *The Duke of Wellington at Waterloo* (plate 5) which he placed in the South-East Sitting Room under the east windows, a room where they were in the company of the previously mentioned portrait of the young Paolina Borghese. The subjects of these portraits of the victor and the vanquished of the battle of Waterloo had been the suggestion of Haydon, a commission that appears from his own account to have resulted primarily from the 6th Duke's kind response to the artist's desperate financial circumstances.[44] The installation of the panels at Chatsworth deliberately evoked poetic resonance: 'Haydon's melancholy and poetical idea of Napoleon in exile would be too good for such a position if it were not an unrivalled one.' Haydon's popular image of exile depicts Napoleon, with his back to the viewer, contemplating the sea from a rocky headland. The 6th Duke makes precise recommendations about how the viewer should both see this work and contemplate nature: 'Sit down at the table with your back to the clear glass window – look at the reflection in the glass of that prospect of earth and water without sky.'[45] He then inserts an unattributed quotation from Goethe's 'Mignon', a poem that opens Book III of *Wilhelm Meisters Lehrjahre* (1795): 'Es stürzt der Fels, und über ihn die Fluth' (the cliff rocks plunge under the rushing flood). He continues, 'Turn then to the Apollo and the Emperor fountain on the South, and say whether this favoured spot can receive too rich or too artistical an embellishment.'[46] The 'glass' in which the reader, his sister, is instructed to look in order to gain a wide-angled complete view of the vista, had originally been placed in the Queen of Scots' Room at Chatsworth, and was moved to the Presence Chamber at Hardwick Hall, before being brought back to its new setting by the 6th Duke. In this setting its elaborately carved wooden frame provided 'projecting scrolls' upon which he placed iron busts of the Emperor and Empress of Russia.[47] This interplay between references to Russia's continuing imperial rule and reflection upon the instruments of Napoleon's defeat and exile is also present in the Sculpture Gallery. Haydon's painting in which Napoleon stands above the seemingly endless ocean, reflecting upon his past glories and present fate is in contrast to actual reflections of the fecund richness of the gardens and the joyful play of water graced by Apollo seen in the mirror by those whose lives continued in freedom

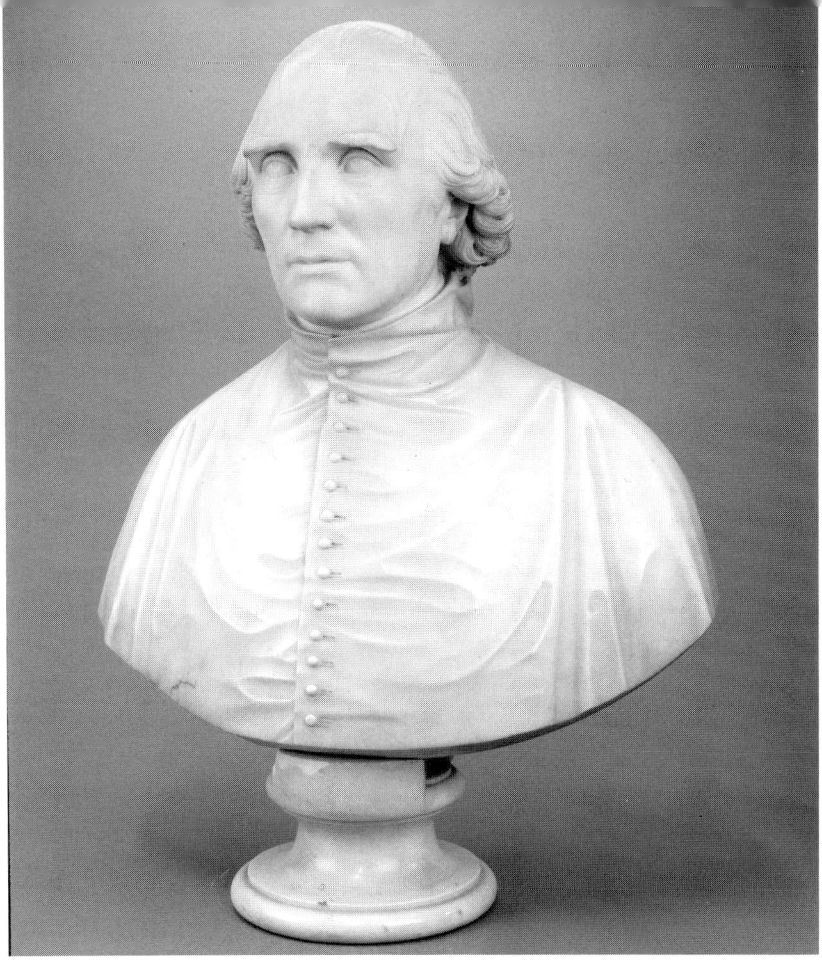

Figure 20 Berthel Thorvaldsen, *Cardinal Consalvi*, 1824.

at Chatsworth. Napoleon's death on 5 May 1821 had occurred at a time when the 6th Duke was planning his sculpture gallery and in 1840, just a few years before the Queen's visit to Chatsworth and the composition of the *Handbook*, his ashes had been returned to France and interred in Les Invalides. Once again the landscape of the 6th Duke's personal life, his friendships and lineage, is superimposed and mixed with the counter histories of aggrandisement, power and defeat, a heady romantic mix.

In the Sculpture Gallery the personal memorialising of the 6th Duke's Roman sojourns continued with Berthel Thorvaldsen's powerful bust of Cardinal Consalvi (1824) placed immediately before the Bonaparte family triumvirate (figure 20). The Cardinal had died in January 1824 and a death mask taken by Thorvaldsen was the basis for the sculptor's portrait of the man whose intellectual strengths are conveyed by the almost phrenological appearance of the forehead and stern set of the face.[48] The Cardinal, often working with Canova, had done so much to shape post-Napoleonic Rome and in particular the successful realisation of the much-admired sculpture gallery, the Braccio Nuovo.[49] Not least he had been a loyal friend to the Duchess Elizabeth and the Duke therefore placed his portrait memorial accordingly, on the west side before the statues of Paolina, Napoleon and Madame Mère. On the opposite side of the gallery he constructed his own memorial to his stepmother, bringing together several items. A 'rocchio of pale Verde Antico was found by Elizabeth, Duchess of Devonshire, in her noble excavation that brought to light the pedestal and history of the column of Phocas, and the surrounding road and pavement in the Roman Forum'.[50] This birthday gift of 1819 given to him by the Duchess Elizabeth, with another surmounting fragment of ancient alabaster, formed the colourful pedestal upon which he placed Canova's *Head of Laura* 'dearly loved by the sculptor, entirely formed by his own chisel', which required all his stepmother's 'powers of persuasion, added to my entreaties, to make him part with her'.[51] Next to this he placed a reduced copy of the Column of Phocas with an inscription memorialising the Duchess Elizabeth's part in its discovery (figure 21).

A Napoleonic theme is therefore present in the gallery, not in an overtly political way as it was at Holland House, but interwoven with Canova's artistic and political involvement with the Emperor and his family as well as the 6th Duke's own connections. The gift of Canova's colossal marble statue of Napoleon to the Duke of Wellington following the victory at Waterloo, and its grand imprisonment in the stairwell at Apsley House was both current and well known when the 6th Duke was planning his sculpture gallery.[52] There is a marked difference between Napoleon's presence at Chatsworth and that at Apsley House. Whilst Napoleon's aggrandisement was engraved on the Iron Duke's and on Europe's soul, the 6th Duke's relationship with the Emperor's mother and sister took place in the polite society circles of Rome when Napoleon was terminally exiled on St Helena: 'the old lady herself used to receive me at Rome, and rather complained of my possessing her statue' the Duke noted in his *Handbook*.[53] The mourning bracelet Paolina wore for her brother who died on 5 May 1821 was placed on the broken wrist of Thorvaldsen's *Venus*, a gift that the 6th Duke states she gave to him for that explicit purpose.[54] *Venus*, whom he describes as 'a perfectly beautiful woman – not at all Goddess', was placed on the opposite bay of the gallery to the statue of Paolina on a beautiful pedestal of *cipollino*, suggestive of the waves from which she was born.[55] The Duke's fondness for small personal souvenirs, jewellery and other

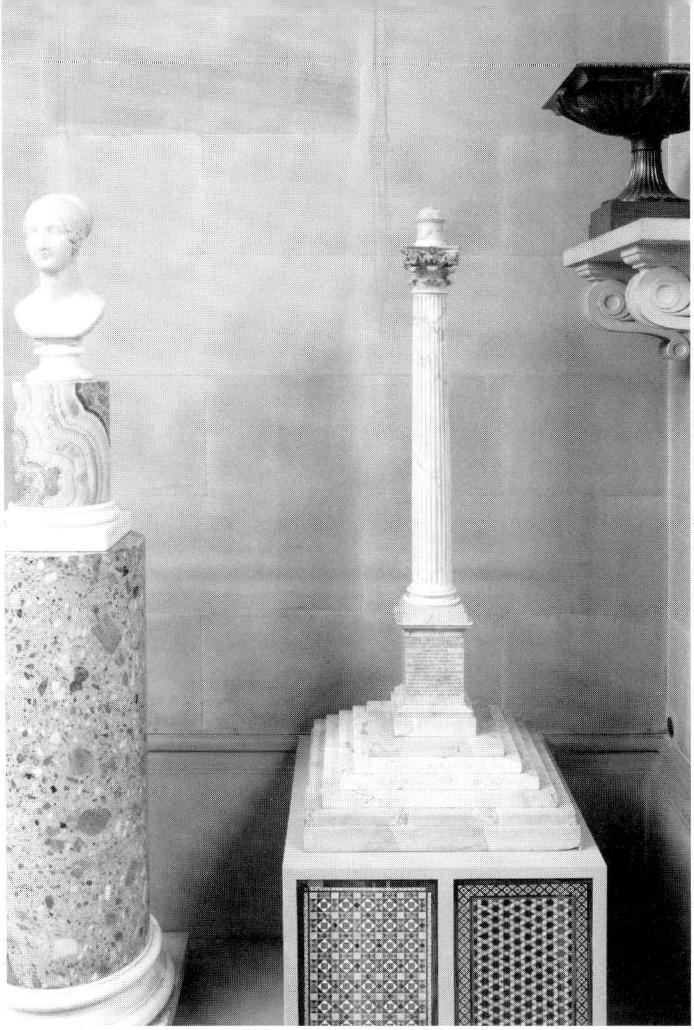

Figure 21
Antonio Canova,
Head of Laura,
1818.

decorative objects often surfaced in the Sculpture Gallery, but most pertinently the Napoleonic medals already mentioned were a reference to the Emperor's first place of exile and to the sisterly devotion that prompted Paolina to join her brother on Elba. The words in ancient Greek that the 6th Duke had painted onto the pedestal of Madame Mère taken from the *Iliad*, 'unfortunate mother of the greatest of men', were selected by Lord Holland and provide a textual reference to the fortunes and misfortunes of this family preserved in marble form, and an example of the pervasive aristocratic Whig interest in Napoleon.[56]

These Napoleonic associations were also sensed in the air at Chatsworth, which in season carried the perfume of the blossom flowering on the four orange trees that came from the Empress Josephine's collection at Malmaison. A sense of bittersweet longing is found elsewhere in the Goethe poem to which the 6th Duke had alluded ('Es stürzt der Fels, und über ihn die Fluth') when reflecting upon Napoleon's exile in his account of the South-East Sitting Room:

> Knowest thou where the lemon blossom grows,
> In foliage dark the orange golden glows,
> A gentle breeze blows from the azure sky,
> Still stands the myrtle, and the laurel, high?
> Dost know it well?
> 'Tis there! 'Tis there
> Would I with thee, oh my beloved, fare.
>
> Knowest the house, its roof on columns fine?
> Its hall glows brightly and its chambers shine,
> And marble figures stand and gaze at me:
> What have they done, oh wretched child, to thee?
> Dost know it well?
> 'Tis there! 'Tis there
> Would I with thee, oh my protector, fare.[57]

It should be emphasised that the experience of viewing sculptures in this location was a sensory one, of touch, sight, smell and sound. In the Orangery, for example, where in the early 1830s Thorvaldsen's and Schadow's reliefs were set in the walls and Baruzzi's *Venus and Cupid* was later placed in the central niche of the west wall, the copy of the Medici Vase at night-time provided a source of artificial and 'magical light', luminous amidst the greenery of rare plants, and animating the figures on its relief. The top-lit Sculpture Gallery bathed the marble figures in light during the day, in particular the highly polished surface of Endymion, giving the impression of the moon's rays and Diana's gaze. As the sun moved on its course so the rays fell on individual works with the effect of a natural spotlight on the players in this theatre of sculpture. Two richly embellished candelabra, bought from the 1822 Wanstead sale,[58] from which the Duke had removed the snakes – the heraldic 'serpent knowed' – in the beaks of the eagles, seeing this as a slight on the ducal coat of arms, lit the area by night and, from time to time, there was the close inspection of these fleshy marble bodies by taper and torchlight. As the 6th Duke's guests moved from dinner in the State Dining Room, heralded by music from the balcony above the anteroom, and looked across the vista of the Sculpture Gallery and its marble forms, Hebe, the cup-bearer to the gods placed on her high porphyry pedestal appears to raise her cup to Campbell's portrait bust of the 6th Duke, suggesting pleasures to come. There is, however, at the same time an undercurrent of melancholy and loss, indicating that these pleasures are by their very nature short-lived and always in the hands of Fate, as Schadow's *Filatrice*, which the 6th Duke had placed upon a pedestal between Hebe and the Duke's portrait, intimates.

Notes

1 W.G.S. Cavendish, 6th Duke of Devonshire (hereafter 6th Duke of Devonshire), *Handbook of Chatsworth and Hardwick* (London: privately printed, 1845).
2 William Adam, *The Gem of the Peak; or Matlock Bath and its Vicinity. An Account of Derby; A Tour from Derby to Matlock; Excursions to Chatsworth, Haddon, Monsal Dale etc.* (Derby: John and Charles Mosley, 1857), p. 102.
3 6th Duke of Devonshire, *Handbook*, p. 1.
4 Ebeneezer Rhodes, *Peak Scenery: or Excursions in Derbyshire Made Chiefly for the Purpose of Picturesque Observation*, 2 vols (London: Longman, Hurst, Rees, Orme, and Brown, and John Murray, 1824), p. 100.
5 Alison Yarrington, '"Under Italian Skies": The 6th Duke of Devonshire, Canova and the Formation of the Sculpture Gallery at Chatsworth House', *Journal of Anglo-Italian Studies*, 10:1 (2009), 41–62 explores and discusses in detail the formation of the ducal collection and the gallery during the 6th Duke's lifetime. The project to redisplay the gallery, completed in 2009, is published in C. Noble and A. Yarrington, '"Like a poet's dreams": The Redisplay of the 6th Duke of Devonshire's Sculpture Gallery at Chatsworth', *Apollo*, 170:570 (November 2009), 46–53. (A second article on the narratives that the redisplay uncovered is currently in preparation.) I am most grateful to the Duke and Duchess of Devonshire for their permission to make use of and quote from the archives at Chatsworth. I would also like to thank colleagues at Chatsworth for their continuing support, and in particular Charles Noble for his suggestions and amendments to this essay.
6 6th Duke of Devonshire, *Handbook*, p. 54.
7 *Ibid.*, p. 29.
8 Adam, *The Gem of the Peak*, p. 143.
9 For the Wanstead sale, see Kate Retford's essay, 'The Topography of the Conversation Piece' in this volume.
10 6th Duke of Devonshire, *Handbook*, p. 108.
11 *Ibid.*, p. 108.
12 Rhodes, *Peak Scenery*, p. 100.
13 *Ibid.*, p. 100.
14 For the 6th Duke's involvement of Chantrey in his sculpture gallery project see Alison Yarrington, 'Anglo-Italian Attitudes: Chantrey and Canova', in Cinzia Sicca and Alison Yarrington (eds), *The Lustrous Trade: Material Culture and the History of Sculpture in England and Italy c. 1700–c. 1860* (Leicester:

Leicester University Press, 2000), pp. 132–55.

15 Adam, *Gem of the Peak*, pp. 92–3. Chantrey's portrait of Canning, commissioned in 1827 by the 6th Duke after the statesman's death at the 6th Duke's residence, Chiswick House, and completed in 1828 is also in the Devonshire collection, see Alison Yarrington, et al., 'An Edition of the Ledger of Sir Francis Chantrey, R.A, at the Royal Academy, 1809–1841', *Walpole Society*, 56 (1991–92), 227. Richard Westmacott, *Marbles, Bronzes and Fragments at Chatsworth* (London: Bradbury and Evans, 1838).

16 6th Duke of Devonshire, *Handbook*, p. 130. For Chantrey's bust of George IV see the entry by Alex Potts, 'His Majesty's Bust', *Walpole Society*, 56 (1991–92), 165–7. Potts cites the mention of the bust in the *Handbook* and also provides details of the other versions and copies that came from Chantrey's studio.

17 6th Duke of Devonshire, *Handbook*, p. 130.

18 Rauch, *Empress Alexandra Feodorovna*, marble, 1833, Dresden, Skulpturensammlung, Albertinium. Wichmann's portrait of the Empress, daughter of Queen Louise of Prussia, marble 1829, St Petersburg, State Hermitage Museum. The 6th Duke also owned 'iron' busts of the imperial couple, see note 47 below.

19 6th Duke of Devonshire, *Handbook*, pp. 96–7: 'while I write, the news is come of a magnificent present of malachite from him; nine cases arrived at Devonshire House.'

20 *Ibid.*, p. 122.

21 *Ibid.*, p. 129.

22 *Ibid.*, p. 97.

23 *Ibid.*, p. 182.

24 *Ibid.*, p. 53.

25 *Ibid.*, p. 53.

26 *Ibid.*, p. 131. Francois-Marius Granet, *Choir of the Capuchin Church in Rome*, 1817, oil on canvas. National Museums and Gallery of Wales, Cardiff.

27 The two terracotta busts are both signed and dated 1769, that to Wynn in the National Gallery of Ireland and that to the 5th Duke at Chatsworth. Together they constitute a record of the two young men's friendly acquaintance during their respective Grand Tours as Ingamells has noted. See John Ingamells, *A Dictionary of British and Irish Travellers in Italy 1701–1800* (New Haven and London: Yale University Press, 1997), p. 296. For a discussion of the previously unpublished bust of the 5th Duke, see Alison Yarrington, 'Christopher Hewetson: Sculpture, Commerce and Sociability in Rome', in Maria Dolorez Sanchez-Jauregui and Scot Wilcox (eds), *The English Prize: The Capture of the Westmorland An Episode of the Grand Tour*, ed. (New Haven and London: Yale University Press, 2012), pp. 106–14.

28 6th Duke of Devonshire, *Handbook*, pp. 6–7. Possibly the Roman head of a flute-playing satyr. See Dietrich Boschung, Henner Von Hesberg and Andreas Linfert, *Die antiken Skulpturen in Chatsworth: sowie in Dunham Massey und Withington Hall* (Mainz am Rhein: Philipp von Zabern, 1997), pp. 39–40 and cat. no. 32.

29 See Malcom Baker's work on busts in country house collections. M. Baker, 'Ancient and Modern, French and English, War and Peace: The Sculpture in

the Duke of Argyll's Gallery at Adderbury', in *Figured in Marble: The Making and Viewing of Eighteenth-Century Sculpture* (London: V&A Publications, 2000), pp. 129–43.

30 Noble and Yarrington, '"Like a poet's dreams"', 50–7.

31 6th Duke of Devonshire Diary, Sunday 29 November 1846, Devonshire MSS, Chatsworth.

32 Everett was American Envoy Extraordinary and Minister Plenipotentiary to the Court of St James until 1845. He had stayed with the 6th Duke at Chatsworth and they were to meet again in Florence, Everett's subsequent posting. It may be that the 6th Duke's commissions for two major gallery pieces from Schwanthaler and Monti in 1846 precluded any further expenditure on Powers' *Slave*.

33 For the 6th Duke's attraction to Lady Alwyne see James Lees-Milne, *The Bachelor Duke: William Spencer Cavendish 6th Duke of Devonshire* (London: John Murray, 1990), p. 179.

34 *Said Abdallah de la Tribu de Mayac, Royaume de Darfour* or *Negre de Tombouctou*, a cast by Simonet & Sons signed and dated 1848, and its pendant the *Venus Africaine*, a cast by Eck & Durand signed and dated 1851. These were not placed in the Sculpture Gallery, where bronze sculpture was almost entirely absent except on a small scale, but in the Painted Hall, their location in 1857 being confirmed in Adam's *Gem of the Peak*, 1857 edition of the guide to the house and its contents.

35 See Helen Smailes, '"Uno sfortunato scultore Scozzese chiamato Campbell":The Correspondence of Thomas Campbell (1791–1858) and His Banking Maecenas, Gilbert Innes of Stow (1751–1831)', *Walpole Society*, 79 (2009), 217–323. On Campbell's procrastination see 224.

36 For the commissions from Bienaimé see Alison Yarrington, 'Turisti britannici a Carrara nella prima metà dell'Ottocento', in Sandra Berresford (ed.), *'Sognando il marmo': Cultura e commercio del marmo tra Carrara, Gran Bretagna e Impero (1820–1920 circa)* (Pacini Editore, 2009), pp. 178–86 and 216–19.

37 The first ground-breaking study of the sculpture collection in its early years and its underlying themes is by John Kenworthy-Browne, 'A Ducal Patron of Sculpture', *Apollo*, 96:128 (October 1972), 322–31.

38 See Yarrington, '"Under Italian Skies"', 41–62 and Noble and Yarrington, '"Like a poet's dreams"', 52–3.

39 Kenworthy-Browne, 'A Ducal Patron of Sculpture', 322 points out that the 6th Duke's sculpture purchases lodged in the Sculpture Gallery made 'reference to living personalities, or else were associated with his experiences, interests and friends'.

40 6th Duke of Devonshire Diary, 30 March 1824, Devonshire MSS, Chatsworth.

41 6th Duke of Devonshire Diary, 31 March 1824, Devonshire MSS, Chatsworth.

42 6th Duke of Devonshire, *Handbook*, pp. 12–13. The portrait, a copy of that by Robert Lefevre (1806) is in the Devonshire Collection. Research by Charles Noble has revealed that the 6th Duke was incorrect in his statement about the period when it was painted. The Duke of Wellington also owned a copy, see C.M. Kaufmann, *Catalogue of Paintings in the Wellington Museum, Apsley House*, rev. Susan Jenkins with contributions by Marjorie E. Wieseman

(London: English Heritage in association with Paul Holberton, 2009), pp. 177–8 and cat. no. 94.

43 'Madame Mère' died 2 February 1836.

44 Malcolm Elwin, *The Autobiography and Journals of Benjamin Robert Haydon* (London: Macdonald, 1850), pp. 626–8. The 6th Duke commissioned the window panels from Haydon on 29 December 1844. Haydon used the money to pay his son Frank's college bill. The work, painted 'with great gusto' was completed by 2 January 1845. The Duke had received them by 11 January when he wrote that he was pleased with the outcome and sent a cheque for £50. Haydon remarked both on the rate of £25 for a day's work as 'not bad', but also mentions the Duke's kindness. The paintings remain in the Devonshire Collection although not in the location described by the 6th Duke.

45 6th Duke of Devonshire, *Handbook*, p. 14.

46 *Ibid.*, p. 15.

47 *Ibid.*, p. 14. A watercolour by William Frederick Lake Price in the Devonshire Collection shows the glass in place in the High Great Chamber, Hardwick. The cast iron busts c.1830 and the glass remain in the Devonshire Collection, although not *in situ* as the 6th Duke describes.

48 See Yarrington, '"Under Italian Skies"', 43. Thorvaldsen's marble bust placed on the Cardinal's tomb in the Pantheon Rome, 1824, was executed from the plaster model (Thorvaldsen Museum, Copenhagen) – also executed Rome, 1824, of which the Chatsworth bust is a version. Thorvaldsen owned a copy of Thomas Lawrence's portrait of the Cardinal (1819) at Windsor Castle.

49 *Ibid.* See also Noble and Yarrington, '"Like a poet's dreams"', 52–3.

50 6th Duke of Devonshire, *Handbook*, p. 103.

51 *Ibid.*, p. 102.

52 Susan Jenkins, 'Buying Bonaparte' *Apollo*, 172:581 (November 2010), 50–5.

53 6th Duke of Devonshire, *Handbook*, p. 95.

54 *Ibid.,* p. 102.

55 *Ibid.*

56 Henry Richard Vassall-Fox, 3rd Baron Holland, a Whig who in 1816 did not support the British government's action in exiling Napoleon to St Helena and subsequently protested against Napoleon's treatment as a prisoner here.

57 Lieder Goethe, 'Kennst du das Land …' from *Wilhelm Meisters Lehrjahre* (1795–96), translation Walter Meyer, 1996, http://www.recmusic.org/lieder/get_text.html?TextId=6461

58 See Yarrington, '"Under Italian Skies"', 41–62 which cites Devonshire MSS, Chatsworth, '6th Duke's Sculpture Accounts', p. 165: 'The items were bought by the Duke's Agent George Ridgeway in June 1822. The pair of "Magnificent carved Gilt" chandeliers were the most costly items purchased at £283. 10s and £309. 15s. The antique statues of Apollo, Domitian and a seated Agrippina with her daughter were purchased for £42, £84, and £105 respectively.'

II

Women's space?

4

Dirty dancing at Knole: portraits of Giovanna Baccelli and the performance of 'public intimacy'

Gill Perry

IN HER BOOK *Knole and the Sackvilles* published in 1922, Vita Sackville-West compares the north side of Knole House with a medieval village. She describes the building as 'heaped' with no attempt at symmetry; it is also 'sombre and frowning'. But she also observes its contradictions. On the garden side – 'the gay, princely side, with flowers in the foreground' … it has 'an indescribable gaiety and courtliness'.[1] Approaching the north side, Knole, with its turreted skyline and gatehouse and grey Kentish ragstone, dating back to the sixteenth and seventeenth centuries, does indeed appear vast and sombre (figure 22). But from the west-facing garden it appears less threatening and more 'mellow'. As Sackville-West writes:

> It is gentle and venerable. It has the deep inward gaiety of some very old woman who has always been beautiful, who has had many lovers and seen many generations come and go, smiled wisely over their sorrows and their joys, and learnt an imperishable secret of tolerance and humour. It is above all, an English house. It has the tone of England; … it stoops to nothing either pretentious or meretricious.[2]

Sackville-West deploys several associations and metaphors that I will consider in this chapter. Firstly, the idea of this venerable, historic house as a woman, albeit a 'gay'[3] older woman. Secondly, the apparently restrained, unpretentious 'Englishness' of Knole. Both associations require some unpacking; in what follows I will I explore these themes through a study of the relationship between this house and one of its most famous eighteenth-century occupants, the dancer Giovanna Baccelli. She was undoubtedly gay and beautiful and according to various accounts, she had many lovers. But she certainly wasn't old when she lived at Knole, near Sevenoaks, between 1779 and 1789. And she was not English, but Italian.

Houses ancient and modern provide some compelling sources of cultural, political and psychic metaphors and anthropomorphic projections.[4] The eighteenth-century country house or 'stately home' offers us a rather more complex notion of 'home' or the supposedly 'private' inhabited domain than does the modern house. Such 'homes' were conceived and built and as symbolic edifices, as an 'expression of artistic, political and economic endeavour', or as what Mark Girouard has described as 'power houses' of the ruling class.[5] Knole House, which was added to and partly renovated in the eighteenth century, was one such 'power house' replete with a strong historic legacy, with buildings

Figure 22 View of Knole House, Sevenoaks, Kent, north side.

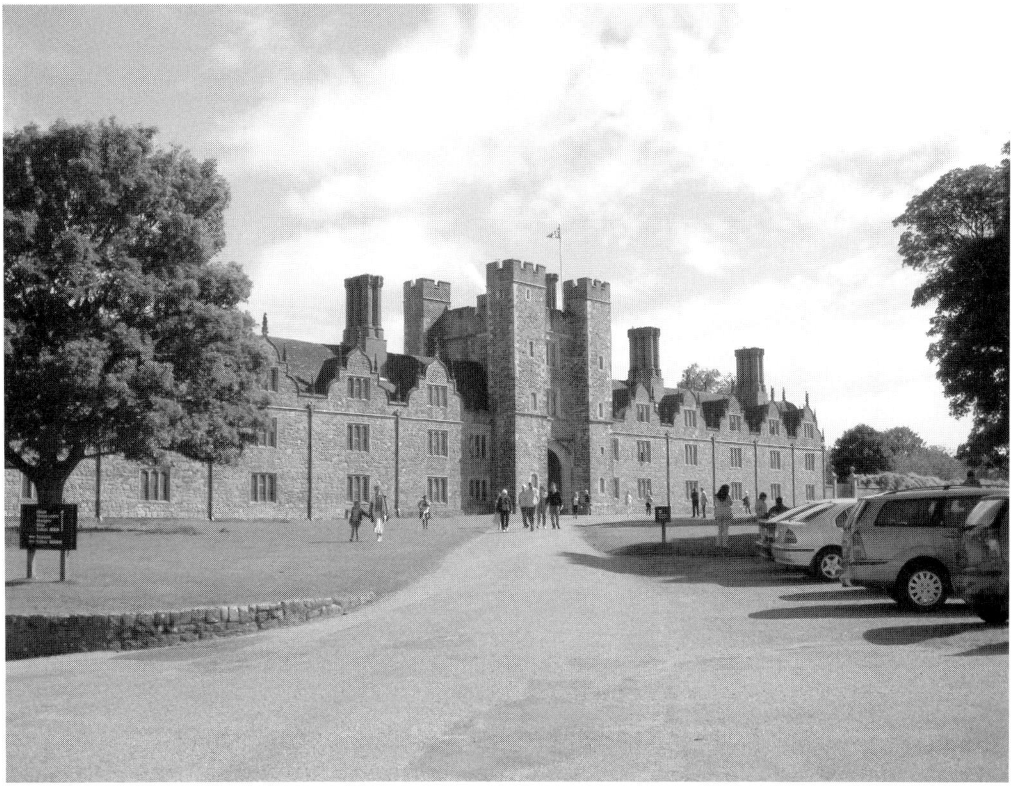

and battlements dating back to the sixteenth and seventeenth centuries, and allegedly beloved of Henry VIII.[6] Moreover, the histories of such 'homes', as Dana Arnold has pointed out, have tended to marginalise their female occupants, despite the traditionally feminine associations of the idea of the home, especially within modern culture.[7] This chapter explores representations of some of those female occupants and considers their likely roles, and visibility, at Knole.

In the early seventeenth century Thomas Sackville, 1st Earl of Dorset, transformed Knole, near Sevenoaks, into a late Renaissance mansion. By the end of the century the 6th Earl, who served as Lord Chamberlain, had added a remarkable collection of Stuart textiles and furniture. And by the end of the eighteenth century the 3rd Duke of

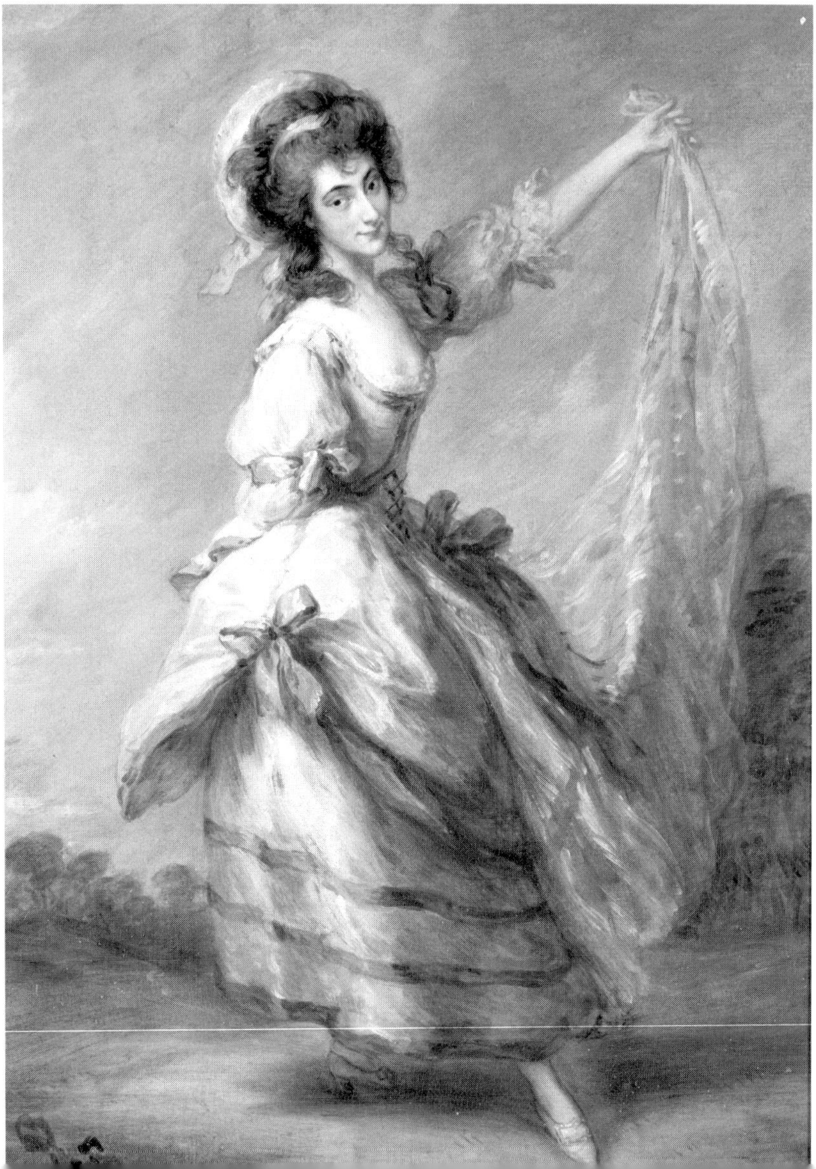

Figure 23 Thomas Gainsborough, *Giovanna Baccelli*, c.1782, oil on canvas, sketch, 56 × 39 cm.

Dorset (1745–99) had added an extensive collection of works gathered on the Grand Tour and commissioned by well-known artists such as Joshua Reynolds and Thomas Gainsborough. By this time Knole was recognised as a major English estate and an historic showcase of cultural capital. The building spoke of rank and dynasty, though to an eighteenth-century audience its historic turreted battlements lacked the magnificence of some newer eighteenth-century 'palaces' such as Blenheim (Sir John Vanbrugh 1705–20) or Castle Howard (Vanbrugh, 1699–1726).[8] In this chapter I shall explore the country house at Knole as a densely coded space in which portraits could contribute to both public and private meanings, and some of their gendered implications. I will consider some of the less well documented aspects of Knole as both a repository of art and precious artefacts, and as a literal and symbolic representation of social power and gender relations. Hence my concern with the roles and representations of one of its most notorious celebrity occupants, the dancer Giovanna Baccelli (plates 6 and 7; figure 23). What was the significance of the portraits of her commissioned by the Duke and placed inside the house? How did her perceived status and her gender contribute to this accumulation and display of cultural capital at Knole? And what was the relationship between Knole and the eighteenth-century celebrity world of the theatre and its female performers? How did the two spheres of English hereditary power and status, and the brash, sexualised and trans-national culture of masquerade and the eighteenth-century theatre, coalesce and even collude in the geography of this building and its valuable contents?

Knole as a woman

The dancer and actress Giovanna Baccelli was born in Venice around 1753. She probably trained in France and then followed an impressive international itinerary performing in London, Venice, Florence and the Paris Opera.[9] Like many successful dancers from the period, she followed a somewhat nomadic peripatetic career, and was in demand for performances in major theatres across Europe. After dancing at the Paris Opera in the 1760s and 1770s, her first recorded performance in London was on 19 November 1774 as Rose in the *Ballet des Fleurs* at the King's Theatre in the Haymarket. She continued to perform intermittently with the King's Theatre until 1789, when it burnt down. By 1779 she could boast one of the best addresses in England. She had moved into Knole as the mistress of John Frederick Sackville, 3rd Duke of Dorset.

And she remained there for ten years until 1789, apart from trips abroad to perform and accompany the Duke. He had inherited his title in 1769, aged only twenty-four and was renowned for his love of art, women and extravagant, jet-setting life style.[10] His good friend Georgiana, Duchess of Devonshire described him in a letter as 'the most dangerous of men ... for what with that beauty he is so unaffected, and has a simplicity and persuasion in his manner that makes one account very easily for the number of women he has in love with him'.[11] Baccelli's predecessors included the celebrated courtesan Nancy Parsons who accompanied him on his Grand Tour, and who had previously been the mistress of the Prime Minister, the Duke of Grafton.[12] But anxieties about the Duke of Dorset's relationship with Parsons, notorious for her series of high-profile lovers, provoked a gossipy discourse on the 'unsuitable' mistress, who might by implication reside one day at Knole. Lady Mary Coke wrote with censure in her diary on 6 January, 1769: 'I shou'd fear he must have the disorder of his father [who had gone mad], to have done so shameful an action, for few people wou'd make a wife of a woman who had been the cast off Mistress of so many other Men. For him he deserves no pity, but for his Family I really grieve.'[13]

Perceptions of Parsons's dangerous feminine sexuality, revealed in her all too visible personal history and her unsuitable class background, fed anxieties about the future of the Sackville family and its historic lineage. Lady Mary need not have worried as the couple parted in 1773 and her place was taken by Mrs Elizabeth Armistead (who later married Charles James Fox), to be followed by Lady Elizabeth (Betty) Hamilton, both before, and apparently after, her marriage to the Earl of Derby. A major scandal was provoked when Lady Elizabeth allegedly left the Earl of Derby and her children for the Duke of Dorset, although the relationship did not last. Although he would not countenance divorce, the Earl of Derby separated from the Countess in 1779. The intricate (and intimate) social relations enjoyed by the aristocracy and actresses were further demonstrated when the actress Elizabeth Farren (1759–1829) later (allegedly) became mistress of the Earl of Derby in 1785/6, and married him in 1797, after the death of the Countess. This chapter also explores some of the remarkably fluid social and sexual boundaries between the worlds of aristocratic power, and the feminine face of eighteenth-century theatre. The Sackville family records indicate that none of the 3rd Duke's affairs lasted as long as his relationship with Giovanna Baccelli, whom he had first spotted dancing at the King's Theatre; according to Vita Sackville-West, he 'lost his head completely over her for the time being'.[14] While living at Knole she bore him a son, John Frederick Sackville, and when they parted officially in 1789, he gave her an annual income of £400, although she left the son behind.[15]

The 3rd Duke shared his father's famous love of opera and the theatre. The 2nd Duke of Dorset, Lionel, who was also Lord-Lieutenant of Ireland, had been passionate about both, and a close friend of the Irish actress Peg Woffington. There is a trail of theatrical portraits and memorabilia at Knole. Apart from the many portraits of Baccelli, commissioned by the 3rd Duke, the eighteenth-century collection included portraits of both the actresses Peg Woffington and Nell Gwyn.[16] According to records in the Knole archive, Woffington made several visits to the house and had a relationship with the 2nd Duke. Vita Sackville-West reports that a playbill for one of Woffington's performances was found stuffed behind the panelling in the Great Hall and the 2nd Duke apparently gave her a command performance at Dublin.[17] Vita Sackville-West also quotes at length a facetious satirical petition found among the Sackville manuscripts, possibly written mischievously by the second Duke's sons, in which Woffington pleads for her suitability for 'any employment he [the Duke] shall graciously please to bestow upon her'. After outlining her suitability for the role of 'housekeeper', the petition ends with an addendum: 'She is ready and willing to act as first Chambermaid to your Grace, to warm your bed and tuck you in, which, as she is advised and verily believes, the present Housekeeper is in no manner qualified to do.'[18]

Apart from its impressive political and ancestral legacies, the history of Knole, whether told by Vita or her descendent Robert Sackville-West, or reconstructed through letters and inventories in the archive, is also a remarkable accumulation of anecdotal narratives about the various Dukes' amorous affairs and mistresses. I suggest that Woffington and Baccelli may qualify as two of those metaphorical 'gay' older women who have had many lovers, with whom Vita Sackville-West compares the house. Knole's relatively hidden history may be found (at last partly) in the various Dukes' love of theatre and feminine celebrities. Perhaps these women are mischievously referenced in veiled form in Sackville-West's metaphor? Like many eighteenth-century country estates, this is a house that, despite the restraint of its façade, is clearly haunted by a lively history of influential, celebrated women. This may be what Sackville-West was implying in her comment that this 'old woman' had learnt an enduring 'secret of tolerance and humour'. Her narrative may also have been intended as a counter to the hierarchical paternalism that dominated the management and inheritance of the English country estate over the centuries. Primogeniture gave enormous powers to one man, often seen as a kind of 'super-father' within and around his estate.[19]

Yet the hidden history of Knole is also a history of and *by* women. Apart from the famous theatrical women who have left their traces, the house is haunted by the memories of inspired and determined women writers, including in the seventeenth century one of the earliest mistresses of Knole, Lady Anne Clifford, and more recently Sackville-West and her close friend Virginia Woolf. Anne Clifford married Richard Sackville, 3rd Earl of Dorset in 1609. However, her refusal to agree to accept a lump sum in lieu of her right to inherit the Clifford estates and title in the north of England, contributed to the breakdown of her marriage and a state of 'melancholy' that she records in her accounts 'The Knole Diary' and her 'Great Book'.[20] 'The Knole Diary' describes her feelings of isolation at Knole caused by her dogged determination to resist the patriarchal control exercised by both her father and husband. Both books reveal her intense obsession with family history, deployed to justify her 'extraordinary resistance to the most powerful patriarchal authorities in her culture'.[21]

Vita Sackville-West's evocative history of the house was also inspired by a sense of melancholy as she had to watch her uncle Charles, the only male heir, inherit her childhood home when her father died in 1928. Her book is partly about her sense of loss, and by implication (and echoing Clifford's protests), the unjust male succession at Knole. That male line is, not surprisingly, subject to her scathing analysis of the various Dukes' buffoonery and foibles. Near the end of the book she describes her ancestors the Sackvilles as 'A rotten lot and nearly all stark staring mad'.[22] Her sometime lover and close friend Virginia Woolf also conjures up Knole in her novel *Orlando*, which she dedicated to Vita to help compensate her for the loss. The two writers met in 1922, and soon after Woolf asked for a copy of the family history she had written. Vita is cast as the eponymous hero and heroine *Orlando*, who changes sex over the three centuries featured. The house and grounds of Knole became the architectural and metaphorical centrepiece of Woolf's novel, and *Orlando* has been described by Sackville-West's biographer as 'a phantasmagoria of Vita's life spread over three centuries'.[23] The flow of the centuries in *Orlando* is grounded by the land, oak trees and house, which as Woolf described it 'looked like a town rather than a house'.[24]

The 'town' of Knole is the stage upon which Woolf performs a complex drama. *Orlando* also has a key theatrical strategy at its heart: role-playing at different sexualities. Transvestism has long been at the heart of theatrical culture and Orlando's change of gender from male to female is staged as if it is a vivid dramatic moment. After falling asleep in Constantinople, an allegorical masque is performed in his room, involving the Ladies of Purity, Chastity and Modesty, preparing the reader for the trumpet blast of 'Truth' as Orlando awakes as a woman.[25] As if in a stage performance in which the disguise of a breeches role is finally exposed, Orlando is now revealed as a woman. Whether conceived as a literal or metaphorical space, Knole is presented yet again as a harbinger of sexual secrets and ambiguities. At the same time, each of these narratives suggests that across the centuries many women have experienced country houses as ambiguous 'homes', as they rarely inherited the houses in which they were born or lived for long periods of time.[26]

'Simply full of stuff'

Knole has been described as a 'Grand Repository' which is 'simply full of stuff'.[27] After declining a visit there in 1791, Edmund Burke wrote that 'It is pleasant to have preserved in one place the succession of the several tastes of ages; a pleasant habitation for the time, a grand repository of whatever has been pleasant at all times. This is not the sort of place which every banker, contractor or nabob can create at his pleasure ... I would not change Knole if I were the Duke of Dorset for all the foppish structures of this enlightened age.'[28]

Despite the fact that Burke was clearly seeking to flatter the Duke, he echoes a contemporary perception. The 'stuff' of Knole House, enmeshed with its long history, was widely seen to be historic, cultured and not foppish or 'nouveau riche'. The remarkable display of ancient ancestors, which offered a rogues' gallery of English aristocracy, clergy and royalty dating back to the sixteenth century, spoke volumes for the historical legitimacy of the *family* and its house or 'home'. And anxieties about the 'tasteless' or showy accumulation of expensive objects which characterised the growing wealth of the middle classes or 'nouveau riche' (whether 'banker, contractor or nabob') haunted the discourse on the English country house during the period.[29] The identity of the house and its political history were inseparable from its collection of 'stuff', especially portraits. The Duke's collection revealed much about his cultural, political and even sexual interests and ambitions. The historical collection provided material evidence of proven noble ancestry and (in Burke's terms) cultured taste. Moreover, its form of display in spaces such as the Great Hall, the Great Staircase and the two long galleries (the seventeenth-century Brown Gallery and the Leicester Gallery) encapsulates some of the problems in defining the relationship between public and private spaces in the interiors of the eighteenth-century country house. As we saw in the Introduction, while modern analyses of the 'home' often explore ideas of 'domesticity' associated with supposedly 'private' family spaces, houses such as Knole were designed to incorporate semi-public spaces which displayed cultural capital and impressed visiting dignitaries and political colleagues. That said, it has been argued that the social geography of the country house changed significantly during the eighteenth century. It has been seen as a period in which, according to Philippe Ariès, the middle classes and nobility began to hold society at a distance, 'pushing it back behind a steadily extending zone of private life. The organisation of the house altered in conformity with this new desire to keep the world at bay.'[30] As we saw in the Introduction, Ariès has argued that this increasing separation of public and private domestic spaces was one of the greatest changes in 'everyday life'. However, the application of this generalised observation, drawn largely from Ariès's experience of French culture and architecture, to the specific spaces of eighteenth-century country houses is a complex exercise, partly dependent on documented knowledge of social uses of spaces during the period. The sixteenth and seventeenth-century architecture of Knole with its use of long galleries and adjoining rooms and 'apartments' makes it difficult to reconstruct an accurate picture of exactly how those public/private distinctions might have been enacted in eighteenth-century daily life. That said, there is some recorded evidence in the archives and in Anne Clifford's 'The Knole Diary' of how the house was organised in the seventeenth century, when there was 'precious little privacy' with servants sleeping 'in dormitories in the attics or on pallet beds at the door to their master's or mistress's bedroom'.[31] Moreover, as I argue, the 3rd Duke's love of entertainment, Knole's proximity to London, and access that was allowed to the general public, enabled a distinctive form of semi-public social exchange around the house and its interior spaces that further complicates (but does not undermine) any analysis of increasing domestic separation. There is also evidence that members of the family and Baccelli herself had private apartments.[32] Given these issues, my focus here is on those works of art which (according to documented evidence) were displayed in particular parts of the house, and on the significance they and their positioning might have held for a contemporary audience.

By the age of twenty-four, the 3rd Duke had restored major parts of the house at Knole, replanted parts of the park and garden and transformed the art collection. He had collected many paintings and marbles on his Grand Tour of Italy, and a surviving notebook lists his many acquisitions bought in Rome and Venice in 1771.[33] His status as a generous patron of the arts was soon established and he commissioned a remarkable number of works from contemporary artists including Gainsborough, Joshua Reynolds, John Hoppner, George Romney, Allan Ramsay, Ozias Humphry and George Opie. The Duke was a friend of Reynolds and pall-bearer at his funeral in 1792, and according to an inventory of 1799 he commissioned at least twenty paintings from the artist, many of which now hang in the so-called Reynolds Room.[34] These include a full-length portrait of the Duke in ceremonial robes, the history painting *Ugolino and his Children in the Dungeon* (RA 1773), portraits of Oliver Goldsmith, Samuel Johnson and David Garrick, and the famous painting of the Duke's Chinese page, *Wang-y-Tong* (plate 8). The Duke's commissions, which included portraits of some of the theatrical and literary stars of his day, proclaimed his position as not merely a beneficent, aristocratic patron of fine art, but also as a figure directly involved with the arts in general. During the Duke's life Knole provided a vivid example of a country house as a kind of 'court' that 'could shelter artists, writers, musicians and even actors'.[35] This engagement with the arts took on some other social and gendered dimensions when the portrait subjects were theatrical women.

It is difficult to reconstruct exactly where different portraits were hung within the house during the Duke's life, although some information can be gleaned from family records. Wang-y-Tong was a Chinese page-boy brought to England by an official of the East India Company who had been a school friend of the Duke. Wang-y-Tong was taken into service at Knole, where the servants allegedly anglicised his name to 'Warnoton'. This cultural appropriation for Englishness was continued when he was sent to the local grammar school at Sevenoaks. Reynolds however, depicts him in full Chinese costume on a bamboo sofa. The conscious exoticism of this portrait, and the worldly and colonial culture which it denotes, sit easily, I suggest, with the visibility of another foreigner at Knole in the late eighteenth century, Giovanna

Baccelli. In a sense, she was yet another 'trophy' of the Duke's wide cultural exploits, travels and interests. Through painted and graphic portraits, copied and disseminated through prints, she herself acquired cultural capital as the celebrated object of visual representation, albeit tinged with sexual innuendo and moral anxiety. During her time at Knole, the Duke commissioned a remarkable number of portraits of the dancer, including works by Gainsborough, Reynolds, Ozias Humphry and John Baptist Locatelli (plates 6, 7; figures 23, 24, 26).[36]

One of the Duke's first commissions was Locatelli's *Giovanna Baccelli Reclining on a Couch*, a life-size plaster of c.1781/2. This reclining statue has been returned to its original position at the foot of the Great Staircase (plate 7; figure 24). The Sackville manuscripts and a Knole inventory of 1799 provide some useful information here. After separating for good from Baccelli in 1789, the Duke married a wealthy heiress, Arabella Cope in 1790. Clearly viewed as a more appropriate social and financial partner, Cope inherited estates worth £140,000 later that year. The inventory tells us that when she took over as mistress of the house the statue of Baccelli was removed from this position and banished to 'the Top of the Stairs next to the wardrobe', and was

Figure 24 John Baptist Locatelli, *Giovanna Baccelli Reclining on a Couch*, 1781, plaster and wood, lifesize. In location at foot of the staircase, Knole.

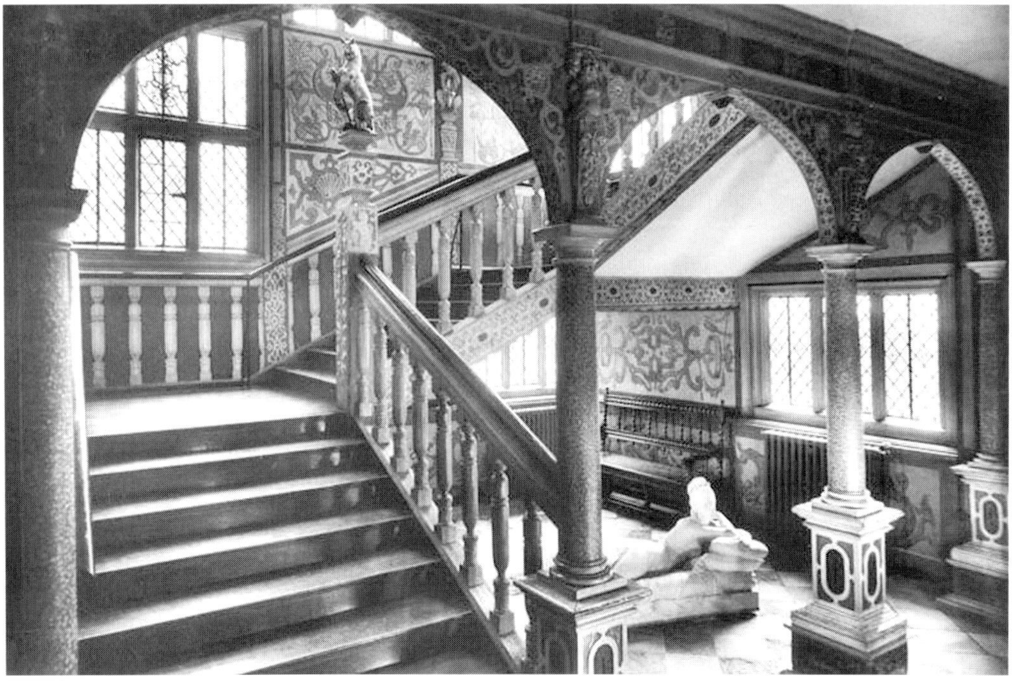

listed anonymously as a 'Naked Venus, whole length, plaster'.[37] But the original position of this overtly sensual work at the foot of the Great Staircase is indicative of a complex domestic and social culture at Knole at the time. Leaning on her elbows, propped up by tasselled pillows, this is a voluptuous image of her body as it sinks deep into the mattress. There is no obvious reference to her status as a dancer; perhaps it was hoped that she would be perceived rather as a Venus to the uninformed visitor. The theme carried a visible currency at Knole as several other copies of standing classical Venuses, some most likely trophies of the Grand Tour, can be found in niches in the galleries.

The positioning of Locatelli's statue guaranteed that it would have confronted all visitors to Knole, both official and more personal. The Great Staircase was at a key point in the formal procession of visitors from the entrance through the Great Hall to the state rooms on the first floor. It reveals a remarkable architectural history: remodelled in 1605–8,[38] it was decorated with classical orders and wall paintings on the themes *The Four Ages of Man*, *The Five Senses* and, on the upper landing, *The Triumph of Peace over War* and *Justice over Evil*. Each panel illustrated recognisable allegorical themes with philosophical and historical resonances, helping to convey the family's claims for political and cultural status. The positioning of Locatelli's statue at the base of this public, processional space raises many questions about the gendered, cultural and political nature of Baccelli's status as 'mistress' of Knole. The public visibility of this statue probably went beyond its presence at Knole, as it seems likely that a plaster version was the reclining sculpture listed in the Royal Academy catalogue of 1781.[39] Naked female bodies, often disguised as figures from classical mythology were, of course, important subjects of painting and sculpture, revealing a gendered discourse that has been interrogated by many scholars over the last few decades. The Royal Academy was a site of viewing that was charged with a specific social function, 'to transform base appetite into refined taste through the production of ideal beauty that was "general and intellectual"'.[40] Although Locatelli's sculpture was commissioned as a portrait of Baccelli, it was not named in the Royal Academy exhibition, allowing the viewing public to seek more idealised classical references.[41] Apart from the possible associations with Venus, the pose directly echoes that of one of the most collected statues of antiquity, the *Hermaphrodite*, a sculpture which was available in sculptural and graphic representation in many eighteenth-century country houses (figure 25). But unlike the conspicuous androgyny of the hermaphrodite, Baccelli was renowned

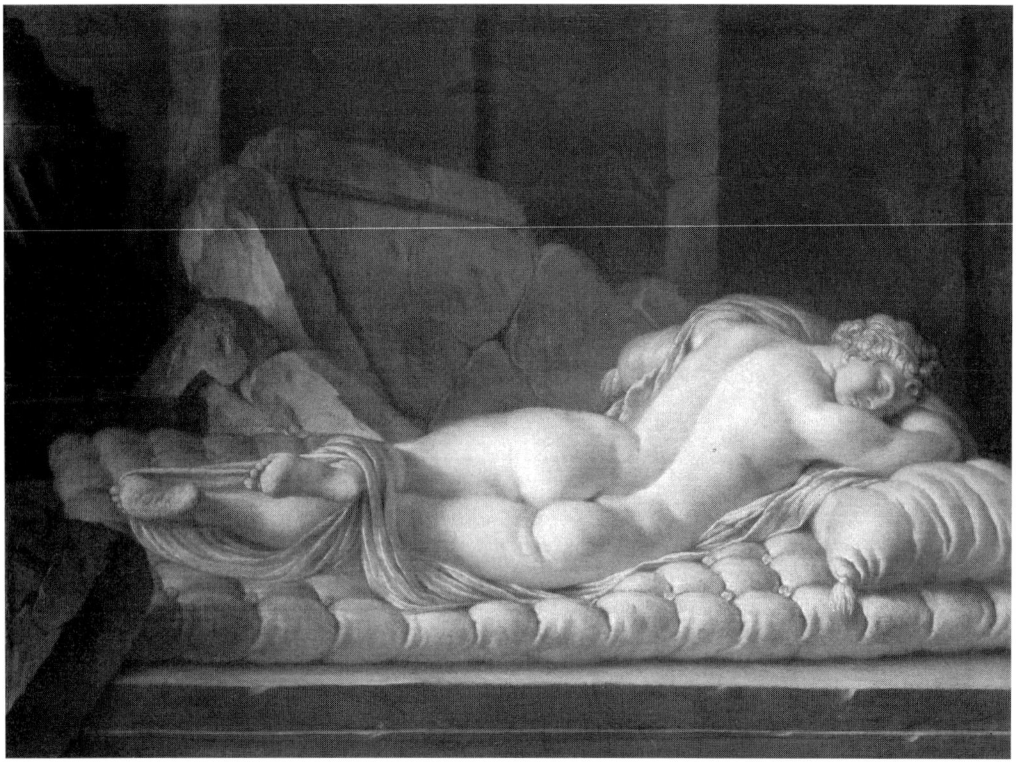

Figure 25 Louis Gabriel Blanchet, *Borghese Hermaphrodite*, 1765. Saltram, Devon.

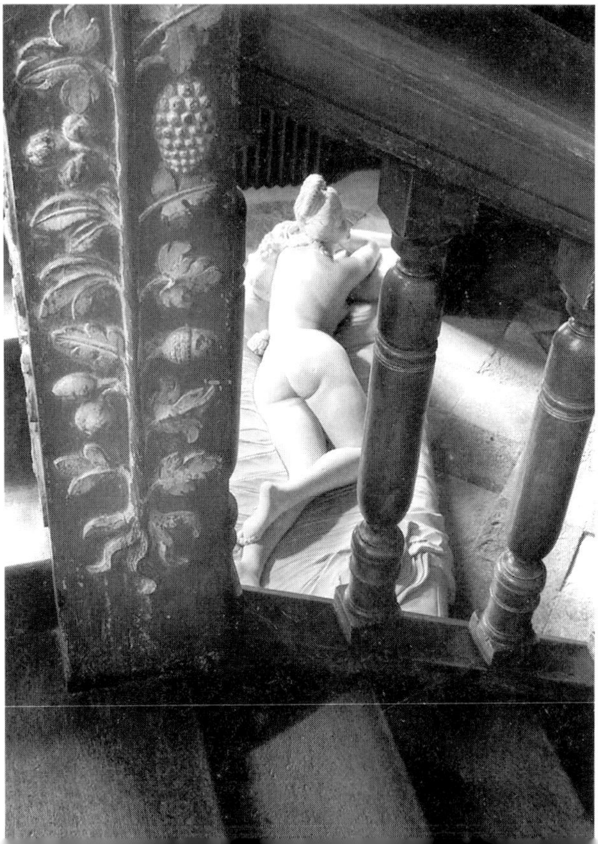

Figure 26 John Baptist Locatelli, *Giovanna Baccelli Reclining on a Couch*, 1781, plaster and wood, lifesize, view from staircase at Knole.

for her feminine sensuality that is clearly in evidence in this reclining sculpture.

Visiting Knole during Baccelli's occupancy would have made it difficult to avoid acknowledging the identity of the subject of this work. The positioning may have been a playful reference to one of the paintings of the five senses on the wall, the allegorical figure of touch. In fact the 3rd Duke does seem to have partly intended this to be displayed as a kind of sexual trophy which his male visitors could admire, and even touch. He presented his closest male friends with small, scaled-down models of the sculpture, so they could literally feel or fondle his mistress. And the positioning at the base of the staircase enabled some further kinaesthetic experiences that would not have been available in more conventional positions of display (figure 26). It provided a range of viewing positions of her body (in representation), including those from above as the visitor ascended the stairs, enabling a better view of her back and buttocks. Apart from their important architectural and social functions, and their symbolic roles linking different interior spaces, staircases enable different viewing positions. They can both provide links between more public, ceremonial spaces and more private apartments, and offer different configurations of the visual spaces of the house and its valuable contents. As Dian Kriz has suggested in her essay on Thomas Rowlandson's satirical drawing *The Exhibition Stare Case*, the display of images of women on and around a public 'stare case' raises many questions about the ways in which 'art and female bodies vied for the male gaze' in eighteenth-century discourse on the fine arts.[42] As a dancer-actress and mistress of the house, Baccelli's potential as an object of erotic titillation for the male visitor at Knole was enhanced by this strategic positioning.

Dirty dancing and celebrity

Despite this positioning, this work does not merely provide erotic evidence of the 3rd Duke's sexual conquests. As I suggest above, its meanings as a sculptural representation that referenced a recognisable cultural iconography, were multivalent for a contemporary audience. Baccelli's identity, like that of other actress-dancers, was a little more complex than just an object – or feminine body – to be fondled. These kinds of mixed or contradictory references were part and parcel of the character profiles that contributed to a growing eighteenth-century culture of celebrity.

And women in particular constituted the highly visible feminine face of the theatre. Painted and sculpted representations of their faces, and their bodies, were much in demand at the time. As is now well documented, the eighteenth century saw a growth in a culture of consumerism, widely identified as marking the origins of modern celebrity culture. I've argued elsewhere that the remarkable visibility of the women who performed on the public stage during the eighteenth century constituted a key part of the literal and symbolic feminine face of that celebrity culture.[43] In combination with her professional achievements, painted and written portraits of Baccelli provide a compelling example of the cultural power of that 'feminine face'.

Popular public exhibitions, an expanding print culture, increasing theatrical and art reviews and puffs, and a growing biographical literature, contributed to the public appetite for images of and information about these 'stars' of the theatre.[44] The sociologist Chris Rojek has argued that a key factor in the construction of celebrities is mass media representation, a development that can be traced back to the dramatic growth of the periodical press and engraved reproductions in the eighteenth century.[45] With the decline in some aspects of organised religion and Court society in the late seventeenth and early eighteenth centuries, the idolatry usually conferred on kings and saints was progressively transferred to secular subjects, especially those who acted out popular roles on the public stage. Stella Tillyard has also developed some of these arguments in relation to the social culture of eighteenth-century London; she describes the 'newspapers, print shops, crowds, coffee houses, theatres, exhibitions, spectacles, pleasure gardens and teeming pavements'.[46] By 1770 there had been a huge expansion in the number of weekly newspapers, with a seemingly insatiable market for biographies of the famous, and an increased dissemination of prints. This public appetite for representations of a recognisable 'face', mixed with scurrilous gossip – and facilitated by weak personal libel laws – contributed to the fantasy of what has been called 'public intimacy'. This term, originated by Joseph Roach, has been adopted by some theatre and cultural historians, to signify an imagined access to private lives that provides the oxygen of celebrity culture.[47] A key feature of this quality of 'public intimacy' is that it operates in the absence of the real person; it is dependent upon representations and myth making, upon an image or a narrative which purports to tell you who the person is, to give you feigned access to private information. It also hinges on contradiction, on the conflation of opposites within these myths. So this imagined access to the famous is enabled largely through the dissemination of painted and written portraits and gossip (both oral and written).

The Duke's many portrait commissions, their appearances in exhibition and their engraved copies, contributed to Baccelli's celebrity status, not to mention her liaison with another form of celebrity, the aristocracy. Visual and written portraits helped to shape the perceived identity or celebrity brand of the performer in question. As is demonstrated by Locatelli's sculpture, they could help to elevate their status through classical or aesthetic allusions, while also enabling or referencing their sensuality or sexual availability. The sculptural medium, with its tactile three-dimensional forms that could literally be touched by the (male) viewer, was especially vulnerable to these struggles for meaning. The potential of the sculptural work to simulate the experience of meeting (or touching) the real person contributed to the confusion of public and private narratives at the heart of feminine celebrity.

Baccelli's career as dancer, although not acknowledged in the statue, was central to her celebrity status. She featured in some of the most reported celebrity events of the decade. In 1781 she was one of the principal ballerinas at the King's Theatre with the famous French dancers Gaeten Vestris and his son Auguste Vestris, and the ballet master Jean-Georges Noverre, who took London by storm. In fact when Auguste Vestris put on a benefit performance that season, the House of Commons adjourned so that its members could be present at this stellar performance, a star-studded event which foreshadows some modern celebrity spectacles. And according to newspaper reports, Baccelli was in several different performances at the King's Theatre the same year that Gainsborough's famous portrait was shown in the Royal Academy exhibition. Theatrical and painted performances mutually reinforced her visibility. The *Public Advertiser* in late April and early May 1782 printed references to her performances only columns away from an assessment of Gainsborough's portrait. In one puff from 1782 she was described as 'the most favourite dancer that ever appeared in England'.[48]

Throughout her relationship with the Duke, Baccelli continued to perform in public; she was often away from Knole performing at the King's Theatre, London, reinforcing her professional identity.[49] She also accompanied the Duke to Paris in 1783 when he was appointed British Ambassador in Paris, where she often danced at the Paris Opera, and the couple were reputedly at the heart of an extravagant social culture of balls and masquerades. Newspapers from the period are full of gossipy, voyeuristic reports. In 1785 the *Morning Herald* included a somewhat patronising account of her Parisian activities: 'Madame Baccelli lives in great splendour in Paris and no lady more truly deserves good fortune than herself. Her house is the resort of all the fashionable English in the gay metropolis; and it is the chief pleasure and study of her life, to shew her gratitude to our nation for the protection with which she was honoured by our nobility.'[50]

The anonymous reviewer emphasises the aristocratic 'protection' that Baccelli had been fortunate enough to enjoy. As mistress of the 3rd Duke, she held a significantly different status to that of many contemporary women performers who married their partners. The latter were often expected to seek feminine respectability by giving up theatrical careers that (for women in particular) continued to carry a social stigma. For example, the dancer Eva Maria Veigel gave up her career after marrying David Garrick in 1749, and the singer Elizabeth Linley also famously gave up performing in public after marrying the playwright and theatre director Richard Brinsley Sheridan in 1777.[51] When actresses married into the aristocracy 'retirement' from paid public performance was the norm, as in the case of Lavinia Fenton who became the Duchess of Bolton in 1751 and Elizabeth Farren who married the Earl of Derby.[52] The dramatic social mobility and assumed role as mistress of a country house involved in such legal marriages usually required this change of status.

Baccelli's status as a professional dancer was itself an ambiguous site of social and sexual status. During most of the eighteenth century the barriers between dancing, musical and straight acting roles were less clearly defined than today; women performing for pay in public was seen as a generic activity that continued to carry a social stigma and still provoked the associations with prostitution and loose morals that had haunted the profession since the seventeenth century.[53] As Richard Leppert has shown, the social functions of music and dancing for women in the second half of the eighteenth century were fraught with tensions, particularly for the middle and upper classes. While respectable women were encouraged to develop a range of accomplishments in music and dance, these were valued primarily in the private domestic sphere.[54] At the same time, the boundaries between 'public' and 'private' spaces were often blurred in the theatrical world, as in the world of country houses. Performances in private homes merged easily into popular invitation-only concerts and balls with extended guest lists.

The actress then was caught between a rock and a hard place. Without the skills of dancing and singing, she could be seen as untrained, but the female performer who practised either activity for money in the commercial theatre, as opposed to indulging an amateur pastime, was vulnerable to claims of overstepping the boundaries of acceptable 'intimacy' on stage. Conduct manuals and courtesy books are full of recommendations to this effect.[55] Displaying and manipulating the body on the public stage was seen as a risky physical pursuit for many women, even when associated with classical ballet, and ran counter to growing ideals of modest femininity, particularly at the end of the century. This may help to account for the fact that there are relatively few surviving exhibition portraits of dancers actually in performance in eighteenth-century British art, although dancing women are more visible in prints and in some private commissions.[56] And the visibility of eighteenth-century actresses and actress-dancers actually contributed to the instability of those boundaries between public and private. Felicity Nussbaum has argued that contemporary culture regarded the feminine as more accessible than the masculine, encouraging an imagined intimacy with actresses in performance.[57] But as I argue, that imagined intimacy – or private access – could be seen to tip towards a more worrying sensual engagement when it involved the physical movement of the feminine body, on stage, or in representation.

Moreover, the increased presence of women in the public sphere contributed to the increase in demand for images of them, not to mention their increased earning power and social mobility. The popularity of women in dance and musical performance contributed to this 'feminine face', and to some of its uneasy contradictions. Such tensions are epitomised in the multiple roles which Baccelli held as mistress of the 3rd Duke, part-time mistress of the house at Knole, professional dancer, and celebrity. Many of these contradictions are enmeshed I suggest in Gainsborough's famous portrait of Baccelli, commissioned by the Duke of Dorset in 1782 (plate 6). The role of this portrait as a visible sign of 'public intimacy' was enhanced by its inclusion in the Royal Academy exhibition of 1782 and its position at Knole.[58] The on-going visibility of the work depended partly on the traffic between Knole and London, the relationship between her public performances and the broader visibility of her painted portraits and engravings, and the position of this work in the house. Walpole, Reynolds and Garrick were among many well-known figures who were regular visitors to Knole. Sevenoaks was relatively easy to get to from London, in comparison with some other notable country seats, and its desirability as a social destination was enhanced by the Duke's love of art and theatre. Baccelli the ballerina, then, enjoyed a remarkable access to the upper classes, the *bon ton* and cultured London society. I've argued that the Locatelli statue would have contributed to her 'well-knownness' partly through its position at the foot of the main staircase. It is less clear exactly where the Gainsborough portrait hung, although records suggest that it was probably in or near the private apartments. When she parted from the 3rd Duke it was apparently moved to a bathroom or closet – the King's Closet.[59] This new position in the visiting sovereign's most intimate, private space contributed to perceptions of Baccelli as the sexually available dancer-courtesan, whose image could straddle the boundaries of public and private life at Knole.

Gainsborough's portrait shows Baccelli in a dance role, yet in a landscape. In this respect it contrasts with two other portraits by Gainsborough that depict actresses in landscapes, his *Perdita – Mary Robinson* of 1781 and *Elizabeth Linley* of 1785–87[60] in which sitters are shown without the trappings of their profession, as women in nature. Unlike Baccelli, both Robinson and Sheridan are shown seated in a landscape, and Gainsborough's characteristically loose brushwork appears to envelop both these sitters and their surroundings. This stylised, evocative nature that seems to enfold some of his sitters has been seen by some critics to contribute to the evocation of desire in the viewer.[61] As Benedict Leca has argued, when applied to the painting of women this 'demonstrative painting meant affective painting, for which Gainsborough expected active, participatory – sensory – looking from the viewer'.[62] However, in the Baccelli portrait, this sensory viewing experience is invited as much by her pose and demeanour, as by her immersive relationship with her landscape. Although painted in his distinctive suggestive style, the background appears more like a stage set, and Baccelli is clearly in role. A print by J. Thornwaite after James Roberts, reproduced in *Bell's Theatre* in 1781 shows Baccelli performing for the ballet *Les Amans surpris*, in one of her most successful roles at the King's Theatre, London that often featured in newspaper reviews and announcements in the period 1781–82.[63] The costume in the Gainsborough portrait, with its hooped, blue ribboned and gathered sections, is close to that of the print, and the slightly raised hemline above the ankle in both works suggests shortened dance wear rather than normal dress length.[64] Although Thornwaite's print clearly depicts the dancer in mid-performance, the Gainsborough represents a seemingly more restrained dance pose, perhaps deemed more appropriate for a large-scale work for public exhibition. She stands with one arm outstretched holding the edge of her skirt, one arm behind her back, and her toe poised for movement. As Eliot has written 'she appears capable of choosing at any moment to bend her well-turned out knee in a *plié* and to step out to balance on the ball of her extended right foot'.[65] Einberg has suggested that the initiative for representing Baccelli in her famous role may have come from the dancer herself. Gainsborough was a keen musician with a close relationship with the King's Theatre, and according to reports had painted two allegorical figures for the side wings of the stage.[66] That Baccelli was in several different performances at the King's Theatre in 1782, the year that Gainsborough's portrait was shown at the Royal Academy, increases the likelihood of a collaboration on this commission. The mythical history of Gainsborough's relationship with both the dancer and with Knole House has been embellished through a nineteenth-century sketch, probably by Joseph Nash, of Baccelli supposedly posing for the artist in the ballroom at Knole (figure 27). However, it seems more likely that Baccelli posed for Gainsborough in his London studio.[67]

Yet, as a ballerina, Baccelli also belonged to a much maligned group of women described by one reviewer in the 1780s as 'the highest order

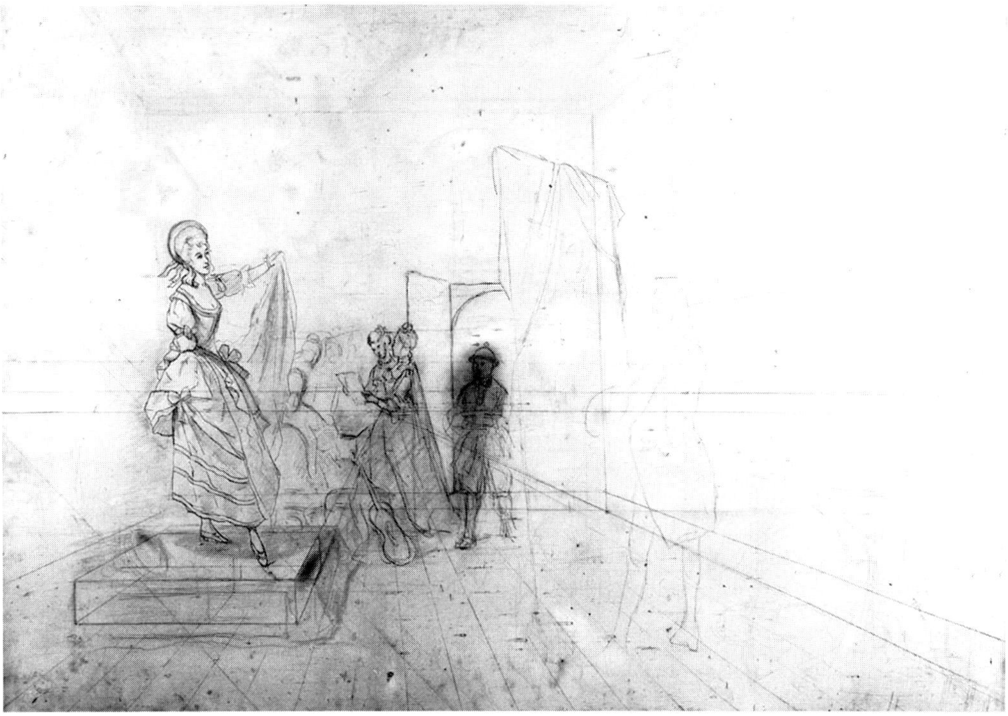

Figure 27 Joseph Nash (attributed), *Sketch of Giovanna Baccelli Posing in the Ballroom at Knole*, nineteenth century, pencil and pen on prepared paper, laid on canvas, 90 × 115.5 cm.

of the impures'.[68] Thus her dancing skills could be perceived as both refined and (to use a modern phrase) 'dirty' or seductive and erotic. Such tensions could also be seen to be revealed in Gainsborough's portrait. While his suggestive brushwork combined with the dancer's gently smiling expression might evoke a sense of intimacy and 'sensory' looking, contemporary critics worried about the feigned or theatrical nature of this intimacy. When Gainsborough's portrait was exhibited at the Royal Academy in 1782, critics noted his fluid brushwork, but continually returned to the problem of whether the painter had achieved an accurate 'likeness', a recurring concern with exhibited images of female performers.[69] When the subject of an exhibited painting was an actress, dancer or courtesan, the 'likeness' debate often took on an overtly sexualised dimension. On the 2 May, for instance, the *Public Advertiser* described Gainsborough's *Baccelli* as 'a good moral likeness'. But what worried this reviewer, paradoxically, was that Gainsborough's picture was *too* close to its subject, as it was seen to betray her lack of moral character. The issue of 'likeness' presented some further problems in relation to images of female performers and theatrical portraits in general. If an individual was to be painted in her or his stage role, how accurate a representation of the dramatic disguise should the artist provide? This dilemma prompted a rather ambivalent assessment of Gainsborough's picture from the critic for the *Gazetteer* (1 May 1782), who explained that in order to represent 'an Italian opera Dancer, the artist was not only obliged to embellish, but if he would be thought to copy the original to *lay on his colouring thickly*; in this he has succeeded for the face of this admirable dancer is evidently paint-painted'. The portrait shows Baccelli rouged and powdered, the exaggerated whiteness of her face and skin appearing in sharp contrast with her dark (Italian) features. But if this was a concession to the 'truth' of her disguise, stage paint, like the activity of acting itself, could also symbolise deception and falsity, the opposite of a natural 'likeness'. In a late eighteenth-century context this form of masquerade was regarded as characteristically *feminine* behaviour and encapsulated the problem of 'public intimacy'. Women – especially women performers – used make-up, or so it was often claimed, to give themselves the look of feminine modesty: but in so doing they simultaneously exhibited their capacity to dissemble and deceive. And stage make-up could exaggerate those powerful cultural symbols of desirable English femininity: the pure white skin of feminine innocence and the modest anxieties revealed by the blush.[70] This false whiteness might also be seen as an attempt to disguise Baccelli's foreignness, her Italian origins. This process of anglicisation was also at work in the traces which she left at Knole. The Duke gave her private apartments in one of the towers, which instead of being called Baccelli's tower, was apparently anglicised by the staff to a more easily pronounced 'Shelley's Tower'.

As Sackville-West suggested, then, Knole is not merely a 'grand repository', full of historical stuff, but is also full of rich metaphorical resonances as a 'gay old woman', harbouring traces of struggles and negotiations for status, in relation to both gender and class. These struggles, for public and social identity and recognition, involved strategies of masquerade and dissembling, both qualities associated with women and the theatre. While Virginia Woolf later turned the story of Knole into the performance of gender struggles, or gender ambivalence, some of its earlier occupants have left their traces in the form of painted performances. We have seen that Baccelli's celebrity brand was heightened by her visible presence in Knole, as a kind of 'mistress of the house'. Moreover, the Locatelli statue and the Gainsborough portrait are both works that invited affective responses from their eighteenth-century viewers. While the Locatelli positioned on the staircase invited a tactile, kinaesthetic response, Gainsborough's Baccelli seductively represents a woman in performance. Both evoke a subject who is both on and off stage in the same image, embodying some of the contradictions inherent in eighteenth-century celebrity culture.

Notes

1 Vita Sackville-West, *Knole and the Sackvilles* (New York: George H. Doran, 1922), pp. 1–2.

2 *Ibid.*, p. 2.

3 Sackville-West is using the term 'gay' here in its traditional sense, as lively, merry or cheerful. According to the OED, the term was often used in the nineteenth century in relation to women, as a conventional epithet of praise.

4 The literature on the psychic and cultural associations of the 'house' or 'home' is now immense, and straddles discipline boundaries. Gaston Bachelard's *The Poetics of Space: The Classic Look at How We Experience Intimate Places* (New York: Beacon Press, 1994) was first published in French in 1958 and has become an established text on our psychic and phenomenological understanding of domestic space in the twentieth century. See his introduction, pp. xv–xxxiv.

5 Christopher Christie, *The British Country House in the Eighteenth Century* (Manchester: Manchester University Press, 2000), p. 4; Mark Girouard, *Life in the English Country House: A Social and Architectural History* (New Haven and London: Yale University Press, 1978), p. 2.

6 Robert Sackville-West, *Knole, Kent* (The National Trust, 2006), p. 4.

7 Dana Arnold, 'Defining Femininity: Women and the Country House', in Dana Arnold (ed.), *The Georgian Country House: Architecture Landscape and Society* (Stroud: Sutton, 1998), p. 79. For an excellent discussion of the complex gendered associations of the idea of the house or home in the eighteenth century see Judith S. Lewis, 'When a House is Not a Home: Elite English Women and the Eighteenth Century Country House', *Journal of British Studies*, 48:2 (April 2009), 336–63.

8 After a visit to Knole in 1780, Horace Walpole commented admiringly 'I worship all its faded splendour and enjoy its preservation', but noted that it needed more of 'the bustling jollity of the old nobility to disperse its gloom'. Cited in Vita Sackville-West, *Knole*, p. 181.

9 Her full name was Giovanna Francesca Antonia Guiseppe Zanerini and her sister Argentine Zanerini was a successful dancer at the Comédie Italienne. Known as 'La Baccelli' Giovanna was fluent in French and English, apart from Italian. However, information on her early life is scarce. The information gathered here is taken largely from: Elizabeth Einberg's catalogue *Gainsborough's Giovanna Baccelli* (London: Tate Gallery Publications, 1976), Ivor Guest, *The Ballet of the Enlightenment: The Establishment of the Ballet d'Action in France, 1770–1793* (London: Dance Books, 1996), and Karen Eliot's chapter 'Giovanna Baccelli', in *Dancing Lives: Five Female Dancers from the Ballet d'Action to Merce Cunningham*) (Urbana and Chicago: University of Illinois Press, 2007), pp. 7–32. I have also used newspaper articles and reviews, information in the Centre for Kentish Studies, Maidstone Archives, Sackville MSS, and Robert Sackville-West's history of Knole, *Inheritance* (London: Walker & Company, 2010), p. 129.

10 Reynolds's portrait *John Frederick, 3rd Duke of Dorset*, 1782, currently hangs in the Reynolds Room, Knole House.

11 Quoted in Sackville-West, *Inheritance*, p. 129.

12 Described in the *Oxford Dictionary of National Biography* as a 'courtesan and political mistress' Nancy Parsons (1735–1814/15) was reputedly the daughter of a Bond Street tailor. According to surviving accounts, she eloped at a young age to the West Indies with a Captain Horton. The marriage failed and she returned to London, and took up with the Duke of Grafton around 1763 and remained with him for four years. That relationship, which the Duke was considered to have flaunted in society, was criticised in contemporary gossip columns. After the separation, Parsons became involved with the Duke of Dorset for two years. Following that separation she became involved with and married Charles, Viscount Maynard in 1776. In 1784 she began an affair with the 5th Duke of Bedford. Despite the scurrilous representation of her as a predatory, serial mistress, provoked by her series of high-profile romantic liaisons, she was known for her 'calm', gentle temperament and was deeply religious. She was also painted by Gainsborough and Reynolds, among others.

13 Cited in Sackville-West, *Inheritance*, p. 131.

14 Vita Sackville-West, *Knole*, p. 188.

15 The Sackville family archive is now in the public record office in Maidstone,

and along with Vita Sackville-West's account is one of the key sources for Robert Sackville-West's *Inheritance*.

16 Portraits of Woffington and Nell Gwyn at Knole are both mentioned by Vita Sackville-West, although neither are at Knole today. The DNB mentions a portrait of Woffington as Penelope, by Reynolds, which 'was lent by Lord Sackville to the Guelph Exhibition', but this portrait is not mentioned in David Mannings's catalogue of Reynolds, *Sir Joshua Reynolds: A Complete Catalogue of His Paintings*, 2 vols (New Haven: Yale University Press for the Paul Mellon Centre for Studies in British Art, 2000) and is probably now lost.

17 Vita Sackville-West, *Knole*, p. 165.

18 *Ibid.*, p. 167.

19 Christie, *British Country House*, p. 99. Christie discusses the effects of primogeniture and the 'deed of settlement' which governed inheritance in large landowning estates with a peerage. This settlement secured the house and the estate for the heir, often on his marriage. During the first decades of the eighteenth century some writers began to question this patriarchal organisation of a 'family', as in Mary Astell's *Reflections on Marriage* of 1731.

20 I am indebted to Mihoko Suzuki for drawing to my attention the history of Anne Clifford at Knole, explored in her article 'Anne Clifford and the Gendering of History', *CLIO: A Journal of Literature, History and Philosophy*, 30:2 (Winter, 2001), 195ff. For an account of Clifford's time at Knole see also Sackville-West, *Inheritance*, chapter 2.

21 Suzuki, 'Anne Clifford', 197. As Suzuki shows, it was precisely because she continually withheld consent to the cash settlement that Clifford was later able to inherit her title and estates thirty-eight years later, after the death of her father George, his brother Francis and his son Henry.

22 Vita Sackville-West, *Knole and the Sackvilles*, p. 201.

23 Victoria Glendinning, *Vita: The Life of Vita Sackville-West* (New York: Quill, 1983), p. 203.

24 Woolf writes: 'There it lay in the early sunshine of spring. It looked like a town rather than a house, but a town built, not hither and thither, as this man wished or that, but circumspectly, by a single architect with one idea in his head. Courts and buildings, grey, red, plum colour, lay orderly and symmetrical; the courts were some of them oblong and some square; in this was a fountain; in that a statue; the buildings were some of them low, some pointed; here was a chapel, there a belfry; spaces of the greenest grass lay in between the clumps of cedar trees and beds of bright flowers; all were clasped – yet so well set out was it that it seemed that every part had room to spread itself fittingly – by the roll of a massive wall; while smoke from innumerable chimneys curled perpetually into the air.' Virginia Woolf, *Orlando* (Ware, Hertfordshire: Wordsworth Editions, 2003), p. 51.

25 *Ibid.*, p. 66.

26 This argument is explored in Lewis, 'When a House is Not a Home', 339. See also the Introduction to this collection.

27 Sackville-West, *Inheritance*, p. 127. Sackville-West titles his chapter on the 3rd Duke of Dorset, 'A Grand Repository (1769–1799)', pp. 127–42.

28 *Ibid.*, p. 127.
29 And informed some contemporary debates on 'taste' and 'luxury'. For a discussion of these debates see Maxine Berg, *Luxury and Pleasure in Eighteenth Century Britain* (Oxford: Oxford University Press, 2005).
30 Philippe Ariès has argued that the modern idea of the family 'home' with all its associations of privacy and intimacy was first developed in the eighteenth century. See *Centuries of Childhood: Social History of Family Life* (New York: Vintage, 1962).
31 Anne Clifford's 'The Knole Diary' provides a vivid account of the claustrophobic atmosphere within the house; see Suzuki. Robert Sackville-West also cites a seating plan for the household which lists more than 120 dependants at Knole between 1613 and 1624. Sackville-West, *Inheritance*, p. 27.
32 A tower in the 'Inner Wicket' courtyard was named Shelley's tower (an English corruption of Baccelli) and contained Baccelli's rooms.
33 The notebook is titled 'An Account of the Number and Value of the Pictures, Busts, etc' and tells us that his acquisitions included ancient marble busts of Antinous and Pompey excavated by Gavin Hamilton at the Villa Adriana, and paintings by Teniers, Garofalo and Wouvermans. The notebook is in the Centre for Kentish Studies, Maidstone Archives, Sackville MSS.
34 The inventory is among the Sackville papers (see notes 15 and 33) and is cited by Sackville-West, *Inheritance*, p. 130.
35 Christie, *British Country House*, p. 2.
36 Reynolds's portrait *Giovanna Baccelli as a Bacchante*, 1783 is in Lord Sackville's collection at Knole House. For other known portraits see Einberg, *Gainsborough's Giovanna Baccelli*.
37 Centre for Kentish Studies, Maidstone Archives, Sackville MSS, U269. See also Sackville-West, *Inheritance*, p. 139.
38 Along with the Great Hall, the Great Staircase was remodelled by Thomas, 1st Earl of Dorset, between 1605 and 1608. The architectural scheme for the staircase was influenced by the Renaissance revival of classical orders, arranged with Doric on the lower floor, Ionic in the middle and Corinthian on the top.
39 The Royal Academy Catalogue for 1781 lists a plaster sculpture of a 'Reclining Nude' by Locatelli that is possibly the same work.
40 K. Dian Kriz, '"Stare Cases": Engendering the Public's Two Bodies at the Royal Academy of Arts', in David Solkin (ed.), *Art on The Line: The Royal Academy Exhibtions at Somerset House, 1780–1836* (New Haven and London: Yale University Press for the Paul Mellon Centre for Studies in British Art and the Courtauld Institute Gallery, 2001), p. 55.
41 This was a common practice in Royal Academy exhibitions in the 1780s in which portraits were listed anonymously in the catalogue as, for example, 'Portrait of a Lady'.
42 Kriz, '"Stare Cases"', p. 57.
43 This issue is explored in the book/catalogue Gill Perry (ed.), *The First Actresses* (London: National Portrait Gallery, 2011).
44 *Ibid.*, chapter 4, 'Star Systems' for a discussion of uses of the term 'celebrity'.
45 Chris Rojek, *Celebrity* (London: Reaktion, 2001).

46 Stella Tillyard, 'Paths of Glory', in Martin Postle (ed.), *Joshua Reynolds: The Creation of Celebrity* (London: Tate Publishing, 2005), p. 61.
47 In his influential book *It* Joseph Roach explores a notion of celebrity through its characteristic manifestations of what he calls 'public intimacy', an illusion of availability that is 'paradox ridden' (p. 8), and that may take on a pseudo-religious characteristic. Celebrities may seem 'at once touchable and transcendent' (p. 16). Joseph R. Roach, *It* (Michigan: University of Michigan Press, 2007).
48 Cited in Ivor Guest, 'The Italian Lady at Knole', *Ballet Annual,* 2:1 (1957), p. 81.
49 Karen Eliot has also researched Baccelli's performances in Italy, especially her returns to Venice. See Eliot 'Giovanna Baccelli', pp. 7–32.
50 *Morning Herald*, 9 February 1785.
51 For an account of Linley's life and debates about her 'retirement' after marriage see Alan Chedzoy's biography, *Sheridan's Nightingale: The Story of Elizabeth Linley* (London: Allison & Busby, 1997).
52 Although many, including Farren, continued to perform and organise amateur dramatics in the private theatricals beloved of the aristocracy. See Gill Perry, 'Star Systems: Then and Now', in Perry, *The First Actresses*, pp. 122ff.
53 Much has now been published on this topic. A key text is Kristina Straub's *Sexual Suspects: Eighteenth Century Players and Sexual Ideology* (Oxford and Princeton: Princeton University Press, 1992). See also Gill Perry, *Spectacular Flirtations* (New Haven and London: Yale University Press, 2007).
54 Richard Leppert has explored some of these issues in *Music and Image: Domesticity, Ideology and Socio-Cultural Formation in Eighteenth Century England* (Cambridge: Cambridge University Press, 1988). See also Perry, *The First Actresses*, chapter 2, 'Divas, Dancing and the Rage for Music', pp. 78–102.
55 See Leppert, *Music and Image*, especially chapters 1, 2 and 5.
56 This subject is discussed in Perry, *The First Actresses*, chapter 2 (see footnote 44). John Hoppner's portrait of *Mlle Hilligsberg*, c.1781, now in the Gallery of New South Wales is an unusual late eighteenth-century portrait of Hilligsberg dancing.
57 Felicity Nussbaum, *Rival Queens: Actresses, Performance and the Eighteenth Century British Theater* (Philadelphia: University of Pennsylvania Press, 2010), p. 16.
58 For an account of some of the portraits in this Royal Academy exhibition see Gill Perry, 'The Spectacle of the Muse: Exhibiting the Actress at the Royal Academy', in Solkin, *Art on The Line*, pp. 113–16.
59 As described in Vita Sackville-West, *Knole*, p. 194.
60 Gainsborough's *Perdita – Mrs Robinson* of 1781 is in the Wallace Collection, London. His *Elizabeth Linley* of 1785–87 is in the National Gallery of Art, Washington DC.
61 Much has now been written about the evocative powers of Gainsborough's later portraits in landscapes. See, for example, Martin Myrone and Michael Rosenthal (eds), *Gainsborough* (London: Tate Publishing, 2002). In a *Guardian* review of works in this Tate exhibition, the critic Jonathan Jones described the 'drugged ecstatic' look of Mary Robinson's portrait and the 'intimacy'

that it suggested. Jones also described 'Nature – the woozy, leafily stylised nature that decorates almost all his portraits – is for Gainsborough a kind of screen on which all manner of desires and fears can be projected. Jonathan Jones, 'Thomas Gainsborough: A Modern Genius', *Guardian*, 19 October 2002.

62 Benedict Leca, 'A Favourite among the Demireps', in B. Leca, A. Ribeiro and A. Ludwig (eds), *Thomas Gainsborough and the Modern Woman* (Cincinnati: Cincinnati Art Museum, 2010), p. 45.

63 The print was published for Bell's Theatre, 15 May, 1781, and is illustrated in Einberg, *Gainsborough's Giovanna Baccelli*, p. 17. According to dance historian Karen Eliot, Simonet's ballet was first produced in London at the King's Theatre on 6 December 1780 and received twenty-two performances during the 1781–82 season, and Baccelli''s performance in the ballet attracted Gainsborough's attention. Eliot, 'Giovanna Baccelli', p. 27.

64 Eliot has discussed the shortening lengths of dance costumes in the eighteenth century in 'Giovanna Baccelli', pp. 18–19.

65 *Ibid.*, p. 8.

66 Einberg, *Gainsborough's Giovanna Baccelli*, pp. 10–11.

67 This drawing, probably from the 1820s, is not referenced in the 1828 Knole inventory. See Einberg, *Gainsborough's Giovanna Baccelli*, p. 33.

68 *Ibid.*, p. 8.

69 While the *Westminster Magazine* of May 1782 identified a 'striking likeness', the *St James's Chronicle* argued that Gainsborough has 'hardly given a likeness', 27–30 April 1782, p. 4.

70 The significance of the blush in representation has been explored in Angela Rosenthal's work, some of which was being prepared for publication before her sad death in 2011. I am indebted to her excellent lectures and conference papers on this subject, especially her lectures series on the subject at University College, London, 2001.

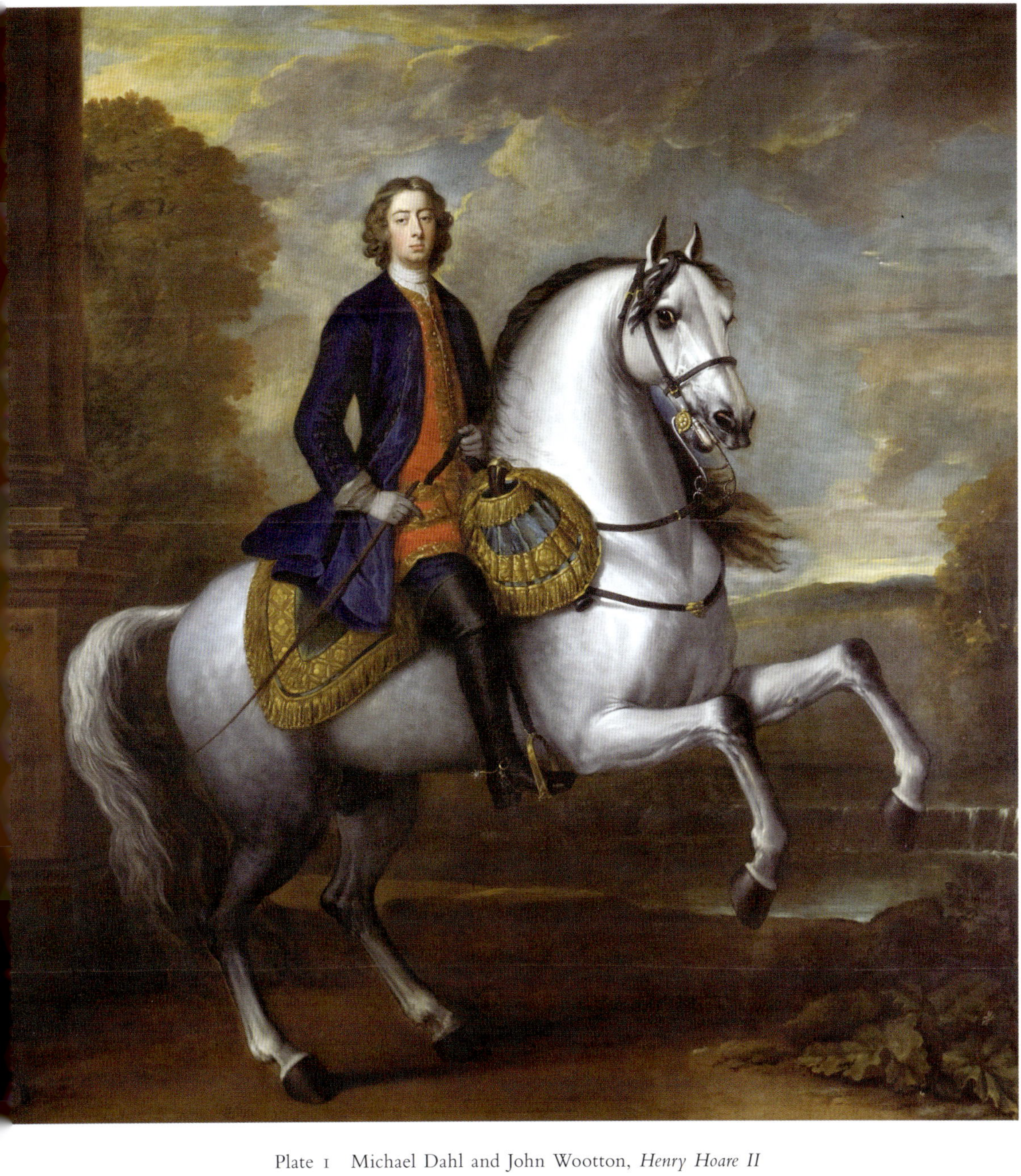

Plate 1 Michael Dahl and John Wootton, *Henry Hoare II 'The Magnificent'*, 1726, oil on canvas, 300 × 307 cm.

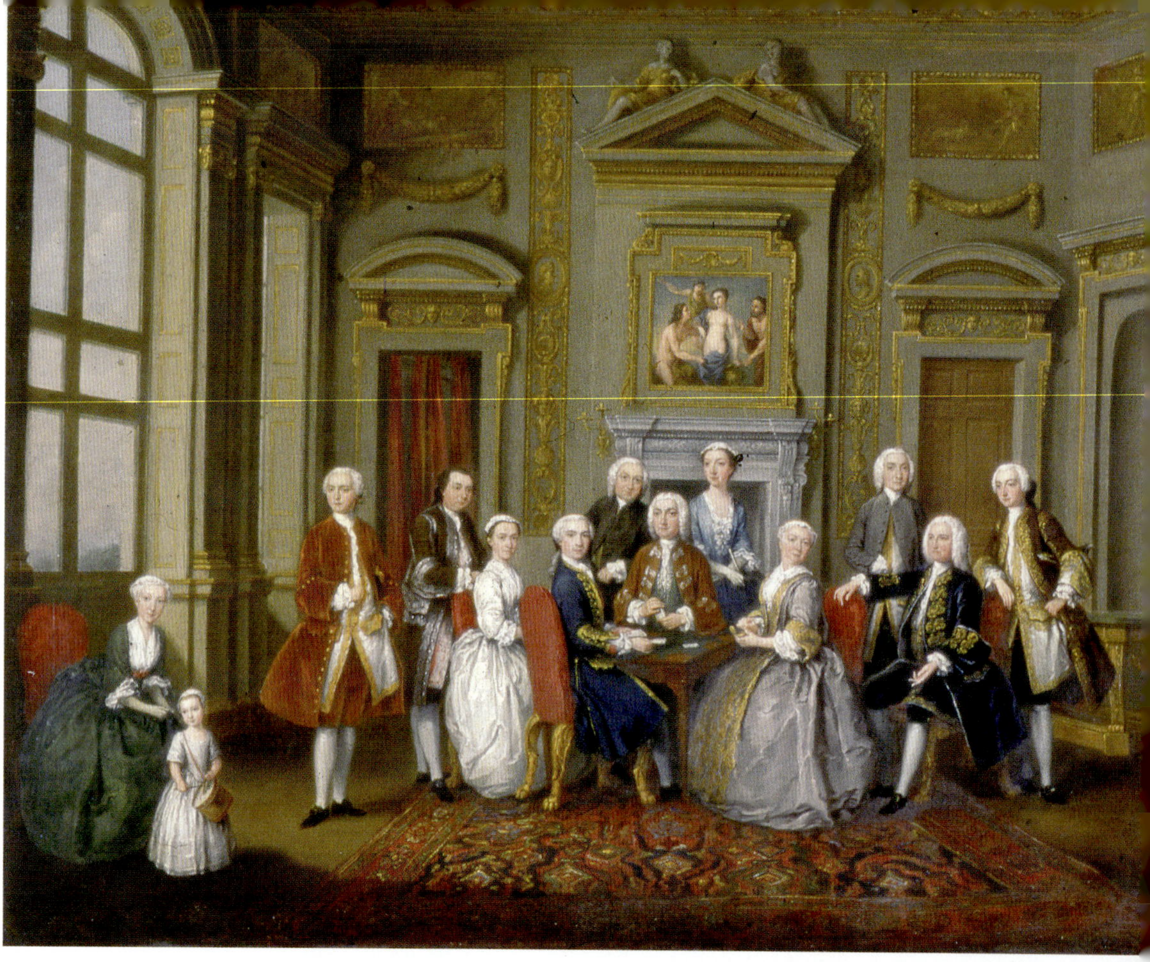

Plate 2
Joseph Francis Nollekens, *The Tylney Family in the Saloon at Wanstead House*, 1740, oil on canvas, 86.3 × 109.2 cm.

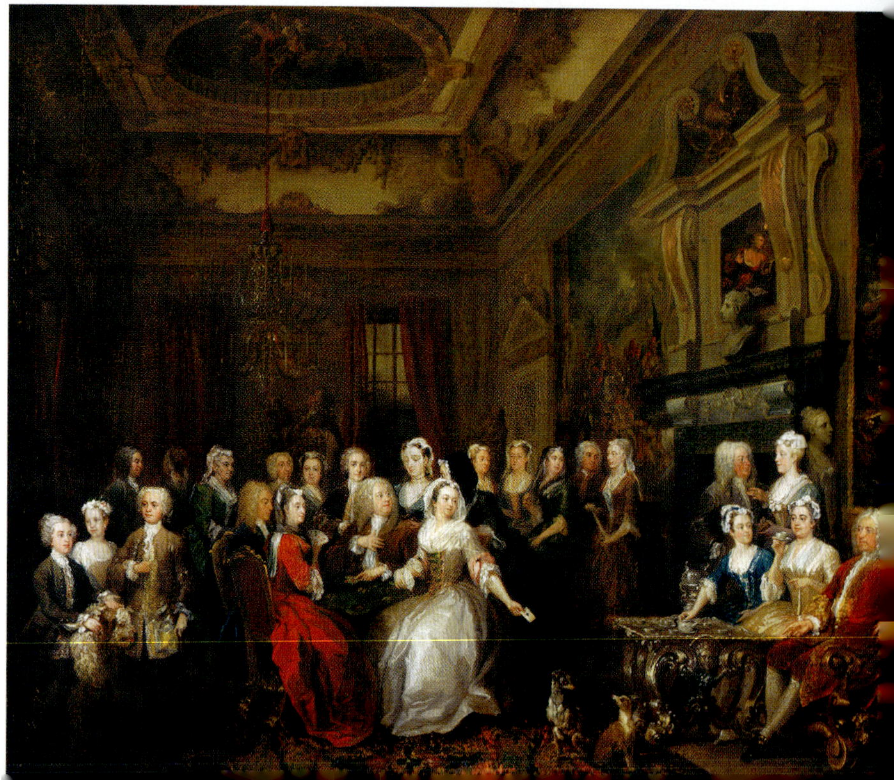

Plate 3
William Hogarth, *Assembly at Wanstead House*, 1728–31, oil on canvas, 64.8 × 76.2 cm.

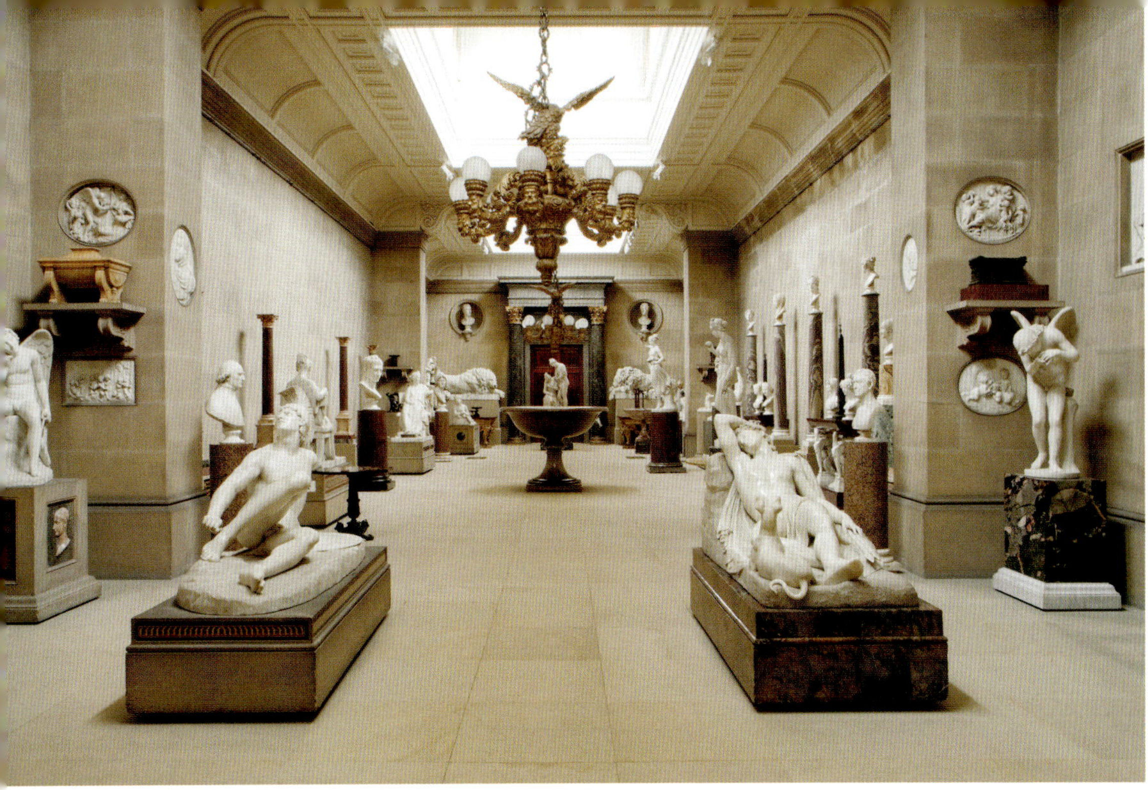

Plate 4
The Sculpture Gallery, Chatsworth, view looking north.

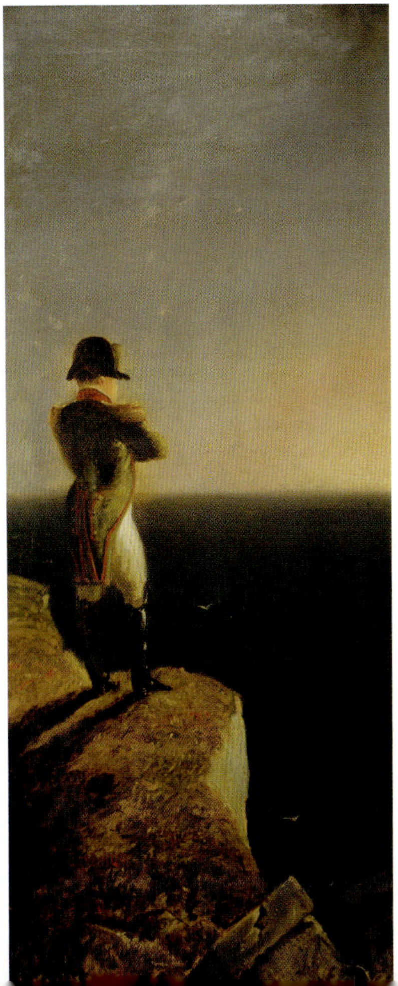

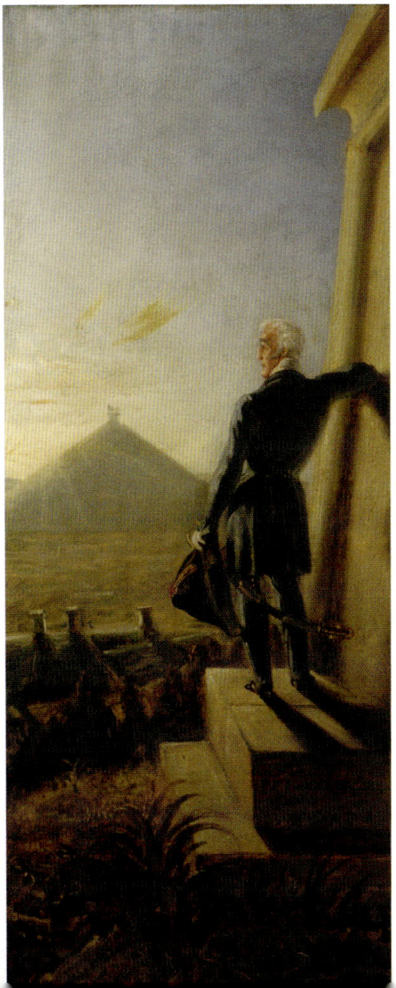

Plate 5
Benjamin Robert Haydon, *Napoleon in Exile* (left) and *The Duke of Wellington at Waterloo* (right), 1844–45, window panels.

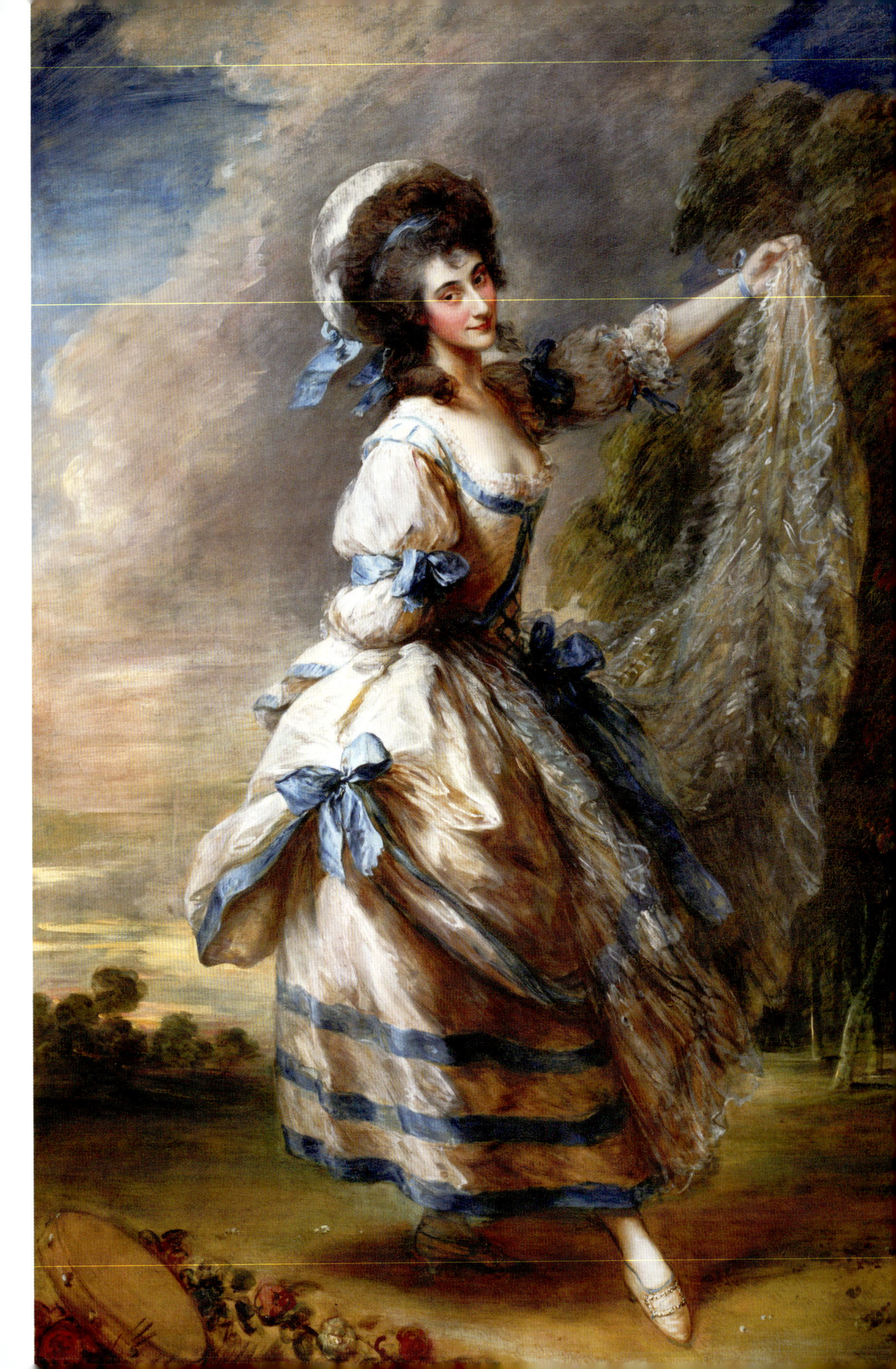

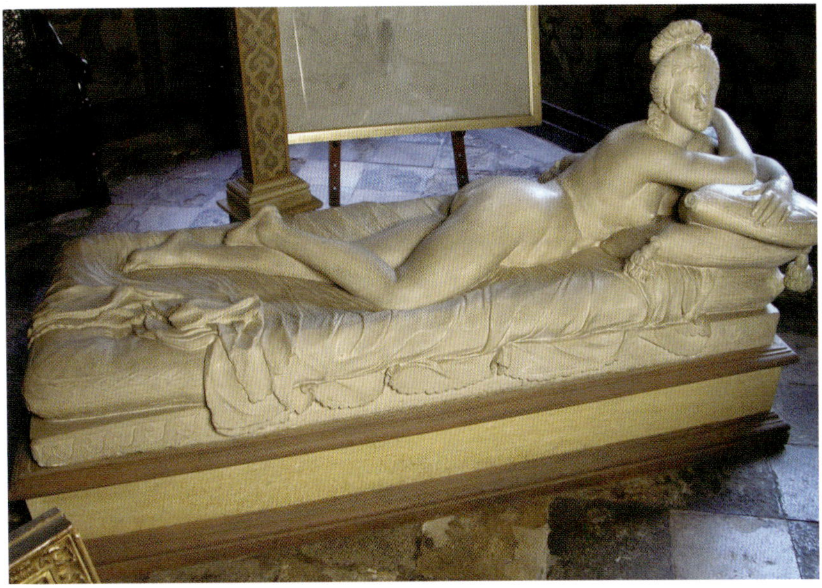

(*opposite*)
Plate 6
Thomas Gainsborough, *Giovanni Baccelli*, 1782, oil on canvas, 227 × 149 cm.

Plate 7
John Baptist Locatelli, *Giovanna Baccelli Reclining on a Couch*, 1781.

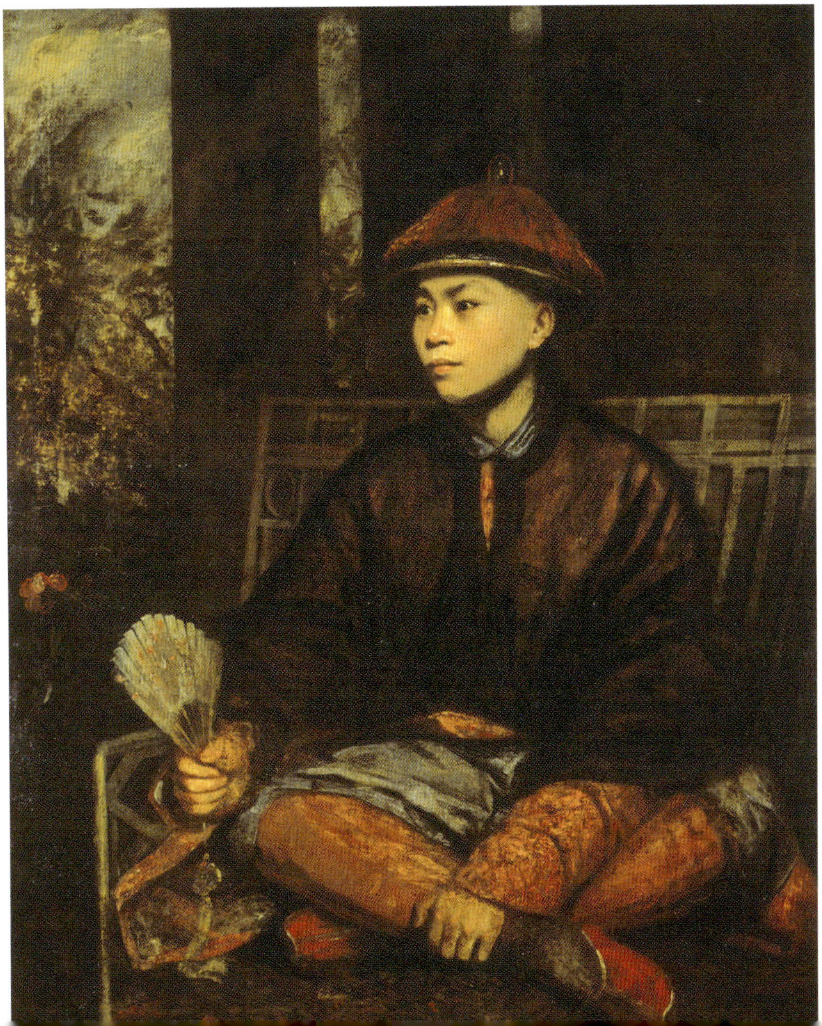

Plate 8
Joshua Reynolds, *Wang-y-Tong*, 1776, oil on canvas, 125 × 100 cm.

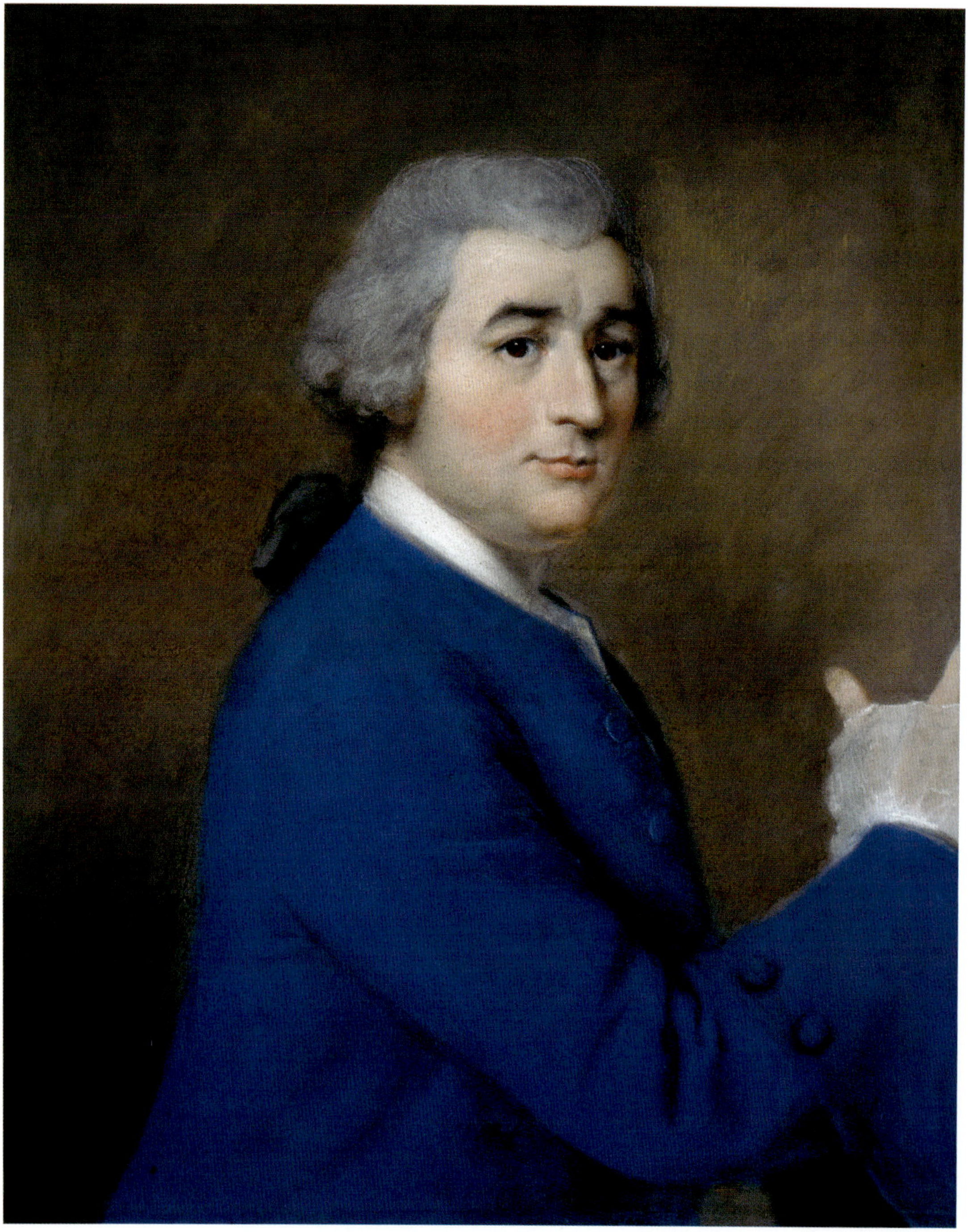

Plate 9 Jean-Étienne Liotard, *David Garrick*, 1751, pastel on paper, 59.2 × 48.3 cm.

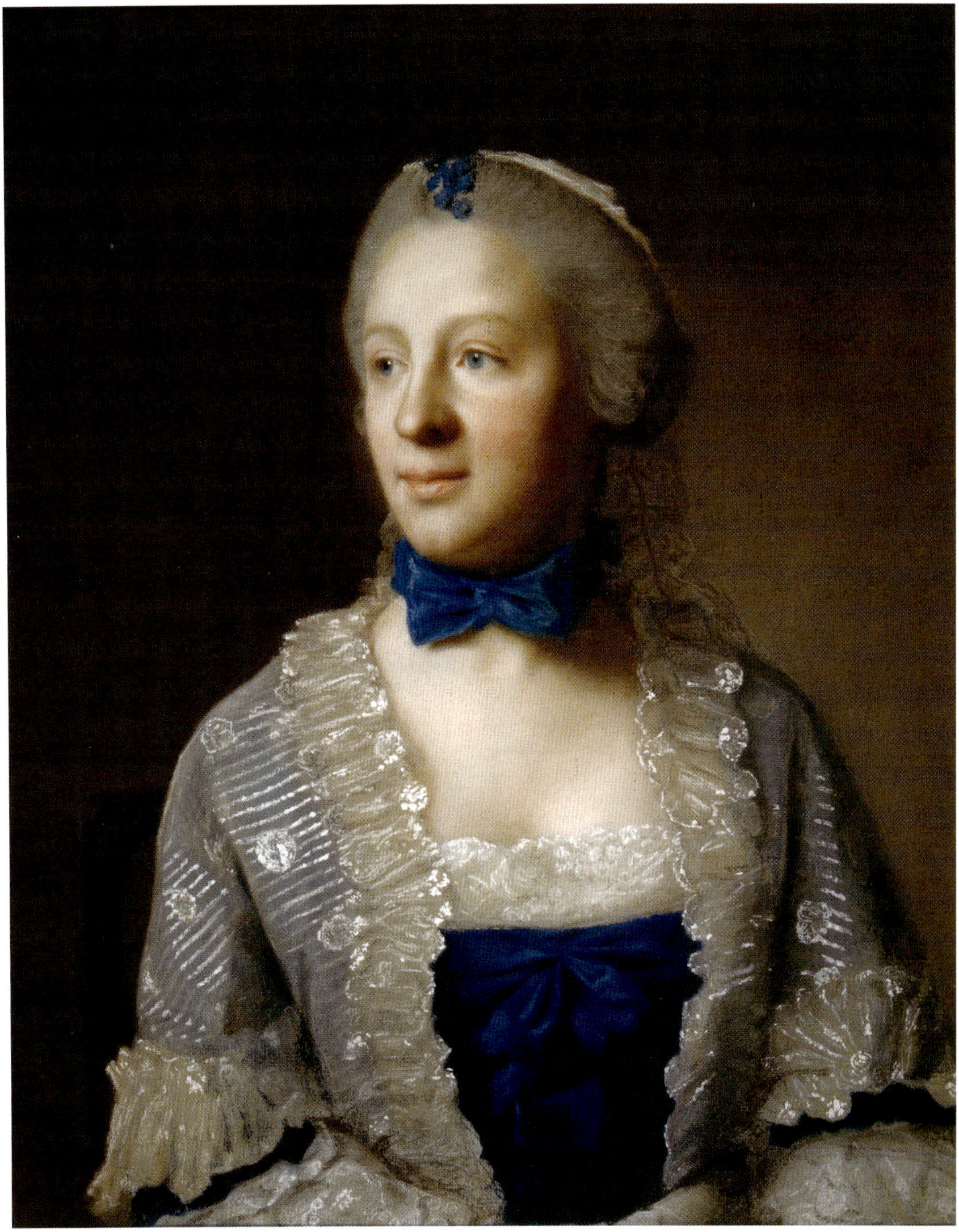

Plate 10 Jean-Étienne Liotard, *Eva Maria Garrick, née Veigel, known as 'Violette'*, c.1754, pastel on paper, 58.2 × 48 cm.

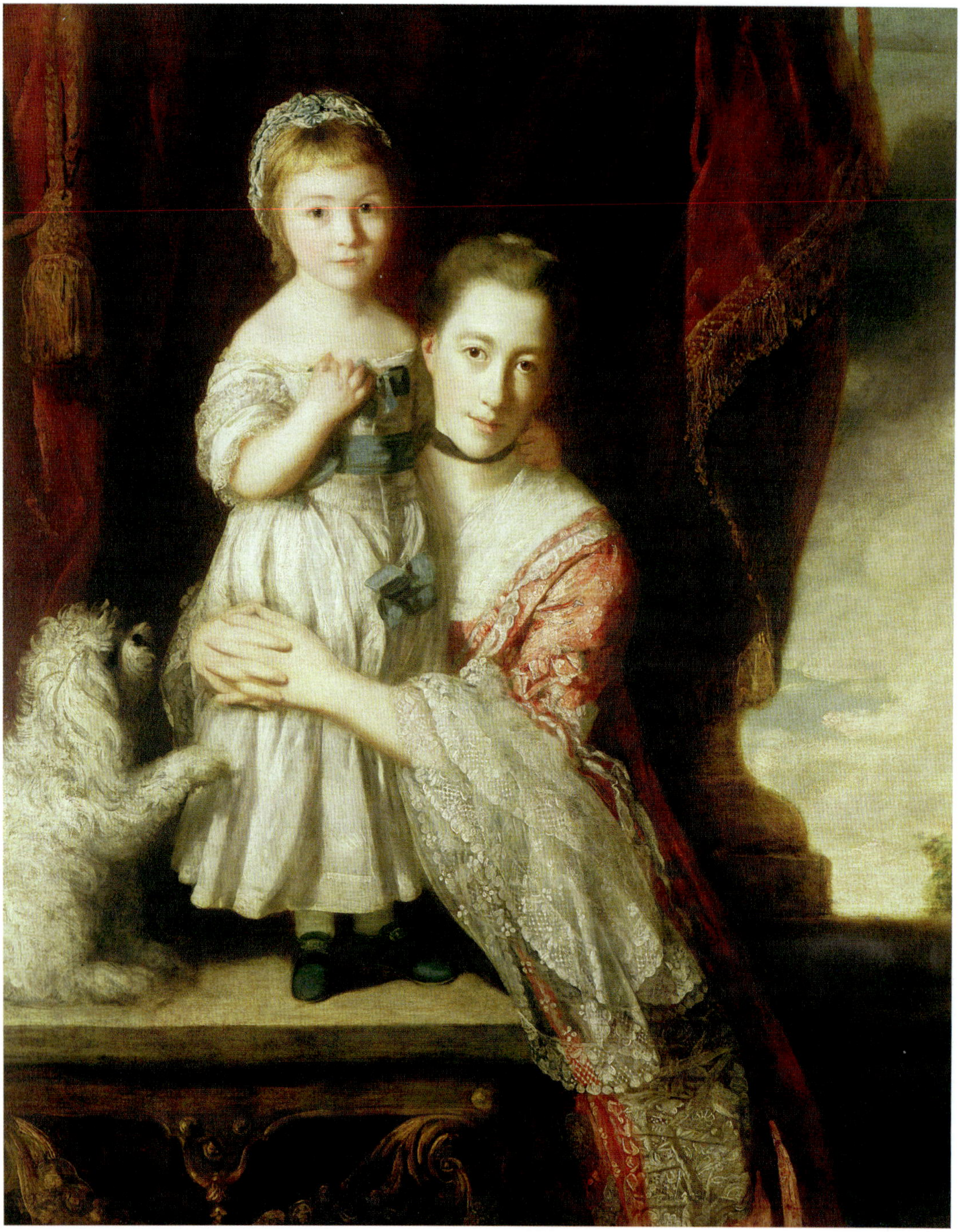

Plate 11 Joshua Reynolds, *Viscountess Spencer with her Daughter Miss Georgiana Spencer*, c.1759–61, oil on canvas, 122 × 115 cm.

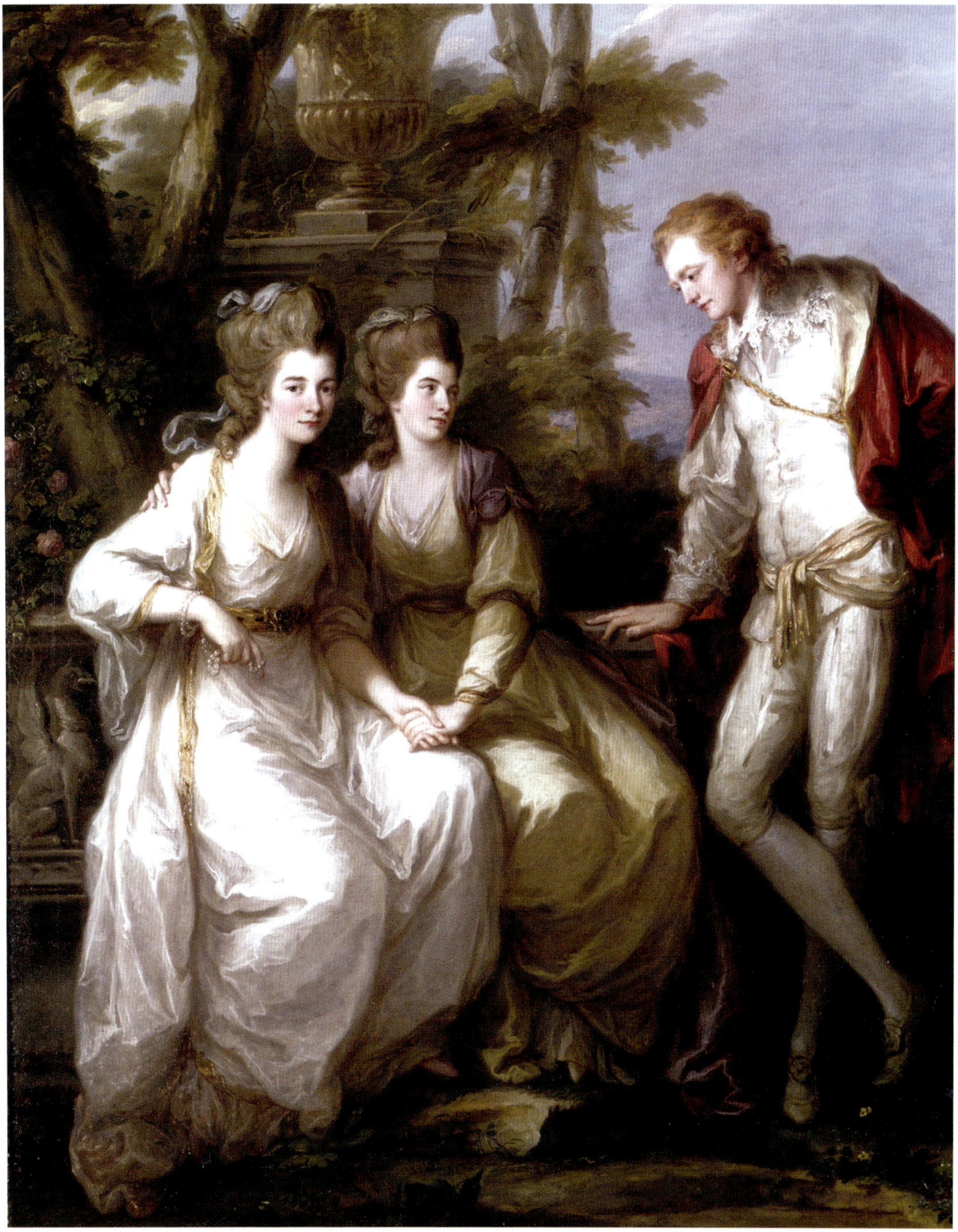

Plate 12 Angelica Kauffman, *Lady Georgiana and Lady Harriet Spencer, with their brother, Viscount Althorp*, 1774, oil on canvas, 125.5 × 101 cm.

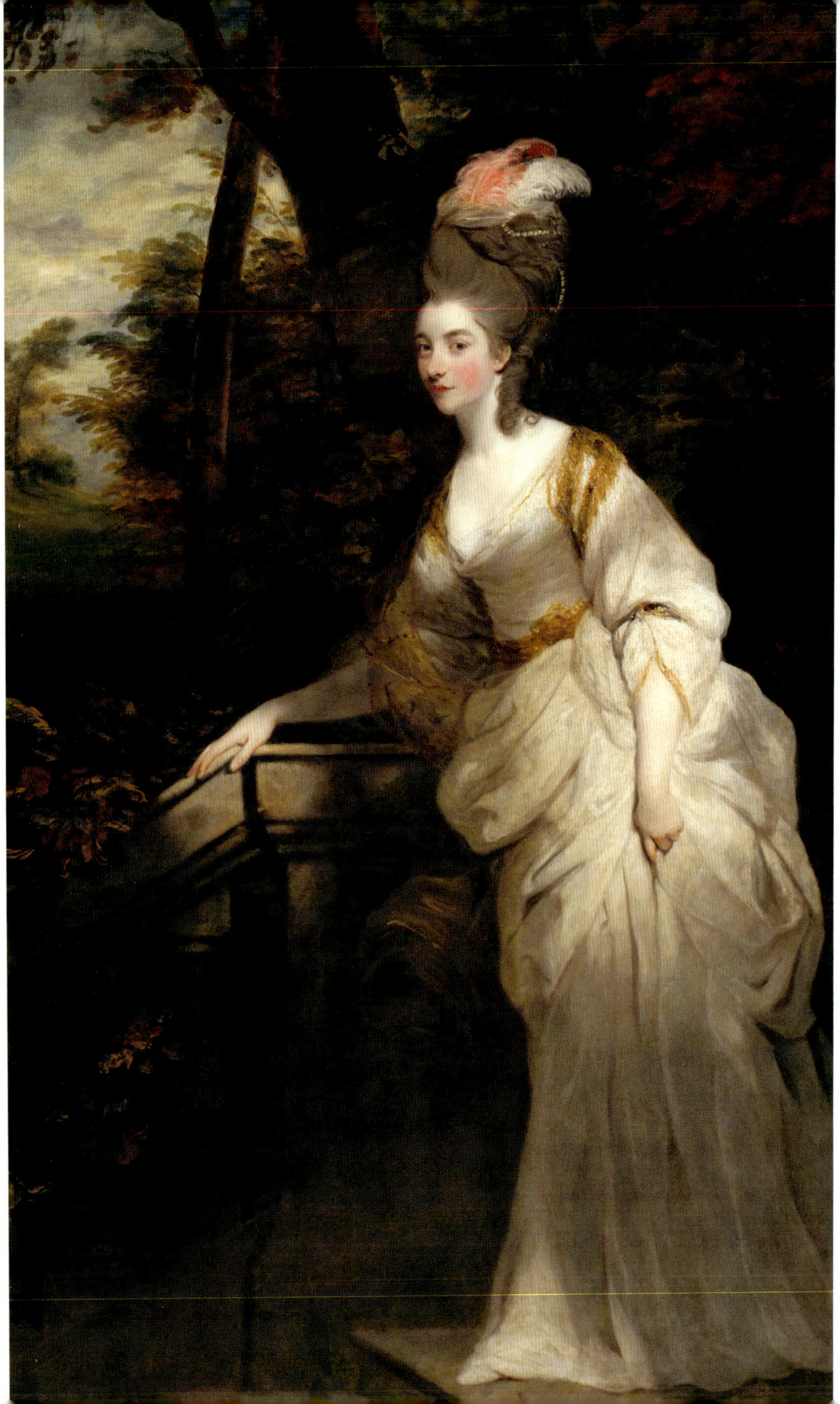

(*opposite*) Plate 13 Joshua Reynolds, *The Duchess of Devonshire*, 1776, oil on canvas, 237 × 145 cm.

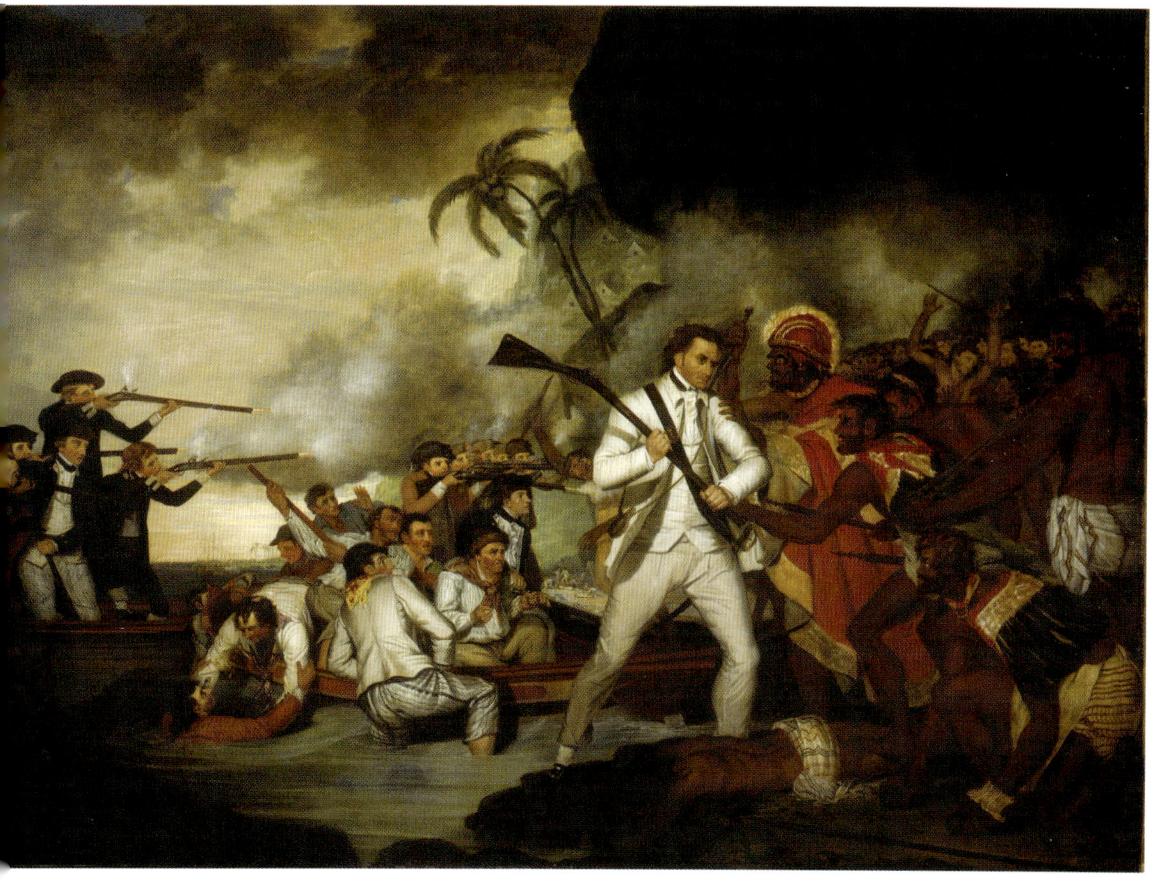

Plate 14 George Carter, *The Death of Captain James Cook*, c.1781–84, oil on canvas, 151.2 × 213.4 cm.

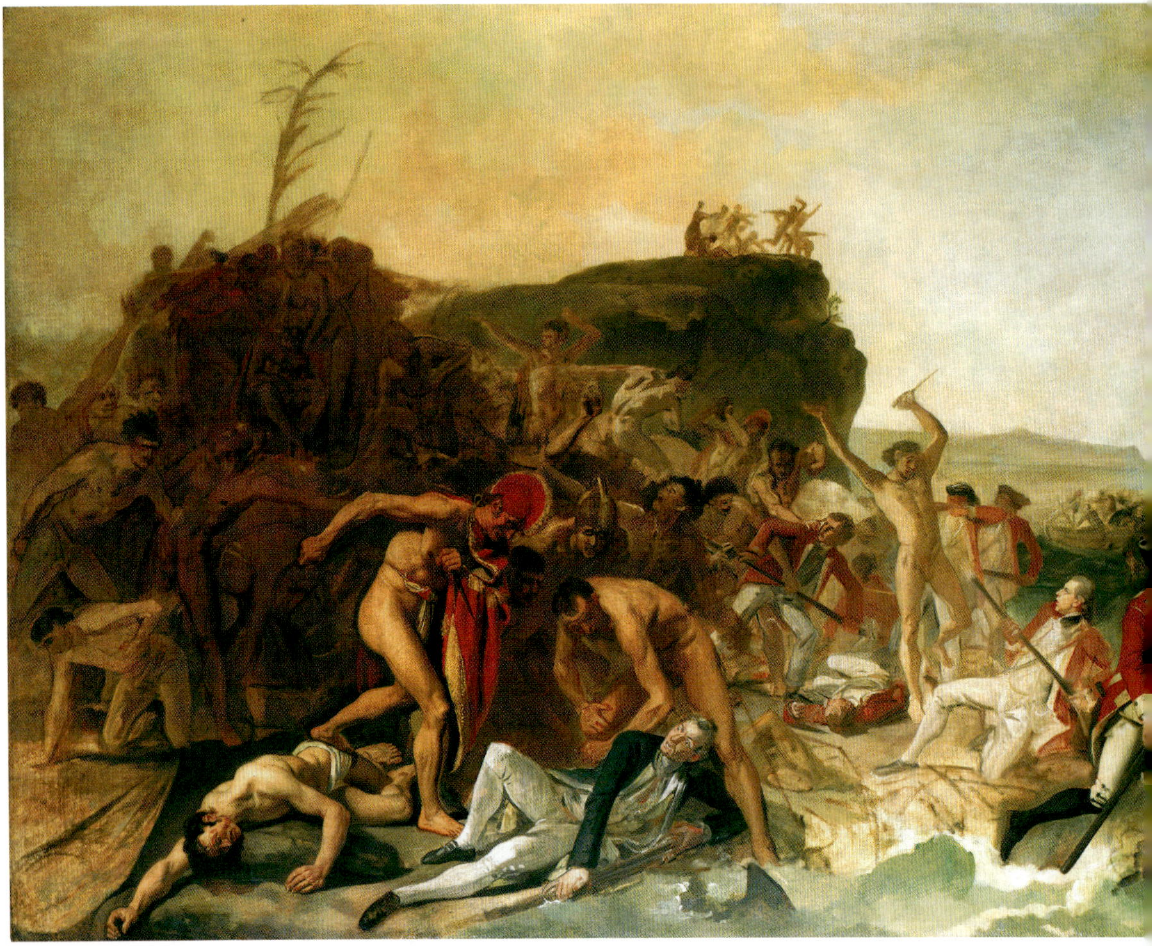

Plate 15 Johan Zoffany, *The Death of Captain Cook*, c.1798, oil on canvas, 137.2 × 182.9 cm.

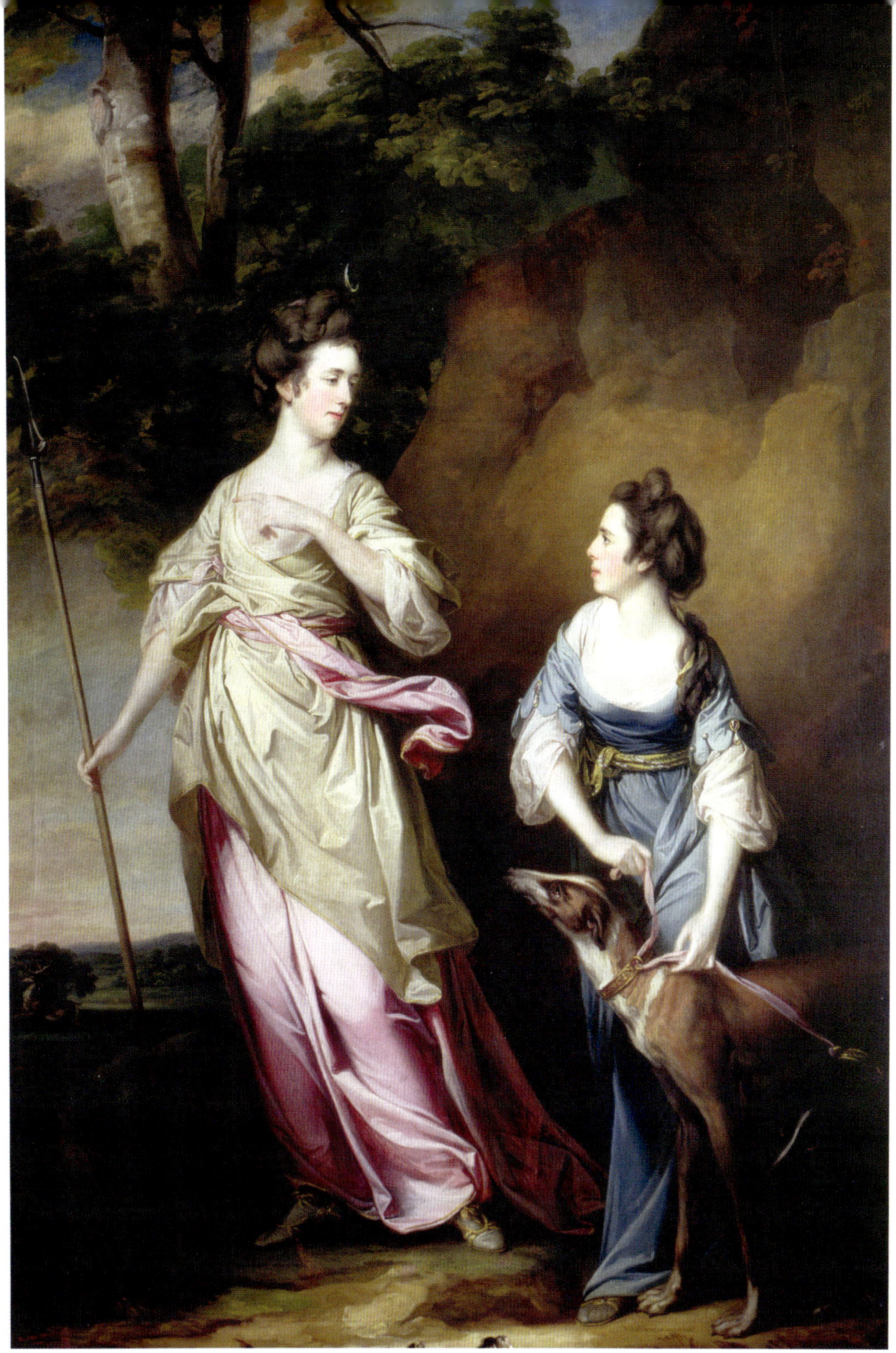

Plate 16 Francis Cotes, *The Honourable Lady Stanhope and the Countess of Effingham as Diana and her Companion*, 1765, oil on canvas, 240 × 152 cm.

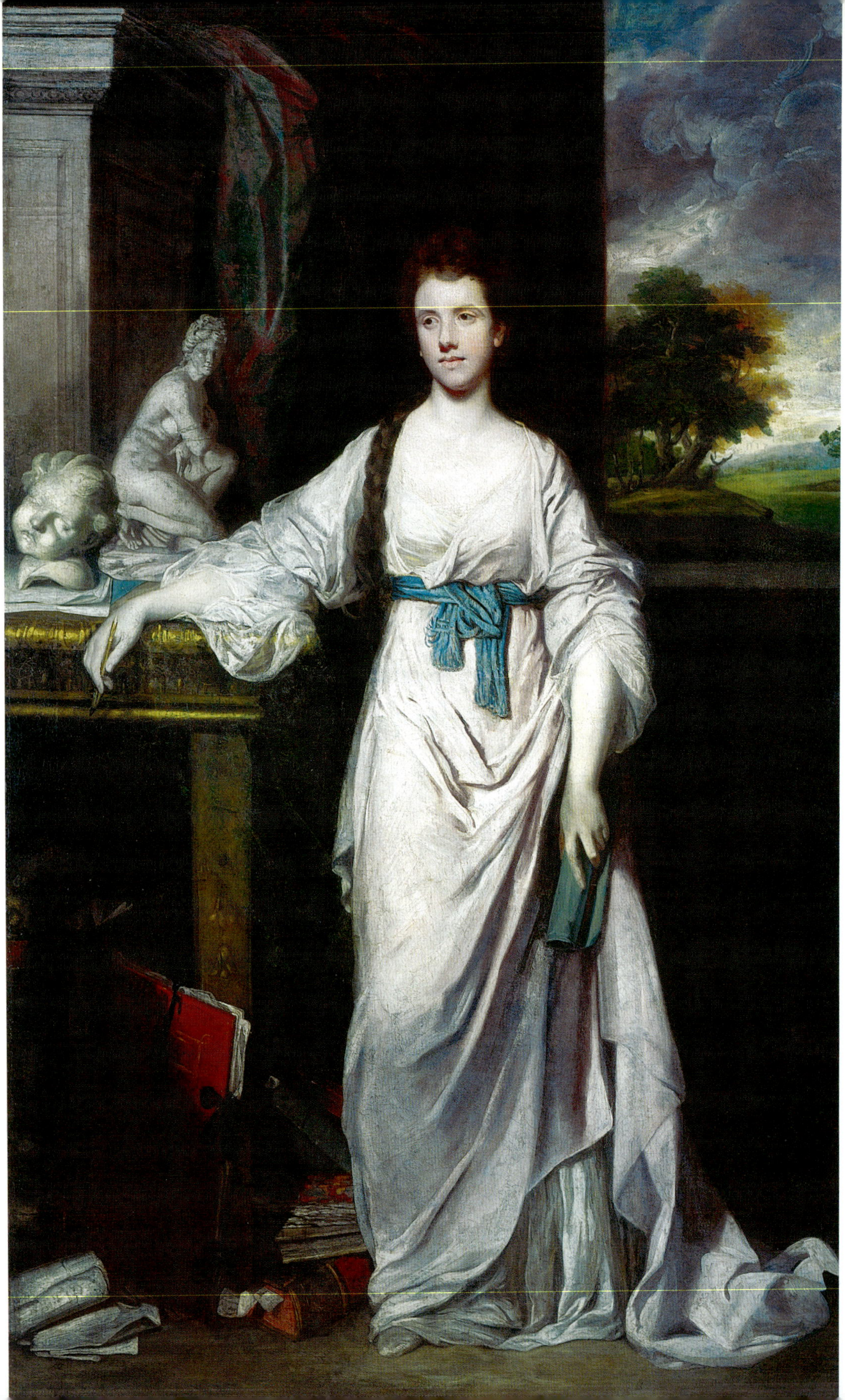

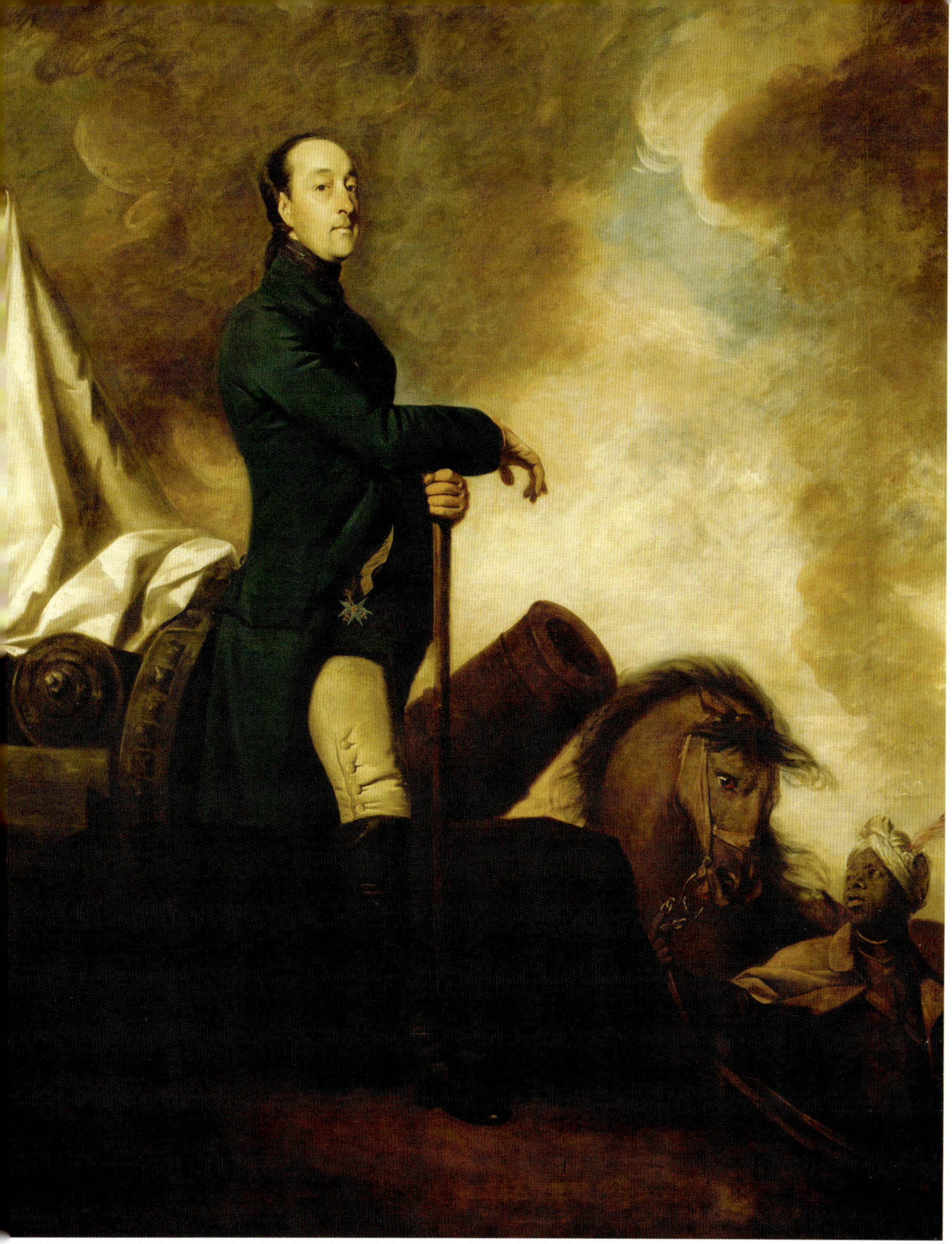

(*opposite*) Plate 17 Sir Joshua Reynolds, *Lady Anne Stanhope as Contemplation*, 1765, oil on canvas, 236.2 × 146.1 cm.

Plate 18 Sir Joshua Reynolds, *Frederick William Ernest, Count of Schaumburg-Lippe*, 1767, oil on canvas, 245.4 × 206.7 cm.

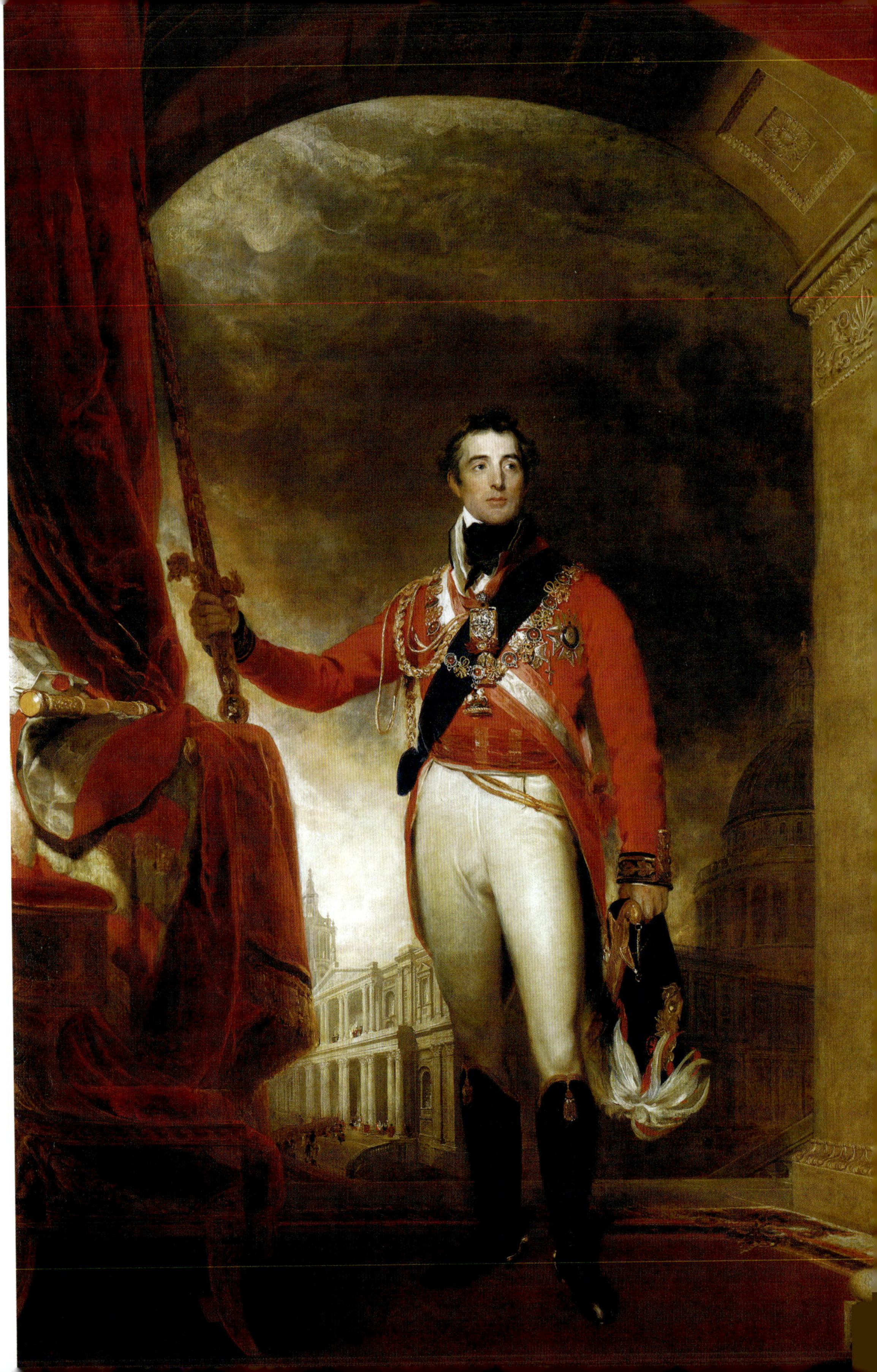

5

'Apartments that are not too large': pastel portraits and the spaces of femininity in the English country house

Ruth Kenny

In September 1756, Mary Delany departed Bulstrode Park, Buckinghamshire with her host and close friend Margaret Bentinck, Duchess of Portland, to pay a visit to the estate of the Duchess's late mother, Welbeck Abbey. During their stay, they toured the house to admire the alterations Lady Oxford had orchestrated at a price of 'above forty thousand pounds'. Yet Mrs Delany's enthusiasm for the house as a whole was rather muted and she was eager to return to the familiar terrain of Bulstrode, where she was often in residence:

> One may truly say this is a fine place, but it wants the agreeableness and sweetness of Bulstrode. Here everything displays the antiquity of the noble race, from whence the owners are descended and the walls are covered with family portraits; but there is a *glare of grandeur* and though I admire the Duchess when receiving princely honours and acquitting herself with dignity, I love her best in her own private dressing room! [1]

The 'dear dressing room' Mrs Delany had in mind was the backdrop against which the most intimate moments of her friendship with the Duchess of Portland were played out: a room directly off the Duchess's bedchamber at Bulstrode, where they enjoyed long 'tête-à-tête', read aloud to each other and worked on their numerous artistic projects.[2] Here the grand family portraits of Welbeck were replaced by a more

(*opposite*) Plate 19 Thomas Lawrence, *Duke of Wellington*, 1814–15, oil on canvas, 318 × 225 cm.

intimate display, dominated by pastel portraits. These were noted with particular care amongst a 'thousand curiosities' by the Duchess of Northumberland when she dined at Bulstrode on 29 May 1760:

> There is a Crayon Picture of Ld. Tichfield and another of Ly. Juliana Penn, a view of Cavendish Lodge in Nottinghamshire, several Drawings by Lady Andover and Mrs Delany, a Basket of Flowers turned in Ivory and Tortoise Shell. Thro this is a small closet; over the doors are Crayon Pictures of Ly. Weymouth and Ly. Harriet Bentinck and a number of pretty things.[3]

The placing of pastel portraits in such a space was, it appears, entirely in keeping with contemporary norms. Several sources suggest that, as recommended by the prominent pastellist Francis Cotes, pastel portraits were indeed hung predominantly in 'apartments that are not too large'; bedchambers, closets and, most commonly, ladies' dressing rooms.[4] At Donington Park, Leicestershire, the country seat of Francis Hastings, 10th Earl of Huntingdon, the ante-chamber – a room between the Green Bedroom and the Closet, fitted up with a mahogany wash stand, armchairs and a table – was adorned with two pastel portraits of the 'Last Theo Earl of Huntingdon', the deceased 9th Earl, and 'Lady Viscountess Kilmory', possibly those by Rosalba Carriera and Katherine Read respectively. Nearby, 'Lady Moira's Dressing Room' likewise contained 'A Lady's Head in Crayons'.[5] At Holkham House in Norfolk, pastels of Lord Coke and the Earl of Leicester by Rosalba Carriera hung in 'Mrs Coke's Closet', while '3 portraits in crayons, framed and glaized' were to be found in the dressing room at Lee, the house of Sir Thomas Fluyder in Kent.[6] A series of small pastel portraits by John Raphael Smith depicting members of the Goodwood Hunt are also known to have hung in the 'Dressing Room off the Scarlet Bed-Chamber' at Goodwood, the country house of Charles Lennnox, 3rd Duke of Richmond, while four 'Family portraits in Crayons by William Hoare Esq. of Bath' hung in the principal bedchamber at Henry Hoare's Stourhead.[7] In addition, at Ham House, the country seat of the Earl of Dysart, the 'Yellow Satin Dressing Room' contained 'two portraits of children in crayons', probably by Lady Dysart's own hand.[8] This chapter, however, will consider in particular detail the dressing rooms of three houses: that of the Duchess of Portland at Bulstrode, Lady Burlington's at Chiswick and two dressing rooms at Lady Buckingham's Stowe, all of which were decorated with pastel images.

Self-fashioning and the dressing room

The central importance of these small rooms to the conduct of upper-class eighteenth-century female life is hinted at by Mrs Delany.[9] They acted as the locus for a wide range of feminine domestic activity, from the reception of guests, through the daily rituals of dressing, to the pursuit of craft work; a span attested to by their assortment of furniture. While the Duchess of Portland's dressing room would have contained a selection of armchairs and at least one table, it also housed her 'Toilet' or dressing table, 'furnished with Boxes and Glass of Red Indian Paper with Landscapes and Flowers in Black and White'.[10] Likewise, Lady Burlington's dressing room, sometimes also known as the 'Garden Room', boasted a pair of matching commodes and mirrors, ten gilt elbow chairs, two sofas, two mahogany reading tables, a mahogany breakfast table and two needlework pole screens.[11] As these descriptions attest, the decoration of these spaces was highly considered. The fabric of contemporary femininity was woven around the activities these rooms hosted and the ability to arrange one's own stage-set, as it were, brought a crucial element of self-fashioning into play. In 1760, Horace Walpole, on a visit to Chiswick House, the Burlington family's summer retreat, took special care to note that Lady Burlington's dressing room was 'Built at her own Expence'.[12] Housed in a free-standing structure between the old and new houses and with contents valued at twice those of any other room, it was liberally decorated with owl motifs, taken from the Savile family crest, which marked the space as Lady Burlington's own.[13] Another country house visitor, Mrs Philip Lybbe Powys of Hardwick House in Oxfordshire paid particular attention to dressing rooms in the detailed notes of interiors she included in her diary, perceiving them to reflect directly on the character and status of their owners. Visiting Fawley Court in Buckinghamshire in 1771, she noted 'There are numberless other more common rooms, but Mrs Freeman's own dressing-room must be mentioned as most elegant … ornamented with pictures and a thousand other curiosities, as one might expect to see in the particular apartment of the mistress at Fawley Court.'[14] Indeed, dressing rooms had long been treated as a metaphor for female identity in the popular imagination, giving rise to a whole genre of 'dressing room poems' – the most famous of which were Alexander Pope's *The Rape of the Lock* (1717) and Jonathan Swift's *The Lady's Dressing Room* (1732) – and their regular appearance in contemporary novels such as Samuel Richardson's *Pamela* (1740) and *Clarissa* (1748).[15]

This fascination was fuelled by the quite intentional confusion between the public and private spheres fostered by such spaces, which allowed the seemingly intimate details of a life to become a subject for public scrutiny. In their unique duality, they became a showcase for feminine virtues – sentimentality, beauty and amateur accomplishment – and were decorated accordingly. Creating the appropriate ambience was crucial to the success of any such performance and the well-considered display of personal items appears to have played a central role.

The positioning of pastel portraits at Bulstrode, Chiswick and Stowe suggests that they played an important part in the creation of these exquisitely self-conscious decorative schemes.[16] Research into the clientele of the artist and dealer Arthur Pond indeed suggests that women were the prime purchasers of pastel portraiture; of his eighty-eight female patrons more than two-thirds bought pastel portraits, roughly twice the percentage of men.[17] As the century progressed the medium was increasingly promoted in gendered terms. Some knowledge of pastel painting came to be seen as a desirable female attribute and newspaper advertisements for London shops such as G. Riley's 'Sliding Patent Pencil Warehouse', which sold ready-made pastels, aimed their wares specifically at such a market. Their sets of 'Portable Colours', of 'elegant shade' were recommended as 'a very desirable acquisition for Young Ladies'.[18] Correspondingly, much contemporary criticism of the medium also came to be framed in gendered terms, with Joshua Reynolds dismissing the work of the fashionable Swiss pastellist Jean-Étienne Liotard as 'just what ladies do when they paint for their own amusement'.[19] Yet women's preference for pastel portraits, in the first flush of their popularity, spoke to a deeper sympathy between these works and the areas of the house which they habitually populated; the particular iconography of pastel portraiture and its unique material properties resonating with the way in which ladies' dressing rooms were conceived, perceived and used. The particular nature of this relationship will be the focus of our discussion here.

Pastel portraits and familial relations

Closer examination of the dressing room displays under scrutiny reveals an emphasis on portraits of children and close relations. At Bulstrode, the wall decoration of the Duchess of Portland's dressing room centred around pastel portraits of her three eldest children: Henrietta, known as Harriot, by Arthur Pond and Elizabeth and William, also probably

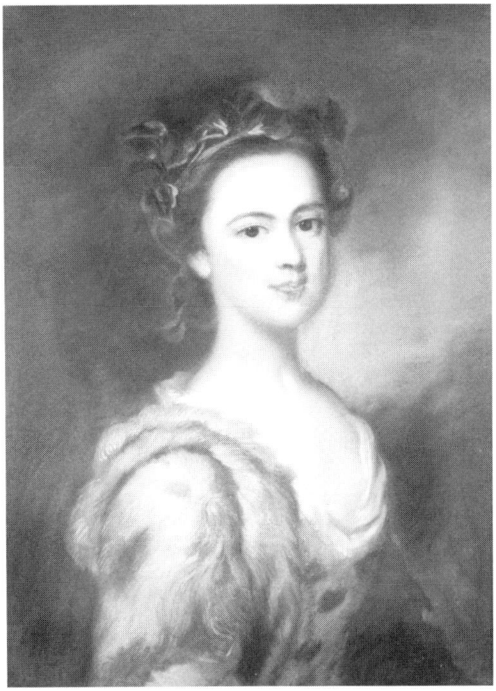

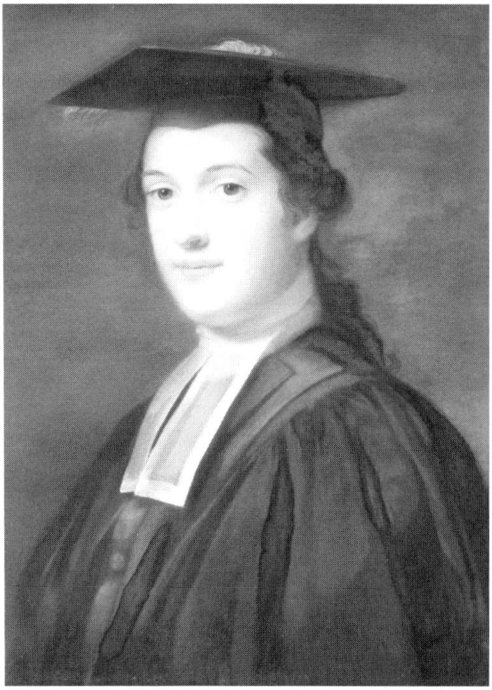

Figure 28
Arthur Pond [?], *Viscountess Weymouth, Marchioness of Bath née Lady Elizabeth Cavendish Bentinck*, c.1750, pastel on paper, 64 × 48 cm.

Figure 29
Arthur Pond [?], *William Henry Bentinck, Marquis of Titchfield*, c.1757, pastel on paper, 64 × 53 cm.

by Pond, though traditionally given to William Hoare (figures 28 and 29). At least the first of these portraits was commissioned and paid for by the Duchess herself, a transaction confirmed by Pond's sitter book, which on 7 May 1744 notes her payment of 7 guineas plus 2½ guineas for the glass and frame.[20] A lightly allegorised portrait of Elizabeth, with a leopard skin over her shoulder and a red ribbon in her hair attached to an ivy wreath, was added circa 1750, while William in an academic cap and gown, presumably marking his graduation from Christ Church, Oxford, joined them around seven years later.[21] At Stowe, home to George Nugent-Temple-Grenville, 1st Marquess of Buckingham and his wife Mary, a dressing room to one side of the main hall, possibly used by Lord Buckingham's late mother Elizabeth Wyndham, Mrs Grenville, was hung with yellow damask and contained several 'crayon pictures' by her hand, subjects unspecified, though possibly including the self-portrait listed in the 1848 Stowe Sale.[22] This was accompanied by another pastel portrait of herself and those of her aunt, the Countess of Thomond and her brother Percy Wyndham O'Brien, the late 1st Earl of Thomond, possibly his portrait by either Francis Cotes or William

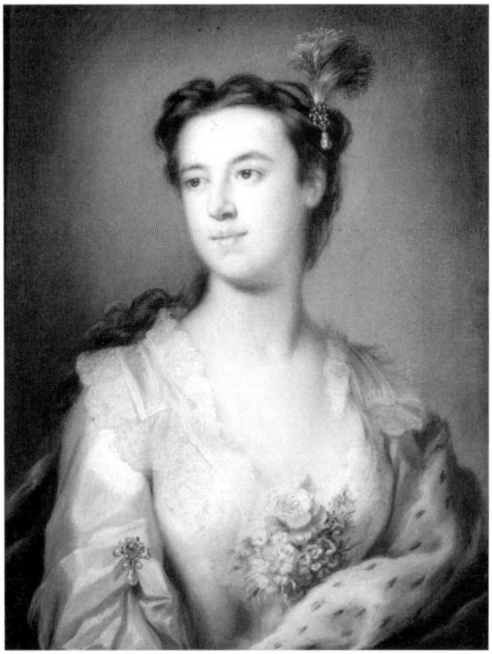
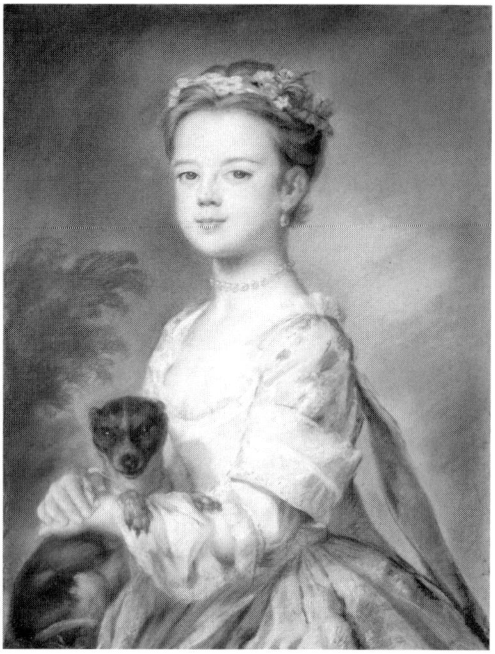

Figure 30
George Knapton,
Dorothy Boyle, Countess of Euston, c.1740,
pastel on paper,
59.9 × 44.9 cm.

Figure 31
George Knapton,
Charlotte Boyle, later Marchioness of Hartington,
c.1740, pastel
on paper,
65.2 × 50.2 cm.

Hoare. Upstairs, Lady Buckingham's dressing room, hung with white Irish damask, was 'decorated with a variety of crayons and drawings' including pastel portraits she had executed herself: an image of her eldest son Richard, Earl Temple 'when young', and two of her other children.[23] Similarly, at Chiswick, Lady Burlington's dressing room contained a pair of pastel portraits of her two daughters Lady Dorothy and Lady Charlotte Boyle by George Knapton (figures 30 and 31).[24]

Further additions to these groupings demonstrate that pastels were also used to map relationships beyond the immediate family. The Duchess of Portland's children hung with a pastel of Lady Juliana Penn, most probably that by Katherine Read – the only known pastel portrait of her. Penn according to Mrs Delany had 'a house in the neighbourhood' and was a frequent dinner guest at Bulstrode.[25] Likewise, Lady Burlington's daughters found company with a Rosalba Carriera pastel portrait of Faustina Bordoni, an Italian singer who Lady Burlington championed, and a further Knapton pastel portrait of another protégée, the Viennese dancer Eva Maria Veigel, known as Violette. After Violette's marriage to David Garrick in 1749, a match in which Lady Burlington had played a significant role, further pastel pendants of the newly-wed couple by Jean-Étienne Liotard joined the display (plates 9 and 10). These were commissioned by Garrick, who, after the formalities of the marriage had been brokered by the Duchess and 'all reserve and distance thus happily got over' became 'as was to be expected, a great favourite'.[26] In a public display of harmony he appears in a bright blue coat, which mirrors the blue neck bow, hair decoration and bodice of his wife's costume. The affection the couple felt towards Lady Burlington is also explicitly acknowledged; as Violette turns to Garrick with an indulgent smile, he gestures towards his wife while looking at the viewer – the Duchess – thus including her in the pictorial record of their happy union.

The inclusion of friends such as Juliana Penn and the Garricks in these dressing room displays highlights the way in which pastel portraiture operated outside the perceived confines of much formal portraiture in oil. Pastel portraits were often not included in household picture inventories; undoubtedly they were seen as less significant than oils due to the friable nature of their delicate surfaces and their alleged emphemerality.[27] Yet, precisely because of their 'not standing', which in the opinion of Fanny Burney was 'the only inferiority they have to oil colours', pastels seemed to escape weighty ideas of lineage and futurity, thus granting their patrons a certain freedom.[28] As Horace Walpole noted with regard to his own historical portrait collection, formal oil paintings celebrated ideas of heredity not only iconographically, but also in their pedigree as objects; 'Such well-attested descent is the genealogy of the objects of virtu; not so noble as those of the peerage, but on a par with those of race-horses.'[29] Pastels, on the other hand, provided a carefree respite from the rather more complex demands and permanency of other media. They were valued for their immediacy and were apparently intended only for the fleeting appreciation of the current generation, whose lively and diffuse sociability they so inimitably captured. Indeed, the flexibility and potential spontaneity of a system of individual portraits in series, executed in quick, relatively inexpensive pastel, must have been a large part of their appeal. Such a series could reflect the natural ebbs and flows of social relations, allowing for additions which mirrored changes in circumstance, the forging of new bonds or the commemoration of an occasion or a memorable guest. Operating on a network rather than linear system they built up a more complex, layered picture of a family and its social life than any single work could achieve. When raised to the status of pictorial record, these social links became powerful signifiers of a life well-led. Such displays acted as credentials for the woman of feeling, bearing physical witness to warm familial relations and fertile networks of friendship in their suggestion of exchange and association. This was particularly the case when pastels were commissioned or given as gifts, a circumstance their small, portable, economical nature readily lent them to. As previously mentioned, Garrick – a man who undoubtedly recognised the exchange value of portraits and often presented engraved versions to friends and admirers – commissioned the Liotard pendants and presented them to Lady Burlington as a gift.[30] Lady Burlington's papers also reveal a long list of pastels by her own hand, annotated with details of their recipients. Of twenty-four works, eight were given away, most often to female friends, such as Lady Fitzwalter, Lady Isabella Finch and Mrs Selwyn.[31] Similarly, a copy of Lady Burlington's portrait of Eva Maria Veigel by Knapton was made for Garrick's niece Arabella, Mrs Schaw, while a copy of Lady Dorothy Boyle's portrait at Chiswick and two copies of Lady Juliana Penn's pastel at Bulstrode are known to exist with slight variations of size and costume to suit the taste of the owner.[32]

Portraiture, space and intimacy

In a concrete way, pastel portraits directly reflected the intimate social interaction that dressing rooms encouraged, mirroring the pared back, if no less regulated, sociability of such spaces. Their power to map the sentimental and affectionate relationships played out beneath them owed much to their unparalleled ability to establish an intimate relationship between subject and viewer, primarily through the reduction of anything that might distract from the face as the central signifier. Their characteristic plain backgrounds condensed portraiture to its very essence, generally dispensing with the iconographic and status bearing accessories that appeared in many contemporary oil portraits and promoting a more psychological engagement with the viewer. The more confined size of the rooms prescribed for the hanging of pastels demanded close physical proximity between viewer and image and it was under such conditions that pastel's unique effects could be fully appreciated. As use of pastel developed and proliferated, the peculiar properties that set it apart from other media were embraced and many artists became interested in developing pastel away from its graphic origins, in order to explore the softer effects that could be achieved. The luminous expanse of *Lady Juliana Penn*'s face and neck amply demonstrate the main appeal of this approach to the medium; pastel's ability to mimic flesh, the portrait artist's holy grail. In accordance with the usual, highly blended style of Katherine Read's pastels, the pigmentation of Penn's portrait appears to have been built up in several careful layers: an application of beige which still acts for the shadow of the sitter's décolletage, then a broad application of heavily stumped white and finally a hint of a pale pink blush on the shoulders. As Fanny Burney noted, while perusing examples of Read's pastel work on her second visit to the artist's studio in February 1775: 'while they are new nothing can be so soft, so delicate, so blooming'.[33] Liotard's *Eva Maria Garrick ('Violette')* demonstrates a similar approach. The artist disliked visible strokes of pastel – they were not found in nature, he argued, and so must be eliminated from faithful representations – but in contrast to Read, pursued realism to a far greater degree.[34] The appeal of his characterful portrait of Violette owes much to the extraordinary veracity of her depiction. From the soft white highlights on the tip of her nose and the translucent skin beneath her eyes to the taut sheen of her gently swelling forehead, Violette's portrait is a virtuoso display of the textural possibilities of pastel and its ability to communicate a very real, almost tangible sense of the sitter's skin. The more generous application of pastel that such effects required necessitated a preliminary roughening of the paper in order to make the pastel stick, with the result that a furry nap, akin to the fine hairs of the face, is evident in many works, further aiding the apparent metamorphosis of crayon into flesh. This is particularly evident under uneven or raking light, which perhaps best mimics the conditions by which these portraits would originally have been seen. Francis Cotes's recommendation that 'by candle-light' pastels 'are luminous and beautiful beyond all other pictures' perhaps had this effect in mind.[35]

Delivering a very real sense of bodily presence, the pastel medium's apparent ability to physically stand in for rather than merely picture its subject was undoubtedly an important component of its intense contemporary popularity. As Liotard's portrait of Violette further demonstrates, such bodily associations also signified in other ways. When hung in dressing rooms, the unique physical qualities of pastels additionally reflected the conduct of the daily toilette, dressing and undressing, that took place beneath them. Most strikingly, their dry surfaces mimicked that quintessential eighteenth-century custom, the liberal use of face and hair powder, so apparent in Liotard's portrait, where Violette's lightly frizzed coiffure is covered in a layer of fine white dust. Indeed, this material interplay was explicitly acknowledged by some pastel artists, not least John Russell, who often used white pastel to record where the white powder from a sitter's dressed hair had stained a collar, a shoulder or the lining of a hat.[36] The considerable cross-over in the physical make-up of pastel and body powders further amplified this playful confusion. According to Robert Dossie's popular *Handmaid to the Arts*, first published in 1758, 'Starch has been frequently used along with some of the other whites for giving a due texture to crayons' while it also provided the main bulk of hair-powder.[37] Similarly 'The true genuine Pearl Powder, for the face' advertised by R. Sangwine, at the sign of the Rose, No. 38, Strand, found its counterpart in 'pearl white' – 'the powder of pearls, or the finer parts of oister-shells' according to Robert Dossie – which was recommended for pastel painting in preference to the lead white or flake white usually used for oil painting.[38]

The wide variety of textural effects which could be achieved with the medium, depending on its formulation and application, also made it particularly suited to the representation of textiles and the detail of fine clothing, which would have been chosen, donned and admired in a dressing room setting. From the lacy edging of Violette's costume and the agitated, feathery lines of Lady Dorothy Boyle's ermine stole, picked out with a fine dry crayon point, to the heavily stumped satin of Lady Penn's dress and the staccato pointilism of Lady Charlotte Boyle's elaborate pink and white brocade – all were recorded with an exacting eye. Here, fashionable 'style' met artistic 'style'. The discerning, well-dressed viewer was invited to delight in how the image was made and revel in the pleasure of pigment, noticing where the edge of a gauzy fichu suddenly looked like the tip of the pastellist's crayon before the illusion worked its magic once again. Indeed, the manner in which pastel was used, its range of supports and a number of its constituent ingredients encouraged a deliberate confusion between material and referent which went beyond the obvious parallels with face and hair powder. Thus, for a medium which so readily recorded the sumptuous variety of contemporary fashions, leading London artists' suppliers Riley's recommended silk, satin or 'the slightest gauze' mounted to a wooden strainer, as alternative supports to paper: 'the whole making a most beautiful assemblage'.[39] When paper was preferred, those purpose-made for pastel, which appeared in the later eighteenth century, often included fibres such as silk and wool to achieve a good 'tooth' for holding the powdery pigment.[40] In a form of playful oscillation between representation and the act of representing, carefully chosen resources and technical bravura were thus used to simultaneously materialise and dematerialise, fuelling a fascination with the doubleness of the pastellist's art and adding to the unique pleasures offered by the medium in a dressing room setting.

Party to the pursuit of beauty as dressing rooms were, whether through the application of cosmetics or a judicious choice of clothing, they can be understood as central ideological spaces in the debate surrounding female identity in the mid-eighteenth century. Their customary decoration with pastel portraits, both criticised and treasured for their perceived fragility – a trait generally associated with female desirability in contemporary discourse – can thus be seen to reinforce certain notions of ideal femininity. In a poem of 1760 by the artist Claude Henri Watelet, it is indeed this quality for which the medium is most cherished, for 'Ainsi de la Beauté, Le Pastel a l'éclat et la fragilité' ('Just like Beauty herself, Pastel is radiant and fragile').[41] The pastel sticks themselves were indeed prone to fracture and had to be carefully protected. John Imison, in his popular guide to amateur artistic practice *The School of the Arts*, counselled that 'bran be used as a bed for the colours, because it not only preserves them clean, but prevents their breaking'.[42] The finished works were also prone to damage as Francis Cotes cautioned: 'Crayon pictures are in their nature more delicate and consequently more liable to injury than almost every other kind of painting.'[43] A letter of 1771 written by the 5th Duke of Argyll to a John Davidson in Edinburgh, regarding the framing and glazing of a pastel portrait by Katherine Read, demonstrates the immense care that had to be taken in their transport:

> [it] is to be sent to Hamilton [Hamilton Palace in East Lanarkshire] with great care. As it is painted in crayons it may be easily hurt and must therefore be carried on a man's back.[44]

A popular song entitled 'To FLAVELLA, occasioned by her Picture in CRAYONS, sent as a Present, but damag'd by the Carriage' was a favourite in the public gardens and theatres at mid-century and clearly demonstrated the dangers of such transfer. Here the parallels between the ephemeral nature of female beauty and that of pastel were spelt out, with a distinctly moralistic cast:

> See there confus'dly blended Tints,
> Which look'd a thousand Charms so late;
> Th'instructive Piece still represents
> Precarious Beauty's transient Fate.[45]

Correspondingly, just as Mrs Delany compared her own pastel portrait of her sister Anne to an oil painting of the same subject and concluded that 'you are much better drawn in a place where the air cannot fade you', the glass frames necessary to protect the friable surfaces of pastels sealed fragile female beauty in, protecting it from pollutants, both physical and moral, and allowing it to be looked at and desired even as its real-life counterpart might spoil or diminish.[46]

Femininity and the amateur

Evidently, the presence of pastel portraiture in dressing rooms also promoted a discourse that went beyond the ambit of fashion and beauty. The heightened appreciation of pastel portraiture in such spaces and the ability to enjoy these works in the sophisticated manner discussed previously, was also facilitated by the intimate knowledge of the medium borne of amateur practice, which Mrs Delany suggests was often undertaken in these rooms. The Duchess of Portland's dressing room, for example, hosted a wide range of female work and became known as 'The Hive', while two sketches of Lady Burlington in her dressing room show that she also used the space as a studio.[47] Mrs Delany experimented with pastel portraiture herself, as indeed did most of the owners of the dressing rooms under consideration – Lady Burlington, Lady Buckingham and Mrs Grenville. Impressed by the efforts of her friend Grace Carteret, Countess of Dysart, who had been receiving instruction from Arthur Pond, Mrs Delany wrote from Bulstrode that she also planned to 'fall into that way. I hope Mr Pond will help me too, for his colouring in crayons is *the best* I have seen of any English painter – it tires my eyes less than work, and entertains me better.'[48] She produced several known pastel portraits, including the portrait of her sister Anne, mentioned previously, and those of various female friends. Her interest was evidently a long-standing one for six years later in December 1740, again at Bulstrode, she wrote to Lady Throckmorton to thank her for sending a box of crayons.[49] Equally, Lady Burlington is known to have drawn 'in crayons', with lessons from William Kent and possibly Charles Jervas.[50] Burlington House, the family's town house, was crowded with her work, predominantly pictures of her daughters, while at their suburban villa, Chiswick, a pastel portrait of her daughter Dorothy, by her own hand, is known to have hung in the 'Closet within the Bed-chamber'.[51] While Horace Walpole confirms that Lady Burlington 'succeeded admirably in likenesses', he also suggests that a dazzling performance and pursuit of a certain *sprezzatura* were often prized above the appearance of the finished piece, for 'working with too much rapidity' she 'did not do justice to her genius'.[52] The variable quality of her extant work suggests that this was indeed the case and that a preference for charming, apparently effortless 'effect' over painstaking execution was an important element of the medium's appeal for this demographic. The much lauded speed with which pastels could be executed, as opposed to the tight control and precision required by watercolour or miniature painting, made the medium a perfect fit for women cultivating the air of accomplishment essential for a member of contemporary polite society.[53]

While the artists who instructed Mrs Grenville and her daughter-in-law Lady Buckingham in the art of pastel are unknown and only two of their portraits in this medium survive, the way in which Mrs Grenville's work was hung at Stowe is instructive. Mixed apparently indiscriminately with purchased pastel portraits in the lower dressing room, its display promoted a mode of viewing which encouraged a direct dialogue between the amateur and the professional. Indeed, the existence of many amateur copies of the works of professional pastel artists suggests that this was the manner in which many women were taught to appreciate the intricacies of the medium.[54] This association undoubtedly worked to pastel's advantage. Pastel portraiture operated outside the confines of classical art theory and was beholden to a different set of imperatives, formed by popular, most usually female, consumer taste rather than connoisseurial diktat. Women, who often had direct experience of the medium and an intimate understanding and appreciation of the skill involved, thus formed a market of knowledgeable patrons. Perhaps most importantly, they had the language in which to discuss these works, culled straight from the proliferation of amateur instruction manuals which they had studied for their own practice. The remarkably uniform vocabulary that sprang up around pastel, no doubt due to the rampant piracy and copying of large chunks of text from one manual to another, undoubtedly aided such appreciation. Pastel patrons could talk readily and knowledgeably about 'sweetening', 'cooling crayons' and 'pearly teints'. Equally, the close viewing conditions prescribed for works in pastel and their highly legible surface geography allowed the kind of aesthetically sensitive viewer who emerged in the eighteenth century the gratification of appreciating stylistic distinctions and the pleasure of aesthetic admiration. Thus the dressing room became a space in which women could formulate and articulate their own brand of cultural expertise, creating a feminine community of specialist knowledge. As one of only a handful of amateur artistic pursuits that were also practised by professionals, pastel portraiture allowed women to be informed consumers, developing and exhibiting their taste and, by extension, helping to establish their social and personal identities with every addition to their carefully calibrated pastel displays.

Within the ambit of these 'apartments that are not too large', women were granted a certain liberty. The way in which they configured these spaces reflected both society's ideas about them and their own nascent self-identity. The widespread popularity of pastel portraits to decorate such rooms suggests that, as a means of artistic expression, they fulfilled a unique function, drawing together different elements of female domestic experience. Central to their appeal was perhaps the fact that, as a fledgling medium with few set rules, pastel was well placed to respond to an evolving social context and track clients' changing desires. With no direct precedent before the seventeenth century, there was little cut and dried in terms of technique and pastel artists were free to innovate, constantly developing new ways to exploit the medium's very particular qualities. The mutable nature of pastel encouraged a uniquely symbiotic relationship with the culture in which it functioned, both facilitating and signifying sentimental attachments, the development of fashionable taste, the pursuit and appreciation of beauty and the attainment of a certain cultural capital. As an examination of their display in the particular context of the dressing room reveals, while undoubtedly 'beautiful and decorative in a very high degree' as Francis Cotes decreed, they also spoke to cultural currents that ran far deeper than their dusty surfaces.[55]

Notes

1 Letter from Mrs Delany to Mrs Dewes, Welbeck, 7 September 1756 in Mary Delany, *The Autobiography and Correspondence of Mary Granville, Mrs Delany*, ed. Lady Llanover, 3 vols (London: Richard Bentley, 1861), III, p. 438.

2 Letter from Mrs Delany to Mrs Dewes, Bulstrode, December 1754. *Delany Autobiography*, III, p. 308.

3 Duchess of Northumberland, 'Diaries', 29 May 1760, Alnwick Castle, Northumberland, MS 121/4, unpaginated.

4 Francis Cotes, 'Notes on crayon painting', *European Magazine* (February 1797), 84–5. This article was 'a copy of a manuscript found among the papers of the late Francis Cotes Esq, the celebrated Crayon Painter'.

5 'An Inventory of Household Goods and Furniture at Donington Park taken

the 9th day of Decemb. 1788', Huntington Library, San Marino, Hastings MS Inventories 3, fo. 8; 'Inventory of Goods at Donnington House', undated (before 1799), Huntington Library, San Marino, Hastings MS Inventories 3, fo. 28.

6 *A Description of Holkham House in Norfolk with a particular of the pictures, statues, bustoes, and other marbles therein. Published by permission of the Hon. Wenman Coke* (Norwich: R. Beatniffe, 1775), unpaginated; *A Catalogue of the large and capital museum of Sir Thomas Fluyder, Knt* (London, 1769), unpaginated.

7 *A Description of the House and Gardens at Stourhead, in the County of Wilts, the seat of Sir Richard Hoare Bart with a Catalogue of the Pictures &c* (Salisbury and London: J. Easton, 1800), p. 19. D. Jacques, *A Visit to Goodwood near Chichester, the seat of His Grace the Duke of Richmond, with an Appendix descriptive of an ancient painting* (Chichester and London: D. Jacques, Messers. [*sic*] Lackington, Hughes & co. and W. Mason, 1822), p. 37.

8 'Paintings, Drawings and Prints (the Earl of Dysart) Ham House', c.1820, British Library, London, Additional MS 2817.

9 See Orest Ranum, 'The Refuges of Intimacy', in Philippe Ariès, Georges Duby, Roger Chartier and Arthur Goldhammer (eds), *The History of Private Life, Vol. 3: Passions of the Renaissance* (eds), (Harvard and London: Harvard University Press, 1989), pp. 207–32; Linda A. Pollock, 'Living on the Stage of the World: The Concept of Privacy among the Elite of Early Modern England', in Adrian Wilson (ed.), *Rethinking Social History: English Society 1570–1920 and Its Interpretation* (Manchester: Manchester University Press, 1993), pp. 78–97; Mark Girouard, *Life in the English Country House: A Social and Architectural History* (New Haven and London: Yale University Press, 1978), pp. 181–212.

10 'Northumberland Diaries', 29 May 1760, MS 121/4, unpaginated.

11 '1770 inventory of Chiswick House', Devonshire MSS, Chatsworth. See also Treve Rosoman 'The Decoration and Use of the Principal Apartments of Chiswick House, 1727–70', *Burlington Magazine*, 77:991 (October 1985), 663–77.

12 Horace Walpole, 'Journals of Visits to Country Seats', *Walpole Society*, 16 (1927–28), 16.

13 Mark de Novellis, *Pallas Unveil'd: The Life and Art of Lady Dorothy Savile, Countess of Burlington 1699–1758* (London: Orleans House Gallery, 1999), p. 9.

14 Emily J. Climenson (ed.), *Passages from the Diaries of Mrs Philip Lybbe Powys of Hardwick House, Oxon 1758–1808* (London, New York and Bombay: Longman, Green and Co., 1899), p. 147.

15 Felicity A. Nussbaum, *'The brink of all we hate': English Satires on Women 1660–1750* (Lexington, KY: University Press of Kentucky, 1984), pp. 94–116. See also Tita Chico, *Designing Women: The Dressing Room in Eighteenth-Century English Literature* (Pennsylvania: Bucknell University Press, 2005).

16 By contrast, it is interesting to note that male dressing rooms were more usually decorated with prints or in the case of Bulstrode: 'My Lord's Dressing Room hung with Tapestry'. Northumberland, 'Diaries', 29 May 1760, MS 121/4, unpaginated.

17 Louise Lippincott, *Selling Art in Georgian London: The Rise of Arthur Pond* (New Haven and London: Yale University Press for the Paul Mellon Centre for Studies in British Art, 1983), p. 68.

18 *The Times*, 30 May 1788; Ann Bermingham, *Learning to Draw: Studies in the History of a Polite and Useful Art* (New Haven and London: Yale University Press, 2000), p. 128. See also Charlotte Turner Smith, *Celestina: A Novel* (London: T. Cadell, 1791), pp. 15–16 for the use of this trope in popular novels.

19 William T. Whitley, *Artists and Their Friends in England, 1700–1799*, 2 vols (London and Boston: The Medici Society, 1928), I, p. 238.

20 Arthur Pond, 'Account of the Receipts 1734–1750', British Library, London, Additional MS 23724.

21 A fourth portrait of their younger brother Lord Edward, similarly sized and framed, is also given to Hoare. It too was in the Bulstrode collection but does not appear in the Duchess of Northumberland's notes on the house. With thanks to Derek Adlam for his thoughts on these pictures.

22 Dukes of Buckingham and Chandos; Stowe, Christie's 15 August – 30 September 1848, Lot 192. www.dukesofbuckingham.org.uk/places/stowe/1848_sale/family_portraits, accessed 8 June 2012.

23 *Stowe. A Description of the house and gardens of the most noble & puissant prince, George Grenville-Nugent-Temple Marquis of Buckingham* (Buckingham: J. Seeley, 1797), unpaginated.

24 Walpole, 'Visits', 23.

25 Letter from Mrs Delany to Mrs Dewes, Bulstrode, December 1754, *Delany Autobiography*, III, p. 308.

26 James Boaden (ed.), *The private correspondence of David Garrick … and a new biographical memoir*, 2 vols (London: Henry Colburn and Richard Bentley, 1831), I, pp. xxiii–xxiv. See Renée Loche and Marcel Roethlisberger, *L'Opera completa di Liotard* (Milan: Rizzoli Editore, 1978), cat. no. 137 for a query regarding the date of the portrait of Eva Maria Garrick. It has been suggested that both portraits were commissioned in Paris in 1751, though the difference in their quality gives credence to the suggestion that Eva Maria's portrait was completed later, in 1754.

27 For example, the 1785 inventory of Stourhead, made on the death of owner Henry Hoare, listed only two pastel portraits, despite evidence from Henry Hoare's accounts that he had purchased many such works from the artist William Hoare by this date. 'Schedule of Pictures at Stourhead as left by Henry Hoare' c.1785, Wiltshire and Swindon History Centre, Trowbridge Stourhead Archive, T(ST)383/9. Kenneth Woodbridge, *Landscape and Antiquity: Aspects of English Culture at Stourhead 1718 to 1838* (Oxford: Clarendon Press, 1970), pp. 43–4.

28 Fanny Burney, *The Early Diaries of Fanny Burney 1768–1778*, ed. Annie Raine Ellis, 2 vols (London: G. Bell & Sons, 1913), II, p. 11.

29 Walpole Library Farmington, 3582, fo. 49; Horace Walpole *A Description of the Villa of Mr Horace Walpole at Strawberry Hill near Twickenham*, extra-illustrated copy (London: printed by Thomas Kirkgate, 1784), p. ii.

30 Heather McPherson, 'Garrickomania: Art, Celebrity and the Imaging of

Garrick', www. folger.edu, accessed 15 June 2012.

31 Included as an addendum at the end of 'Paintings in the New House at Chiswick', undated, Devonshire MSS, Chatsworth.

32 Neil Jeffares, *Dictionary of Pastellists before 1800* (London: Unicorn Press, 2006), www.pastellists.com, accessed 28 May 2012. Knapton executed two portraits of both Dorothy and her sister Charlotte and it is no longer possible to say which of the pastels are those mentioned by Walpole, hanging in the dressing room in 1760; Walpole, 'Visits', 23. The two portraits of Dorothy are very close to each other, with differences only in details of the dress and hair-piece, in which feathers replace flowers. Charlotte's two portraits show more variation. However, the age of the sitter, the characterisation of the faces and similar pink and white brocade dresses and crowns of flowers do link the two. With thanks to Charles Noble for his thoughts on these works.

33 Burney, *Diaries*, II, p. 11.

34 Jean-Étienne Liotard, *Traité des principes et des règles de la peinture*, ed. Pierre Cailler (Geneva: Pierre Cailler, 1945; first published 1781), pp. 81–2.

35 Cotes, 'Notes on crayon painting', 84–5.

36 For example Russell's *George de Ligne Gregory*, 1793, Getty Museum, California; *John Godbold*, 1794, Hove Museum, Brighton; *John Bannister*, 1799. National Portrait Gallery, London; *William Radford*, 1799, Temple Newsam House, Leeds to name only a few.

37 Robert Dossie, *Handmaid to the Arts* (London: J. Nourse, 1764), p. 202.

38 General Advertiser and Morning Intelligencer, 6 May 1778; Dossie, *Handmaid to the Arts*, pp. 127, 194; John Imison, *The School of the Arts or an Introduction to Useful Knowledge*, 4th edn (London: J. Murray and S. Highley, 1796), p. 66.

39 *The Times*, 30 May 1788 and the *World*, 22 March 1791.

40 Thea Burns, *The Invention of Pastel* (London: Archetype, 2007), p. 113.

41 Claude Henry Watelet, *L'Art du peindre: Poëme* (Paris, 1760), unpaginated.

42 Imison, *School of the Arts*, p. 75.

43 Cotes, 'Notes on crayon painting', 84–5.

44 Letter from John (5th) Duke of Argyll to John Davidson, 16 August 1771, University of Edinburgh, Laing MS 2, 511.

45 *The Bull-Finch. Being a choice collection of the newest and most favourite English songs most of which have been sett to music and sung at the public theatres and gardens* (London: I Hinton, [c.1750]), pp. 65–6.

46 Letter from Mrs Delany to Anne Granville, 5 August 1731, *Delany Autobiography*, I, p. 280.

47 Letter from Mrs Delany to to Mrs Dewes, Bulstrode, 9 March 1755, *ibid.*, III, p. 328. Lady Burlington in the Garden Room, Chiswick and Lady Burlington painting in the Garden Room, Chiswick, William Kent, c.1740, pen and wash. Devonshire Collection, Chatsworth.

48 Letter from Mrs Delany to Anne Granville 30 June 1734, *ibid.*, I, p. 485.

49 Letter from Mrs Delany to Lady Throckmorton, Bulstrode, 5 December 1740, *ibid.*, II, p. 133.

50 Kim Sloan, *A Noble Art: Amateur Artists and Drawing Masters c.1600–1800* (London: British Museum Press, 2000), pp. 230–2.

51 Thomas Martyn, *The English Connoisseur: containing an account of whatever is curious in painting, sculpture, &c in the palaces and seats of the nobility and principal gentry of England, both in town and country* (London: L. Davis and C. Reymers, 1766).

52 Horace Walpole, *Correspondence*, ed. W.S. Lewis, 48 vols (New Haven and London: Yale University Press, 1937–83), XXIV, p. 475.

53 See Ann Bermingham 'The Aesthetics of Ignorance: The Accomplished Woman in the Culture of Connoisseurship', *Oxford Art Journal*, 16:2 (1993), 3–20.

54 For example at Ham House, where Grace Carteret, Countess of Dysart executed a copy of William Hoare's exemplary pastel portrait of her son Lionel Tollemache.

55 Cotes, 'Notes on crayon painting', 84–5.

6

Georgiana at Althorp: Spencer family portraits 1755–83

Emma Barker

RECENT scholarship has explored the historical significance of Georgiana, Duchess of Devonshire, as an early example of the modern celebrity. She was one of the most high profile of the prominent individuals who gained an unprecedented visibility in later eighteenth-century Britain, their likenesses circulating in the public realm not only through the exhibition of portraits at the Royal Academy but also in the form of graphic images over which they had no control. When the Duchess campaigned in Westminster on behalf of Charles James Fox during the election of 1784, the outpouring of often savage caricatures reached such a pitch as to prompt her to commission a portrait of herself in the role of a devoted mother to her infant daughter, which was duly exhibited at the Royal Academy.[1] However, this celebrated painting is only one of many portraits executed throughout Georgiana Spencer's life. She is exceptional, perhaps unique, in having been painted by both Reynolds and Gainsborough whilst still a child as well as in adulthood.[2] Both of these early likenesses form part of a remarkable group of Spencer family portraits dating from the 1750s to the 1780s, most of which remain to this day at their country house, Althorp, in Northamptonshire. Although many of these works have been discussed individually, no existing study has considered them together, with reference to the patrons rather than the artists.

In this essay, I seek to make good this lacuna, building on the earlier work of Kenneth Garlick, who catalogued the Althorp collection as it existed in 1976.[3] In so doing, I shall pay attention not only to the famous paintings by Reynolds and Gainsborough now (or formerly) in the collection, but also to those by other artists, including two women painters, Katherine Read and Angelica Kauffman, who were both commissioned to paint Georgiana and her siblings. The aim is to explore the processes by which this group of portraits came into being, the functions that they were intended to perform and (so far as is possible) the spaces within which they were displayed. More specifically, it will be argued that it was not solely or even primarily Georgiana's father, the 1st Earl Spencer, who commissioned them, as is generally assumed; rather it was his wife, née Georgiana Poyntz, who played the more active role in the development of the family portrait collection.[4] Furthermore, the relative prominence among these paintings of likenesses of their eldest daughter, her mother's namesake, as opposed to their son and heir, tends to support the thesis that a patriarchal, hierarchical and dynastic conception of the family was modified (if not actually challenged) during this period by a new sentimental model of domestic intimacy and affection. However, the portraits of the Spencer family also need to be understood in terms of the self-fashioning of the Whig oligarchy as it came under increasing pressure to justify its hereditary power and privilege.

Althorp and the Spencers

What must be emphasised here is that Althorp was not simply a rural retreat and a family home, but also a dynastic seat and, as such, a power base. The 1st Earl Spencer was debarred from a political career by the terms of the will of Sarah, Duchess of Marlborough, who, on her death in 1744, left the bulk of her property to her favourite grandson, the Hon. John Spencer, younger son of the 3rd Earl of Sunderland (see the family tree on p. xvii), on condition that neither he nor his son were to accept any office or pension from the crown.[5] Nevertheless, her great-grandson, also named John Spencer, who succeeded to his father's inheritance on the latter's death in 1746, took a keen interest in politics. Elected MP for Warwick in December 1756, he was elevated to the rank of viscount in 1761 and received an earldom in 1765. As well as being active in the House of Lords, Lord Spencer used his great wealth to support the Whigs in the boroughs in which the family had an 'interest'. He scored his greatest success at Northampton in 1768, when he managed to break the hold of the local Tory magnates in one of the most expensive, that is to say, corrupt, elections of the century.[6] Lady Spencer described their triumphant entry into the town with the MP in a letter to her children, one of many testifying to the importance of politics to the whole family. She herself campaigned regularly at election time, both in Northampton and in St Albans, where the Spencers had inherited the Duchess of Marlborough's 'interest', together with her childhood home, Holywell House (but not, it should be noted, in London, outside the realm of family interest, as her daughter controversially did in 1784).[7] Her son, George John, the 2nd Earl, continued the family political tradition, free of the constraints that the Duchess's will had imposed on his father, serving as First Lord of the Admiralty in the 1790s and later (briefly) as Home Secretary.

Throughout this period, Althorp was only one, and by no means the grandest, of several residences between which the Spencers divided their time. Nevertheless, as the dynastic seat, it contained the majority of the family portraits, which had been inherited, together with the house, from the Earls of Sunderland (who instead succeeded to the Marlborough dukedom and the property that went with it). By contrast, Spencer House, the splendid London mansion that John Spencer had built in the years following his marriage in December 1755, served as a showcase for some of the grandest old master paintings that he owned.[8] Other Spencer residences, notably Holywell House and Wimbledon Park, the latter also inherited from the Duchess of Marlborough (see the Introduction), contained some portraits, but nothing like the hundred or so at Althorp.[9] Picture lists produced in the mid-eighteenth century show that, in accordance with established practice, most of them hung in the long gallery on the first floor. Elizabethan in origin, it was given its present form in 1682 by the 2nd Earl of Sunderland, who had the walls panelled in oak and ordered frames of a distinctive scalloped design to be made for all the pictures to create a uniform display.[10] Presenting as it did a grand array of Spencer ancestors, their kinsfolk among the great noble families of England and other notable figures, as well as a fair few unidentified sitters, the gallery functioned to assert the status and power of the dynasty. Described by Horace Walpole on the occasion of a visit to Althorp in 1760, as 'a gallery of all one's acquaintance by Vandyke and Lely', it served its purpose more particularly by associating the Spencers with the pomp and glamour of the Caroline courts, even though the Whig loyalties they had since adopted put them at odds with Stuart absolutism.[11] In other words, the illusion of continuity mattered more than ideological consistency.

For the eighteen-year old Georgiana Poyntz, visiting Althorp for the first time during the autumn before her marriage to John Spencer, it was the gallery that particularly attracted her attention. In a letter to her friend Theodora Cowper ('Thea'), she describes the house as 'very large but very old. The picture gallery 114 foot long. A fine room for walking about in. We always breakfast there. There are vast Quantities of Pictures. Some fine Ones'.[12] By this date, she had already sat in London for her own portrait, painted in miniature by the Swiss artist Jean-Étienne Liotard; in a letter probably written in May 1754, she reports that she had gone to sit for him in her riding habit, which 'made me look better than I have done for months ... though I sat but half an hour today my Picture is more improved than if I had sat for hours another day'.[13] The same letter also refers to a love letter she had received from Spencer, of whom Liotard also painted a miniature around the same time. Since the compositions indicate that they were not conceived as pendants, it is possible that the two pictures were exchanged as tokens of an affective bond that transcended material interest, in accordance with the conventional significance of miniature portraits during this period.[14] Such an exchange would have been in keeping with the conspicuous ardour with which Spencer courted Miss Poyntz, regardless of her inferior rank and fortune.[15] Another letter written by Georgiana refers not only to a final sitting to Liotard, but also to a visit to 'two painters, Mr Reynolds and Mrs Read to see Pictures'.[16] The future Lady Spencer was thus already familiar with two of the artists whom she and her husband later commissioned to paint members of their family.

No doubt many, if not most, of these commissions were in some sense collaborations between the two Spencers. They seem to have been an exceptionally close couple, at any rate by the standard of most aristocratic marriages of the period; they shared a love of art, literature, music and sport, as well as each other and their children.[17] However, Lord Spencer remains a shadowy figure by comparison with his wife, partly because she destroyed his private papers after his death, but also because of his persistent ill health and more reserved personality. A young French nobleman who met them in Montpellier in 1772, the comte d'Antraigues, was struck by the contrast between the charming and cultivated Lady Spencer and her morose and taciturn husband. He describes her as a 'devotee of the Methodist sect', one who was 'methodical in everything related to sentiment', but otherwise lenient and tolerant.[18] She certainly had evangelical sympathies, later becoming a friend of Hannah More, whose vision of a reformed aristocratic order, based on Christian piety and *noblesse oblige*, she shared.[19] Although Lady Spencer saw herself as the loyal executor of her husband's wishes, conscientiously promoting his ideals and values, she had more than a little in common with the 1st Earl's ancestress, the Duchess of

Marlborough, who also combined deep devotion to her husband with strongly held convictions of her own; the will that prevented Lord Spencer entering politics reflected Sarah's fierce commitment to Whig ideals and accompanying distrust of the crown.[20] The family portraits commissioned between 1755 and 1783, when her husband died, are shaped, I shall argue here, by Lady Spencer's at once dutiful and forceful personality.

Lady Spencer and her portraits

After their marriage, the Spencers did not commission full-length portraits of themselves, such as had been painted of previous residents of Althorp, up to and including the 1st Earl's parents.[21] In fact, the first portrait they commissioned was not intended to hang at Althorp at all. A painting by Reynolds of Lady Spencer with her daughter, Georgiana (plate 11), it was given to her brother, William Poyntz, who, in turn, presented a portrait of himself by Gainsborough to his sister. In other words, as may have been the case with the miniatures by Liotard, the two paintings were exchanged in order to mark the affective bonds between the sitters. The exchange of portraits with her eldest brother, the head of the Poyntz family since the death of her father, may have been initiated by the then Mrs Spencer in order to confirm and reinforce her ties to her own kindred, as a demonstration of love and loyalty, even a kind of guarantee of the benefits that would accrue to them as a result of her marriage into a considerably grander and wealthier family. At any rate, her portrait was begun first, probably in 1759, though it may have been conceived immediately after the younger Georgiana's birth in 1757.[22] By the time that Mrs Spencer began to sit for Reynolds, however, she also had a son, so that the decision to be painted with her daughter must have been deliberate. The painting may reflect changing attitudes towards girls, particularly given that the elder Georgiana wrote to Thea after George John's birth in September 1758: 'I will own I feel so partial to my Dear Little Gee that I think I never shall love another so well.'[23] It should be noted, however, that she made this statement in a letter to a close friend, at a time of great rejoicing at the birth of a Spencer heir; as Ingrid Tague argues, aristocratic mothers probably found it easier to express such a preference for a daughter once the pressure to produce a boy was off.[24]

Furthermore, the Spencer lineage did not matter so much in this case, given that Reynolds's painting was not intended to hang at

Althorp. Nevertheless, it is illuminating to compare it with the one earlier portrait then in the house of a Spencer mother and daughter, Charles Jervas's painting of Anne Churchill, wife of the 3rd Earl of Sunderland, with Lady Diana Spencer, painted around 1715. Although she too was deeply concerned by the welfare of her children, not least her daughters, Lady Sunderland's full-length portrait emphasises her courtly elegance rather than her maternal attachment; she stands in a formal garden, one hand held out to a bullfinch which flies towards her, her other arm extended to support her youngest daughter, who is seated on a rock to the right.[25] By contrast, Lady Spencer (as she had become by the time the picture was completed in 1761) is shown at three-quarter length, with both arms clasped around her daughter, who in turn places a hand on her mother's shoulder, so as to leave no doubt as to their closeness to each other. Although the typically baroque column and curtain behind them, together with the carved and gilded table base at lower left, indicate their high rank, the way that their heads are nestled within a dark fold of curtain reinforces the sense of intimacy. Despite the fashionable dress they wear, the composition recalls that of a madonna, as Ellis Waterhouse long ago pointed out. More specifically, by depicting the child standing on a table supported by her mother, Reynolds seems to allude to those in which the Virgin presents the infant Christ to be venerated.[26] The effect is solemn and dignified, suggesting that the mother-child bond is something sacred, but also playful and ironic, not least because of the presence of the fluffy white dog, who paws at the little girl's dress, evidently trying to attract her attention.

In depicting Lady Spencer in this way, Reynolds at once pays tribute to her maternal devotion and to her good taste while also suggesting that she does not take herself too seriously. On the one hand, the painting accords with the growing sentimentalisation of motherhood in evidence by the 1750s; on the other hand, at the same time it testifies to the unrivalled prestige of Italian art in the age of the Grand Tour.[27] On the latter point, it should be noted that Lady Spencer sat to Reynolds at a time when she and her husband were both engaged in planning the decoration of their new London house, for which purpose Lord Spencer paid large sums of money to buy paintings by such artists as Guido Reni and Andrea Sacchi. From 1763 to 1764, before the house was completed, they travelled to Italy, where Lady Spencer, like her husband, admired the famous works of the High Renaissance and seicento; a painting that particularly attracted her attention was Raphael's *Madonna 'della*

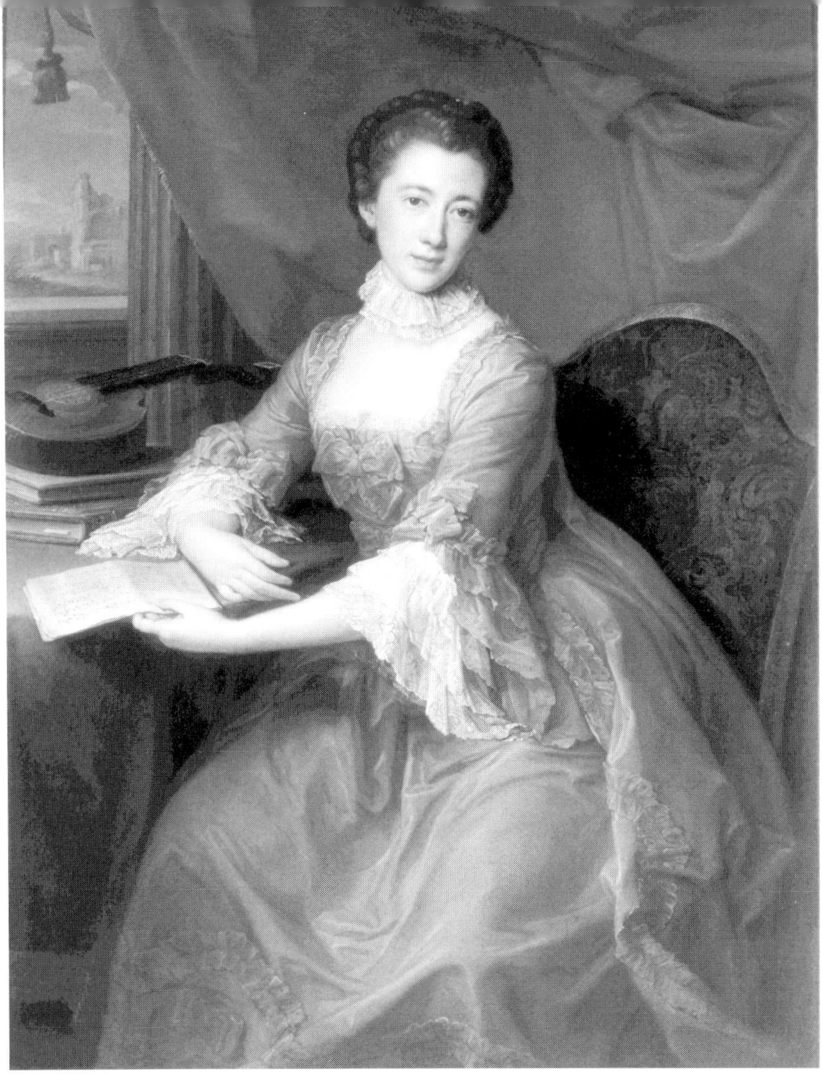

Figure 32
Pompeo Batoni, *Viscountess Spencer*, 1764, oil on canvas, 137 × 123 cm.

Sedia in Florence.[28] While they were in Rome, she sat for her portrait to Pompeo Batoni, who did not usually depict British female sitters (as opposed to male Grand Tourists) in the presence of antiquities (figure 32). The view of the Colosseum that appears behind her must therefore have been deliberately included to signal her appreciation of the city's glories: 'Rome and Rome only', she declared to Thea, 'is the place to see and admire the perfection to which painting, sculpture and architecture have been carried.'[29] Since Batoni's portrait shows her seated with a musical score in her hands beside a table on which lie a guitar (though her usual instrument was a viola da gamba) and two books (one with a bookmark tucked in its pages), it more broadly represents her as a cultivated and even learned woman. This, it seems, was Lady Spencer's own preferred image, perhaps also her husband's of her; it is first documented in 1802 at Althorp in Lord Spencer's dressing room.[30] By then, the 1st Earl was long dead, but the picture could have been there ever since it first arrived in the house.

Reynolds's portrait of Lady Spencer and her daughter, by contrast, only came to Althorp in 1840, after another Miss Poyntz married the 4th Earl. Before then, the picture presumably hung at Midgham, the Poyntz family's house in Berkshire, where it would have functioned as a statement of the grandeur of their connections, especially after the younger Georgiana married the Duke of Devonshire in 1774. Whereas the artist's animated portrait of the latter with her own daughter, yet another Georgiana, was intended to recuperate her moral reputation in the eyes of the public, his depiction of the Duchess's mother as a modern madonna serves to ennoble Lady Spencer in both senses of the term; combining as it does moral authority with cultural prestige, the painting transcends the conventional gentility of earlier aristocratic portraiture by transforming the sitter into an ideal model of patrician femininity.[31] Although Reynolds applied much the same formula to other female portraits around this date, its use was especially apt in this case, since Georgiana Poyntz seems to have been widely regarded by her contemporaries as an exemplary figure, as good as she was beautiful (even if her reputation for virtue also provoked some scepticism; she certainly struggled with the tensions between her Christian faith and her love of gambling). When she became engaged to John Spencer, Mrs Delany declared that, for all his rank and fortune, it was he who was the lucky one in the match: 'a happier choice he could not have made. She was born a gentlewoman, greatly allied by her mother's side, well educated, a most sensible, generous, delicate mind, and I think a very agreeable person [that is, appearance].'[32] On the occasion of a visit to Althorp in 1779, the Earl of Bristol wrote:

> Lady Spencer you know is my model of women, and having seen her in retirement and in all her domestic employments, my admiration and respect of her increase; she has such a decided character that nothing can warp it, and then such simplicity of manners one would think she had never lived out of the country, with such elegance, 'tis as if she had never lived in it.[33]

(He goes on to praise her charitable activities; the significance of which will be discussed below.) Moreover, if Horace Walpole was being at least partly ironic in dubbing her 'the goddess of wisdom', it only

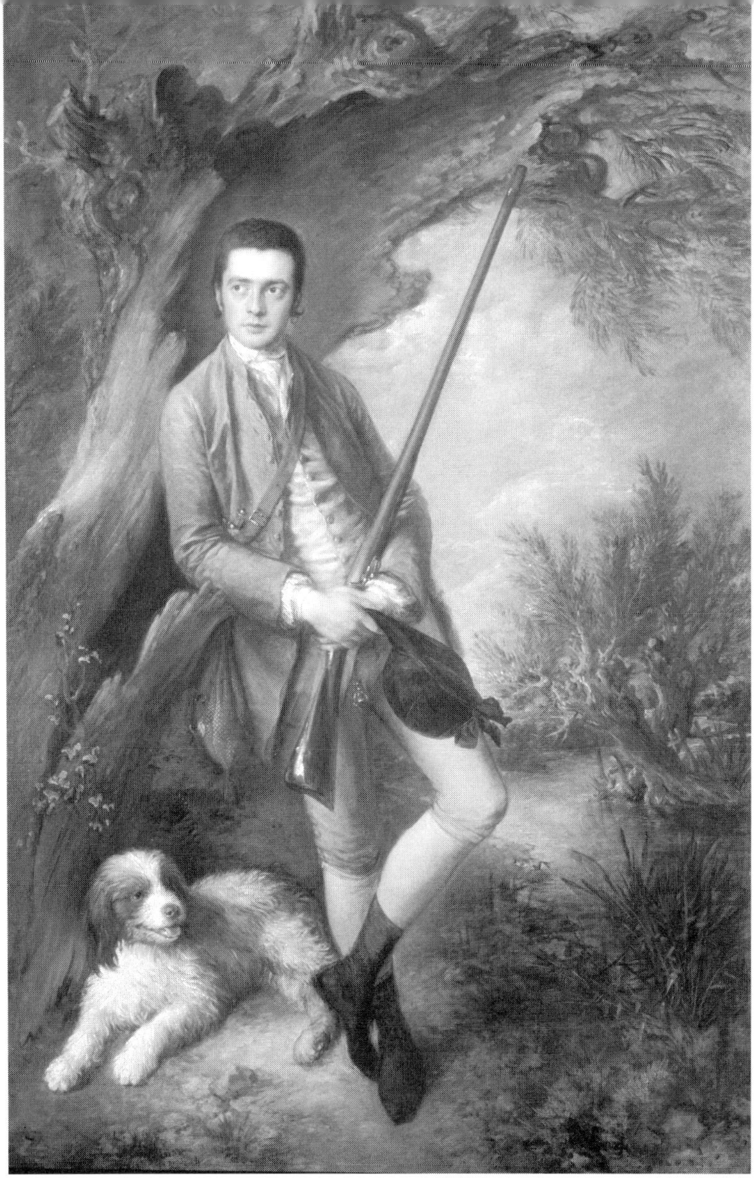

Figure 33 Thomas Gainsborough, *William Poyntz*, 1762, oil on canvas, 235 × 152.5 cm.

serves to point up the resemblance between such a characterisation and Reynolds's painting.[34]

However, the full significance of the portrait of Lady Spencer can be grasped only by bearing in mind that her brother gave her in return one of himself by Gainsborough. By showing William Poyntz with a gun (figure 33), the painting asserts his status as a landowner, since only those with an income of at least £100 a year enjoyed the right to go shooting. It thereby confirms a relatively recently acquired status, since the estate of Midgham had been bought by their father, Stephen Poyntz, in 1736 or thereabouts.[35] By displaying the portrait at Althorp, alongside those of the Spencers, Georgiana upheld the dignity of the Poyntzes, an old landed family whose fortunes had declined to the point where her grandfather had earned his living as an upholsterer (that is, a supplier of furniture and fabric). However, the painting also breaks with previous conventions of aristocratic portraiture, as can be seen by comparing it to the portrait of the Hon. John Spencer out shooting painted in 1745 by George Knapton. The 1st Earl's father appears a commanding figure, as he stands upright, gun in hand, observed by his son and heir, who is shown on horseback, and a black servant, whose subordination is underlined by his crouching position.[36] By contrast, William Poyntz leans against a picturesquely decrepit tree, looking dreamily upwards while a spaniel pants at his feet; called Amber, and said to have been a favourite of his master, it certainly appears more amiable pet than noble hound. Like other Gainsborough portraits of sitters with their dogs, it suggests that he deserves respect not simply for his landed status but also for his tender sensibility. Although the placing of the gun has been interpreted as a lewd joke, any such innuendo would hardly have been calculated to appeal to the painting's intended recipient.[37] On this point, it may be noted that, in 1762, the year it was exhibited at the Society of Artists in London, Laurence Sterne, with whom Lord and Lady Spencer had struck up a friendship, dedicated to the latter one of the most touching sections of *Tristram Shandy*, the story of Le Fever, perhaps as part of a strategy of appealing to respectable female readers by downplaying the novel's bawdiness.[38]

Both Reynolds's portrait of Lady Spencer and Gainsborough's of William Poyntz can thus be seen to present a new kind of patrician image, one that emphasised inner, moral qualities as much as external markers of status, though not without a touch of playfulness in each case. Like pendant portraits of a husband and wife, they do so in accordance with conventional gender roles: through motherhood and sporting pursuits respectively.[39] Like such portraits, they thereby omit less normative aspects of the sitters' lives: most obviously, the fact that Lady Spencer was an enthusiastic horsewoman, who went out with the local hunts. Only later, in a portrait commissioned from Gainsborough as a present for her son on his marriage in 1781, did she have herself painted in her habitual riding habit. In the same portrait, she also wears a rose in her coat, presumably to signify her maternal love.[40] In all three cases, the portrait functions to reinforce family ties following a marriage that would inevitably distance the sitter from the recipient. Such a portrait continued to serve its function long after it was painted.

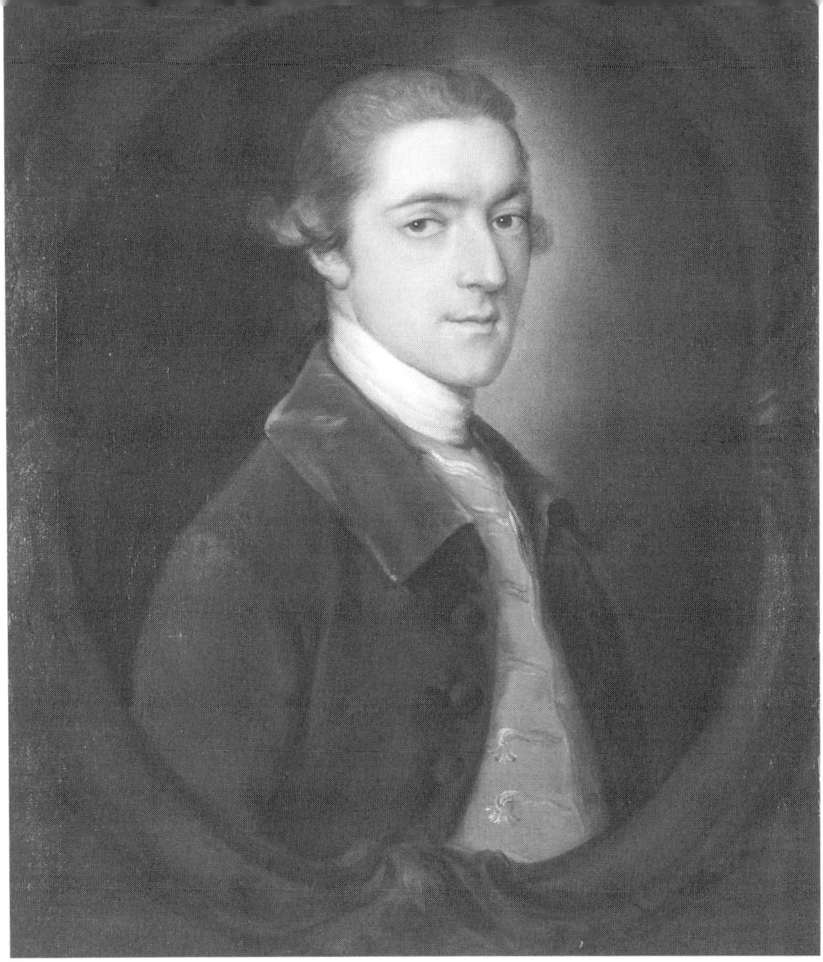

Figure 34 Thomas Gainsborough, *Viscount Spencer*, c.1763, oil on canvas.

Thus, after her husband died in 1783, Lady Spencer took her brother's portrait with her to Holywell House, where she lived until her own death in 1814.[41] Two other portraits painted by Gainsborough in the 1760s, neither of which appears in the 1802 Althorp picture catalogue, probably also accompanied her to Holywell as a reminder of beloved family members now separated from her by marriage or death. In the case of Gainsborough's portrait of her husband (figure 34), this is made likely by the fact that it is the only known full-scale picture of the 1st Earl as an adult.[42] It must have been painted while the Spencers were in Bath, one of numerous spas that they frequented in the vain hope of finding a cure for his ill health.[43] In contrast to the full-length of his brother-in-law, it is one of the artist's standard head and shoulders portraits, which, as Susan Sloman notes, would have been readily affordable to most visitors to the city.[44] As such, it offers only a simple likeness, with almost nothing to indicate the sitter's wealth and status.

The 1st Earl thus omitted to add a portrait of himself to the succession of imposing full lengths of his predecessors at Althorp and indeed seems to have been disinclined to be painted at all. Although his friend George Simon Harcourt, Viscount Nuneham, entreated him not 'to forget your most obliging promise of making me that very acceptable present of your picture', presumably in return for the gift of Nuneham's own portrait, he failed to sit to Reynolds as requested.[45] Lord Spencer's reluctance to be painted can be attributed to his ill health, combined with his reserved, withdrawn character. He was described by another friend, the 2nd Viscount Palmerston, as 'a man whose value few people know. The bright side of his character appears in private and the dark side in public … it is only the few who live in intimacy with him who know that he has an understanding and a heart that would do credit to any man'.[46] However, the explanation for the paucity of likenesses of Lord Spencer surely lies not in purely personal factors, but also in the will that prevented him following family tradition by becoming a minister of the crown. At a time when the aristocracy was seeking to justify its hereditary power and privileges by adopting an ethos of public service, he may have felt that his inability to add lustre to the family name in the political arena made it inappropriate for him to be commemorated in a formal portrait.[47] His son provides a telling point of contrast; having accepted political office out of a sense of patriotic duty, the 2nd Earl was painted by John Singleton Copley in 1800, in the grandest possible manner, wearing the robes of the Order of the Garter, with which he was invested the previous year in recognition of his services as First Lord of the Admiralty, with Windsor Castle in the distance. After being exhibited at the Royal Academy, Copley's portrait was hung in the gallery at Althorp.[48]

Portraits of the Spencer children

In the light of these considerations, it is tempting to speculate that the 1st Earl was persuaded to sit to Gainsborough by Lady Spencer, who surely would have wanted to have a likeness of her husband, not least in view of the constant worry about the prospect of his early death. He presumably did so at the same time that his daughter, Georgiana, sat to Gainsborough for her portrait (figure 35), probably in 1763, a date based on the child's apparent age in the picture.[49] It too is a standard head and shoulders portrait, with the sitter set within a painted oval frame, but, whereas Lord Spencer's picture is one of many of this type that the artist painted of adult male sitters, Georgiana's seems to be the only such painting that he executed of a child, apart from one of his own niece. Whereas Reynolds had idealised her, along with her mother, turning the little girl into an embodiment of wide-eyed innocence, Gainsborough painted the six-year-old Miss Spencer (not yet Lady Georgiana) in a far more matter of fact manner, offering not so much a picture of childhood as a likeness of an individual, who happens to be a child. The portrait has been related to the ideals of sensibility, which required parents to attend to the unique qualities of each child, and to the progressive educational values of Lady Spencer, more specifically.[50] However, Gainsborough surely depicted Georgiana as he did primarily because he approached the task in hand as he would have done a portrait in this format of an adult sitter. As with comparable portraits of women, he has carefully rendered the elaborate details of her clothes. The commission most likely came about because she had accompanied her parents to Bath; they are known to have taken her with them when they travelled to Spa, in the Ardennes, in the summer of 1763, leaving her younger siblings behind in England.[51] The painting's very existence thus testifies to her status as a favourite child, in whose company her parents delighted.

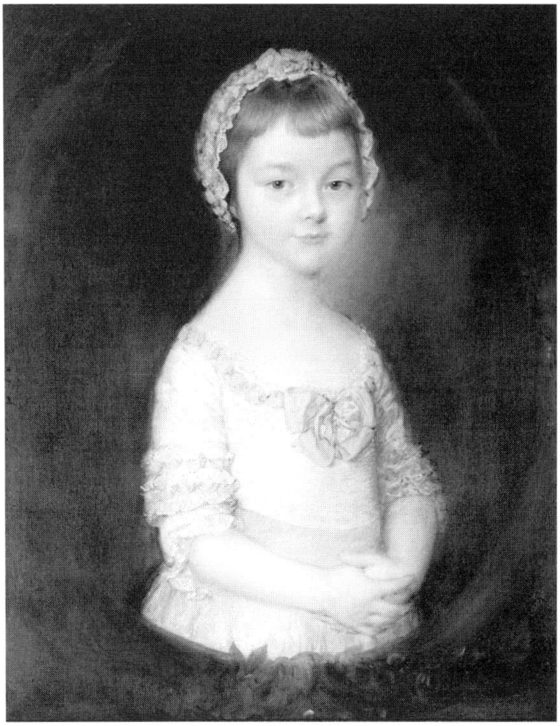

Figure 35 Thomas Gainsborough, *Miss Georgiana Spencer*, c.1763, oil on canvas, 73 × 60 cm.

As with Reynolds's portrait of Lady Spencer and her daughter, Gainsborough's portrait of the six-year-old Georgiana had few, if any, precedents among the portraits inherited by the Spencers. The only one that offers a direct comparison is Kneller's portrait of Henrietta and Anne Churchill, the eldest daughters of the future Duke and Duchess of Marlborough, painted in 1688.[52] At the time, they would have been aged seven and five respectively, but look significantly older; Henrietta, in particular, appears more a young lady than a little girl. In her elegant dress, gracefully holding out a flower with one hand as she looks out at the spectator, she seems already to be presented as a prospective bride; Anne, seated at her sister's feet and gazing up at her, plays a subordinate role. Like the Countess of Sunderland, as Anne became, the Duchess of Marlborough was a devoted mother, which, for her, involved striving to ensure that her daughters had dowries large enough to allow them to make grand marriages. In some respects, little had changed four generations later, despite the growing pressure on parents to act in their children's best interests.[53] Although Lady Spencer, like the Duchess, claimed to be reluctant to allow her daughter to marry at too early an age, she and her husband nevertheless accepted a grand match for her while she was still in her mid-teens. The only real difference seems to have been that they needed to persuade themselves that Georgiana's marriage was based on love, like their own, before doing so.[54] Nevertheless, it is significant that, while Kneller's picture of Henrietta and Anne Churchill has a male counterpart in the artist's portrait of their brother, John, Marquess of Blandford, Gainsborough's of Georgiana is not matched by any comparable portrait of her brother.[55]

However, the reason for this omission lies not just in the Spencers' preference for their eldest daughter, but also in the fact that the artist whom they regularly employed to paint their children during the 1760s was the then highly successful pastel painter, Katherine Read. As previously noted, Georgiana Poyntz visited the artist before her marriage, and it is likely that she played the major role in commissioning portraits from Read. As Ruth Kenny points out in her essay in this volume, women provided a significant proportion of the patronage for pastels, which typically hung in their private apartments, notably dressing rooms. At Althorp in 1802, the dressing room of the by then Dowager Countess contained pastels by Read of George and Georgiana. The former can be identified as a portrait showing him at the age of seven or eight; he had previously been painted by Read at the age of about two, while still in skirts, stroking the head of a large dog. His sister was first painted by Read as an infant in her mother's arms, but the pastel in Lady Spencer's dressing room can be identified as one showing her at the age of eight executed in connection with a large pastel of the Spencer children (she looks much the same in both).[56] The large pastel must have been commissioned to commemorate the birth of Lady Charlotte ('a sweet little girl', her mother reported) in the autumn of 1765. It shows Georgiana with her little sister in her arms, while George holds up a scroll inscribed with the alphabet, as if trying to teach the baby to read; the Spencer's second daughter, Lady Harriet, completes the scene by cuddling up to the latest addition to the family. Read exhibited the picture at the Free Society of Artists in 1768 under the title, *A Nobleman's Children*, but by then Charlotte was dead.[57]

Commemorating as it did a joyful moment in her family life, before it was shattered by the death of Charlotte, this large pastel is likely to have held a special significance for Lady Spencer, who wrote in November 1766 to Thea: 'you who know the perhaps uncommon tenderness I have for my children will know but too well what I must have suffer'd from this stroke'.[58] Its absence from the 1802 picture list suggests that she took it with her to Holywell; after her death, it hung at Althorp in the bedroom of the 2nd Earl's wife, née Lady Lavinia Bingham, together with other portraits of the Spencers and her own family.[59] In choosing pastel as the medium for her children's portraits, the first Lady Spencer followed the precedent set by the 1st Earl's mother, Lady Cowper, who owned one by Knapton of her son with his sister Diana, who died in 1743 at the age of seven, which she bequeathed to her son in her will. For Lady Cowper, the portrait of her children, one of them dead, no doubt held the same kind of emotional resonance as the pastel by Read did for Lady Spencer, but the pictorial idiom is very different, since Knapton depicted his sitters in mythological guise, John as Bacchus, Diana as Ceres; they smile and hold hands, but are otherwise poised and still.[60] Once again, an earlier style of aristocratic portraiture can be seen to give way after 1750 to a new sentimental mode, central to which is the demonstration of affection for a vulnerable, dependent being, whether a small child or a pet animal. Rather than having a purely personal, strictly private significance, Read's large pastel of the Spencer children suggests (as Margery Morgan argues of another portrait of aristocratic children by the artist) 'the values and sympathies nurtured within the family overflowing to promote a good society'.[61]

More specifically, the typically sentimental characterisation of the sitters' ties with each other in the Spencer portraits, particularly the one by Reynolds and those by Read, needs to be understood in relation to the patrons' philanthropic activities. For both Lord and Lady Spencer, such activities played a crucial role in their self-fashioning as responsible patricians, whose power and privilege was justified because of the good use they made of it. In 1768, for example, it was reported that Lord Spencer had given 200 guineas for the poor of Wimbledon and Roehampton.[62] However, though such gifts were made in his name, it seems to have been Lady Spencer who acted as his agent in charitable matters. After her husband's death, she became renowned for her philanthropy, contributing money and offering advice to a range of organisations. As with her political activities, the moral framework for her endeavours in this domain was provided by her family loyalties; in typically paternalist fashion, she felt a particular sense of obligation to anyone with some kind of connection to the Spencers, notably those who had worked for them or lived on or near their estates, as the example quoted above indicates. However, as Donna Andrew has shown, she also recognised more general ties based on simple fellow feeling, such as the appeal from a supplicant 'to the sensibility of Lady Spencer', 'too well acquainted with the tender duties of a wife and mother not to feel for a wretched one'.[63] So far as her own children were concerned, she welcomed such signs of fellow-feeling in them, writing to a friend in 1769, when both George and Harriet had been ill, that Georgiana had shown 'upon this as upon every other occasion such charming sensibility that it is impossible not to be pleased with it'. Later, she wrote to her daughter expressing delight 'with the idea that your unaffected good humour, civility and attention to everyone will draw all hearts towards you' and pity for those who 'have not that Vivifying spark of benevolence about them, nor know what it is to love their fellow creatures abstracted'.[64]

The hopes that Lady Spencer invested in her children, her desire for them to become exemplars of an aristocratic status based on sensibility and benevolence as much as on lineage and landowning, found expression in a portrait of the young Spencers (plate 12) painted by Angelica Kauffman shortly before Georgiana's marriage to the Duke of Devonshire. The Spencers had first met Kauffman in Rome in 1764; when she arrived in London in 1766, Lady Spencer visited the artist in her lodgings and bought a portrait of Reynolds that she had painted. Given her sense of obligation to people with whom she had a prior connection, Lady Spencer no doubt did so as much out of a desire to be of service to Kauffman as to possess the portrait of Reynolds, which she, in any case, appears to have relinquished to John Parker of Saltram.[65] Moreover, as with Read's portraits of the Spencer children, there can be little doubt that it was their mother, rather than their father, who played the leading role in commissioning Kauffman to paint them. Both artists indeed seem to have been particularly favoured by female patrons; for example, Queen Charlotte also commissioned portraits from Read and Kauffman.[66] Whereas the earlier portrait commemorated an addition to the family, the 1774 picture served to reinforce the bonds between the siblings in the face of the approaching marriage, which represented at once a personal loss and a dynastic triumph. Seated on the left, the future Duchess of Devonshire rests her elbow on a relief of a griffin, the Spencer crest, as if to assert that she will always belong to them even once she has married a Cavendish; in this respect, the picture echoes Spencer House, the decoration of which was full of symbolic griffins.[67] Above the relief appear roses, symbolic of love, and, behind, a large urn signifies eternal fidelity.

More broadly, Kauffman's portrait of the Spencers exemplifies the ideals of sensibility in the way that it focuses attention on an interior world of feeling. As Angela Rosenthal has observed, the figures are engaged in a 'sympathetic exchange', in which the two sisters can be seen to take the lead.[68] Seated side by side, they affirm their affection for each other; Georgiana clasps Harriet's hand, as if to reassure her, while the latter in turn puts an arm around her sister's shoulder. Both girls wear a version of what Aileen Ribeiro terms Graeco-Turkish dress, one that combines classical elements with a residual exoticism; the pale colours and flowing lines reinforce their characterisation as creatures of exquisitely refined feeling, far removed from the commonplace world of everyday life.[69] Their brother similarly embodies a highly idealised version of masculinity; standing with his legs crossed in what had become the archetypal pose of gentlemanly politeness, he looks almost deferentially down at his sisters. Harriet in turn looks tenderly towards him, as if to share her own sadness at the imminent loss of their sister. George wears Van Dyck dress, which was not simply a popular masquerade costume, but also evoked a vanished world of refinement and gallantry supposed to have existed at the court of Charles I. As with the heroine's '"whole-length picture in the Vandyke taste' in Richardson's *Clarissa*, this costume could signify allegiance to a high-minded aristocratic code at odds with the self-seeking materialism of the modern world. In its archaic elegance, it locates George in a timeless elsewhere, a realm of sensibility, in much the way as the Graeco-Turkish dress does his sisters.[70] The attitudes and costumes of the young Spencers thus identify them as true aristocrats, whose hearts are as noble as their ancestry.

Furthermore, each of Lady Spencer's children is depicted by Kauffman in a way that makes them at once recognisable individuals and sentimental stereotypes. The fair-haired Georgiana, clad in white, dominates the composition, not least by being the only one of the three to look out at the spectator, in accordance with her status as the family beauty as well as a future duchess. The artist was reported to have said 'that 'she looks so like one of the graces as to realize in her own person all of the ideas of the most fervid imagination'.[71] Georgiana also appears the embodiment of the sentimental heroine, a Clarissa or a Julie, as she was no doubt aware; the novel of which the latter is the heroine, Rousseau's *Julie ou la Nouvelle Héloïse*, had enthralled her during a stay in France with her family in 1772 to 1773, at least according to the comte d'Antraigues, who claims that his reading aloud of it led her to fall in love with him.[72] Somewhat overshadowed by her sister, Harriet is recognisable as the daughter whom Lady Spencer described at her birth as 'a little ugly girl [with] … an abundance of brown hair'; as her gestures suggest, she was devoted to Georgiana, even justifying her choice of the Duke of Devonshire's cousin as her husband on the grounds that, 'by marrying him she made no new connections, for now her sister's and hers would be the same'.[73] Both in this respect and in the dark hair that makes her a foil for her sister, Harriet resembles Julie's cousin, the 'inseparable' Claire, who declares at one point in Rousseau's novel: 'Cousin, forever, forever, until death'.[74] With his height and red cloak, George vies with his elder sister for attention, testifying to his status as the heir; he too is recognisable as the boy of whom his mother reported at his birth: 'As for his hair I think the little he has is absolute carrots.'[75] Both in his costume and his demeanour he appears a truly gallant gentleman, comparable to Rousseau's hero, Saint-Preux, whose name, redolent of the 'preux chevalier', suggests that he belongs to the aristocracy of feeling.

Reynolds at Althorp

Of course, Lady Spencer would not have viewed Kauffman's painting of her children in exactly these terms, though she would certainly have been familiar with *La Nouvelle Héloïse*, however much she may have disapproved of novel reading in theory.[76] Nevertheless, a Rousseauian account of the picture serves to convey something of the high aspirations (and inevitable disappointments) that must have entered her mind as she looked at it in the years that followed. Absent from the 1802 picture list, it presumably accompanied her to Holywell; after her death, it hung over the chimney in Lady Spencer's bedroom at Althorp, along with the pastels by Read and other family portraits.[77] When the 1st Earl and his wife lived there, the various portraits of Georgiana and her siblings most probably hung in their mother's bedroom or dressing room. Although they spent only four or five months of the year in Northamptonshire, the Spencer seat had something of the character of a family home in the modern sense; regarded by the Duchess of Marlborough as her ideal country house, it was 'dear Althorpe [*sic*]' to Lady Spencer, who also described it as 'this place, which I must always love preferably to any other'.[78] She and her husband habitually held a large house party there over Christmas and the New Year. A guest at one such party, the Earl of March ('Old Q'), writing to George Selwyn on 31 December 1767, reported:

> I like everything here so much, that I have no inclination to leave the place. I wish you were here. It is just the house you would wish to be in. There is an excellent library; a good parson; the best English and French cookery you ever tasted; strong coffee, and half crown whist. The more I see of the mistress of the house, the more I admire her and our landlord improves very much upon acquaintance. They are really the happiest people I think I ever saw in the marriage system. *Enfin c'est le meilleur ménage possible.*[79]

From an art-historical point of view, the irony is that this happiest of aristocratic marriages was never commemorated in a pair of pendant portraits, let alone one of husband and wife together. Although they appear to have been on good terms with Reynolds, the only portrait he painted of either of them after 1761 was a modest bust-length one of Lady Spencer, who had perhaps come to regard having one's portrait painted as a form of self-indulgence. At any rate, in June 1772, she told Thea she had to come to town, 'on a very foolish errand to sit for my picture … perhaps you will meet me at Sir Joshua Reynolds's on Leicester fields'.[80] It is also worth noting that none of the portraits of Lady Spencer was ever publicly exhibited in London.

However, Lord and Lady Spencer did commission the artist to paint a pair of full-length portraits, not of themselves, but of their two elder children. Exhibited together at the Royal Academy in 1776, Reynolds's portraits of the Duchess of Devonshire (plate 13) and Viscount Althorp (figure 36) were paid for only in 1783, shortly after the death of the 1st Earl, by his widow. She hung that of Georgiana in her bedroom at Althorp, but took that of George to her new residence outside St Albans, where it was paired with a full-length portrait of his sister by Gainsborough.[81] By the 1820s, however, Reynolds's portrait of the 2nd Earl and that of the Duchess hung in the gallery at Althorp on either side of the grandest of the Van Dycks, the double portrait of the 2nd

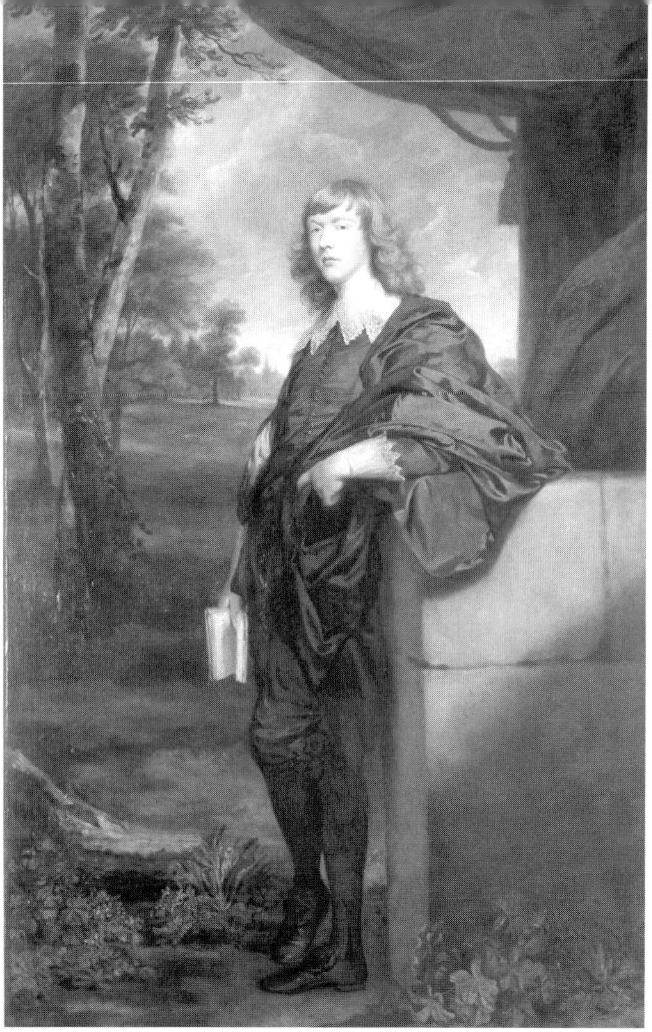

Figure 36
Joshua Reynolds, *Viscount Althorp*, 1776, oil on canvas, 239 × 147 cm.

Earl of Bristol and 1st Duke of Bedford, at the South end of the room, facing visitors as they entered at the North end. According to Nicholas Penny, 'this arrangement is likely to have been planned by the artist'.[82] It would certainly help to explain the black Van Dyck costume that George wears, which otherwise appears strangely at odds with the disdain that Reynolds expresses for 'this fantastick dress' in his seventh discourse (delivered the very year that the painting was exhibited at the Academy).[83] By contrast, though also echoing the way that she appears in Kauffman's portrait, Georgiana is shown dressed in a fanciful ensemble that combines Turkish details with classical elements[84]. It may be assumed her dress was intended to harmonise with the loose, flowing costume worn by many of the Lely beauties in the gallery. Reynolds also exhibited in 1776 a small portrait of the Duke of Devonshire; since it too hung in the gallery in 1822, it would seem that all three pictures formed part of a commission conceived very much in the spirit of the existing array of imposing portraits of Spencers and their distinguished kinsfolk.[85]

Such a commission would, however, have represented not so much a continuation as a revival of the gallery's dynastic function. The mid-eighteenth-century picture lists suggest that the hang had hardly changed at all since the 2nd Earl of Sunderland had transformed the space at the end of the seventeenth century. Recent portraits such as Knapton's of the Hon. John Spencer and his son hung elsewhere in the house. Although Walpole boasted of his familiarity with the sitters in the portraits by Van Dyck and Lely, he spoke as much as an antiquarian as an aristocrat; in his *Anecdotes of Painting*, he refers to 'the gallery at Althorp, one of those enchanted scenes that a thousand circumstances of history and art endear to a pensive spectator'.[86] It probably remained much as Walpole saw it in 1760, a relic of times past, for the next twenty years or so, given that the 1st Earl and his wife focused their picture buying on Spencer House; the comparatively few portraits of family and friends that they acquired are all likely to have hung in the more private spaces of Althorp. Only after George became the 2nd Earl do significant changes seem to have been made to the hang in the gallery. Already, in 1782, in a letter to Georgiana, his mother reported: 'Lavinia has made some very good alterations in the hanging of the pictures' (though where is not specified) and, in general, 'has a great many pretty ideas and seems really fond of Althorp'.[87] By 1802, the mostly seventeenth-century pictures in the gallery had been joined not only by Copley's portrait of the 2nd Earl in his Garter robes, but also by Knapton's of his father and grandfather, suggesting a desire to continue the array of Spencers up to the present day. In placing the portraits by Reynolds of his sister and himself in the gallery, George could have been following the artist's intentions, but the various changes he made to the hang more certainly testify to his own interest in historical portraiture, which led him to collect sixteenth and seventeenth-century pictures of sitters with no connection to the Spencers.[88]

Nevertheless, in asking Reynolds to paint a pair of full-length portraits of their elder children, the 1st Earl and his wife undoubtedly intended to make a public statement about the Spencers in a way they had not done with any of the family portraits they had previously commissioned. Since the artist started work on the pictures in 1775, they functioned to commemorate Georgiana's recent marriage to the

Duke of Devonshire, but the commission also served to mark a turning point in George's life, since he left Harrow in that year. In 1776, when they were exhibited at the Academy, he was admitted to Trinity College, Cambridge. Like the portraits of Lady Spencer and William Poyntz, this pair of pictures of a brother and a sister thus accords with conventionally opposed gender roles, but they do so in such a way as to emphasise the personal qualities by means of which, it was hoped, the two young Spencers would add lustre to the family name. As well as celebrating her new status as a duchess, the portrait of Georgiana seeks to convey her celebrated beauty, a task all the more difficult given that it resided more in her personality than in her appearance. 'Without being handsome or having a single good feature in her face', her mother reportedly remarked, 'she is one of the most showy girls I ever saw.'[89] By contrast, her brother's portrait attests to his parents' pride in their son's serious, scholarly disposition, which had been encouraged by his tutor, the Orientalist scholar William Jones; George is shown with an open book, leaning on a low wall in a contemplative, even brooding attitude.[90] It was, however, above all her children's refined sensibility, their moral integrity, that mattered to Lady Spencer, who hoped that they would set an example to their peers and thereby help to reform society.

In this ambition, she was to be disappointed, at least so far as Georgiana and Harriet were concerned. As their lives became steadily more troubled, George at least lived up to her expectations, prompting his mother once to lament: 'What would not my daughters have been with husbands like him.'[91] In so far as the portraits by Reynolds give expression to Lady Spencer's high ambitions for her children as they reached adulthood, they would certainly have been intended to hang in a relatively public space at Althorp. It is even possible that she and her husband (who presumably shared her views, though the loss of his private papers makes it hard to tell) did contemplate rehanging the gallery in order to make room for them. However, the locations in which the portraits were actually placed demonstrate that they came to be endowed with a more private significance, particularly Georgiana's, which must have served as an increasingly poignant reminder to Lady Spencer of her favourite daughter in her heyday (especially after the latter's death in 1806). Furthermore, the parkland setting against which Reynolds painted both of the young Spencers would have resonated with their mother's preference for country life. According to Lord Bristol, 'Nothing could tempt Lady Spencer to London but the restlessness of her poor husband and I heard her say before him she hated even the sight of Town.'[92] Her choice of residence after Lord Spencer's death does suggest that, during her later years at least, she did prefer a life of comparative retirement. A modest establishment, without 'the appearance of a house of nobility', it 'looked intirely into the country, incommoded by the town'; there, she concerned herself particularly with botany.[93] The portraits at Holywell included not only Reynolds's of George, but also Gainsborough's of William Poyntz, the most obviously rural of those that belonged to her.

Although a far less well-known figure than her daughter and namesake, Lady Spencer has as much claim to historical importance. Whereas the Duchess of Devonshire came to exemplify in the public eye the vices for which both conservative and radical critics increasingly attacked the aristocracy, the elder Georgiana was in the vanguard of those who sought a new moral basis for oligarchic rule, one in which domestic virtue and charitable endeavour went hand in hand.[94] Just as her electioneering served to uphold the Spencer family's interests in their local power bases, so her self-fashioning as an exemplary patrician worked to similar effect in the larger political context of the public sphere.[95] As I have argued, her commitment to sensibility and benevolence helped to shape the portraits that she and her husband commissioned of members of their family, but unlike the portrait that their eldest daughter commissioned of herself in the role of a loving mother, the Spencer family portraits were not primarily intended to impress the image of their virtues on the public. Rather than being conceived with public exhibition in mind, the portraits of Lady Spencer, her husband, her brother and her children were intended to hang on the walls of the rooms at Althorp (even if several of the pictures then spent the better part of three decades at Holywell). There they functioned to reinforce affective bonds between them and to embody their own aspirations (or, at any rate, hers for them). In this respect, she was followed by her son and his wife, who proved fiercely loyal patrons of Reynolds, so much so that, when the 2nd Earl's college asked for a portrait of him in 1787, Lavinia declared: 'I can't bear the idea of anybody having a picture by Sir Joshua of you beside myself, and I think a daub by Gainsborough would do full well as another for them.'[96] In fact, the 1776 portrait is the only one Reynolds did of George, but the artist did paint several portraits of Lavinia and her eldest son, John Charles, including a notably tender one of mother and child.[97] This painting follows the precedent set by the portrait of the previous Lady

Spencer and her eldest child, though with the difference, of course, that the child in the earlier work was not the son and heir, but a favourite daughter. The dazzling but unhappy future that awaited that daughter testifies to the limited nature of the challenge to traditional dynastic values represented by her mother.

Notes

I would like to thank everyone at Althorp who provided assistance during my research for this essay, especially Ruth Coverdale, Caroline Dwyer, Marion Scott and Sophie Slater.

1 Kate Retford, *The Art of Domestic Life: Family Portraiture in Eighteenth-century England* (New Haven and London: Yale University Press for the Paul Mellon Centre for Studies in British Art, 2006), pp. 196–203; Michael Rosenthal, 'Public Reputation and Image Control in Late Eighteenth-Century Britain', *Visual Culture in Britain*, 7:2 (Winter, 2006), 79–86. See also, more generally, Stella Tillyard, 'Paths of Glory: Fame and the Public in Eighteenth-Century London', in Martin Postle (ed.), *Joshua Reynolds: The Creation of Celebrity* (London: Tate Publishing, 2005), pp. 61–9 and Gill Perry's essay in this book.

2 For her iconography (excluding prints), see John Ingamells, *The National Portrait Gallery: Mid Georgian 1760–1790* (London: National Portrait Gallery, 2004).

3 Kenneth Garlick, 'A Catalogue of the Pictures at Althorp', *Walpole Society*, 45 (1974–76), henceforward known as CPA.

4 For this assumption, see, for example, Joseph Friedman, *Spencer House: Chronicle of a Great London Mansion* (London: Zwemmer, 1993), p. 41. For a case comparable to that of the Spencers, see Kate Retford, 'Patrilineal Portraiture? Gender and Genealogy in the Eighteenth-Century English Country House', in John Styles and Amanda Vickery (eds), *Gender, Taste and Material Culture in Britain and North America, 1700–1830* (New Haven and London: Yale Center for British Art 2006), pp. 322–3.

5 Frances Harris, *A Passion for Government: The Life of Sarah, Duchess of Marlborough* (Oxford: Clarendon Press, 1991), pp. 285–6, 309, 322, 346–7, 349.

6 Friedman, *Spencer House*, pp. 36–7; Charles Spencer, *The Spencer Family* (London: Viking, 1999), pp. 118–19.

7 Elaine Chalus, *Elite Women in English Political Life c. 1754–90* (Oxford: Oxford University Press, 2005), pp. 23–4, 192, 226. See also Judith S. Lewis, *Sacred to Female Patriotism: Gender, Class and Politics in Late Georgian Britain* (New York and London: Routledge, 2003), pp. 47, 52, 134, 144. Both authors emphasise that Georgiana's electioneering in Westminster was, in fact, far less unorthodox than Fox's political enemies made out.

8 Friedman, *Spencer House*, pp. 41–4, 142, 154.

9 The Duchess also rebuilt her family home; see Frances Harris, 'Holywell House, St Albans: An Early Work by William Talman?', *Architectural History*,

28 (1985), 32–9. For a list of pictures at Wimbledon in 1751, see Horace Walpole, 'Journals of Visits to Country Seats', *Walpole Society*, 23 (1927–28), 13–15.

10 Picture Lists of 1746 and 1750, in CPA, pp. 96–8 and pp. 113–15 (for pictures in the gallery). See also Rosalys Coope, 'The "Long Gallery": Its Origins, Development, Use and Decoration', *Architectural History*, 29 (1986), 53; Christopher Hussey, *English Country Houses: Mid Georgian 1760–1800* (London: Antique Collectors' Club, 1956), pp. 204–5.

11 Horace Walpole, *Correspondence*, ed. W.S Lewis, 48 vols (New Haven and London: Yale University Press, 1937–83), IX, p. 299 (1 September 1760). See also Walpole, 'Visits', 31–3.

12 Althorp papers, British Library, London (henceforward AP BL) 75691 (1755; letter dated in pencil in another hand).

13 AP BL 75691.

14 See Marcia Pointon, '"Surrounded with Brilliants": Miniature Portraits in Eighteenth-Century England', *Art Bulletin*, 83:1 (March 2001), 53–4, 63–5, 68.

15 Both were at Althorp, but have since been sold; see Marcel Roethlisberger and Renée Loche, *Liotard: catalogue, sources et correspondance*, 2 vols. (Doornspijk: Davaco, 2008), pp. 440–1, cat. nos. 263 and 264. On Spencer's courtship, see Mary Delany, *The Autobiography and Correspondence of Mary Granville, Mrs Delany*, ed. Lady Llanover, 3 vols (London: Richard Bentley, 1861), III, p. 305 (18 November 1754) and p. 319 (15 January 1755); Friedman, *Spencer House*, pp. 56–7.

16 AP BL 75691 (1754). This is the probable date.

17 Friedman, *Spencer House*, pp. 38–43, 54–5.

18 Colin Duckworth, 'Georgiana Spencer in France: or The Dangers of Reading Rousseau', *Eighteenth-Century Life*, 7:3 (Spring, 1982), 86–8.

19 She must have met Hannah More soon after the latter arrived in London in 1774, probably through her friend, David Garrick, who promoted More's career as a playwright, though the first reference to the Spencers in the latter's correspondence appears in a letter of 1776; see William Roberts, *Memoirs of the Life and Correspondance of Hannah More*, 2nd edn, 4 vols (London: R.B. Seeley and W. Burnside, 1834), I, p. 54. Anne Stott, *Hannah More: The First Victorian* (Oxford: Oxford University Press, 2004), pp. 40, 44–5, 65, 73.

20 I am grateful to Elizabeth McKellar for suggesting the parallel.

21 For Knapton's portrait of the Hon. John Spencer, see below. Full-length portraits of Lady Georgina Spencer, later Countess Cowper, were painted by both John Vanderbank and John Robinson, see CPA, p. 72, cat. no. 555 and p. 84, cat. no. 650. It is probably the former that Walpole mistakenly refers to as 'Countess Cowper ... by Knapton in a Spanish dress', see Walpole, 'Visits', 21–2.

22 David Mannings, *Sir Joshua Reynolds: A Complete Catalogue of his Paintings*, 2 vols (New Haven and London: Yale University Press for the Paul Mellon Centre for Studies in British Art, 2000), I, pp. 427–8, cat. no. 1677. Mrs Spencer's name in Reynolds's pocket book for 9 June 1757 can't refer to a visit by her to the artist, as Mannings assumes, since she had given birth to Georgiana only two days previously.

23 AP BL 75691 (30 September 1758).

24 For a report of the 'joy and magnificence' that attended George's birth, see Spencer, *The Spencer Family*, p. 111. See also Ingrid Tague, 'Aristocratic Women and Ideas of Family in the Early Eighteenth Century', in Helen Berry and Elizabeth A. Foyster (eds), *The Family in Early Modern England* (Cambridge: Cambridge University Press, 2007), pp. 196–8.

25 CPA, p. 40, cat. no. 312. For Lady Sunderland's concern about her children, see Ingrid H. Tague, *Women of Quality: Accepting and Contesting Ideals of Femininity in England, 1690–1760* (Woodbridge: The Boydell Press, 2002), pp. 85–6. Significantly, she was also painted by Kneller with her eldest son; see CPA, p. 45, cat. no. 352 and, for a reproduction, Georgina Battiscombe, *The Spencers of Althorp* (London: Constable, 1984), p. 64.

26 Ellis Waterhouse, *Painting in Britain 1530 to 1790*, 4th edn (Harmondsworth: Penguin Books, 1978), p. 225.

27 See Retford, *The Art of Domestic Life*, pp. 83–114.

28 Friedman, *Spencer House*, pp. 41–2. On the use made of the *Madonna della Sedia* as a model for portraits of mothers with their children, see Retford, *The Art of Domestic Life*, pp. 92–3.

29 Quoted in Friedman, *Spencer House*, p. 55. See also CPA, p. 4, cat. no. 21; Edgar Peters Bowron and Peter Björn Kerber, *Pompeo Batoni: Prince of Painters in Eighteenth-Century Rome* (New Haven and London: Yale University Press, 2007), pp. 70–1; Sabrina Norlander Eliasson, *Portraiture and Social Identity in Eighteenth-Century Rome* (Manchester: Manchester University Press, 2009), p. 128. (Eliasson fails to consider that the portrait of Lady Spencer does have close parallels in Batoni's male Grand Tour portraits, even if the setting is less elaborate than that of his grandest portraits of this kind.)

30 1802 Picture List, in CPA, p. 119 (as by 'Pompeus'); E.K. Waterhouse, 'The Exhibition of Portraits from Althorp at Messrs. Agnews', *Burlington Magazine*, 89:528 (March 1947), 77. On Lady Spencer as a player of the viola da gamba, an instrument often associated with sensibility, see BL AP 75691 (letter of 7 May 1762); Peter Holman, *Life after Death: The Viola da Gamba in Britain from Purcell to Dolmetsch* (Woodbridge: The Boydell Press, 2010), pp. 235, 247–8, 254.

31 My argument here is indebted to David Solkin, 'Great Portraits or Great Men? Reynolds, Male Portraiture, and the Power of Art', *Oxford Art Journal*, 9:2 (1986), 42–9.

32 *Delany Autobiography*, III, p. 340 (3 March 1755). The more sceptical view of Lord Lansdowne is quoted in Battiscombe, *The Spencers of Althorp*, p. 79.

33 Earl of Bristol, quoted in Spencer, *The Spencer Family*, p. 129; Lord Spencer omits a crucial phrase in this passage, which I have reinserted on the basis of a briefer quotation from the same letter in Friedman, *Spencer House*, p. 55. I have been unable to trace the original source. I assume the writer was the 4th Earl, the father of Georgiana's friend (and her husband the Duke of Devonshire's mistress), Lady Elizabeth Foster, who inherited the title in 1779.

34 Walpole, *Correspondence*, XXXV, p. 357 (9 September 1780).

35 CPA, p. 31, cat. no. 228. Philip Woodfine, 'Poyntz, Stephen (*bap.* 1685,

d. 1750)', *Oxford Dictionary of National Biography*, Oxford University Press, 2004; www.oxforddnb.com/view/article/22694, accessed 2 September 2012.

36 CPA, p. 42, cat. no. 331.

37 See Michael Rosenthal, *The Art of Thomas Gainsborough* (New Haven and London: Yale University Press for the Paul Mellon Centre for Studies in British Art, 1999), pp. 46, 234; Martin Myrone and Michael Rosenthal (eds), *Gainsborough* (London: Tate Publishing, 2002), p. 96, cat. no. 37. Lord Spencer's own favourite dog, Mouton, was painted by George Stubbs; see CPA, p. 81, cat. no. 623; Friedman, *Spencer House*, p. 39.

38 Arthur Cash, *Sterne: The Later Years* (London: Methuen, 1986), pp. 81–2, 108–9, 226–7; Ian Campbell Ross, *Laurence Sterne: A Life* (Oxford: Oxford University Press, 2001), pp. 268–9; Friedman, *Spencer House*, pp. 40, 55, 200.

39 Retford, *The Art of Domestic Life*, pp. 19–47. For the archetypally masculine character of the 'picture with spaniel and gun', see Joseph Addison, *The Spectator*, as quoted in Alison Conway, *Private Interests: Women, Portraiture and the Visual Culture of the English Novel, 1709–1791* (Toronto and London: University of Toronto Press, 2001), p. 9.

40 CPA, p. 31, cat. no. 230; Lady Spencer did not actually ride to hounds, but accompanied the hunt in a cabriolet; see Battiscombe, *The Spencers of Althorp*, pp. 77–9.

41 Spencer, *The Spencer Family*, p. 128; Edward Wedlake Brayley, *The Beauties of England and Wales. Vol. 7, Hertfordshire, Huntingdonshire and Kent* (London: Vernor and Hood, 1808), p. 108.

42 The only other known portraits of him are small in scale, like the miniature by Liotard. Another is mentioned in Lady Spencer's correspondence with her friend Caroline Howe; described both as 'Hamilton's little picture' and as a drawing, it was presumably a small oval portrait in pastel by Hugh Douglas Hamilton. Both it and the Gainsborough portrait were used by Joseph Nollekens as a source for the likeness of the Earl on the monument in Great Brington church near Althorp where he is buried; see BL AP 75631, letters dated 15, 17, 20 and 21 April 1787. I am grateful to Martin Price for drawing my attention to these references. The portrait by Hamilton (now untraced) may have been the source for the engraved likeness of the Earl now in the National Portrait Gallery (NPG D8044).

43 CPA, p. 31, cat. no. 229.

44 Susan Sloman, *Gainsborough in Bath* (New Haven and London: Yale University Press for the Paul Mellon Centre for Studies in British Art, 2002), pp. 41, 46, 69.

45 BL AP 75683 (letter of December 1756). The portrait of the 2nd Earl Harcourt (Nuneham's later title) by Benjamin Wilson is at Althorp; see CPA, p. 89, cat. no. 693.

46 Quoted, together with other comments, in Friedman, *Spencer House*, p. 38.

47 See Paul Langford, *Public Life and the Propertied Englishman, 1689–1796* (Oxford: Oxford University Press, 1991), pp. 510–81.

48 CPA, p. 14, cat. no. 101, and (for the 1802 picture list, which places it in the gallery), *ibid.*, p. 123. On the 2nd Earl's career of public service, see Malcolm Lester, 'Spencer, George John, second Earl Spencer (1758–1834)',

Oxford Dictionary of National Biography, Oxford University Press, 2004; www.oxforddnb.com/view/article/26125, accessed 2 September 2012.

49 CPA, p. 31, cat. no. 231. Her age is given as six in the earliest known document referring to the picture; see BL AP 78030: Catalogue of paintings at Althorp, compiled between 1821 and 1831, with notes in the hand of Lavinia, Countess Spencer, 1821–31.

50 Myrone and Rosenthal, *Gainsborough*, p. 188, cat. no. 97. See also Rosenthal, *The Art of Thomas Gainsborough*, p. 219.

51 Amanda Foreman, *Georgiana Duchess of Devonshire* (London: HarperCollins, 1998), p. 11.

52 CPA, p. 44, cat. no. 344.

53 On this pressure, see Joanne Bailey, 'Reassessing Parenting in Eighteenth-Century England', in Berry and Foyster, *The Family in Early Modern England*, pp. 209–32.

54 Harris, *A Passion for Government*, pp. 78, 81, 94, 97, 109; Foreman, *Georgiana*, pp. 18–19.

55 Moreover, the version of the Kneller portrait at Althorp is only a copy; see CPA, p. 43, cat. no. 338. It is said there to be a copy of a painting now at Blenheim, but the picture is described as lost in J. Douglas Stewart, *Sir Godfrey Kneller and the English Baroque Portrait* (Oxford: Oxford University Press, 1983), pp. 69, 95. His parents were utterly devastated by the death of their only son; see Harris, *A Passion for Government*, p. 98.

56 CPA, p. 66, cat. nos. 512–15, 517; Neil Jeffares, *Dictionary of Pastellists before 1800* (London: Unicorn Press, 2006), pp. 431, 433 (with illustrations); www.pastellists.com, accessed 28 May 2012. For Lady Spencer's response to Charlotte's birth, see AP BL 75691 (letter of 6 December 1765).

57 CPA, p. 66, cat. no. 516; Jeffares, *Dictionary of Pastellists*, pp. 433–4 (with illustration).

58 AP BL 75691 (letter of 26 November 1766).

59 Thomas Dibdin, *Supplement to the Biblioteca Spenceriana: or a descriptive catalogue of the books printed in the fifteenth century in the library of George John Earl Spencer* (London: W. Nicol, 1822), p. 240.

60 CPA, p. 43, cat. no. 333; Jeffares, *Dictionary of Pastellists*, p. 266 (with illustration). She left the pastel to her son in her will, so must have taken it with her when she married Lord Cowper in 1750.

61 Margery Morgan, 'Katherine Read: A Woman Painter in Romney's London', *Transactions of the Romney Society*, 4 (1999), 17.

62 Spencer, *The Spencer Family*, p. 119.

63 For a detailed study of Lady Spencer's charitable activities, see Donna T. Andrew, '*Noblesse oblige*: Female Charity in an Age of Sentiment', in John Brewer and Susan Staves (eds), *Early Modern Conceptions of Property* (London: Routledge, 1995), pp. 275–300.

64 Foreman, *Georgiana*, pp. 14, 149.

65 Letter from Kauffman dated 10 October 1766, quoted in Angelica Goodden, *Miss Angel: The Art and World of Angelica Kauffman* (London: Pimlico, 2005), pp. 82, 139; Angela Rosenthal, *Angelica Kauffman: Art and Sensibility* (New Haven and London: Yale University Press, 2006), p. 99.

66 See Heidi Strobel, 'Royal "Matronage" of Women Artists in the Late Eighteenth Century', *Women's Art Journal*, 26:2 (2005–6), 3–4.
67 Friedman, *Spencer House*, pp. 119, 148–9.
68 Angela Rosenthal, 'Kauffman and Portraiture', in Wendy Wassyng Roworth (ed.), *Angelica Kauffman: A Continental Artist in Georgian England* (London: Reaktion Books 1992), p. 106. See also Rosenthal, *Angelica Kauffman*, p. 213.
69 Aileen Ribeiro, *The Art of Dress: Fashion in England and France 1750 to 1820* (New Haven and London: Yale University Press, 1995), pp. 223–4.
70 Samuel Richardson, *Clarissa, or the History of a Young Lady*, ed. Angus Ross (Harmondsworth: Penguin, 1985; first published 1747–48), p. 509. On Van Dyck dress in eighteenth-century portraiture, see Ribeiro, *The Art of Dress*, pp. 183–213; Deborah Cherry and Jennifer Harris, 'Eighteenth-Century Portraiture and the Seventeenth-Century Past: Gainsborough and Van Dyck', *Art History*, 5:3 (1982), 287–309; Conway, *Private Interests*, pp. 82–90.
71 Johann Wilhelm von Archenholz, *A Picture of England: containing a description of the laws, customs, and manners of England* (London: Edward Jeffery, 1789), p. 38.
72 Duckworth, 'Georgiana Spencer in France', 89–90.
73 AP BL 75691 (letter of 29 June 1761); Foreman, *Georgiana*, p. 74.
74 Philip Stewart and Jean Vaché (eds), *Collected Writings of Jean-Jacques Rousseau*, vol. 6: *Julie, or The New Héloïse* (London and Hanover: University Press of New England, 1987), p. 490.
75 AP BL 75691 (letter of 30 September 1758).
76 Her library at her death includes a 1762 edition of Rousseau's work; see 'Catalogue of Georgiana, Countess Spencer's library at Holywell House, St Albans', AP BL 78007.
77 Dibdin, *Supplement*, p. 240. Garlick mistakenly says it is included in the 1802 picture list, but, in fact, it is Kauffman's portrait of Lavinia's mother, Lady Lucan, that appears; see CPA, p. 42, cat. no. 328 and p. 119.
78 Harris, *A Passion for Government*, p. 82. AP BL 75691 (letter of 22 August 1759); letter of unknown source quoted in Spencer, *The Spencer Family*, p. 120.
79 John Heneage Jesse, *Memoirs of George Selwyn and his Contemporaries*, 4 vols (London: Richard Bentley, 1843–44), II, pp. 215–16. On this letter, see also Betty Rizzo, *Companions without Vows: Relationships among Eighteenth-Century British Women* (Athens, GA: University of Georgia Press, 1994), p. 373, note 29.
80 AP BL 75691 (letter of 9 June 1772); CPA, p. 70, cat. no. 541; Mannings, *Sir Joshua Reynolds*, p. 427, cat. no. 1677. This portrait shows Lady Spencer in 'Persian' dress, leaning her head against her hand in the traditional pose of melancholy, in such a way as to characterise her as a high-minded Sibyl.
81 CPA, pp. 68–9, cat. no. 529; Mannings, *Reynolds*, I, pp. 426–7, cat. no. 1675. On the portrait of Georgiana by Gainsborough, which was painted for Lady Spencer and exhibited at the Royal Academy in 1783, see John Hayes, *National Gallery of Art: British Paintings of the Sixteenth through Nineteenth Centuries* (Washington and Cambridge: Cambridge University Press, 1992), pp. 95–7.

82 Dibdin, *Supplement*, pp. 243, 266–8; Nicholas Penny (ed.), *Reynolds* (London: Tate Publishing, 1985), p. 273, cat. no. 102.
83 See Ribeiro, *The Art of Dress*, pp. 205–7.
84 For further exploration of the parallels between Reynolds's and Kauffman's likenesses of the Duchess, see Mark Hallet, *Sir Joshua Reynolds: Portraiture in Action* (Yale University Press, forthcoming).
85 CPA, p. 69, cat. no. 531; Mannings, *Reynolds*, I, p. 126, no. 336; Dibdin, *Supplement*, pp. 249–50.
86 Horace Walpole, *Anecdotes of painting in England; with some account of the principal artists; and incidental notes on other arts; collected by the late Mr. George Vertue; and now digested and published from his original MSS*, 4 vols (Twickenham: Printed by Thomas Farmer at Strawberry Hill, 1762), III, p. 18.
87 Quoted in Spencer, *The Spencer Family*, p. 131.
88 Kenneth Garlick, 'The Earls Spencer, Althorp, England', in Douglas Cooper (ed.), *Great Family Collections* (London: Weidenfeld and Nicolson, 1965), p. 211.
89 See the detailed discussion of the painting in Robyn Asleson, *British Paintings at the Huntington* (New Haven: The Huntingdon Library, Art Collections, and Botanical Gardens in association with Yale University Press, 2001), pp. 336–41, cat. no. 73. Nobody seems ever to have traced Lady Spencer's remark about her daughter to a contemporary source; it is always quoted from William T. Whitley, *Artists and Their Friends in England, 1700–1799*, 2 vols (London and Boston: The Medici Society, 1928), II, p. 397.
90 See Spencer, *The Spencer Family*, pp. 155–6, 171.
91 Foreman, *Georgiana*, p. 276.
92 Quoted in Spencer, *The Spencer Family*, p. 120.
93 Samuel Egerton Brydges and Stebbing Shaw (eds), *The Topographer for the Year 1789, containing a variety of original articles, illustrative of the local history and antiquities of England*, 4 vols (London: Robson and Clarke and J. Walker, 1789–91), I, p. 393. See also Brayley, *The Beauties of England and Wales*, Vol. 7, p. 108. During this period, Lady Spencer also found a substitute daughter in her young companion, Elizabeth Preedy; see Rizzo, *Companions Without Vows*, pp. 255–65.
94 For Hannah More's disapproval of the Duchess, see Stott, *Hannah More*, pp. 64–5. On these issues more broadly, see Clarissa Campbell Orr, 'Countesses and Courtesans', *History Workshop Journal*, 61 (2006), 278–92.
95 For an assessment of her historical importance, one which, however, characterises her too simply as 'middle class', see Langford, *Public Life*, pp. 571–3, 575.
96 Letter of 24 May 1787, quoted in E.K Waterhouse, *Reynolds* (London: Kegan Paul, 1941), p. 17.
97 CPA, pp. 68–9, cat. nos. 525, 528 and 530; Asleson, *Paintings at the Huntington*, cat. no. 81. 382–7; Mannings, *Reynolds*, I, pp. 428–9, cat. nos. 1681–4.

III

Imperial designs

7

Commemorating Captain Cook in the country estate

Harriet Guest

Cook and the American crisis

James Cook died at Kealakekua Bay, Hawaii, on 14 February 1779. Rumours of a possible mishap circulated in Britain over the late summer and autumn of that year, but it was not till early January 1780 that the London press reported that confirmation of his death had been received by the Admiralty. In the following weeks and months, as this news was chewed over and digested, the press was rather more concerned with the progress of the transatlantic war with the American colonies and their European allies; with events which seemed to take place not just in a different ocean, but on a different timescale. Speculative and increasingly detailed commentary on Cook's death appeared in paragraphs juxtaposed in an apparently fortuitous or casual manner with reports of naval events which seemed of more pressing significance, and though the connection between Britain's imperial adventures in the Pacific and those across the Atlantic was not entirely ignored, Cook's fate was usually treated as a discrete narrative apparently linked only by the accident of simultaneity.

An article from the *Morning Chronicle*, published within about a week of the confirmation of Cook's death, gives a flavour of how the coincidence of the skirmish in the Pacific and war in the Atlantic was handled. It carried paragraphs which reflected that while the loss of Cook, with four of his men, was regrettable, it was hardly surprising.

Cook, the journalist pointed out, might well have appeared to the islanders as 'an invader, a pirate' whom it was their duty to attack, just as, say, the inhabitants of fifteenth-century Plymouth had been justified in resisting the French raiders who frequently menaced them from the Channel, or the ancient Britons would have been in repulsing 'any Roman Captain Cook'. He concluded: 'Put the Spanish massacre into the other scale; nay, put Captain Cook's own necessary (I know not what to call them) into the other scale, to which self-defence obliged him – Will they not weigh more than five men?'[1] The acts of violence carried out by Cook and his men towards the islanders were to the journalist indescribable – 'I know not what to call them' – but he could begin to come to terms with them and with the reaction they provoked by recontextualising the scene, transforming its position in time and space.[2] Having played around with history, geography and national identity in comparing the Hawaiians to late medieval Devonians, as well as to ancient Britons, the article seems to have sealed off Cook's fate in a pre-modern era which knew nothing of the transatlantic war.

But the journalist also hinted that this containment was not secure or impermeable. He teased his readers with the suggestion that it was the current war he had in mind rather than French and Spanish invaders of the fifteenth and sixteenth centuries, though this was not a suggestion he cared to spell out or make good. Throughout much of the previous year, south coast ports had been on the alert, looking out for Spanish and French invasion fleets. The paragraphs of the article in which the discussion of Cook appeared have more continuity in their style and in their focus on maritime news than those short disconnected comments that made up so much newspaper gossip and comment of the period; and the paragraphs immediately preceding those on Cook discussed the demolition of part of the Spanish battery and 'dreadful slaughter' of its defenders by the British garrison besieged at Gibraltar. The journalist seemed almost to invite his patriotic readers to identify their position on the one hand with that of the Hawaiians as islanders threatened with invasion, as well as with Cook on the other.

News of Cook's death arrived in Britain as an almost completely de-contextualised event. Newspaper accounts were confused about where and why he had died, and even if they had been confident about whether he had met his end in Hawaii or Kamchatka (on the coast of north-eastern Russia) these were remote and exotic locations with few if any clear associations. The immediate context in which the news appeared, or in which Cook was memorialised, shaped the significance of his death a good deal more urgently and distinctively than could cloudy apprehensions of distant places.[3] In this essay I will explore how representations of his death move implicitly towards enmeshing its narrative into the dominant and consuming narrative on the war, and yet hesitate, hold back from indicating more than an accidental relation between the two. This ambiguous contextual relation gives an indication of the nature of Britain's vision of global empire in the period, and I claim that this is important to an understanding of the monuments to Cook that did appear at the time of his death. I will focus on the monuments constructed at Stowe and the Vache, and argue that the situation of the monument to Cook at Stowe in particular suggests that he was understood primarily as an antitype or even an antidote to the imperial vision that had gone so badly wrong in America, and that it was this idea of him, alongside the waning political status of his most powerful patrons, that resulted in the absence of any grand public memorial to his achievements.

George Carter's national heroes

The shaping role of the transatlantic and European conflict on the commemoration of Cook, and yet the tenuous and indirect nature of the links between the two sets of events, are suggested by two of the earliest representations of his death. These were George Carter's painting of the death scene (plate 14), and Anna Seward's *Elegy on Captain Cook*, in print in April 1780 – the second of these I have already written about quite extensively elsewhere, and will comment on quite briefly here.[4] Carter implied that he had completed his ambitiously large image of the *Death of Captain James Cook* by March 1781, when he put forward proposals to publish by subscription a print after the painting, though no print was to appear till January 1784.[5] Seward and Carter both made names for themselves in the 1780s in those genres, so characteristic of the period of the American War, appropriate to the expression of public grief and, for both, work on Cook was important to their reputations, and resonated with the representation of the war. Carter's *Cook* was the fourth in his series of images of national heroes, which he began with his print of the death of Captain George Farmer, published in October 1780 (figure 37), and continued with representations of the *Immortality of Garrick* (1783) and the *Death of Sidney* (1782). His major painting of the *Siege of Gibraltar* (1784), which was the centrepiece of his one-man show in Pall Mall in April 1785, was the culmination of

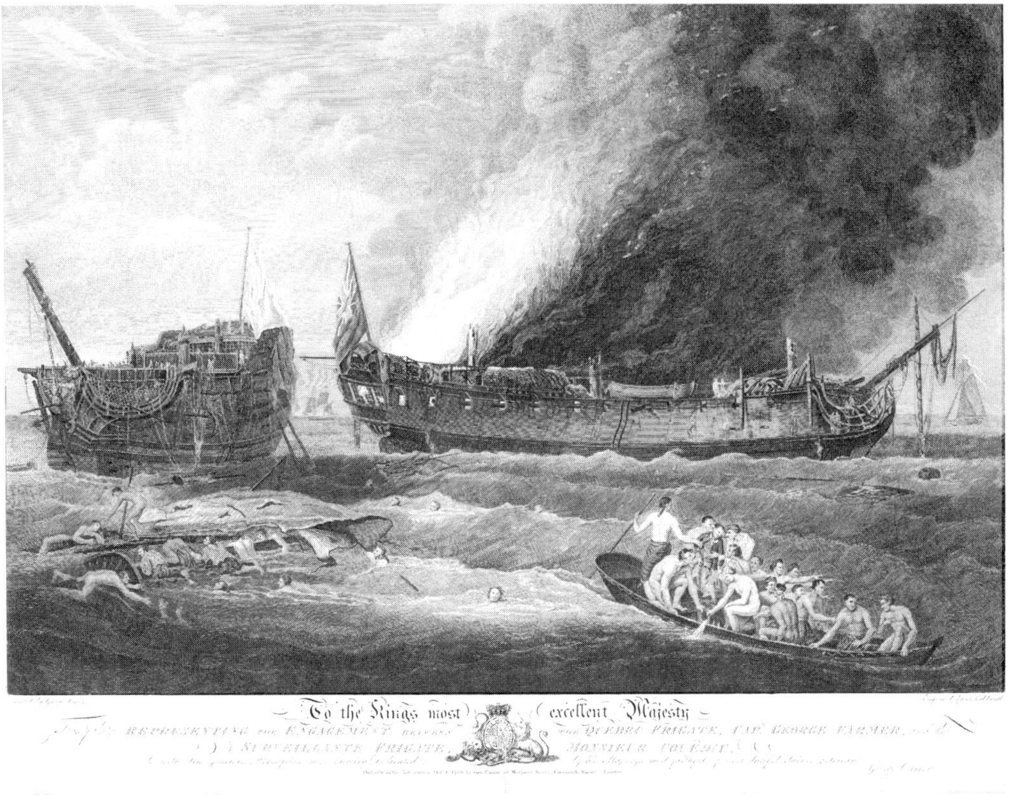

Figure 37
J. Caldwell after George Carter, *The plate Representing the Engagement between the Quebec Frigate, Capn George Farmer, and the Surveillante Frigate, Monsieur Coëdic* (London: G. Carter, 1 October 1780).

this patriotic theme in his work, but, as far as I know, it did not result in a print.[6] The siege painting celebrated the victory of General George Augustus Eliott, the Governor of Gibraltar, and later Baron Heathfield, who is shown receiving news of the destruction of the French and Spanish floating batteries in September 1782, and whose heroism and humanity were also celebrated by Seward in her *Ode on General Eliott's return from Gibraltar* (1787). The painting belongs to that characteristic genre of the period which attempted to combine history painting with multiple portraiture, and thus to endow its figures with both individual specificity and the capacity to represent something more universal or at least national. A similar tension is apparent in the topographical specificity of both Carter's and Seward's representations of Cook: these are records of an individual fate, and a particular event, but they are also about what or whom the nation chooses to revere in a time of war, and about the nation's capacity to mourn. In this work images of the war and of Cook keep pace with one another, each lending the other depth and significance.

Seward established her claim to express the grief of the nation with her *Elegy on Captain Cook*, which, as a reviewer commented in July 1780, had 'a claim to higher praise than can be be derived from mere literary fame', as it revealed the 'spirit of benevolence which could prompt the Authoress to lament and celebrate a person she never saw, or knew nothing of, except from those useful and commendable endeavours exerted by him in the service of his country'.[7] It established her praise-worthy attachment to that service, as well as her capacity to give voice and form to the country's loss. With her *Monody on Major André* (1781), Seward consolidated her place as the muse of the nation's grief, and confirmed that the melancholy lamentations in which she specialised embraced the public response to the American conflict. Carter similarly established the transatlantic war as the motif or centre of gravity for his constellation of national heroes. The first of his prints, the *Death of Farmer*, as it was usually titled in advertisements, represented a famous encounter between French and British frigates off Ushant in October 1779. The gallant Captain Farmer is shown remaining with his ship, the *Quebec*, and refusing to strike its colours, though it was about to explode. It had been dismasted by the superior forces of the French frigate *Surveillante*, also shown as a dismasted hulk.[8] Farmer's heroic action was widely celebrated and very publicly rewarded – his eldest son was made a baronet and his wife and nine children all received pensions – in hopes that his example would raise 'the drooping Spirits of every true Englishman'. The *St James's Chronicle* conjured its readers fiercely, 'May all our Farmers become Sailors, and may every British Tar prove himself a Farmer.'[9] He was an exemplary hero of the present moment, much as was Seward's Major André, and gave a contemporary immediacy to the theme of self-sacrifice in Carter's series.

Carter was not the only artist and publisher to rush a representation of Farmer's death into print. His image competed with that by John Boydell after the marine artist Richard Paton, and both advertised their prints as suitable pendants to Woollett's engraving after Benjamin West's *Death of Wolfe*, which Boydell had published in 1776 (figure 38). Boydell's decision to commission a fresh etching of the death of Wolfe so soon after the onset of the American War could obviously be seen as an attempt to transpose the glory of the British victory in Quebec in 1759 to the present conflict, and Carter uses it to fold Farmer, and later Cook, within the mantle of Wolfe's masculine heroism, and the

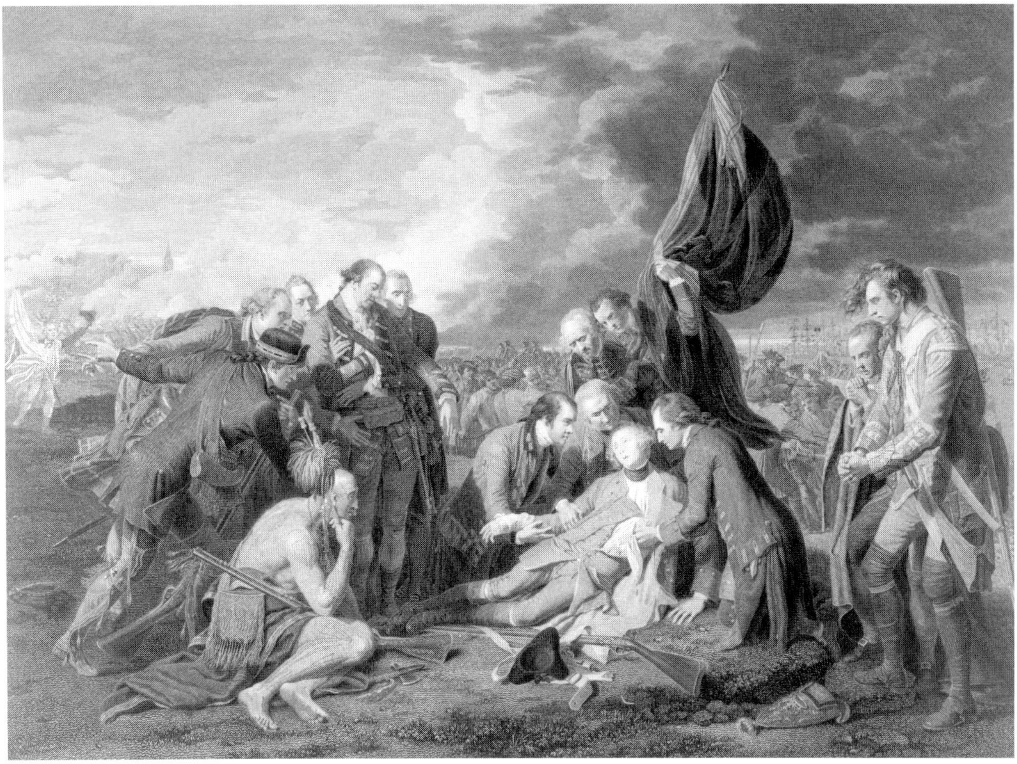

Figure 38 William Woollett after Benjamin West, *The Death of General Wolfe* (London: John Boydell, 1776).

imperial project that the Quebec campaign had reinforced.[10] Carter's print of Farmer was published some months before Boydell's, but re-advertised after the latter appeared, with the pointed claim that it was 'with deference, submitted as a proper companion' to the death of Wolfe, and a reminder that 'This Print cannot be had at Mr. Boydell's.'[11] His subsequent prints of Sidney, Garrick and Cook were all advertised for subscription for some time before they appeared – Garrick and Cook in particular were advertised for several years – and the advertisements stressed that the plates were all of a size. The proposal to publish the *Death of Cook* followed the advertisement for the *Death of Farmer* in noting that 'Mr. Carter has painted it with a view to give a proper companion' to Wolfe.[12]

The *Death of Farmer* seems an appropriate pendant for Wolfe because it revisits scenes of conflict with the French about North America, but the only obvious reason to pair the two prints is thematic, whereas the *Death of Cook* echoes that of Wolfe in its composition as well as in its transposed imperial theme: the advertisement points out that the figures are of an appropriately complementary size, and the disposition of the figures is similar in both prints. The figure of the sailor in the shallow water pushing out the boat picks up and reverses the posture of Wolfe; the crouching islander to the right of the Carter's print has some similarity to West's native American, and the group of officers directly above the seated Indian are reflected in the composition of the group made up by Cook and his two assailants. Wolfe, of course, is reclining in a Christ-like pose, whereas Cook, upright, and threatening a hostile islander with the butt of his musket, might seem contrastingly active and aggressive. But to contemporary audiences this image would more probably have confirmed Cook's status as a figure for the benevolence of Britain's imperial ambitions. As David Samwell, the voyage surgeon, was to explain in his influential account of events at Hawaii, when an islander had threatened Cook with his spear, the captain, 'being still unwilling to take away his life, instead of firing with ball, knocked him down with his musket'.[13]

It was an enormously important aspect of Cook's reputation that he was famed for his reluctance to take lives, and indeed many of the accounts of the fateful return to Kealakekua Bay dwell on the possibility that the captain was the victim of his own humanity. John Webber's print of the scene, for example, shows Cook turning his back on the islanders to order the men in the boats to stop firing, focusing on the moment that led Captain King to remark in the official account of the voyage that it was 'not improbable, that his humanity, on this occasion, proved fatal to him'.[14] Seward's *Elegy on Cook* and *Monody on Major André*, as well as her later *Ode on General Eliott* praise the sentimental humanity of these heroes as a national trait, and Carter's patriotic memorials may attempt something similar, affording their viewers the pleasures of nostalgic melancholy by wrapping contemporary heroes in the glories of the past and linking them with the softer cultural associations of Garrick and Sidney. Both Seward and Carter represent Cook as though his achievements and early death were continuous with a national and imperial narrative of manly heroism, of ambition and its price. This is a narrative that seems big and bold enough barely to be troubled by, for example, Cook's social origins as the son of a day labourer, or the violence and confusion surrounding his death at Kealakekua Bay.

The imperial project

If Cook posthumously becomes the embodiment of an idea of the British imperial project as dedicated to ideals of enlightened humanity, as various people (including myself) have argued over the last decade or so, then it may seem puzzling that he was not honoured for this more publicly and explicitly. John André, Anna Seward's next elegiac subject, had a monument in Westminster Abbey by the autumn of 1782, designed by Robert Adam and erected at the expense of the King, but Cook was not conspicuously honoured with a national monument, though the King was reported to have been moved to tears by the news of his death.[15] Seward mentioned in passing, in her *Elegy*, her assumption that a grateful Britannia, 'to his virtues just, / Twines the bright wreath, and rears th'immortal bust'.[16] Eight years later, Helen Maria Williams, in her elegiac ode, *The Morai* (1788), still imagines in the concluding lines that the nation will wish to raise 'immortal wreaths' to Cook's memory in the shape of 'the marble tomb, the trophied bust'.[17] But there were no public monuments to Cook till a memorial obelisk and sea-mark was erected on Easby Moor in North Yorkshire in 1827 – and that was built at the expense of the local lord of the manor, Robert Campion, rather than of the King or the nation.[18]

Figure 39 Monument to the Memory of Captain James Cook at The Vache, Chalfont St Giles, Bucks.

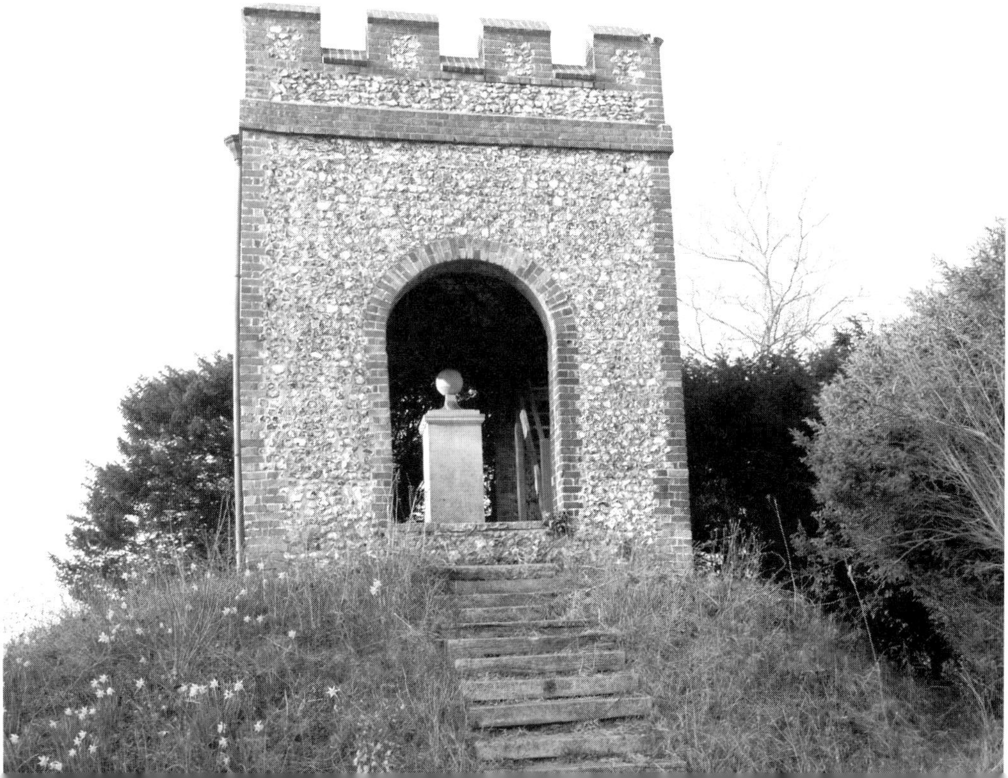

In 1781, almost immediately after Cook's death, his patron, Admiral Sir Hugh Palliser, built a private monument in the grounds of the Vache, his seat near Chalfont St Giles in Buckinghamshire (figure 39), and this was, for decades, the most substantial memorial to Cook in Britain – indeed, Andrew C.F. David, writing in the online DNB, claims that though there are now many monuments to Cook across the world, this is still 'perhaps the most significant'.[19] It is an odd structure; a moated mound topped by a small fort resembling a Georgian hunting lodge, and protecting a heavily inscribed stone block or plinth, the English text of which concludes with the sentence: 'If public services merit public acknowledgements, if the man who adorned and raised the fame of his country is deserving of honours, then Captain *COOK* deserves to have a monument raised to his memory, by a generous and grateful nation.' The quotation from the Roman historian Valerius Maximus which follows underscores the point, reminding readers that honour is the most productive food of virtue.[20] Palliser's monument praises Cook's achievements, and its design defends or protects his memory, but it also functions as a milestone or waymark indicating a direction beyond itself. It gestures towards the Pacific, to what it enumerates as 'islands, people and productions of which we had no conception', and it reminds its viewers of the need for a further, public monument in Britain.[21] The long inscription, which has been attributed to Admiral John Forbes, was reprinted frequently in the introduction to various editions of the authorised account of the third voyage.[22] But in 1790 John Adams still found it necessary to lament in his collection of *Modern Voyages* that 'no plan has yet been formed for erecting a monument', although 'sound policy, as well as gratitude, requires a tribute of this kind'.[23]

(*opposite*) Figure 40 Thomas Banks, *Design for a National Monument to the Memory of Captain Cook*, 1781.

A *Design for a National Monument to the Memory of Captain Cook* had in fact been proposed by Thomas Banks, and included in the Royal Academy exhibition of 1780 (figure 40). The great navigator was represented by an elongated and heroic nude figure, draped over a globe. Above him, as in Seward's poem, Britannia 'twines the bright wreath' as a trophy on a memorial obelisk bearing his name, and below him putti representing Castor and Pollux point to Hawaii, and the most northern latitude to which he had sailed, on the globe. On the sarcophagus the scene of Cook's death is depicted in relief. Cook has fallen and is being attacked by islanders with clubs while one is in the act of stabbing him in the back with a spear. Despite his peril, Cook raises his hand apparently in an attempt to halt the firing of the marines in front of him. The only surviving evidence of Banks's

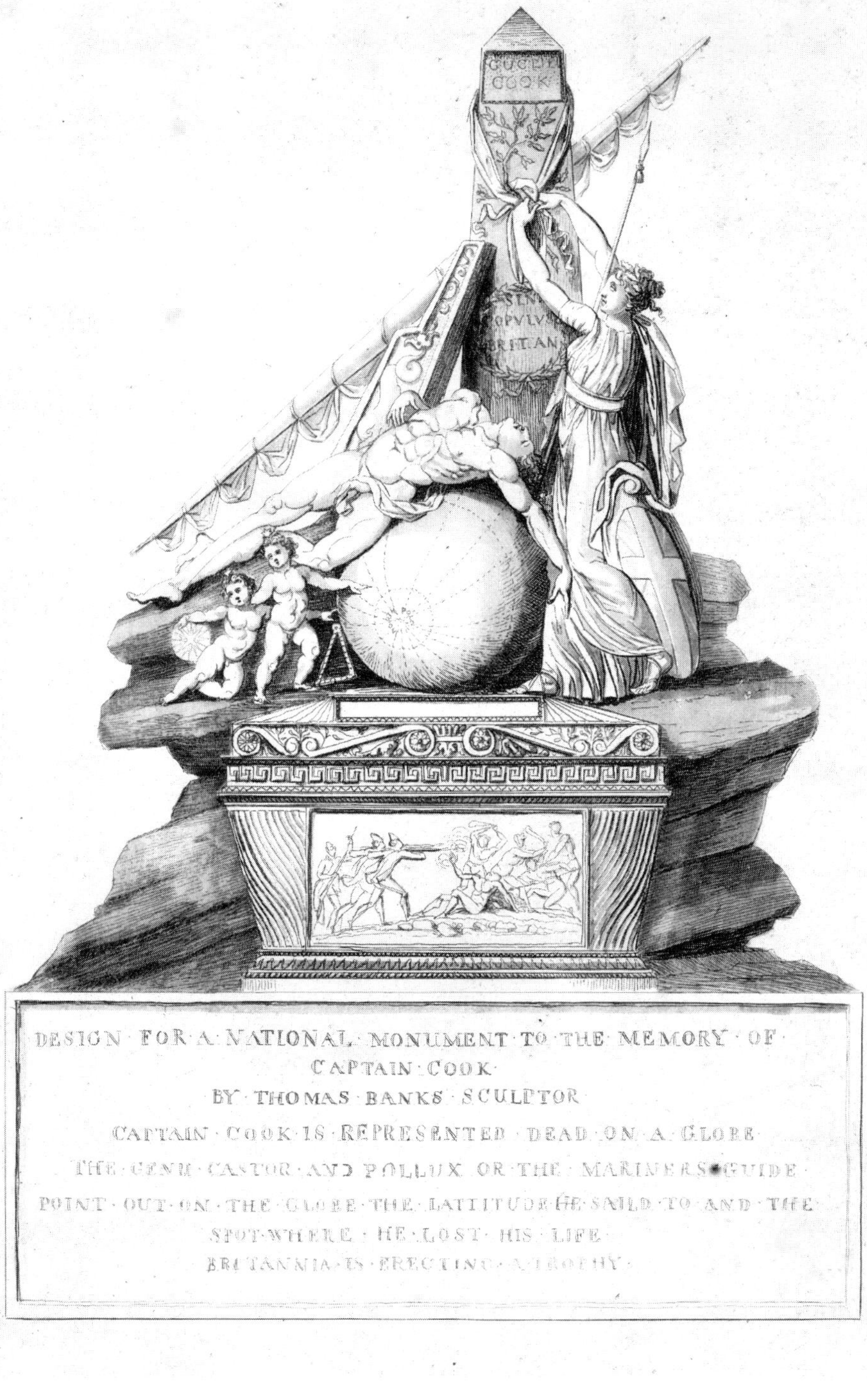
DESIGN · FOR · A · NATIONAL · MONUMENT · TO · THE · MEMORY · OF ·
CAPTAIN · COOK ·
BY · THOMAS · BANKS · SCULPTOR
CAPTAIN · COOK · IS · REPRESENTED · DEAD · ON · A · GLOBE ·
THE · GENII · CASTOR · AND · POLLUX · OR · THE · MARINERS · GUIDE ·
POINT · OUT · ON · THE · GLOBE · THE · LATTITUDE · HE · SAILD · TO · AND · THE ·
SPOT · WHERE · HE · LOST · HIS · LIFE ·
BRITANNIA · IS · ERECTING · A · TROPHY ·

design is his small etching, and the monument itself never advanced beyond the stage of a terracotta model, but the heroic proportions of the figures suggest that it might have had more in common with Zoffany's representation of Cook's death, painted in the late 1790s, than with most of the paintings produced in the 1780s (see plate 15). While small images in books, such as the print after D.P. Dodd from the published account of the third voyage, or the print reproduced in John Rickman's unauthorised voyage narrative, showed Cook fallen, of the larger prints and oil paintings from the 1780s only one – the lurid image exhibited by J.H. Ramberg at the Royal Academy in 1784 – did. Reviewers derided Ramberg's use of colour, and expressed mocking sympathy for Cook as the artist's victim: 'O-why-he! – poor Cook, what an unhappy fate, doomed to be murdered all over the world'.[24] But in Banks's proposed design, Cook is tragically defeated, both in heroic mode above the globe and with more pathos – or perhaps even bathos – in the relief below.

At the Academy exhibition, as Julius Bryant notes, the Cook model 'played a supporting role' to Banks's marble of *Caractacus before Claudius*.[25] Here the Welsh leader is shown addressing to the Emperor Claudius the defiant words 'If you want to rule the world, does it follow that everyone else welcomes enslavement?' – a comment the radical Banks may have intended to be addressed to the British king in ironic reference to the claims of the American colonists in 1777 (when Banks's relief was finished). The reference would have been strengthened by the performance at Covent Garden, a few months earlier, of William Mason's play, *Caractacus*, which may also have used the Welsh leader's defiance to express the Whig poet's sympathy for the American cause.[26] Banks's marble had been commissioned by George Grenville (later 3rd Earl Temple and Marquess of Buckingham) for the collection at Stowe, when he was in Rome as part of his post-university Grand Tour in 1774. At that stage, Grenville might have seen Caractacus's attitude of masculine defiance as appropriate to his own attempts to distance himself from his father's policy of opposing taxation on the American colonies – a policy that dogged his own reputation after his father's death.[27] But by 1777 Caractacus's speech had perhaps become rather too pointed for Grenville's cautious opposition to the American War, and he refused to pay the sculptor the price that had been agreed, treating Banks, as he commented bitterly, 'with too much Contempt both as an Artist & a Man'.[28] Grenville kept the sculpture, but Banks might have been cautious about soliciting his patronage again. The design for the

Cook monument might instead have been intended to catch the eye of his uncle, Richard Grenville, the 2nd Earl Temple.

There is a monument or tribute to Cook on an island in the gardens at Stowe – a large globe, bound with bronze strips signifying the latitude and longitude, on a pedestal bearing an unrecognisable portrait profile. It is clearly dated 1778, too early to commemorate his death, but if the date is accurate the monument would already have been in place when Banks produced his design. The globe and plinth had probably been commissioned by Richard Grenville, who took a keen interest in the expansion of Britain's empire, both as a landowner and as a patriot Whig. He had served as First Lord of the Admiralty briefly from 1756–57, making connections that allowed him to amass considerable wealth through trading in Navy and Victualling Bills, but his interest in Cook's achievements later in his life, after he had retired from politics to focus on developing his estate, probably had more to do with his extensive holdings in stocks and shares. His extensive redesigning of Stowe was built on his success as 'perhaps the ablest financier in Europe', manipulating investments in the East India and South Sea companies.[29] After being thrown from his chaise the Earl had died in September 1779. But before that Banks might have hoped that his ambitious design would appeal to the Earl because of his admiration for Cook's achievements. But the monument Richard Grenville had installed at Stowe is very different in character to the one Banks proposed, and appeals to a distinct vision of the nature of empire.

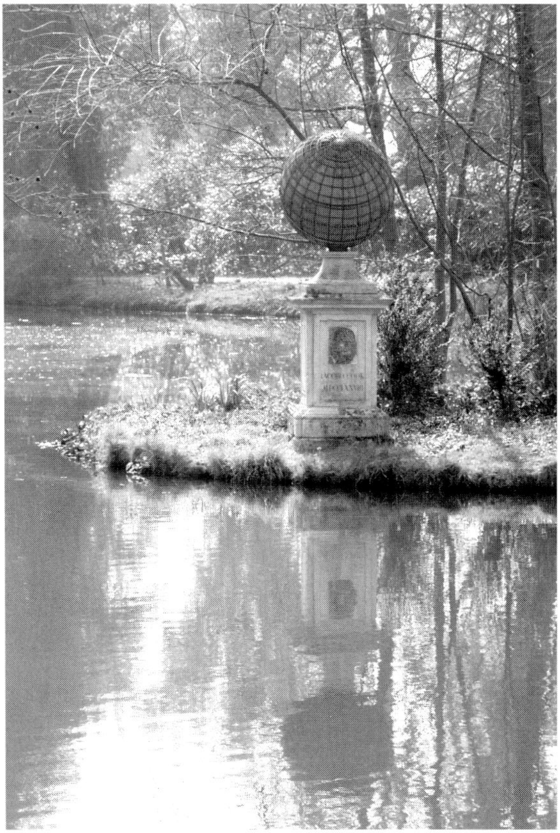

Figure 41 Monument to Captain Cook at Stowe.

Though the Cook monument at Stowe is dated 1778, no guidebook or tourist has been found who comments on its position there before 1788 (figure 41). It is tempting to speculate about the date on the monument, not in the vein of those historians who have read into its position and inscription a commentary on Cook's burial at sea, but as signalling an attempt to celebrate Cook the successful living navigator, rather than the slain victim of imperial ambition.[30] The monument is positioned so that the viewer, strolling along the bank of the river between the Grotto and the Temple of British Worthies, can glance from the globe up to the Grenville Column, which commemorates the death at sea of Captain Thomas Grenville, a scion of Lord Cobham's family who had died in action against the French in 1747. But the column stands considerably above the river, and though the tourist may be invited to see a relation between the two sailors, it is primarily one of contrast. There is no mistaking the more elevated social status of Grenville, as a member of the Temple family whose heroic martial deeds are proclaimed by the Muse of History surmounting his rostral pillar. As Patrick Eyres has pointed out, the 'naval column represents the patriotic union of the Grenville dynasty with the national interest'; it proudly celebrates Britain's maritime supremacy, and the role of the Grenville family in achieving that dominance over rival European powers.[31] The two monuments face away from each other, and in contrast to the Doric splendour of the naval column the monument to the explorer seems almost anti-heroic. It no more seems comparable to the column than it does to more distant monuments, such as General Wolfe's Obelisk, or the Temple of Concord and Victory, though the National Trust's guide to Stowe links the navigator's globe with these celebrations of the imperial triumphs of the Seven Years War.[32] Grenville's Column is visible from the temples of Ancient Virtue and of British Worthies, and from the house itself; it belongs in a coherent visual narrative of epic grandeur populated with large and prominent landmarks.[33] Cook's pedestal and globe in contrast seems unassuming, modestly turning away from association with grander constructions in a secluded landscape of retirement and reflection.

The character of the valley had been marked until the 1770s by the presiding Temple of Contemplation, and for the tourist its shade offered a pleasing respite from contemplation of the nobler theme of patriotic ambition; a spot where it could be conceded that 'there is no better Preservative of good Principles than a little Retirement now and then from the Glare of Life, a little Contemplation *de contemptu mundi*'.[34] This mood was confirmed by the construction of the Seasons fountain – a modest affair (a recycled marble chimneypiece) – before the visit of the Prince of Wales in 1805. The fountain was positioned close to the former site of the Temple so that the Cook monument, which faces it, is directly before the tourist who has turned to obey the lines from Thomson's *Spring* on the fountain:

> Here pause in Silence, while beneath the Shade
> Of solemn Oaks, that tuft the swelling Mounts,
> You pensive Listen to the Plaint of Rills,
> That Purling down their dewy Murmurs shake
> On the Sooth'd Ear.[35]

The lines are adapted from the frequently reprinted and cited passage in which Thomson's patron Lord Lyttelton wanders through Hagley Park, enjoying its shaded and retired spaces and the opportunity they offer to reflect on philosophy, history and poetry. The closest he comes to action in this retreat is to ponder patriotic projects to improve the country and 'from the venal Gulph / To raise her Virtue'. He also here enjoys the company of his wife, and acts as the ideal friend and family man, for whom 'all the Tumult of the a guilty World, / Tost by ungenerous Passions, sinks away'.[36] Cook's monument is sheltered within an enclosed and peaceful space which the Seasons fountain rededicated to philosophical reflection and familial affection. It is a site which caters to the need of great public men for contemplative retirement, either, in Lyttelton's case, to recharge their energies and reburnish their ideals for the fight against corruption, or, in Grenville's, to reward them for past labours.

The setting and nature of the monument to Cook at Stowe combine to confirm that he is here celebrated not as a hero of imperial and martial prowess comparable to Captain Grenville or General Wolfe, but as a figure for the more modern idea of empire, which expands the field for British benevolence and philosophical enquiry – fortunately also a field that enriched the Grenville family; and this was a narrative of Cook's achievements that might well have seemed praiseworthy in the aftermath of his first two circumnavigations, when he had become a member of the Royal Society and accepted a post at the Greenwich Hospital. If the globe was installed after news of Cook's death reached England, on the other hand, it might have had the merit of wiping his memory clean of associations with violence or resistance to imperial expansion. It celebrated Cook for his contribution to the sorts of study that Thomson had imagined Lyttelton carrying out in the retirement of Hagley, where he would be soothed by the sounds of 'rural Peace', and

> From these abstracted oft,
> You wander thro' the Philosophic World;
> Where in bright Train continual Wonders rise,
> Or to the curious or the pious Eye.[37]

This is a Cook whose achievements appeal to the 'warm Benevolence of Mind' that distinguishes the true patriot because they are imagined to transcend party or national conflict. They position him as a private man who selflessly contributes to the advancement of knowledge in the service of 'curious' natural philosophy and 'pious' religion.

Cook and modernity

Banks's proposed monument in contrast might have seemed to insist on Cook's status as a sacrifice to Britain's imperial ambitions, and to provide too strong a reminder of the excessive cost in lives as well as money that opponents of the American War claimed it demanded; it might have been understood to echo the implications of *Caractacus before Claudius*, and to draw further contextual significance from a range of representations of Cook's death. For Cook's fate at Kealakekua Bay resonated strongly with the British representation of the transatlantic war in two of its most distinctive and familiar registers. The war was repeatedly understood as a conflict within the family, between parents and children – and Cook was of course celebrated for his fatherly care for his own men, and for the more implicitly but unmistakeably paternalist benevolence of his attitude to the islanders they encountered. Palliser's monument, for example, praised him as 'a father to his people', and David Samwell emphasised in his eulogy that 'He was beloved by his people, who looked up to him as to a father, and obeyed his commands with alacrity.'[38] And persistent representations of the war as a conflict between pale and civilised Europeans and dark and savage Native Americans made readily available a visual and verbal vocabulary which coloured the Hawaiians as rebellious and brutal. The islanders were understood as directly analogous to American Indians, but visual images of Cook's death drew on the registers of familial relations and of savagery which representations of the war defined, though their implications for the way his fate was understood were complex.

In Carter's and Webber's images of Cook's death he is the modern and enlightened opponent of savage energy and aggression. In Carter's painting – as in Ramberg's – Cook's white clothing and upright masculine

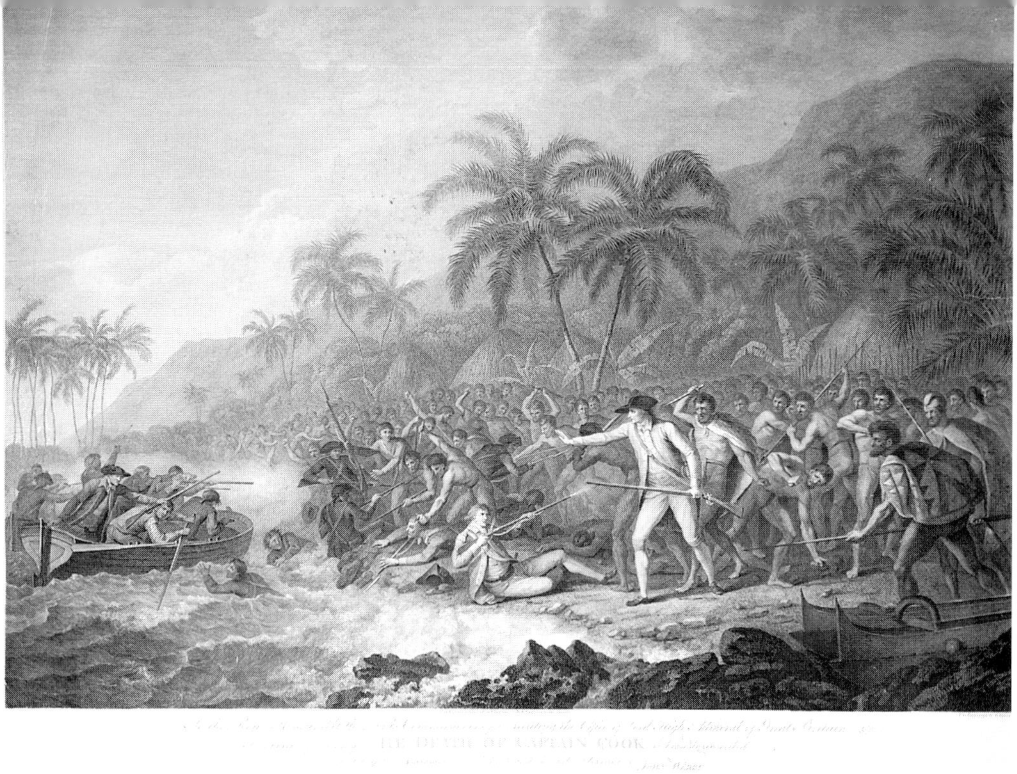

Figure 42 Francesco Bartolozzi and William Byrne after John Webber, *The Death of Captain Cook* (London: John Webber and William Byrne, 1784).

shape stand in clear contrast to the darker shapes of the islanders facing him, their features contorted with passion, and their bodies twisted to suggest a sort of muscular servility. In Webber's painting different coloured clothing works to individualise the Europeans, and also to give their bodies a softer and less masculine definition than that of Cook's immediate assailants, while most of the islanders are a seething horde, a barely discriminated meld of brown torsos and limbs (figure 42). In both these paintings the contrast between Cook and the islanders works as it were to confirm their containment within a benighted primitivism from which no escape or progress seems possible, and the division of space underscores this. In Carter's this is direct and perhaps rather crude: the left half of the picture space is filled with Europeans, and the right third with islanders, and the two groups are kept well apart by the figure of Cook. The European voyagers behind Cook fire freely into the crowd on the beach, but their humanity seems guaranteed by the care with which the artist has detailed the expressive features of the sailors, and has indicated, in the detail of the sailor helping the marine, their civilised concern for one another. In Webber's painting the division is horizontal rather than vertical. Cook and the uniformed figure of Lieutenant Molesworth Phillips, at his feet, appear in front of the crowd, in a plane they share only with the islander on the right, who is excluded from the unearthly light in which they are bathed, and with the assassin, who seems to catch a little of Cook's glow.

In Banks's sketched scene for the relief on the sarcophagus, in contrast, as well as in Zoffany's unfinished painting, Cook has fallen, and the space occupied by his prone form is less clearly demarcated from that of the threatening islanders whose well-muscled bodies tower over him. The Hawaiians too are much more ambiguous figures than they were in Carter's or Webber's paintings. Kate Davies has pointed out that British representations of American Indians in the context of the war draw together 'narratives of liberal modernity's losses and gains'. They could seem to represent 'that political liberty, masculine virtue, and independence' which had been exchanged for the more sentimental comforts of commercial modernity, with its increased investment in the values of commerce, humanity and familial domesticity.[39] The heroic proportions of Zoffany's islanders, and particularly the man with the headdress above Cook in the pose of the Discobulus which Charles Townley had recently added to his collection, draw on a similar set of notions of antique or savage nobility (plate 15). Though Cook is given the pose of the Ludovisi Gladiator, which should work to define his fallen state as that of a tragic warrior in defeat, the image is too brutally violent and, perhaps because of its unfinished state, too confused for manly heroism to be the dominant and unambiguous characteristic of his pose. Cook's clothing gives his outline an indeterminacy, a softness, an incongruous note of modernity that disrupts and detracts from the grandeur of the scene.[40] The Europeans are all lower than the islanders, as though diminished by their greater ferocity and muscular prowess, and overwhelmed as it were by the forceful diagonals that contain them to the lower, subordinate sector of the composition. Whatever Zoffany's intention, the contrast between the physical grandeur of the islanders and the cowering or retreating forms of the Europeans suggests that modernity is impoverished or emasculated by its lack of freedom and independence. The conventions of high art seem inevitably to dictate that the powerful forms of the islanders indicate virtuous masculinity, in contrast to which modern Europeans appear degenerate and perhaps corrupted by commercial progress.

Banks's planned monument does not emphasise the violence and confusion of the scene of Cook's death to this degree, and nor does it turn so centrally on the contrast between Europeans and islanders, but Zoffany's image nevertheless provides a suggestive context for considering the representation of Cook here. The relief on the sarcophagus opposes the muscular forms of the islanders to the much more rigid figures of the armed and uniformed marines on the left, and shows Cook the passive focus of the mêlée, his hand raised in the gesture of characteristic humanity that was commonly believed to have been fatal to him. The figure draped across the globe above is certainly heroic in physique, but its posture seems almost sacrificial. A well-informed correspondent to the *Morning Chronicle* who named himself 'Columbus' provided an early summary of many accounts of Cook's policies in a letter published within a fortnight of the news of his death. Columbus praised the 'humanity with which he treated the natives of all places', but went on to lament that 'it is to this humane and laudable disposition that the loss of his life is most probably to be attributed, as he seems to have fallen a sacrifice to his having put himself foremost' in danger, 'having placed too much confidence in the return of benevolence which uncivilized people so generally make to those who treat them like fellow-creatures'.[41] The idea of Cook as sacrificial victim is here tellingly bound up with the other features of his modernity: his humanity, and the sense in which he is a prototypical commercial agent, a sort of salesman for modernity, in his expectation that confidence will be repaid, that sentiments and indeed goods can be traded between people who have faith in each other's humanity or status as fellow-creatures. Columbus's letter to the *Morning Chronicle* suggests that by putting himself in danger in order to show his trust in the islanders, Cook offers his own body as a sacrificial gift for which he expects the return of benevolence.

Cook's own crew, at least after his death, seem to have regarded him as an object of veneration of a saintly and sacrificial kind, as is suggested by the relic some of them made for Mrs Cook: a coffin-shaped ditty box, containing a lock of Cook's hair, and a small watercolour of the scene of his death. A silver plate on the top of the box is inscribed 'Lono and the Seaman's Idol'.[42] That notion of Cook as sacrificial victim is important to Seward's comparison of his death with that of Orpheus at the hands of the Thracian women, and to her eucharistic notion that 'on his limbs the lust of hunger feeds!'[43] And it resonates in Samwell's panegyric to him as 'the animating spirit of the expedition', who, 'in every situation ... stood unrivalled and alone; on him all eyes were turned; he was our leading-star, which at its setting, left us involved in darkness and despair'.[44]

Banks's representation of Cook as a soft and youthful elongated nude may suggest that he is a national sacrifice to imperial ambition in return for which Britannia expects new markets to replace those of North America. The inscription on the pedestal precludes the possibility that the figure on the globe might be understood as a personification – here 'CAPTAIN COOK IS REPRESENTED DEAD', and the relief on the sarcophagus duplicates the point, showing the scene and the 'SPOT WHERE HE LOST HIS LIFE'. The large-scale reclined figure lacks the suggestion of lingering brave life, or imminent resurrection, that might be seen in West's *Death of Wolfe* or Zoffany's Cook. If it does invite any allegorical reading, its context seems to determine that allusions to modernity, humanity and sacrifice should predominate. But the insistence of the proposed monument on the very deadness of Cook may imply that his modernity and humanity have been sacrificed to the imperial project in the Pacific; that Britain's imperial ambitions are incompatible with enlightened modernity and have resulted in its denial and death. This is hardly a message Britain would have wanted to think about in a period in which success in the American War seemed to hang in the balance. Cook's death was an uncomfortable reminder of the moral consequences of empire which the nation could not afford to acknowledge, though it haunted news of the American War.

The Cook monument at the Vache

The transatlantic conflict with the thirteen colonies and their European allies complicated the commemoration of Cook in ways that I have suggested were relatively indirect. But for a few years at least celebration of Cook was overshadowed by that conflict in a more immediate sense that has a specific relation to the politics of the American War in Britain. As we saw earlier, the first monument erected to Cook after news of his death reached Britain was that built at the Vache, the country house of Sir Hugh Palliser at Chalfont St Giles in Buckinghamshire. The monument is directly opposite to the main door of the north side of the house, and is near enough, and large enough, to be the focus of the prospect from the house. I suggested earlier that the monument in its tower seemed to gesture beyond itself, perhaps towards the extensive land and seascapes of Cook's voyages, but its most obvious and immediate relationship is with the house, and with the man Cook had first met soon after he enlisted in the Royal Navy in 1755, and with whom he had worked closely in the surveying of Newfoundland. Palliser's influence, as Cook's friend and patron, was enormously important to Cook throughout his career, as Palliser became successively Governor of Newfoundland (1764–66), Comptroller of the navy (1770–75) (as Comptroller he presided over the Navy Board, responsible for commissioning), and subsequently Vice-Admiral of the Blue. By 1778 Palliser was senior Naval Lord of the Board of Admiralty, as well as MP for Scarborough. He worked closely with Lord Sandwich, who was First Lord of the Admiralty 1763–65, and again from 1771, and whose influence and approval had been essential to Cook's circumnavigations – as Cook acknowledged in naming the Hawaiian islands after him.

By early 1780, when news of Cook's death was circulating in London, Palliser's successful career as a naval officer, administrator and politician had come to an abrupt end following his catastrophic row with his senior Admiral of the Blue, Augustus Keppel. In November 1780 Charles James Fox described Palliser in the House of Commons as 'that object of universal detestation', and numerous newspaper attacks on him bear out Fox's judgement. A brief summary of the events that caused the row will suffice: in a naval battle with the French off Ushant in July 1778, Keppel, who was commanding the British fleet, had been disappointed to secure only an indecisive outcome – though his supporters were to celebrate it as a victory anyway.[45] Back in London the newspapers reported that Keppel blamed this on the slowness of Palliser, who had ignored – or as he was to claim had been unable to see – his superior officer's signal commanding him to fall into line to attack. Keppel, Palliser and Sandwich had up to this point been on reasonably good terms, despite their political differences: Keppel supported the Rockingham Whigs, who opposed Lord North's administration and sympathised with the American cause, while Palliser and Sandwich were both government supporters. Palliser responded to Keppel's rumoured remarks about the battle through the press, and used his position on the Board of Admiralty to have Keppel brought before a court martial, which in February 1779 dismissed the charges against him as 'malicious and ill-founded'. In London, streets were lit up in celebration, Palliser's house was gutted and he was burnt in effigy. In York his sister's house was demolished by the mob. In Bath flags were put out, church bells were rung, and, according to one newspaper correspondent,

> Whigs and Tories, Aldermen and Constables, Ladies and Gentlemen, Tars and Trulls, Boys and Girls, all united, and with one Voice, showed their unfeigned Satisfaction, that a brave, a good, and a great Officer, had triumphed over a mere *Log-man*, whose Effigies were led about the City with a Cord

round his Neck, and a dilapidated *Log-book* in his hand, as a Momento of his approaching Fate in a *Feu de joye* prepared for its reception.[46]

Palliser resigned from all his public positions and tried to recover his reputation through a court martial in which he defended his actions, but though he was not found guilty of misconduct he was not acquitted with honour. Though he asked to be reinstated in his offices, he was unable to return to public life, and when Sandwich appointed him Governor of Greenwich Hospital in July 1780 newspapers and public prints held both of them up to ridicule and claimed that his appointment was a dishonour to the naval veterans of Greenwich. Thomas Rowlandson's caricature of November 1780, commenting on the affair, can be taken as representative of this (figure 43). *Naval Triumph or Favors Confer'd* (London: J. Harris, 1780) shows Sandwich and Palliser proceeding in triumph through Greenwich, Sandwich mounted on the back of an aged, peg-legged naval pensioner who supports himself on

Figure 43 Thomas Rowlandson, *Naval Triumph or Favors Confer'd* (London: J. Harris, 1780).

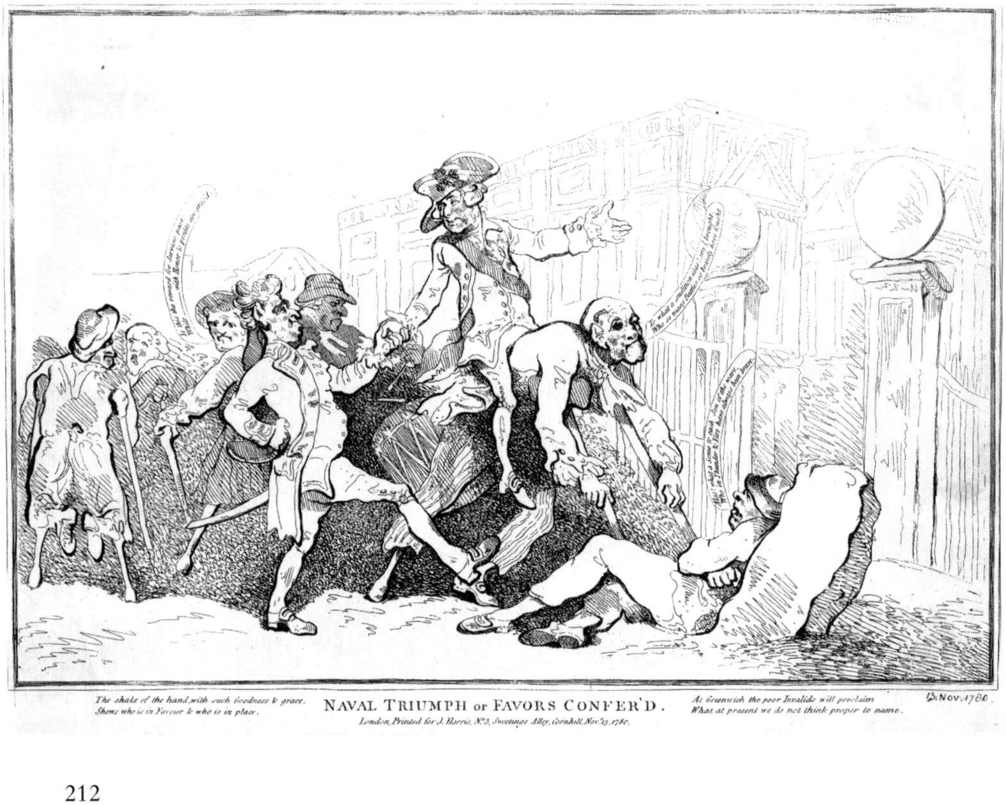

crutches while lamenting 'To what a condition alas! am I brought, / Who so many battles so bravely have fought.' The verse beneath the image hinted broadly at a corrupt agreement between Sandwich and Palliser, at the expense of the Greenwich pensioners.

Keppel also came in for some criticism. He was repeatedly reminded in caricatures of his failure to secure victory at Ushant, and satirists repeatedly suggested that he and his party had betrayed the constitution through their American sympathies.[47] But nevertheless the destruction of Palliser's reputation following the Keppel trial was thorough, and this had serious implications for Sandwich, making it more difficult for him to avoid accepting some responsibility for Britain's imminent defeat. After the fall of the North administration in 1782, neither man was able to regain public office. The dispute between Palliser and Keppel dramatised party political hostilities which could be fought out in the public prints, and enacted by the crowds in the streets of London, York or Bath. It associated the memory of Cook with the damaged reputations of his friends, and with the loss of the American colonies. It seems unlikely that Cook shared their interest in party politics; he had after all spent most of his life at sea. But Palliser's monument at the Vache tried to appropriate Cook's reputation as a cover for his own. The first monument erected to Cook was intended to assert the priority of Palliser's right to a share in Cook's virtues and achievements.

The monument at Stowe offered a modest visual spectacle, and the lettered and capped block at the Vache was even more undecorated and unembellished – little more than a stone mason's rendition of the printed page. For nearly half a century after this death Cook received no grander or more public memorial in Britain, though there were medals inscribed with his image, and his portraits seem to have been widely reproduced. In the absence of a single and dramatic positive achievement on which to hang his posthumous reputation, it was shaped or inhabited by the historical events with which accounts or images of his death were juxtaposed in newspapers and prints, as well as by the sites and relationships in which monuments to him were placed at Stowe and the Vache. In an age that wanted heroes, but whose notion of heroes was of men distinguished by some grand defining event, Cook remained a private man, out of step with the narrative of the transatlantic war whose monuments crowded the aisles of Westminster Abbey.

Notes

1 *Morning Chronicle*, 17 January 1780.

2 Immediately before he was stabbed, Cook had killed a man in the fracas on the beach. For detailed accounts of the circumstances leading to Cook's death, and discussion of the extent to which violence towards the islanders provoked his assassination, see Nicholas Thomas, *Discoveries: The Voyages of Captain Cook* (London: Allen Lane, 2003), chapter 21, and Anne Salmond, *The Trial of the Cannibal Dog: Captain Cook in the South Seas* (London: Allen Lane, 2003), chapter 17.

3 For an excellent account of the reception and dissemination of the news of Cook's death in newspapers as well as a range of other media, which explores the implications of cultural context much more fully than I can here, see Ruth Scobie, 'The Many Deaths of Captain Cook: A Study in Metropolitan Mass Culture, 1780–1810' (PhD Dissertation, University of York, 2013). I am grateful to Ruth for her advice on this essay.

4 See Harriet Guest, *Small Change: Women, Learning, Patriotism, 1750–1810* (Chicago: Chicago University Press, 2000), chapter 10, 'Britain Mourn'd: Anna Seward's Patriotic Elegies'.

5 The earliest advertisement I have found for Seward's *Elegy* is in *London Chronicle*, 20 April 1780. For the proposal of Carter, Robert Sayer and John Bennett, see *Morning Chronicle*, 12 April 1781. See J. Hall and J. Thornthwaite after George Carter, *The Death of Captain James Cook, by the Indians of O,why,ee one of the Sandwich Islands* (London: G. Carter and Sayer & Bennet, 1784).

6 It might have been too overshadowed by the competition of works by marine painters Paton and Serres, as well as by Wright and Copley. For further discussion of representations of this subject see John Bonehill, 'Laying Siege to the Royal Academy: Wright of Derby's *View of Gibraltar* at Robins's Rooms, Covent Garden, April 1785', *Art History*, 30:4 (2007), 521–44.

7 *Whitehall Evening Post*, 27 July 1780.

8 The lettering identifies the image more cumbrously as *The plate Representing the Engagement between the Quebec Frigate, Capn George Farmer, and the Surveillante Frigate, Monsieur Coëdic* (1 October 1780). For fuller versions of Farmer's heroic death see John William Piercy, *An Epistle to the Right Honourable John, Earl of Sandwich, &c. or, the British Hero Displayed. A Poem* (London: J. Rivington & Sons, H. Payne and J. Deighton, 1780), pp. 16–17, and *History and Antiquities of the County of Norfolk. Vol. IX* (Norwich: J. Crouse, 1781), pp. 107–10. John André was the British officer charged with handling correspondence with the American traitor, Benedict Arnold. He was hanged in October 1780, having been captured behind enemy lines in civilian dress.

9 *St James's Chronicle*, 16 October 1779.

10 See Kathleen Wilson, *The Sense of the People: Politics, Culture and Imperialism in England, 1715–1785* (Cambridge: Cambridge University Press, 1998), p. 195.

11 See, for example, the advertisement for Boydell's print in *General Evening Post*, 26 February 1780; Carter's print was re-advertised in *Gazetteer and Daily Advertiser*, 30 December 1780. Boydell's print is dated 12 December 1780,

while Carter's is dated 1 October 1780. De Loutherbourg later suggested something similar with his design for *The Apotheosis of Captain Cook* (1794), where Cook reclines in a pose that echoes that of West's Wolfe.

12 *Morning Chronicle*, 12 April 1781. Carter explained that the large number of portraits involved in the *Immortality of Garrick* had slowed its production.

13 David Samwell, *The Death of Captain Cook and Other Writings*, ed. Martin Fitzpatrick, Nicholas Thomas and Jennifer Newell (Cardiff: University of Wales Press, 2007), p. 75. Samwell's account was first published as a pamphlet in 1786.

14 James King, *A voyage to the Pacific Ocean. Undertaken, by the command of His Majesty, for making discoveries in the Northern Hemisphere. Performed under the direction of Captains Cook, Clerke and Gore, in His Majesty's ships the Resolution and Discovery; in the years 1776, 1777, 1778, 1779, and 1780, Vol. III* (London: G. Nicol, 1784), p. 46.

15 On André's monument see Dean Eric Abbott et al., *Westminster Abbey* (Radnor, PA: Annenberg School of Communications, 1988; first published 1972), pp. 228–9.

16 Anna Seward, *Elegy on Captain Cook. To which is Added, an Ode to the Sun. By Miss Seward* (London: J. Dodsley, 1780).

17 Helen Maria Williams, *The Morai. An Ode*, App. 2, in Andrew Kippis, *Narrative of the Voyages Round the World, Performed by Captain James Cook. With an Account of his Life during the previous and intervening periods* (London: J. F. Dove, 1788), p. 526.

18 See *Proposal for erecting a monument, on Eston-Nab, in Cleveland, in memory of the celebrated navigator, Capt. James Cooke* (Stockton: Christopher and Jennett, 1811).

19 Andrew C.F. David, 'Cook, James (1728–1779)', *Oxford Dictionary of National Biography*, Oxford University Press, 2004; www.oxforddnb.com/view/article/6140, accessed 2 July 2012.

20 '*Virtutis uberrimum alimentum est honos. VAL MAXIMUS, Lib. 2 Cap. 6.*'

21 The text of the inscription is reproduced in Andrew Kippis, *The Life of Captain James Cook* (London: G. Nicol, 1788), pp. 490–2. The upper floor with castellated walls is a later addition, but the moat was probably part of the original construction. I am grateful to Ian Boreham for his advice, and for sending me an extract from the structural survey carried out by Christopher Wallis. See *Cook's Log*, 26:4 (2003), 12 for Boreham's detailed account of the monument, and also *Cook's Log*, 28:4 (2005), 17.

22 For the attribution see J.C. Beaglehole, *The Life of Captain James Cook* (London: Hakluyt Society, 1974), p. 696. The inscription is reprinted in, for example, *Voyage to the Pacific Ocean. Undertaken by command of His Majesty for making discoveries in the Northern Hemisphere. Performed under the directions of Captains Cook, Clerke, and Gore. In His Majesty's ships the Resolution and Discovery; in the years 1776, 1777, 1778, 1779 and 1780. In Three Volumes. Vol. I and II written by Captain James Cook, F. R. S. Vol. III by Captain James King, L. L. D. and F. R. S.* (London: G. Nicol and T. Cadell, 1785), Introduction, pp. lxxxv–lxxxix; and *A Compendious History of Captain Cook's Last Voyage, Performed in the Years 1776, 1777, 1778, 1779, and 1780; in which all the*

interesting transactions are recorded, particularly those relative to his unfortunate death (London: G. Kearsley, 1784), pp. xviii–xix. A monument in the form of an ornamented sarcophagus, originally at Manby Hall, in the parish of Broughton in Linconshire, was the work of local statuary Richard Hayward for Charles Anderson Pelham (created 1st Baron Yarborough in 1794). Cook stayed at Manby prior to his last voyage. The monument was destroyed by vandals in 1909, and the remaining fragments were moved to Brocklesby Hall, the principal seat of the Anderson Pelham family. Charles Anderson Pelham was an MP and wealthy landowner, Master of the celebrated Brocklesby Hounds and a long-standing patron of George Stubbs. This private monument, apparently testament to personal respect, left little trace either in the past or more recently. See National Maritime Museum, 'Memorial: M1675', *Maritime Memorials: Commemorating Seafarers and Victims of Maritime Disasters*, www.nmm.ac.uk/memorials, accessed 1 September 2011; Willoughby Maycock, 'Captain Cook: Memorials', *Notes & Queries*, 12 S, viii, (26 February 1921); *Warwick Times*, 22 May 1909; John Lord, 'Richard Hayward: An Early and Some Later Commissions', *Church Monuments: Journal of the Church Monuments Society*, 12 (1907), 67–79; Judy Egerton, *George Stubbs, Painter: Catalogue Raisonné* (New Haven and London: Yale University Press for the Paul Mellon Centre for Studies in British Art, 2007), pp. 57, 376. I am grateful to Jordan Vibert for alerting me to this monument.

23 John Adams, *Modern Voyages*, 2 vols (London: G. Kearsley, 1790), I, p. 325.

24 *British Gazette and Sunday Monitor*, 16 May 1784, and see also *Morning Post*, 14 May 1784. See Johann Heinrich Ramberg, *The Death of Cook*, in the Mitchell Library Reading Room at the Library of New South Wales, and reproduced and discussed in Martin Myrone, *Bodybuilding: Reforming Masculinities in British Art 1750–1810* (New Haven: Yale University Press, 2005), pp. 213–14. I am grateful to Ruth Scobie for drawing this image to my attention.

25 See Julius Bryant, *Thomas Banks, 1735–1805: Britain's First Modern Sculptor* (London: Soane Gallery, 2005), p. 48; and *A Candid Review of the Exhibition (being the twelfth) of the Royal Academy, MDCC LXXX. Dedicated to his Majesty. By an Artist* (London: H. Reynell for T. Evans, 1780).

26 Mason's poem was originally published in 1759, but was revised for performance in 1777, when it was also published as *Caractacus. A Dramatic Poem. Written on the model of the Antient Greek Tragedy* (York: A Ward, 1777).

27 See, for example, the satirical print, *The Curious Zebra. alive from America. 'walk in Gem'men and Ladies, Walk in'* (London: G. Johnson, 1778), British Museum.

28 Letter from Thomas Banks to Ozias Humphry, 30 September 1778, in David Bindman, 'Thomas Banks's "Caractacus before Claudius": New Letters to and from Ozias Humphry', *Burlington Magazine*, 142:1,173 (December 2000), 769–72.

29 This anonymous contemporary comment is cited in John Beckett, *The Rise and Fall of the Grenvilles: Dukes of Buckingham and Chandos, 1710–1921* (Manchester: Manchester University Press, 1994), p. 37, and see chapter 2 'Richard, Earl Temple, and the Building of the Family Fortunes'.

30 The Cook monument at Stowe is first mentioned in Benton Seeley's

guidebook of 1788. This has led some commentators to argue that it was placed there after Cook's death. See, for example, Richard Wheeler, 'Captain Cook's Long Journey to Elysium' *Apollo*, 160:513 (November 2004), 78–81.

31 Patrick Eyres, 'Fleets, Forests and Follies: Supremacy of the Seas and of the Eye', in Patrick Eyres (eds), 'Hearts of Oak', *New Arcadian Journal*, 35/36 (1993), 10.

32 See Michael Bevington, et al. (eds), *Stowe: The People and the Place* (Swindon: National Trust, 2011), pp. 48–50. John Martin Robinson's earlier guide, *Temples of Delight: Stowe Landscape Gardens* (Andover: Pitkin in association with The National Trust, 1994), pp. 140–2, was yet more emphatic on this point.

33 For fuller discussion of the Grenville column see Joan Coutu, 'Stowe: A Whig Training Ground', in Patrick Eyres (ed.) 'The Political Temples of Stowe', *New Arcadian Journal*, 43/44 (1997), 66–78.

34 *Stow: the gardens of the Right Honourable the Lord Viscount Cobham* (London: B. Seeley, 1751), p. 13 (anon.). See William Gilpin, *A dialogue upon the gardens of the Right Honourable the Lord Viscount Cobham, at Stow in Buckinghamshire* (London: B. Seeley, 1748), pp. 29–33, where a landscape of retirement is enjoyed without direct reference to the Temple. In Seeley's composite volume, *Stow*, pp. 12–13, a paraphrase of Gilpin's comments is applied to the landscape and the Temple. On the exact location of the Temple and the date of its demolition see 'Buckinghamshire', *South Midlands Archaeology*, 26 (1996), 16–18.

35 The lines are adapted from James Thomson, *Spring The Seasons*, ed. James Sambrook (Oxford and New York: Clarendon Press and Oxford University Press, 1981).

36 Thomson, *Spring*, 930–1, 939–40, and see 904–49. This passage is also cited in the description of Thomson's Seat at Hagley, in *A companion to the Leasowes, Hagley and Enville; with a sketch of Fisherwick, the seat of the Right Hon. Earl Donegall* (London, 1789), p. 74. It is recommended as a suitable inscription for a shady garden in Samuel Felton, *Miscellanies, on ancient and modern gardening; and on the scenery of nature* (London: printed for the author, 1785).

37 Thomson, *Spring*, 918, 922–5.

38 Samwell, *Death of Captain Cook*, p. 82. See also J.C. Beaglehole (ed.), *The Journals of Captain James Cook on his Voyages of Discovery. III. The Voyage of the Resolution and Discovery 1776–1780: Part One* (Cambridge: Cambridge University Press for the Hakluyt Society, 1967), p. 551 note 1.

39 Kate Davies, *Catharine Macaulay and Mercy Otis Warren: The Revolutionary Atlantic and the Politics of Gender* (Oxford: Oxford University Press, 2005).

40 Zoffany's painting has been much discussed, but the essay which set the terms for most subsequent comment is Charles Mitchell, 'Zoffany's *Death of Captain Cook*', *Burlington Magazine*, 84:492 (March 1944), 56–63. See also Bernard Smith, *European Vision and the South Pacific* (New Haven and London: Yale University Press, 1985), pp. 119–20.

41 *Morning Chronicle*, 22 January 1780.

42 See *Carved ditty box shaped like a coffin on silver stand, containing a rough watercolour sketch of the death of Cook, including a lock of Cook's hair, ca. 1779/*

carved by sailors on Cook's last ship HMS Resolution, in State Library of New South Wales, at http://acms.sl.nsw.gov.au/. The inscription suggests a parallel between the sailors' idolatrous veneration for Cook, and the islanders' supposed identification of him with the god Lono.

43 See Seward, *Elegy on Captain Cook*, p. 15.

44 Samwell, *Death of Captain Cook*, p. 82.

45 See the droll of *The Honourable Augustus Keppel, Admiral of the Blue Squadron, and Commander in Chief of His Majesty's Fleet which engaged and defeated the French on the 27 & 28 of July 1778 off Ushant* (London: Carrington Bowles, 1779), British Museum.

46 Letter from 'NO PARTY MAN', in *St James's Chronicle*, 13 Febuary 1779.

47 See, for example, *Who's in fault? (Nobody) A view off Ushant* (London: W. Humphrey, 1779), mocking Keppel for his imagined refusal to accept responsibility for the outcome at Ushant. Also James Gillray's *Britania's assassination. or – the Republicans amusement* (London: E. Darchery, 1782), which satirises the Whig ministry for the loss of America, shows Keppel lowering the national flag while reflecting that 'He that Fights & runs away, / May live to fight another day'.

8

Framing Sir Francis: Lady Anne Stanhope and the corruption of civic masculinity[1]

Jordan Vibert

Framing

In the main stairwell of the York City Art Gallery hangs a portrait that may seem, to a casual observer, quite unremarkable (plate 16) – simply another 'grand manner' costume piece amongst the many that decorated the walls of country houses in the eighteenth century, and which still dominate in collections today. Painted by Sir Francis Cotes in 1765, the portrait shows Lady Anne Stanhope (1737–1812) and Katherine, Countess of Effingham (1746–91) in the guise of Diana and nymph, hunting a stag in a wooded landscape, and represents a vogue for such mythological guises in elite female portraiture of the period, and for Diana portraiture more specifically. Allan Ramsay and Sir Joshua Reynolds each produced at least three such 'Dianas' between 1735 and 1768, and similar portraits were also painted by French premiers Nicolas de Largillière and Jean-Marc Nattier in this era.[2] This vogue has been linked to the popularity of mythological costumes at masquerade balls, and it is perhaps no coincidence that Anne, who assumes the role of Diana here, attended a masquerade ball at the Haymarket Opera House in 1769 dressed as 'Diana ... with a bow in her hand, and a quiver at her back'.[3] At the same time, the portrait also plays to a popular fantasy of female retirement, offering to transport the viewer away to peaceable pastoral groves inhabited by goddesses and nymphs, conjuring the idyllic ideal of retired country life that so many portraits of the period expressed through the pastoral mode. One of the oddities of this portrait is the richly decorated frame that surrounds it. This frame is emblazoned with overtly martial and maritime emblems – swords, shields, helmets, hand-axes and an armillary sphere – which seem puzzlingly incongruous with the subject matter of the portrait, apparently having little to do with two women hunting as Diana and nymph.[4]

In the contemporary surroundings of the York City Art Gallery, it is difficult to make much sense of this portrait and its frame. Stripped of its original context, Cotes's portrait runs the risk of becoming simply another one of many portraits, generic and unremarkable, displayed in a baffling frame. But there is another story to tell about this portrait, a story that involves restoring some of the original contexts of its production and display, and reflecting on how such contexts might have shaped its meaning for a contemporary audience. The frame surrounding this portrait is crucial to this story because it provides important evidence of where and how this portrait was displayed within a country house and of its potential relationship to various narratives at work in its surroundings. The frame was one of a series of identical frames, of which six are known to have survived, in the possession of Anne's family, the Delavals of Seaton Delaval Hall in Northumberland.[5] Using surviving evidence, Richard Green has suggested that these frames originally formed part of a designed scheme at Doddington Hall in Lincoln, another country estate in the family's possession which had been inherited by Anne's second eldest brother, Sir John Hussey Delaval (1728–1808). He began an extensive scheme of renovation on the property in the early 1760s, alongside rebuilding Ford Castle, a third inherited estate. Green argues that it's likely that part of the renovations at Doddington involved installing these six frames in the Long Gallery. In 1766, in fact, a year after Cotes painted Anne and Katherine, London papier mâché frame and ornament maker Peter Babell sent a bill to John Hussey Delaval for seventy feet of 'Paper machee Rich Border Gilt in Oil Gold', explaining the price for this was higher than quoted because 'the Moulding being so Bold did take more Gold, than I thought', and that he had 'sanded the ground of the Border to give a Relief to the Ornaments'.[6] It seems likely that these richly gilded and boldly ornamented frames were the martial frames which were intended for the gallery at Doddington Hall, with the dating suggesting that one was intended as a frame for Cotes's portrait, painted just a year before. Such a scheme of martial and maritime frames would obviously be

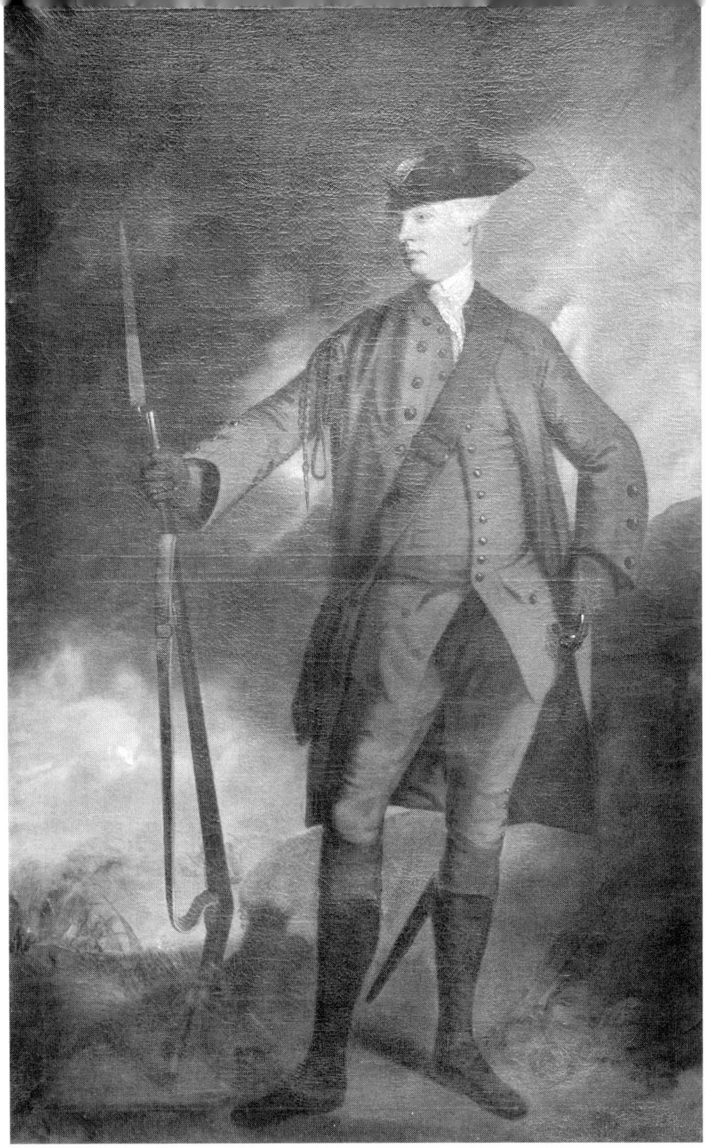

Figure 44
[Copy of?] Sir Joshua Reynolds, *Francis Blake Delaval*, 1759, oil on canvas, 225 × 143.5 cm.

intended, in part, to celebrate the Delaval family's naval ancestry, which spanned several generations. Seaton Delaval Hall, the family's principal residence, had been built for Admiral George Delaval (1660–1723) and inherited by his nephew and Anne's father, Captain Francis Blake Delaval (1692–1752), an officer in the Royal Navy.[7] Green points out that one of these frames probably originally contained a military portrait of Anne's eldest brother, Sir Francis Blake Delaval (1727–71), participating in an assault on the French coast during the Seven Years War. A portrait matching its description which hangs at Doddington today may be the original by Reynolds or a copy of it (figure 44).[8]

Marcia Pointon has already shown how Cotes's portrait could have contributed to such an aggrandising familial narrative of naval glory, suggesting that the bellicose frame surrounding it subsumes the woman into a 'frame-work … of masculine signifiers'.[9] The stag hunt thus becomes a complementary foil to the naval offensive – peace and war, respectively. Significantly, Doddington Hall contained just such a playful pairing in the rich early seventeenth-century tapestries which Sir John installed in the state bedrooms in the 1760s – one set, in the Holly Room, depicting bucolic scenes of rural life (figure 45) and the other, in the Yellow Room, showing battle scenes from the Trojan War.[10] These tapestries, with their competing yet complementary representations of bucolic peace and violent conflict, may certainly have provided a

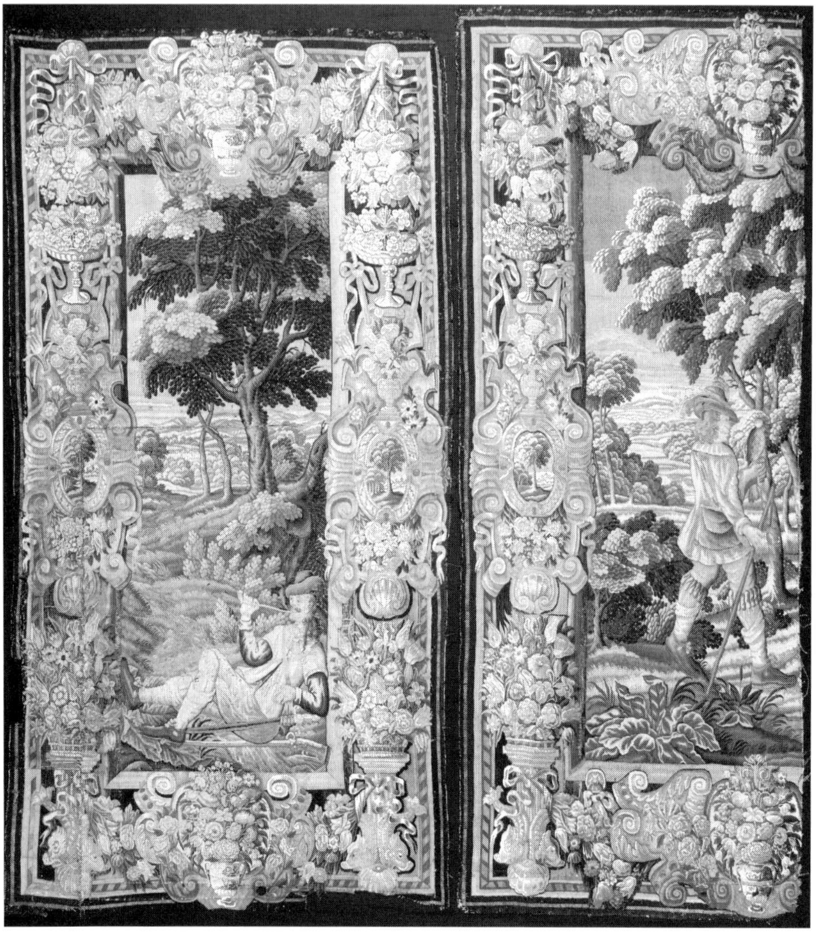

Figure 45 Flemish tapestry in the Holly Room at Doddington Hall, seventeenth century.

broader narrative framework for reading Cotes's portrait on similar terms – as offering up peaceable pastoral femininity as a foil to bloody masculine warfare. It's this sense of how Cotes's portrait, its frame and 'frameworks', may have functioned within the walls of Doddington Hall that I explore here. I want to tell a more careful and nuanced story about the interplay between peace and war in this portrait, pinning it more specifically to the lives of the women it represented and to the men and their martial deeds it helped to glorify. Doddington is an essential part of this story in its dual function as the site of a particular kind of female retirement and sociability, and also of masculine displays of martial heroism, ancient and modern. Both offer frames of reference for interpreting Cotes's portrait, potentially shaping how it was understood by those familiar with the house and by the people who inhabited its rooms and whose faces graced its walls.

Pastoral retirement and sentimental preservation

The first part of this essay concerns the story that Cotes's portrait tells about the women it represents, Lady Anne Stanhope and Katherine, Countess of Effingham – a story about their lives and their relationships with each other. We know very little about these women beyond a few scraps of biographical information and other surviving fragments, perhaps because neither had children to preserve their correspondence in a family archive. Anne was the daughter of Captain Francis Blake Delaval and Rhoda Apreece (1724–59), members of the landed though untitled gentry. In 1759, she had married Sir William Stanhope (1702–72), but had separated from him four years later, in 1763, for reasons which remain unclear.[11] Katherine came from humbler origins as the daughter of Metcalfe Proctor and Martha Disney of Thorpe Hall, near Leeds, with what survives of the house suggesting that the family were reasonably wealthy, though not to the extent of being established landed gentry like the Delavals.[12] In 1765, the year Cotes's portrait was painted, Katherine stepped up in the world, marrying Thomas Howard, the 3rd Earl of Effingham (1747–91) in Scotland, the couple presumably having eloped there to escape the need for parental consent, both being under age at the time.[13] Objections to the marriage possibly arose, we may speculate, from the obvious disparity in the couple's social status. How and why these two women from such different backgrounds and regions came to be painted together has proved something of a puzzle, particularly as double portraits of women from this period usually represented familial relationships – depicting sisters or mothers and daughters – and Anne and Katherine were not related by either birth or marriage. A number of critics have proposed that the women were friends who had met through the amateur theatricals that the Delaval family were famous for, with the guise of Diana and nymph suggesting their involvement in a play.[14] But I agree with Pointon that this does not look much like a scene from a play, and I think the mythological guise the women take on in this portrait may have yielded a rather different meaning to a contemporary audience familiar with the sitters, particularly if the portrait was displayed at Doddington Hall.[15] I want to consider how, rather than suggesting masquerade, allusions to Diana in this portrait mean something more particular to these women, referring to a bond of friendship between them conducted around a shared engagement with a contemporary cultural discourse of retired rural living. When understood in these more private and sentimental terms, I argue that the portrait functions as a commemoration of the friendship between its sitters, which preserves their relationship against the threat of impending sentimental loss.

In 1714, some fifty years before Cotes painted Katherine and Anne, Nicolas de Largillière produced a comparable double portrait of the Comtesse de Montsoreau and her sister as Diana and attendant nymph. As with Cotes's portrait, the mythological guise of Diana and nymph in this portrait was, Donald Posner has explained, part of a vogue for 'mythological or allegorical costume pieces'.[16] At the same time, the guise of Diana and nymph also develops other resonances in relation to its sitters. Largillière bases the compositional arrangement of his portrait on Louis de Boulogne's roughly contemporaneous *Diane et ses compagnes se reposant après la chasse*, a painting depicting Diana and her nymphs resting together after a hunt within a secluded, pastoral space. While Boulogne's painting is evidently designed to titillate the male viewer-voyeur, who might gaze at leisure on these scantily clad virgins, it also suggests female companionship: a private space of female intimacy, where women co-exist in companionable unity. Through Diana's associations with female companionship as disseminated in Boulogne's *Diana et ses compagnes*, then, Largillière may be seen to represent the sisterly companionship of his subjects.

Like Largillière's comparable double portrait, Cotes's work also calls to mind artistic representations of Diana and her nymphs. The mythological hunt in which Katherine and Anne participate might be read in relation to any number of paintings depicting Diana hunting with her nymphs, many of which were in circulation as prints in the eighteenth

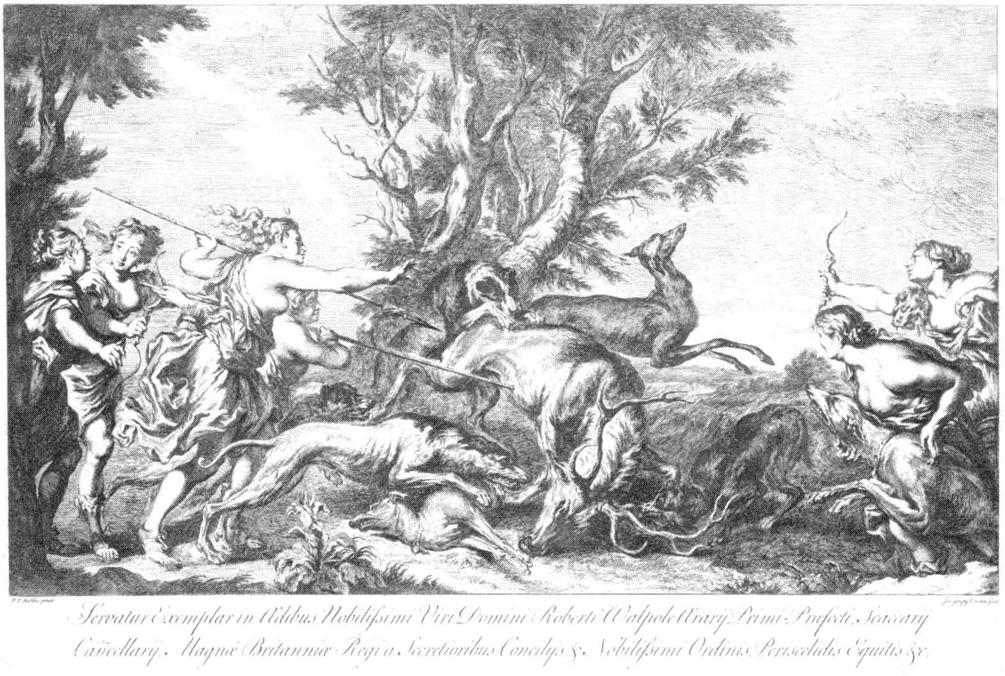

Figure 46
Joseph Goupy
after Peter Paul
Rubens, untitled,
1720–50,
etching,
33.7 × 51.5 cm.

century: for example, Joseph Goupy's early to mid-eighteenth-century etching after a painting by Peter Paul Rubens (figure 46) owned by Sir Robert Walpole. In a similar way to Largillière's portrait, connections to artistic representations of Diana and her companions could suggest contemporary companionship in Cotes's portrait. In these paintings, the shared physical unity of hunting suggests female companionship – a sport the women engage in together, each forming a part of a whole, with their bodies and movements synchronising in perfect harmony. Cotes's portrait, emptied of all other figures, offers a more specific and intimate version of this motif. Anne and Katherine mirror each other – profile to profile, arm to arm – moving in perfect synchronicity to form a single action, an invisible line of sinew seemingly connecting Anne's arm as it gestures to the stag, and Katherine's arm as it responds by releasing the hounds. Their faces are, indeed, not displayed to the viewer – as are those of the Comtesse de Montsoreau and her sister – but only to each other. Here, too, the bodily sympathy between Anne and Katherine might be seen to hint at Adam Smith's close identification between the body and sympathetic connection.[17] This physical synchronicity between Anne and Katherine offers a more intense and intimate version of the physical unity between Diana and her band of nymphs in paintings of the hunt, suggesting a close bond of companionship.

As well as suggesting this intimate connection between Anne and Katherine, the mythology of Diana has another set of resonances, associating the women, and their friendship, with the retirement of country life. The portrait employs motifs of pastoral seclusion common to artistic depictions of Diana and her nymphs, positioning the friends within an intimate space, sheltered and hidden from the wooded landscape by a rocky outcrop and an overhanging tree. This kind of pastoral seclusion was part of a contemporary and fashionable cultural discourse, which privileged virtuous country life over corrupt city living, particularly with regard to women and notions of fashionable display.[18] In 1764, for example, the year before Cotes's portrait, Mary Darwall had published a volume of poetry, which included a celebration of just such virtuous rural retirement in 'Rural Happiness. To a Friend'.[19] Darwall personifies '*Retirement*' as a 'musing Nymph! in russet Vest array'd', and goes on to position a retired, pastoral setting – with 'silent Shades', 'twilight Woods' and 'dusky Gro[ves]' – against the various corruptions of the 'noisy Town'.[20] Instead of this corrupt city life, Darwall seeks, rather, to 'Tread *Virtue's* paths' in a 'Sylvan scene', where 'social Converse' crown[s] the Day's Decline, / And Folly's Slaves divide their Haunts from mine'.[21] Cotes's portrait resonates with this kind of pastoral fantasy, presenting a similar vision of sociable rural retirement, articulated through the mythology of Diana and nymph.

Such a reading of Cotes's portrait would have been all the more possible in the context of Doddington Hall, and what the place meant to Anne and Katherine and their wider social circle. While we know very little about these women and their relationship, surviving evidence strongly suggests that they belonged to a social group invested in retired country living. In November 1766, Katherine wrote to Anne's sister-in-law, Susanna Hussey Delaval, the wife of John Delaval, at Doddington Hall expressing her marked disdain for London, and preference for country life:[22]

> We don't go to Town till Febry which I am heartily glad of you know how I like London … Pray tell me if you leave [D]oddington before we go to Town. I hope not for I think you enjoy the country as much as I do & I am very certain the only people that go to London are those which can not find themselves any Rational amusements elsewhere.[23]

A year later, in December 1767, Katherine articulated these sentiments to Susanna still more vehemently. Ruminating on her and her husband's impending removal from Yorkshire to London, Katherine writes glumly:

> I daresey [*sic*] you will regret leaving the country as much as we do, the weather has been delightfull [*sic*] for the time of the year, which makes it still more meloncholy [*sic*], to think of leaving all air & exercise whatever, to be confin'd within the walls of that shocking place call'd London. I can not think of it with patience tho I ought, for the Time draws near.[24]

In these letters, Katherine is clearly engaging with a discourse of virtuous, rural retirement in opposition to the corruptions of city life: she positions herself as avowedly preferring the outdoor pursuits – the 'air & exercise' – of the country, setting herself apart from those 'people that go to London' to engage in its '[irr]ational amusements'. Through Katherine's suggestion that Susanna 'enjoy[s] the country' as much as she does, and will 'regret leaving the country as much as' she will, we can see the two women sharing in these views and values. Here, Doddington features as the site of sociable retirement for Katherine and Susanna, and this shared association can be extended to Anne, who was described in a similar way at the time of Cotes's portrait. In a letter written by Anne's brother-in-law, Philip Stanhope, 4th Earl of Chesterfield in 1765 – the year of Cotes' portrait – Anne is remembered as:

> a young woman of a retired disposition ... bred up prudently under an old grandmother in the country; she hated and dreaded a London life, and chose to amuse herself at home with her books, her drawing, and her music.[25]

What's interesting about this account is that the 'old grandmother in the country' must refer (unless Chesterfield is using grandmother in an archaic sense to mean any female ancestor) to Anne's maternal grandmother, Sarah Hussey Apreece (1700–49), since Anne's paternal grandmother, Mary Blake Delaval (1664–1711), died before she was born.[26] Apreece inherited Doddington Hall, along with her two sisters, from her father in 1706 and became sole owner of it in 1724.[27] It thus seems likely, based on the comments about Anne's upbringing in Chesterfield's letter, that Anne's early years were spent in quiet retirement with Apreece at Doddington.[28]

Significantly, Anne had been represented in paint by Reynolds (plate 17) in the terms Chesterfield described her at Doddington at around the time Cotes was painting her.[29] The portrait shows Anne, holding a pen and scroll, beside a table bearing a selection of books, papers and statues – including a miniature version of Lely's *Crouching Venus*. Reynolds's portrait is very obviously a complementary showcasing of Anne's beauty and talents. The statue of Lely's Venus – from which Anne's own hair is modelled – both indicates her beauty by identifying her with the alluring form of the goddess, and reinforces the status of her engagement in artistic pursuits. The portrait, moreover, situates those pursuits within a rural setting – within the leafy trees, rolling hills and expansive sky of the countryside visible through the window in the background, suggesting Anne's retirement from the bustle of city life. This impression is also carried through in the comparison between Anne and Lely's Venus. This Venus – unlike, say, the Venus de Medici – completely covers her body from view. Anne similarly seems to have hidden away her beauty and talents in her virtuous retreat into country life.

Cotes's portrait offers another version of this theme, drawing on the mythology of Diana to suggest Anne's retirement to the country, this time with Katherine. This mythological model could also represent the women's actual participation, as friends, in the sporting pursuits of retired country living. Surviving evidence shows that Katherine, at least, participated in the outdoor pursuits associated with such rural retirement. Apocryphally, she was famed for her ability to jump a five-barred gate on horseback.[30] She herself also recounts twice daily rides in the hills of Liège in 1768 in a letter to Susanna, and, in 1790, the breeding of pointer puppies, and a 'Hearty gallop of three miles' in the heat of a Jamaican spring.[31] And, in 1787, in a portrait that is perhaps intentionally reminiscent of Cotes's, George Haugh painted Katherine hunting in contemporary dress, with a fowling piece in her hand and two spaniels at her side.[32] While there is no available evidence that Anne was similarly inclined, this could well be suggested by her shared participation in the hunt in Cotes's portrait, which may offer a mythological rendering of an activity which she and Katherine shared as part of their retired country life. Such a reading would have been all the more apparent to those familiar with Doddington and the life these women enjoyed there.

But while the mythology of Diana and her nymphs suggests a friendship between Anne and Katherine, formed in the context of virtuous, rural retirement, it also develops another set of associations. The allusions to Diana in this portrait could also indicate Katherine's transition away from this relationship and towards marriage. By the middle of the eighteenth century, Diana was being deployed in portraiture to suggest just such a transition from chastity to marriage. Reynolds's *Rebecca Boyd, Countess of Erroll* (1748–49), Allan Ramsay's *Lady Anne Dawson* (1754) and Charles-Amédée-Philippe van Loo's *Luise Henriette Wilhelmine von Anhalt-Dessau* (1765), each showing the sitters as Diana, were all produced within a year of these sitters becoming engaged or married.[33] In this context, Anne's role as Diana in Cotes's portrait may allude to her separation from Sir William Stanhope, just two years earlier, when she retreated to singleness and female companionship. Interestingly, something similar may have been suggested in Claude Lefèbvre's portrait of Louise de La Vallière, Louis XIV's mistress, in the guise of Diana, painted in 1676. The portrait was painted following a difficult few years during which La Vallière had been replaced in the King's affections.[34] In 1674, seeking to escape the public humiliation she had experienced and to repent for her sins, La Vallière had fled to a Carmelite convent with the blessing of the King.[35] La Vallière's transformation into Diana in Lefèbvre's portrait registers a parallel retreat from public life. Anne's identification as Diana in Cotes's portrait may suggest a similar retirement – or perhaps even banishment – into the country, and possibly even to Doddington, following her separation from her husband and the scandal that may well have accompanied it. 'She was young and indiscreet,' Chesterfield wrote rather bluntly following the couple's separation; 'he was old and jealous.'[36]

While Katherine's positioning as a nymph similarly suggests singleness, read within the context of eighteenth-century Diana portraiture it also indicates her imminent marriage, which took place in the October of the year Cotes's portrait was painted. By alluding to both female friendship and a transition towards marriage through Diana, Cotes's portrait may also indicate Katherine's movement from the female companionship of her life as a single woman at Doddington, where Anne must stay behind, to the conjugal bonds of married life. The mythology of Diana also contributes to this narrative through the tale of Diana and Actaeon. The stag in the background of Cotes's portrait, while clearly being pursued as part of the hunt, also evokes Actaeon's intrusion into Diana's grove, and his consequent metamorphosis into a stag, killed by his own hounds, as recounted in Ovid's *Metamorphoses*.[37] The subject of Actaeon's intrusion was disseminated in eighteenth-century engravings: in 1764, for example, the year before Cotes's portrait, John Boydell published William Woollett's engraving of Filippo Lauri's seventeenth-century *Diana and Actaeon* (figure 47), showing Diana's nymphs covering themselves at the entrance of a partially transformed Actaeon. Through associations with this myth, Cotes's portrait may similarly register male intrusion into the private world of female companionship that Katherine and Anne inhabit at Doddington, perhaps most obviously in terms of the 3rd Earl of Effingham – a man who would have been in a position to gaze on the private world of female intimacy as an Actaeon-like spectator.

Through the mythological resonances of Diana and nymph, Cotes's portrait suggests a contemporary friendship between Anne and Katherine centred on a shared engagement with a discourse of virtuous rural retirement, and a shared participation in country life. At the same time, however, these mythological resonances also cast a shadow of impending

Figure 47 William Woollett after Filippo Lauri, *Diana and Actaeon*, 1764, etching and engraving, 40.3 × 51.3 cm.

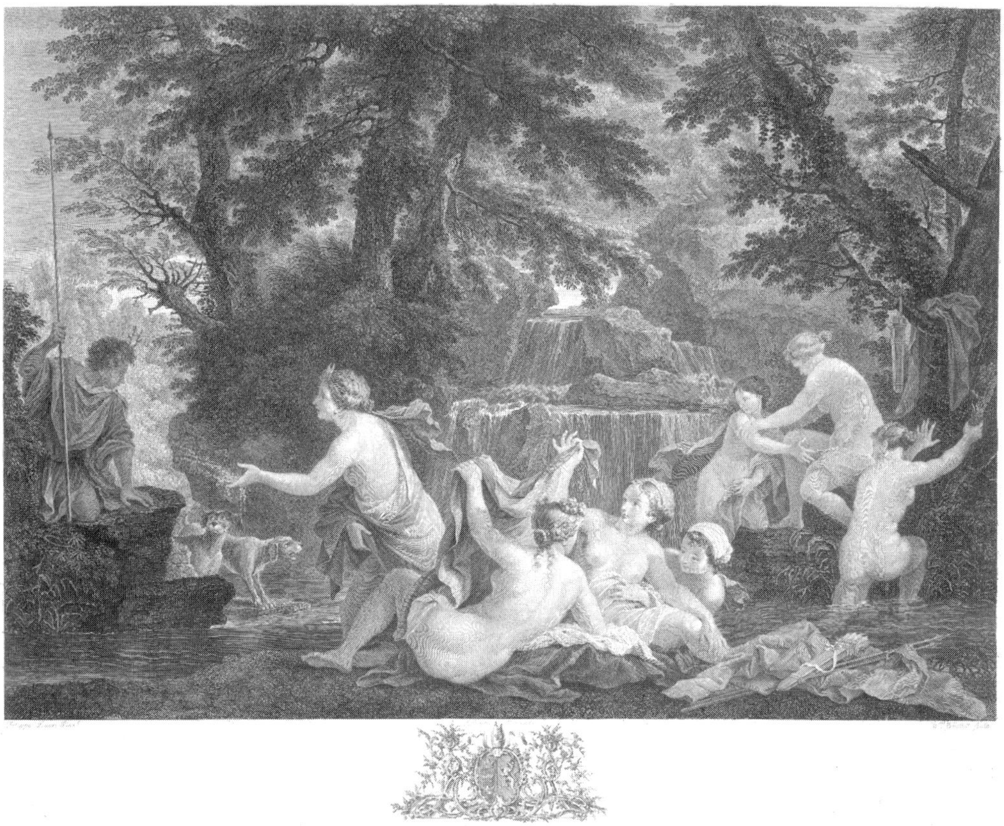

disruption and loss over this friendship through associations with male intrusion, acting as a reminder of Katherine's imminent marriage, and removal from this retired world of female companionship. Cotes's portrait seems to emerge from the quite private sentimental context of Anne and Katherine's friendship; the portrait was, indeed, probably commissioned by Anne herself, who owned it until her death in 1812.[38] Thus Cotes's portrait seems to serve a commemorative function, attempting to capture and fix in time a close relationship between Anne and Katherine that will soon be compromised by Katherine's marriage and her literal and symbolic removal from the retired world of female companionship. The portrait functions then as an act of preservation – the preservation, in paint, of a friendship against the looming threat of sentimental loss.

Pastoral retirement and the defence of the nation

While Cotes's portrait possesses a quite private and sentimental meaning and function, it also has the potential to acquire a much more public and masculine meaning and function in the context of its display at Doddington Hall. Read alongside the military portrait of Anne's brother – and probably displayed in the same space within an identical frame – this representation of pastoral retirement and female friendship has the potential to speak to themes of familial involvement in the defence of nation and empire during the Seven Years War. Katherine and Anne's shared participation in the stag hunt can be seen, I argue, as an allegory of the shared involvement of Anne's brother and Katherine's father-in-law in a series of campaigns on the French coast during this recent conflict. Turning to a series of other texts, I will explore how the pastoral space could come to stand in for the imperial space, leading to the development of analogies between sentimental and imperial defence and preservation.

Reynolds's portrait of Anne's brother (see figure 44) celebrates his participation in an attack on the French harbour of St Malo in June 1758.[39] Reputedly, Delaval had been at the forefront of this attack, as the first volunteer to land and the first Grenadier to proceed up the beach, for which he was created Knight of Bath in 1761.[40] What is interesting about this representation of Delaval is how Cotes's later representation of Anne seems to mimic certain elements of it. Anne's face is similarly shown in profile, her feet are in the same position as Delaval's, and she too holds a pointed weapon in her right hand. Similarly, the rock behind Anne echoes the rock behind Delaval, and the stag is at the same point on the horizon as the activity on the shore in Reynolds's portrait. These similarities may simply be the product of a shared language of portraiture, and dismissed on these terms as coincidental. But the familial relationship between the sitters draws, I think, these portraits into a more meaningful dialogue, particularly if Green is right in suggesting that the same design of frame that surrounds Cotes's portrait of Anne surrounded Reynolds's portrait of her brother, and that both portraits were displayed in proximity.[41]

When these portraits of Anne and her brother are viewed side by side, surrounded by identical frames that allude to warfare, Anne's participation in the mythological stag hunt has the potential to slip into a representation of her brother at St Malo. The similarities between these portraits suggest another possible reading of this huntress as Delaval, and of the hunt she is participating in as the offensive on the French coast that Delaval participates in. At the same time, Katherine also has the potential to become part of this analogy. Katherine's shared participation in this stag hunt could suggest shared familial involvement in the same campaign at St Malo. While Katherine's husband hadn't seen active service during the Seven Years War, her father-in-law – Thomas Howard, 2nd Earl of Effingham (1714–63) – had been actively involved in the early stages of this war.[42] More pointedly, the 2nd Earl had participated in the same campaign on the French coast as Delaval: early in June 1758, the 2nd Earl had arrived with his regiment at Cancalle Bay, where they entrenched themselves – along with the Grenadiers, to whom Delaval was attached – before marching towards St Malo the next day.[43] In this context, Anne and Katherine's shared participation in the hunt could resonate with and suggest the shared involvement of their male relatives in this particular attack on St Malo.

Moreover, this allusion to shared familial involvement in more recent martial activity suggests an older shared ancestral heritage of national defence. The pairing of Katherine and Anne also has resonance with the inclusion of their respective ancestors in a text published just a year before Cotes's portrait was painted. In 1764, the careers of Baron Howard of Effingham (1536–1624) and Admiral Sir Ralph Delaval (1641–1707) – who came from a junior branch of the Delaval family – had been recounted in *Lives of Illustrious British Seamen*.[44] While the men hadn't fought in the same campaigns, this text highlights the role each had played in defending the nation against threats from both France and Spain: Baron Howard in July 1588, when he sailed against the encroaching Spanish Armada near Plymouth; Sir Ralph in June 1692, at Cherbourg, during the Battle of La Hogue, as British fleets suppressed a French, Jacobite invasion.[45] Anne and Katherine's shared participation in the stag hunt could also resonate with this contemporaneous textual pairing of their ancestors, suggesting an ancestral heritage of naval heroism and martial activity in the defence of the nation shared by both their families. Surrounded by a bellicose frame which refers to the naval exploits of the women's families, this portrait could also be framed by textual narratives of these exploits. Through a process of association, Anne and Katherine's shared participation in the stag hunt could thus resonate with these past naval exploits in the defence of the nation.

Interestingly, this ancestral narrative of national defence has something else in common, aside from a familial link, with the naval offensive at St Malo. Like the conflicts Sir Ralph and Baron Howard participated in, the attack on St Malo and associated campaigns on the French coast were perceived as acts of national defence against threatened invasion. While the main purpose of these attacks was to aid Frederick II of Prussia against invading French forces, the campaigns were also incorporated into broader celebrations of the defence of nation and empire against threatened French invasion, particularly during the invasion scare of 1759.[46] When this broader perception of the attack at St Malo enters the frame, the mythological stag hunt that Katherine and Anne participate in slips quite fluidly into a representation of shared familial participation, not only in a single naval offensive, but in the broader defence of nation and empire against foreign invasion. Stag hunting is, indeed, a particularly appropriate and resonant metaphor because of its long-standing associations with landownership: the sport had long been the preserve of the landed elites who owned the deer parks and forests necessary for rearing and pursuing this animal.[47] In Cotes's portrait, this association between stag hunting and private landownership translates quite easily into notions of national and imperial landownership, with the land the stag traverses evoking Britain and her North American colonies, and the hunt the defence of these territories from the French by Delaval and the second Earl during the Seven Years War.

The potential of this portrait to suggest the defence of nation and empire might be further activated through the pastoral space in which this stag hunt takes place – more specifically, through contemporary links between such pastoral spaces and security from invasion.

In Darwall's 'Rural Happiness' (1764), for example, which I discussed above, the pastoral space is not only associated with virtuous rural retirement, but also with peace and security:

> Hail! fair Abodes of *Freedom, Joy* and *Peace!*
> Where Treasure flows, and useful Arts increase;
> No direful Arms these calm Retreats annoy,
> No barb'rous Bands the fruitful Plains destroy
> [...]
> No Coasters ravage, and no Tempest spoils.[48]

Here, the 'calm Retreats' of the pastoral are configured as a place far removed from the 'direful Arms' of war, secure from its destructive and invading forces. This space is closely identified with Britain – as Darwall comments in a footnote, the description refers to 'The famous town of *Birmingham*, near which the scene of this Poem is laid'.[49] Published, and presumably written, against the backdrop of the recent Seven Years War, Darwall's peaceful and secure pastoral haven seems to articulate, more pointedly, the safety of Britain from invasion – specifically, it seems likely, the safety of Britain following the successful defence against a threatened French invasion of Britain in 1759.[50] Looked at through this lens, the pastoral space in Cotes's portrait has the potential to reinforce and augment an understanding of the portrait as a celebration of national defence.

This analogy was also extended to Britain's colonial possessions in North America. In April 1756, in the early stages of the Seven Years War, a poem was published in the *London Magazine*, entitled 'On the Present State of America, and General Braddock's Defeat', which drew an overt association between the horrific massacre and defeat of British troops in North America and the destruction of the pastoral:

> No more I'll paint in soft descriptive strain
> The lofty mountain, or the sunny plain;
> Nor vernal meadow, nor embowering grove,
> Once the known seats of innocence and love
> But now pale terror haunts the secret shade,
> And hostile bands each wish'd retreat invade.[51]

Here, the 'hostile bands' of war enter and invade the pastoral, transforming an idealised site of retirement, with its 'embowering grove[s]' and 'secret shade[s]', into a place of 'terror'. This pastoral space, unlike that of Darwall's poem, is evidently North America, where the conflict referred to in its title – Braddock's Defeat – had taken place.[52] While the poem associates this 'terror' with the bloody massacre of British troops, the destruction of this pastoral space seems equally to encode a threat to Britain's North American possessions; more specifically, the threat posed to them by the French, who had defeated the British during this engagement. As Mark Hallett comments, this poem 'testifies to the growing anxieties concerning Britain's colonial and domestic security' in this period.[53] Through such associations between the pastoral and ideas of national and imperial security, the setting of the mythological hunt cum naval offensive in Cotes's portrait could come to suggest the defence of Britain and also of her North American colonies from French invasion, of which this naval offensive at St Malo was part and parcel.

The potential of the pastoral space in Cotes's portrait to suggest this threat to and defence of the nation is also engendered, I think, through the fear of sentimental loss communicated through the pastoral mode. The pastoral space that Anne and Katherine inhabit is the site of their friendship – a space of retired female intimacy, set apart from men. Yet as I have argued, the portrait also suggests the threatened loss of this friendship, arising from Katherine's marriage, through the threat of male intrusion – or, indeed, invasion – into the pastoral space. This dual meaning of the pastoral in Cotes's portrait produces a curious and potentially resonant coincidence, with the threat of sentimental loss imbricating with the threat of national and imperial loss during the Seven Years War. This coincidence works on the level of paint on canvas – on the level of the act of painting the pastoral as an act of preservation. In committing this pastoral fantasy of Anne and Katherine's friendship to canvas the portrait comes to guard it against the threat of loss – to fix and preserve it. By association, the act of painting this pastoral space also preserves the nation and empire against the threat of loss. In 'Braddock's Defeat', the realised threat of French invasion in North America means the poet/artist is no longer able to 'paint' in the pastoral mode. In Cotes's portrait, the very act of painting in the pastoral mode could be read as suggesting the defence and preservation of just such an imperial and domestic space.

Placed in a series of literal and figurative frames – the text and contexts that surround it, some in situ at Doddington Hall – Cotes's representation of two women engaged in a mythological stag hunt has the potential to unfold into a complex series of allegories, operating on a number of levels. A portrait that serves an apparently quite private and sentimental function in commemorating the friendship between two women could also come to serve a more public and masculine function in commemorating the military heroism of two men associated with these women.

Effeminacy and civic corruption

But if Cotes's portrait has the potential to slip into a celebration of active, masculine virtue and the successful defence of the nation, it also has the potential to turn tail and slip into something quite different. While Britain had emerged victorious from the Seven Years War as the prime imperial power in Europe, the conflict had also been the site of considerable anxiety surrounding military defeats to the French, attributed to the effeminacy and corrupted virtue of Britain's ruling elites. Effingham had, in fact, been implicated in an event that had been viewed as the most terrifying example of aristocratic corruption and effeminacy: the loss of Minorca to the French in May 1756 at the hands of Admiral John Byng (1704–57).[54] As Horace Walpole recorded at the time, Effingham's position in Admiral Byng's council of war had put him very much out of favour:

> By all one learns, Byng, Fowke, and all the officers at Gibraltar, were infatuated! They figured Port Mahon lost, and Gibraltar a-going! a-going! Lord Effingham, Cornwallis, Lord Robert Bertie, all signed the council of war, and are in as bad odour as possible.[55]

Between 1756 and 1757, Effingham had featured in a satirical print of Byng's council of war, published as part of a broadside. He is seated to Byng's left, wearing a coronet and fool's cap, and exclaiming 'Pray let us go back to Gib and there invent a Fib' – a reference to the allegedly cowardly and effeminate withdrawal of British troops to Gibraltar, and the effective handing over of Minorca to the French.[56] Here, then, we find Effingham placed at the heart of the loss of Minorca, dressed in the kind of clothing common to effigies of Byng – the 'bag-wigs and gorgeous uniforms', as M. John Caldwell identifies – so suggestive of luxury and effeminacy, and surrounded by Byng's collection of porcelain that was similarly deployed to suggest 'effeminacy and cowardice' in visual and written satires.[57] While Effingham was subsequently acquitted of any wrongdoing in relation to Minorca, his involvement in this catastrophic defeat lingered on. It was this, and not the subsequent campaigns on the French coast, for which he was remembered in two accounts of the Seven Years War published in 1764, the year before Cotes's portrait was painted.[58]

When framed by the loss of Minorca, Cotes's portrait has the potential to suggest the anxieties surrounding aristocratic effeminacy and national emasculation that had followed this event. As Kathleen Wilson explains, the loss of Minorca 'constituted the symbolic emasculation of the British nation' through military failure, perceived to have arisen from the effeminacy of the nation's aristocratic leadership and nouveau-riche elites.[59] In representing two military men – both landed elites – through two women in the guise of Diana and nymph, Cotes's portrait could bring to mind just these kind of anxieties for a contemporary audience, familiar with these narratives. The slippage between female and male in the portrait blurs gendered boundaries, suggesting precisely the 'collapse of distinctions between … men and women' that Wilson shows commentators were linking to the effeminacy of the ruling elites, and the emasculated nation, in the wake of Minorca.[60] That these women are dressed as Diana and nymph places further emphasis on this sense of effeminacy and emasculation: much of the Diana mythology – and particularly the tale of Actaeon – deals with emasculation, literal or symbolic, in the goddess's rejection and destruction of men. By associating these two military men with, and visually subsuming them into, Diana and nymph, the portrait seems to imply not heroic masculinity but emasculation and effeminacy.

In fact, Delaval's supposed heroism at St Malo had been undermined in a contemporary newspaper report, published twice in June 1758, which associated him with precisely the kind of vice that was being implicated in the effeminacy and corruption of Britain's ruling elites at this time.

> We hear a wager of 1000 l was depending between Francis Blake Delaval, Esq; and another Gentleman, both Volunteers in the present expedition, who should first land on the French coast; which was won by Mr Delaval.[61]

This act of betting serves as a reminder of Delaval's generally extravagant and dissolute lifestyle, positioning him as the antithesis of the patriotic hero, who rejects such corrupt pleasures in order to engage in a patriotic defence of the nation. Delaval's actions at St Malo, this report suggests, did not arise from a disinterested patriotic impulse, but from a vested interest in winning a bet. This attack can also be understood as part of a broader discourse in this period about the perceived corruption of the nation's aristocratic and landed elites. In November 1756, for example, two years before this harangue on Delaval, and on the heels of the loss of Minorca, an address from the people of the County of Brecon attributed the inability of the King to defend either the nation or its colonies to the effects of 'luxury and gaming [which] have introduced an almost universal venality and corruption, whereby every spark of private and public virtue is ... nearly extinguished'.[62] The June 1758 newspaper report is a version of this kind of attack, drastically undermining Delaval's supposedly heroic actions at St Malo by distancing him from the virtuous, masculine patriotism that this offensive was celebrated as evincing, and associating him instead with notions of corruption.

Cotes's portrait, and its relationship to Reynolds's portrait of Delaval, could become quite radically undermined and subverted by such knowledge about Delaval. Delaval was not, indeed, the epitome of public, masculine virtue by any stretch of the imagination. He was, according to first-hand accounts of him, a high-living gambler and womaniser, who had been tried for and found guilty of both adultery and prostitution.[63] In 1756, two years before he fought at St Malo, Delaval had also been forced to turn over the family's estates to his younger brother, Sir John Hussey Delaval, in order to pay off the vast debts he had accrued through his gambling and generally extravagant lifestyle.[64] Delaval was, in short, engaging in precisely the kind of corrupting pleasures that the masculine patriot was supposed to reject. Given this context, the association of Delaval with his sister in Cotes's portrait – and the representational blurring of boundaries between them – could be read as suggesting not his masculine virtue but the erosion and corruption of it. The mythological stag hunt could also play a part in this. I have suggested that associations between stag hunting and landownership in Cotes's portrait could be read as an analogy of the defence of Britain and its territorial possessions by Delaval and Effingham. It might also serve to suggest that Delaval and Effingham – and, perhaps, most pointedly Delaval – are in possession of the land upon which patriotic virtue was contingent. But knowledge of Delaval's loss of his estates as a result of his extravagant and dissolute lifestyle could also lead to a collapse of the analogies between stag hunting and the virtuous defence of the nation's territories from a French threat. Indeed, the housing of these two portraits at Doddington – the home of the now-owner of the Delaval estates – could have acted as an inadvertent reminder of Delaval's dispossession. When viewed in this context, Cotes's portrait offers up some contradictory meanings. Instead of suggesting the successful defence of the nation and empire by two virtuous patriots, the portrait has the potential to dramatically turn tail and present a contemporary viewer with a troubling and uncomfortable allegory, which 'frames' Delaval and Effingham as corrupt and effeminate elites who pose a dangerous threat to the nation's territorial safety and security.

Notes

1 This essay is based on the first chapter of my thesis 'Women, Portraiture and Political Representation, 1765–1787' (PhD dissertation, University of York, 2011), pp. 13–46. My thanks to the many people who have commented on and contributed to this work at various stages, particularly: Kate Davies, Harriet Guest, Mark Hallett, Robert Jones, Gill Perry and Kate Retford.

2 Alastair Smart, *Allan Ramsay: a Complete Catalogue of his Paintings*, ed. John Ingamells (New Haven and London: Yale University Press for the Paul Mellon Centre for Studies in British Art, 1999), cat. nos. 155, 237, 309; David Mannings, *Sir Joshua Reynolds: A Complete Catalogue of His Paintings*, 2 vols (New Haven and London: Yale University Press for the Paul Mellon Centre for Studies in British Art, 2000), cat. nos. 494, 495, 1328. For examples of Jean-Marc Nattier and Nicolas de Largillière's 'Diana' portraits, see: *The Masterpieces of Nattier* (London and Glasgow: Gowans and Gray, 1920), pp. 21, 54; Myra Nan Rosenfeld, *Largillierre and the Eighteenth-Century Portrait* (Montreal: Montreal Museum of Fine Arts, [c.1982]), pp. 216, 219, 242.

3 Aileen Ribeiro, *The Dress Worn at Masquerade in England, 1730–1790, and Its Relation to Fancy Dress in Portraiture* (New York: Garland, 1984), pp. 261–4; 'A particular Account of the grand Masquerade-Ball given by the King of Denmark' in *The Ladies' own Memorandum-book; or, Daily Pocket Journal, for the Year 1769. Designed as a Methodical Register of all their Transactions of Business, as well as Amusement* (London: Robinson and Roberts; Newcastle, T. Slack, [1769]), no page.

4 John Hayes, *The Portrait in British Art* (London: National Portrait Gallery, 1991), pp. 101–2; Richard Green, '"The Hon. Lady Stanhope and the Countess of Effingham as Diana and her Companion" by Francis Cotes', *National Art-Collections Fund Annual Review* (1988), 109.

5 Green, '"The Hon. Lady Stanhope"', 106–9.

6 Peter Babell, London, to John Hussey Delaval, Doddington Hall, Lincoln, 24 July 1766, as quoted in: National Portrait Gallery, *The Art of the Picture Frame*, 'British Picture Framemakers, 1630–1950', s.v. 'Peter Babell', www.npg.org.uk/research/conservation/directory-of-british-framemakers/b.php, accessed 20 July 2012.

7 Stafford M. Linsley, 'Delaval family (per. c.1520–1752)', *Oxford Dictionary of National Biography*, Oxford University Press, 2004; www.oxforddnb.com/view/article/73888, accessed 22 July 2012.

8 Mannings, *Reynolds*, II, p. 164.
9 Marcia Pointon, *Hanging the Head: Portraiture and Social Formation in Eighteenth-Century England* (New Haven and London: Yale University Press for the Paul Mellon Centre for Studies in British Art, 1993), p. 36.
10 R.E.G. Cole, *History of the Manor and Township of Doddington: otherwise Doddington-Pigot, in the County of Lincoln, and its Successive Owners, with Pedigrees* (Lincoln: J. Williamson, 1897), pp. 221–2. My thanks to Claire Birch at Doddington Hall for photographs of these tapestries and an enlivening correspondence about them.
11 Francis Askham, *The Gay Delavals* (London: Jonathan Cape, 1955), pp. 97–9.
12 John Burke, *A Genealogical and Heraldic History of the Commoners of Great Britain and Ireland*, 4 vols (London: Henry Colburn, 1833–38), I, p. 253, www.archive.org/stream/genealogicalheralo1burk#page/n27/mode/2up; 'Thorpe Hall, Middleton Lane', *Leodis: A Photographic Archive of Leeds*, www.leodis.org/display.aspx?resourceIdentifier=200568_34081668, accessed 16 August 2011.
13 *Public Advertiser*, 19 October 1765. At the time of this marriage, both Katherine and Thomas were under age according to Hardwicke's Marriage Act of 1753, hence an elopement to Scotland in order to escape the need for parental consent seeming highly likely. Thomas and Katherine were subsequently married by banns in August 1766 in Rothwell Parish Church: *Yorkshire Marriage Registers: West Riding*, ed. C.S. James (London: issued to the subscribers by Phillimore & Co., 1914), p. xii, 20.A.
14 Edward Mead Johnson, *Francis Cotes* (Oxford: Phaidon, 1976), pp. 30–1; Hayes, *British Art*, p. 101; Andrew Wilton, *The Swagger Portrait: Grand Manner Portraiture in Britain from Van Dyck to Augustus John, 1630–1930* (London: Tate Gallery, 1992), p. 126.
15 Pointon, *Hanging*, p. 36.
16 Donald Posner, 'The "Duchesse de Velours" and Her Daughter: A Masterpiece by Nattier and Its Historical Context', *Metropolitan Museum Journal*, 31 (1996), 134, www.jstor.org/stable/1512976, accessed 5 May 2011.
17 Adam Smith, *The Theory of Moral Sentiments*, 2nd edn (London: A. Millar; Edinburgh: A. Kincaid and J. Bell, 1761), pp. 2–5.
18 For an early example of this discourse, still in circulation at the time of Cotes' portrait, see: Joseph Addison and Richard Steele, *The Spectator*, 8 vols (London: J. and R. Tonson, 1765), I, pp. 65–8. See, also, the discussion of Mary Wortley Montagu's engagement with this discourse, in: Stephen Bending, 'Mrs. Montagu's Contemplative Bench: Bluestocking Gardens and Female Retirement', *Huntington Library Quarterly*, 69:4 (2006), 557, 569–72, 577–8, www.jstor.org/stable/4497977, accessed 4 June 2010.
19 Mary Darwall, 'Rural Happiness. To a Friend', in *Original Poems on Several Occasions. By Miss Whateley* (London: R. and J. Dodsley, 1764), pp. 29–33.
20 *Ibid.*, pp. 29, 32, 31.
21 *Ibid.*, pp. 32, 33.
22 Susanna was the first wife of Anne's second eldest brother, Sir John Hussey Delaval (1728–1808): Stafford M. Linsley, 'Delaval, John Hussey, Baron Delaval (1728–1808)', *Oxford Dictionary of National Biography*, Oxford

University Press, 2004; www.oxforddnb.com/view/article/39337, accessed 22 July 2012.

23 Katherine Howard, Countess of Effingham, Holmes Hall, to Susanna Hussey Delaval, Doddington, 9 November 1766, Social Letters, Seaton Delaval Manuscripts, Northumberland Archives, Woodhorn Museum, Northumberland. Hereafter, this collection will be referred to as Seaton Delaval Manuscripts.

24 Katherine Howard, Countess of Effingham to Susanna Hussey Delaval, 22 December [1767], Seaton Delaval Manuscripts.

25 Philip Stanhope, 4th Earl of Chesterfield to Arthur Charles Stanhope, 12 October 1765 in *Letters of Philip Dormer Fourth Earl of Chesterfield to his Godson and Successor*, ed. the Earl of Carnarvon, 2nd edn (Oxford: Clarendon Press, 1890), p. 368. Also quoted, without citation, in: Askham, *Delavals*, p. 97.

26 Cole, *Doddington*, p. 127.

27 *Ibid.*, pp. 112–13.

28 Cole also states this was the case: *ibid.*, p. 147.

29 Mannings, *Reynolds*, II, pp. 430–1.

30 John Goodchild, 'Matters of Concern: the Life Story of the Third Earl of Effingham' in Melvyn Jones (ed.), *Aspects of Rotherham: Discovering Local History* (Barnsley: Wharncliffe Publishing, 1995), p. 105.

31 Katherine Howard, Countess of Effingham to Susanna Hussey Delaval, 24 May 1768, Seaton Delaval Manuscripts; Katherine Howard, Countess of Effingham to Mr. Ingram, 18 April 1790, photocopy of an unidentified published source, Papers Relating to the Earl of Effingham, John Goodchild Collection, Wakefield.

32 Judy Egerton, *British Sporting and Animal Paintings, 1655–1867: A Catalogue* (London: Tate Gallery for the Yale Center for British Art, 1978), p. 151. For a more developed discussion of this portrait in relation to Cotes' portrait and in itself, see: Vibert, 'Women, Portraiture and Political Representation', pp. 171–202.

33 G.E. Cokayne (ed.), *The Complete Peerage of England, Scotland, Ireland, Great Britain and the United Kingdom, Extant, Extinct or Dormant*, 6 vols (Gloucester: Alan Sutton Publishing, 2000), V, p. 100; L.G. Pine, *The New Extinct Peerage, 1884–1971: Containing Extinct, Abeyant, Dormant and Suspended Peerages With Genealogies and Arms* (London: Heraldry Today, 1972), p. 98; *Allgemeine Deutsche Biographie*, 56 vols (Munich: Historische Kommission, Bayerische Akademie der Wissenschaften, 1875–1912), XVIII, pp. 357–8. My thanks to Mette Harder for sourcing and translating this information on Luise von Anhalt-Dessau.

34 Antonia Fraser, *Love and Louis XIV: The Women in the Life of The Sun King* (London: Weidenfeld and Nicolson, 2006), pp. 113–16.

35 *Ibid.*, pp. 147–8.

36 Philip Stanhope, 4th Earl of Chesterfield to Arthur Charles Stanhope, 27 September 1763 in *Letters of Philip Dormer*, p. 341. Also quoted in: Cole, *Doddington*, p. 146.

37 Most contemporaneously with Cotes's portrait, see: Ovid, *A New Translation of Ovid's Metamorphoses into English Prose* (London: Printed for J. Robinson,

[etc.], 1759; first published, 1748), pp. 102–5.
38 Hayes, *British Art*, p. 102.
39 Mannings, *Reynolds*, II, p. 164.
40 Askham, *Delavals*, pp. 91–2.
41 Green, '"The Hon. Lady Stanhope"', 109.
42 The 3rd Earl's first military commission was as an ensign in the Coldstream Guards, but came in 1761, after the regiment's major involvement in the conflict: R.E. Wilson, 'Notes on the Howards of Effingham' in *Transactions of the Historical Society Volume Seven: 1951–1957* (Sheffield: J.W. Northend, 1957), p. 338. For an overview of the Coldstream Guards' involvement in the Seven Years War, see: Julian Paget, *Second to None: Coldstream Guards 1650–2000* (Barnsley: Pen & Sword Books, 2000), pp. 18–22. After being promoted to Colonel of the 1st Troop of Horse Grenadier Guards in 1760, the 2nd Earl spent the remainder of the war in command of the camp and garrison at Winchester: *Public Advertiser*, 15 July 1760; *General Evening Post*, 2 July 1761; *Public Advertiser*, 12 June 1762.
43 *A Journal of the Campaign on the Coast of France, 1758*, 2nd edn (London: J. Townsend, 1758), pp. 10, 49–51.
44 Admiral Sir Ralph Delaval should not to be confused with Sir Ralph Delaval, first baronet (1622–91). *Lives of Illustrious British Seamen* (Edinburgh, 1764), pp. 2–13, 158–163. See, also, an earlier comparable account of Sir Ralph and Baron Howard in: John Entick, *A New Naval History: or, Compleat View of the British Marine* (London: R. Manby, [etc.], 1757), pp. 701–2, 333–5.
45 *Illustrious British Seamen*, pp. 2–3, 158–60.
46 Fred Anderson, *The Crucible of War: The Seven Years War and the Fate of the Empire in British North America, 1754–1766* (London: Faber and Faber, 2000), p. 299; Tobias George Smollett, *The History of England*, 6 vols (London: R. Scholey, [etc.]; Edinburgh: J. Ballantyne & Co., 1810–11), V, pp. 240–1; 'English Heroism against French Invaders', in *The Apollo: or, the Muses Choice: being a Collection of the most Celebrated New Songs, Sung at Ranelagh, Vauxhall, Marybone-Gardens &c. &c.* (London: J. Pridden, [1759]), pp. 68–70 and *The Muse's Delight: or, the Songster's Jovial Companion. Being a Collection of Three Hundred of the Most Celebrated New Songs, Sung at Several Societies of Choice Spirits* (London, Bristol, Darlington and Salop: J. Pridden, [etc.], 1760), pp. 68–70.
47 Donna Landry, *The Invention of the Countryside: Hunting, Walking, and Ecology in English Literature, 1671–1831* (Basingstoke and New York: Palgrave Macmillan, 2001), p. 12. For a discussion of the development of deer parks and forest enclosure in the context of hunting, see: Anthony Vandervell and Charles Coles, *Game and the English Landscape: The Influence of the Chase on Sporting Art and Scenery* (London: Debrett's Peerage, 1980), pp. 11–15, 23–8.
48 Darwall, 'Rural Happiness', p. 30.
49 *Ibid.*, p. 30n.
50 Smollett, *History*, V, pp. 551–63.
51 'On the Present State of America, and General Braddock's Defeat', *The London Magazine; or, Gentleman's Monthly Intelligencer. For April 1756* (London: R. Baldwin, 1756), p. 189. Quoted in: Mark Hallett, 'From out of the Shadows: Sir Joshua Reynolds' *Captain Robert Orme*', *Visual Culture in Britain*,

5:2 (Winter, 2004), 44, www.manchesteruniversitypress.co.uk/uploads/docs/s3_24.pdf, accessed 1 March 2010.

52 For an account of Braddock's Defeat, see Hallett, 'From out of the Shadows', 43–4.

53 *Ibid.*, 45.

54 See: John Byng, *An Appeal to the People: Containing, the Genuine and Entire Letter of Admiral Byng* (London: J. Morgan, 1756), p. 21.

55 Horace Walpole to John Chute Esq, 8 June 1756 in Horace Walpole, *The Letters of Horace Walpole, Earl of Orford: Including Numerous Letters Now First Published From the Original Manuscripts*, ed. J. Wright and George Agar-Ellis Dover, 1st Baron Dover, 6 vols (London: Richard Bentley, 1840), III, p. 222, http://books.google.com/.

56 Frederic George Stephens and Mary Dorothy George, *A Catalogue of Prints and Drawings in the British Museum: Division I. Personal and Political Satires*, 11 vols (London: Chiswick Press by order of the Trustees of the British Museum, 1870–1954), III, p. 986; M. John Caldwell, *Arts and Arms: Literature, Politics and Patriotism during the Seven Years War* (Manchester: Manchester University Press, 2004), pp. 50, 52, 86.

57 Caldwell, *Arts and Arms*, pp. 66, 62.

58 *A Complete History of the Present War, from its Commencement in 1756, to the End of the Campaign*, 2 vols. (London: J. Knox, 1764; first published 1761), II, pp. 93, 176; John Entick, *The General History of the Late War: Containing it's [sic] Rise, Progress, and Event, in Europe, Asia, Africa, and America*, 5 vols (London: Edward Dilly and John Millan, 1763–64), I, pp. 281, 290, 308, 326, 462.

59 Kathleen Wilson, *The Sense of the People: Politics, Culture and Imperialism in England, 1715–1785* (Cambridge: Cambridge University Press, 1998), pp. 195, 185–9.

60 *Ibid.*, p. 188.

61 *Lloyd's Evening Post and British Chronicle*, 26 June 1758 – 28 June 1758; *London Chronicle*, 27 June 1758 – 29 June 1758.

62 'Instructions from the High Sheriff, Gentlemen, Clergy, and Freeholders of the COUNTY of BRECON, to the Honourable Thomas Morgan, Esq; their Representative in Parliament' in *The Voice of the People: a Collection of Addresses to His Majesty, and Instructions to Members of Parliament by their Constituents* (London: J. Payne, 1756), pp. 54–5.

63 See: Richard Lovell Edgeworth and Maria Edgeworth, *Memoirs of Richard Lovell Edgeworth*, 2 vols (London: R. Hunter, 1820), I, pp. 142–8; Miss [E.] Ambrose, *The Life and Memoirs of the Late Miss Ann Catley, the Celebrated Actress: with Biographical Sketches of Sir Francis Blake Delaval, and the Hon. Isabella Pawlet, Daughter to the Earl of Thanet* (London: J. Bird, [1789]), pp. 13–14, 20, 22, 26–9, 34–5.

64 See: Linsley, 'Delaval, John Hussey'; Parliament of Great Britain, *An Act for Vesting Divers Manors, Lands, and Hereditaments, Part of the Settled Estate of Francis Blake Delaval Esquire, in Trustees, for Raising Money to pay off and Discharge several Debts and Incumbrances; and for other Purposes therein Mentioned* (London, 1756).

9

The Waterloo Chamber before the Battle of Waterloo

Desmond Shawe-Taylor

THE creation of a distinctive tradition of heroic full-length portraiture intended for public display was one of the most significant achievements of British artists during the Georgian period.[1] The Waterloo Chamber at Windsor Castle, assembled in the 1830s, the last years of that age, is surely the greatest show-case of that achievement. Unfortunately it is not as easy to trace the history of the display and interpret its meaning as might be expected from such a high-profile commission. Part of the difficulty lies in the fact that the two creators of the Chamber, Sir Thomas Lawrence and George IV, both died in 1830 (Lawrence on 7 January and the King on 26 June) before the space had been built or the paintings moved to Windsor. Neither creator ever therefore 'signed off' the scheme. It is not the purpose of this paper to discuss the accuracy of the present appearance of the Chamber, except to say that the fundamentals of the architecture certainly date from the time of George IV. Sir Charles Long's brief for the transformation of the Castle, dateable to 1823, specifies the creation of a room 'for the purpose of a Picture Gallery, to be called the Waterloo Gallery, and to contain the Portraits painted for his Majesty by Sir T. Lawrence'.[2] This space was created by covering over an existing courtyard (called 'Horn Court'). Jeffry Wyatville submitted an estimate of £18,000 for the 'Waterloo Chamber' on 29 May 1829.[3] The Royal Library holds a set of five drawings by him, which show a vault with sky-lights, essentially as it appears today, one of which is dated 18 February 1830.[4]

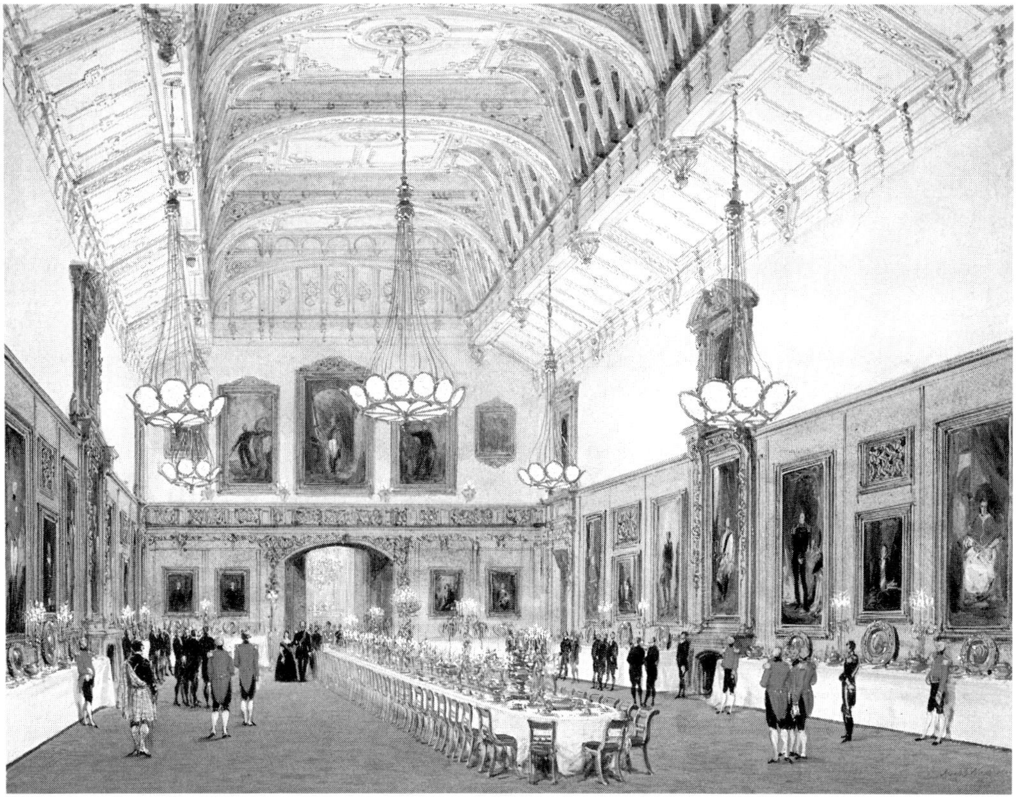

Figure 48
Joseph Nash,
Waterloo Chamber, Windsor Castle, 5 June 1844.

Hanging the Royal Collection

The first reliable record of the appearance of the space as built is provided by Joseph Nash's watercolour depicting the state banquet of 5 June 1844 (figure 48). It can be assumed that in broad outline this reflects George IV's intentions at the time of his death. The purpose of this chapter is to examine how those intentions might have developed by restricting the discussion to the very first phase of the project – to that which occurred before the Battle of Waterloo itself on 18 June 1815. Whatever George IV had in mind at this stage it certainly cannot have been a space called the Waterloo Chamber! Particular attention will be paid to those aspects of George IV's earlier patronage which anticipated the Chamber and therefore give some insight into how the ideas developed.

The difficulty in this venture lies in the fact that George IV had access to royal sums of money for many years and to royal residences for relatively few. The Prince of Wales had begun to purchase works of art by 1780; he came of age in 1783, at which point he acquired and remodelled Carlton House and began collecting in earnest. He learned quickly that he could with impunity spend unlimited sums on both activities.[5] He was made Prince Regent in 1811, but this did not allow him to take over the official or private residences of his father. It was only upon George III's death in January 1820 that he got his hands upon the great royal public spaces. The energy with which he then set about transforming them gives some idea of how important their acquisition must have seemed. During his ten-year reign (1820–30) an enfilade of state rooms was created within St James's Palace; Windsor Castle and Buckingham Palace were entirely re-created inside and out, in both cases providing brand new sequences of interiors (including the Waterloo Chamber). The brief for the Windsor Castle project was drawn up in 1823; George IV took up residence there in 1828, but the work was not completed until well into the next reign. Building at Buckingham Palace started in 1825, by which time George IV had decided to change it from private residence to public palace and it was completed in time for Queen Victoria to take up residence there in 1837.[6] George IV had fifty years during which to acquire works of art and ten years in possession of the great royal palaces worthy of their display, for almost all of which they were building sites. It is perhaps for this reason that Carlton House seems to have been treated as an ever-changing 'Ideal Palaces Exhibition' rather than a definitive architectural statement or site of a coherent picture display.

Carlton House lacked wall space for any part of George IV's collection, but was especially ill-suited to the display of full-length portraits, having no great hall or long gallery. Because wall space was so much at a premium it is worth examining the full lengths he did hang and the arrangements he created with them. The information for such a reconstruction comes from a variety of sources, including watercolour illustrations, many prepared for Pyne's *Royal Residences* of 1819, and inventories, the two most important dated 1816 and 1819 on the title page, though in both cases compiled throughout the 1820s and much annotated subsequently.[7]

The two façades of Carlton House, recorded in William Westall watercolours for use in Pyne (Royal Library, RC 922169–70) were very different in character. The north façade faced a courtyard by Pall Mall, protected from this thoroughfare by a railing and sentries on duty. It presented an appropriately public, severe and military character through its entirely rusticated wall treatment and use of the Corinthian order for the free-standing portico. The ground floor containing the state rooms is very slightly raised with a partly concealed service basement below. The south façade on the other hand was private and protected by the garden, which permitted an open and domestic character, expressed through an undecorated wall treatment and French windows along its entire length on both the ground and first floor. The sloping site meant that the basement became the ground floor for the garden façade, which allowed state rooms of apparently equal prestige to occupy two floors, with the Prince's more important private rooms laid out above.[8] The most formal room on the garden façade was the Throne Room at the west end on the first floor. This was decorated with mirrors which allowed no space for paintings to hang. The Ante Chamber to this Throne Room was the only room on the garden façade to display full-length portraits and contained Allan Ramsay's pair of state portraits of George III and Queen Charlotte (OM 996–7), paired off with Reynolds's portrait of Frederick, Duke of York (OM 1018), commissioned by the Prince of Wales in 1788 and Hoppner's portrait of the Prince himself (OM 834), painted in 1796.[9] Otherwise with one exception the rooms along the garden façade on both main floors were densely hung with George IV's best Dutch and Flemish paintings.[10] More Dutch and Flemish masterpieces were found in the third-floor suite of rooms along the garden, where they mingled with French eighteenth-century and even some English works; the Prince's Bedroom and 'Old Bedroom' were hung with small enamel copies, taken from portraits (many by Reynolds and Hoppner) and Old Master paintings in the collection.[11]

George IV's military full lengths, those that could be displayed at all, hung in the rooms on the courtyard façade of Carlton House, especially in the East and West Anti Rooms (the rooms which lay in the recessed bays on either side of the portico). The West Anti Room (seen in a watercolour after Charles Wild, RC 922175) contained five full lengths and two head and shoulders all depicting members of the British and French royal families. It included Reynolds's influential portrait of the greatest warrior of the Guelf dynasty, William Augustus, Duke of Cumberland, 1721–65 (OM 1010), first recorded hanging at Carlton House in 1792. This portrait is of special significance because of its oversize format (measuring approximately 9 ft by 6 ft rather than 8 ft by 5 ft, which was standard for the period); it was sent to Lawrence's studio in 1819 where it remained during the 1820s (whether to restore or study is not recorded) and was hanging among the Lawrences in the Waterloo Chamber in 1835.[12] Every full length in the spaces so far mentioned at Carlton House depicted a royal sitter; the only non-royal full lengths hung in the East Anti Room across the hall from the West Anti Room and in the Crimson Drawing Room next to that room. No images survive of the East Anti Room so we can only guess at the arrangement of the works listed, which included four full lengths by Hoppner, two statesmen and close associates of the Prince – the Duke of Bedford (OM 842), and Marquess of Hastings (OM 842) and two Admirals – Horatio Nelson (OM 849) and Earl St Vincent (OM 851). The depiction of the two naval heroes is obviously inspired by Reynolds's portraits of Admirals Keppel (OM 1024) and Rodney (OM 1026), works commissioned by George IV at the end of the artist's life in 1786 and 1788 respectively. A diagram in Farington's diary for 26 June 1811 indicates these two Reynolds portraits hanging in the Crimson Drawing Room (see below).[13] It must be assumed that Hoppner's pair was intended to complete the set of four: in 1808 the frame maker, Edward Wyatt, was paid £135 for three 'new whole length frames made [to] Match [whichever frame served as the original model, probably Keppel's] for Paintings of Admirals' and £260 for 'carving and Gilding' 16 corners for '4 frames for Paintings of Admirals' including 'Dolphins, Anchors, Coral, Oak &c'.[14] These matching fames are still visible round all four paintings, with all these decorative elements, alluding to the sea and also binding the sitters' images with victorious wreaths of oak as one might have bound their brows in ancient times.

George IV clearly planned a species of 'Trafalgar Chamber' to celebrate the victory of 1805 which concluded the naval element of the Napoleonic Wars.[15] But Carlton House could not find space even for such a significant group; at some time around 1815 the Reynolds pair was moved from the Crimson Drawing Room, where Farington saw them, and sent to store.[16] As the great building schemes mentioned above reached their conclusion this group could be reassembled, but only by a circuitous route. On 24 July 1828 the two Hoppners were sent to the 'New Gallery' at Windsor Castle, according to an annotation on an inventory.[17] This must refer to the 'New Corridor' (now Grand Corridor), where George IV generally hung half-lengths of his friends and political associates rather than full lengths of national heroes. The same inventory is further annotated with the next move of the Hoppner pair – to St James's Palace in 1832, where they presumably joined the two Reynolds portraits, described as 'In the King's Closet St James palace 1832'.[18] It is at this point that another interesting royal and military

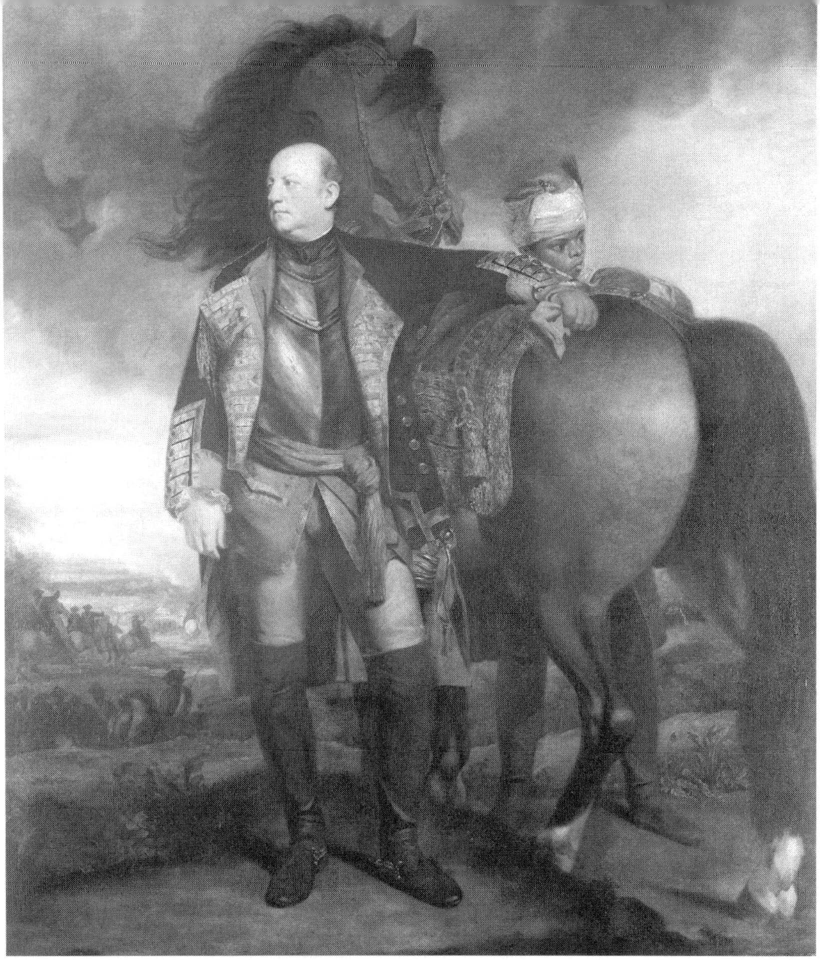

Figure 49
Sir Joshua Reynolds, *John Manners, Marquess of Granby*, 1767, oil on canvas, 245.5 × 207 cm.

image comes into play: Morier's equestrian portrait of George II on the battlefield of Dettingen (OM 591), which George IV acquired in exchange for a portrait of himself and hung on the staircase at Carlton House.[19] In the 1819 Inventory this painting is annotated exactly as the two Reynolds portraits as 'In the King's Closet St James palace 1832'; presumably in this arrangement Keppel and Rodney hung on either side of the King George II, the monarch in whose service they began their naval careers.[20]

The most important military display at Carlton House was unquestionably in the Crimson Drawing Room where a pair of Reynolds portraits were hung, depicting Frederick, Count of Schaumburg-Lippe (1724–77) and John Manners, Marquess of Granby (1721–70) (plate 18 and figure 49). The composition of the portrait of the Marquess of Granby dates from 1763 or 1764 when the French general at the battle of Vellingshausen 15–16 July 1761, the duc de Broglie, sportingly commissioned a portrait of his admired opponent; the resulting painting (now in the Ringling Museum of Art, Sarasota) was exhibited at the Society of Artists in 1766.[21] At this time and in a similar spirit of honouring valour, George, 1st Marquess Townshend (1724–1807), commissioned the autograph replica in the Royal Collection (OM 1022), for which Granby sat on three occasions in 1766, as a pair to the new portrait of the Count of Schaumburg-Lippe (OM 1027), both men under whom Townshend had served.[22] All three portraits were oversize: a standard full length was roughly 8 ft by 5 ft (245 × 150 cm); these are nearly 8 ft by 7 ft (245 × 210 cm), the extra width allowing the battle field to play a complementary role in relation to the figure. George IV may have been aware of the composition of the Granby portrait before acquiring it as it provides the model for his own oversize portrait by Reynolds (Lloyd-Webber Collection) painted in 1783, exhibited at the Royal Academy in 1784 and given away to Lord Melbourne in that year.[23] Whenever George IV first became aware of the pair he actually acquired them from the commissioner's widow, Lady Townshend, on 16 July 1810. He hung them in the Crimson Drawing Room, the room occupying the north-west corner of the palace. They are marked here in a sketch diagram in Farington's diary recording his visit of 26 June 1811 on either side of the door into the West Anti Room and next to Reynolds's full lengths of Admirals Keppel and Rodney (discussed above, OM 1024 and 1026), which hung immediately behind the three (blind) windows on the rusticated block to the right of the courtyard façade.[24] At some date the two army heroes were moved into this latter position, where they appear hanging in their current frames on either side of a mirror in the drawing of the marriage of Princess Charlotte in 1816 (attributed to William Westall, RC 917629).[25] The Carlton House Inventory of 1819 gives a particularly vivid impression of the importance of these paintings, describing the portrait of the 'Count de la Lippe' as 'most Capital' and valuing both at an astonishing £1,050 (1,000 guineas) each.[26]

Portraiture and History Painting

It is not surprising that these works were so highly valued, especially at the time of the conception of the Waterloo Chamber: they provide such an obvious model for that project. They are excellent examples of Reynolds's work at the height of his powers and reputation and in the type of battlefield portrait which would seem to stray into that elusive higher genre of the period – History Painting. The portraits celebrate the victorious alliance of German and British forces during the Seven Years War and more generally suggest the idea of comradeship, between the sitters and the commissioner. In the circumstances of the duc de Broglie's commission one even sees a comradeship between foes. The two portraits are clearly designed to face each other and have always been hung this way round. They are also perhaps intended to contrast different characteristics: artillery and cavalry; aristocratic German elegance and bluff Englishness. The Marquess of Granby was famous for having lost his hat and wig in the impetuosity of his cavalry charge at the Battle of Warburg on 31 July 1760; Reynolds's decision to present him bare-headed may have been intended as reminder of this episode, an example of soldier-like banter. The eighteenth century accepted this combination of praise and mockery as a rhetorical device called 'raillery', defined in the *Spectator* as ridicule upon 'an Excess in something which is in itself laudable' – in Granby's case patriotic zeal and courage.[27] Needless to say this Reynolds 'railles' with dignity, modelling his modern soldier's bald head on that of one of the greatest generals of antiquity, Scipio Africanus, whose features were then believed to be recorded in a bust at the Versailles museum, much reproduced in prints (figure 50).[28] It might be said that Reynolds's paintings evoke the dignity of history and the rough comedy of comradeship.[29]

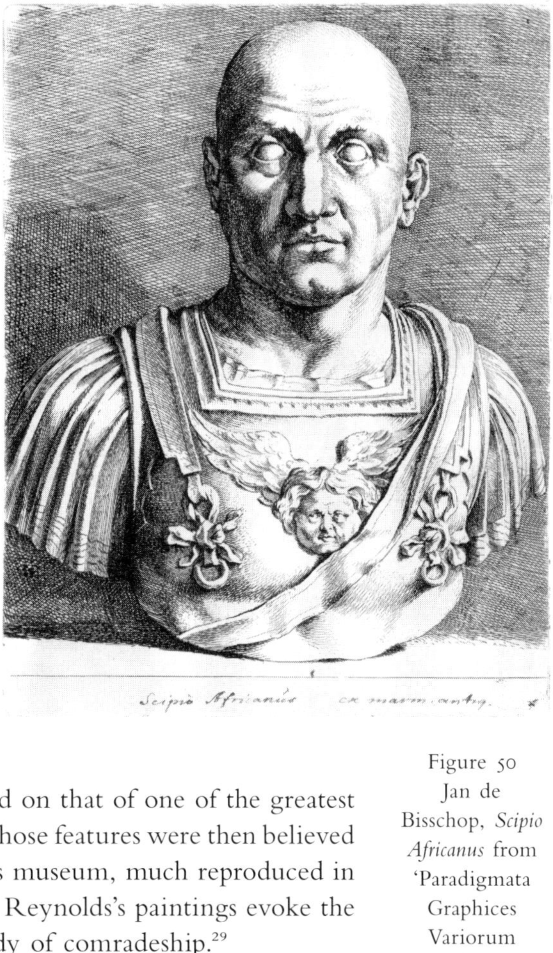

Figure 50 Jan de Bisschop, *Scipio Africanus* from 'Paradigmata Graphices Variorum Artificium', c.1672–89.

On 11 April 1814 the Treaty of Fontainebleau was signed between France and the allied powers, Austria, Prussia and Russia (though not Britain), forcing Napoleon to abdicate as Emperor and accept exile in Elba. In June of that year allied sovereigns visited London in order to celebrate the end of a series of wars against revolutionary France lasting off and on for twenty years and the restoration of the French King Louis XVIII. For two weeks, from 7 to 22 June, the Emperor of Russia and the King of Prussia, with their generals and ministers were together in London; this was part of a larger celebration which culminated in a pageant on 1 August to mark the centenary of the Hanoverian dynasty.[30] The first indication that Thomas Lawrence might be considered as a suitable recorder of these events occurred on 2 May 1814, the date of a letter written to him by the socialite, painter and travel writer, Lady Anne Barnard (1750–1825).[31] Lady Anne tells Lawrence that 'I should feel deeply sorry if such an occasion was lost in handing down to posterity by such a pencil as yours, the noblest events that the history of the world has to produce.' She therefore proposes two paintings: one depicting the event on 20 April 1814 when the restored King Louis XVIII bestowed the order of the St Esprit on the Prince Regent with the words, 'To you Sir I have owed my all!'; the other depicting the forthcoming London visit. 'With respect to the other painting,' she writes, 'you know better than I do, that the two Emperors, the King of Prussia and some of the greatest generals the world can boast are likely to be here soon to see our Regent and to visit this country – what a noble assemblage on such an occasion for your imagination to groupe.' She further suggests that Lawrence should include the Princess Charlotte in the group, to add 'female softness and beauty' and his own portrait, following the examples of Titian and Reynolds. She concludes by observing that 'if the *present opportunity is lost*, its strength and force from collecting the countenances as they *now are*, will be lost for ever'. Lady Anne mentions in the letter that she hopes to 'see the Regent shortly', but it is obvious from her tone that she has the talent to suggest rather than the power to effect this commission. It would seem however that she set the thing in motion. On the 5 June 1814 Lawrence wrote to Colonel MacMahon enclosing Lady Anne's letter offering his services to the Prince Regent much as she suggested.[32] On 9 June 1814 Joseph Farington reported in his diary that Lawrence had shown him a request from Sir Charles Stewart 'informing Him that the Prince Regent desired to have two whole length Portraits of General Blucher and Genl. Platoff and that he shd. Bring Genl. Blucher to Lawrence to sit for His portrait at 12 o Clock on Friday the 10th. Inst.'[33] Charles Stewart, later 3rd Marquess of Londonderry (1778–1854) was half-brother to the famous politician, Lord Castlereagh (1769–1822), an intimate of the Prince and an enthusiastic patron of Lawrence; he may have done more than anyone to reconcile the Prince to the idea of employing an artist cited in the enquiry into the conduct of his estranged wife.[34] However it came about, Lawrence obtained sittings (presumably very few) from Generals Blücher and Platov during their London stay. The resulting portraits (figures 51 and 52) were exhibited to great acclaim at the Royal Academy on 7 May 1815 (nos. 155 and 163); thereafter they remained in the artist's possession until claimed after his death.[35]

This 1814 commission also gave rise to four other full-length portraits: the Duke of Wellington sat on the 6 July 1814, the resulting painting (OM 917, plate 19) was exhibited at the Royal Academy in 1815 (no. 109). The Emperor of Russia and King of Prussia both granted sittings during their London visit but neither portrait (OM 883 and 898) was completed until Lawrence had obtained further sittings at the Congress of Aix-la-Chapelle in 1818; the Prince Regent himself sat in

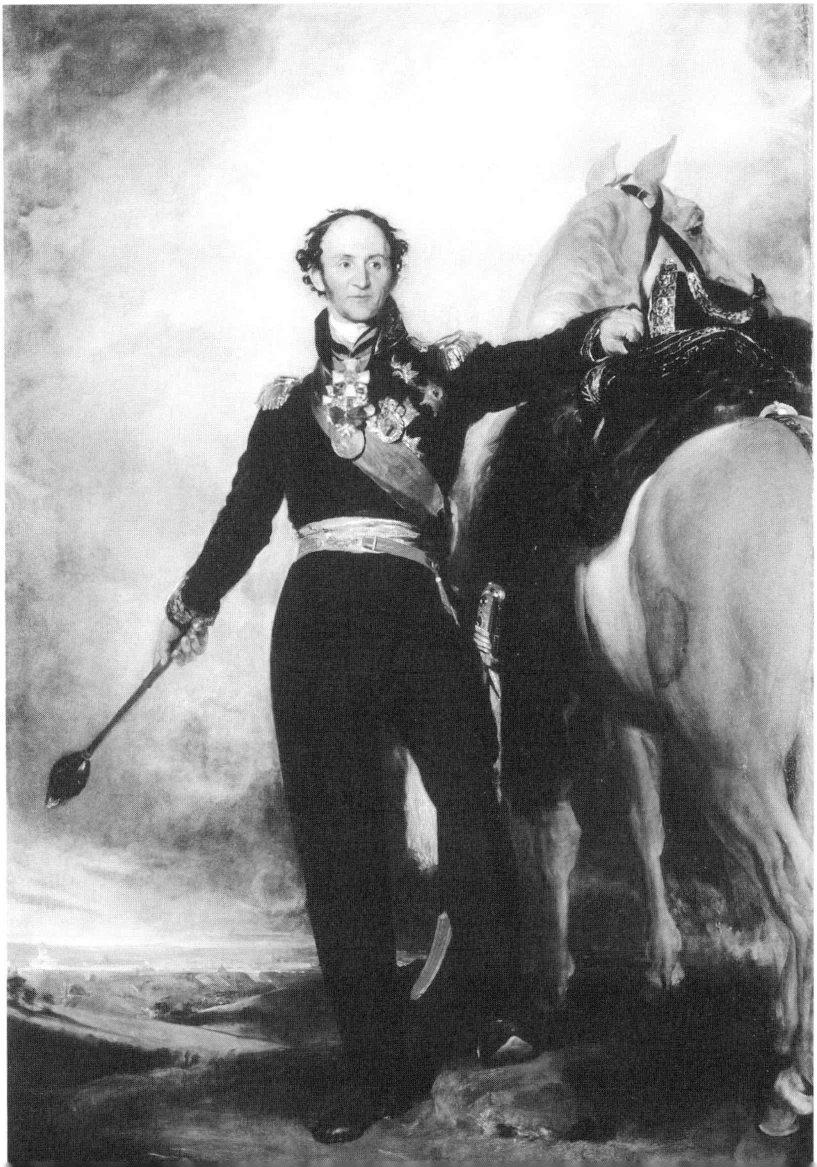

Figure 51 Thomas Lawrence, *Matvei Ivanovitch, Count Platov*, 1814, oil on canvas, 270 × 178 cm.

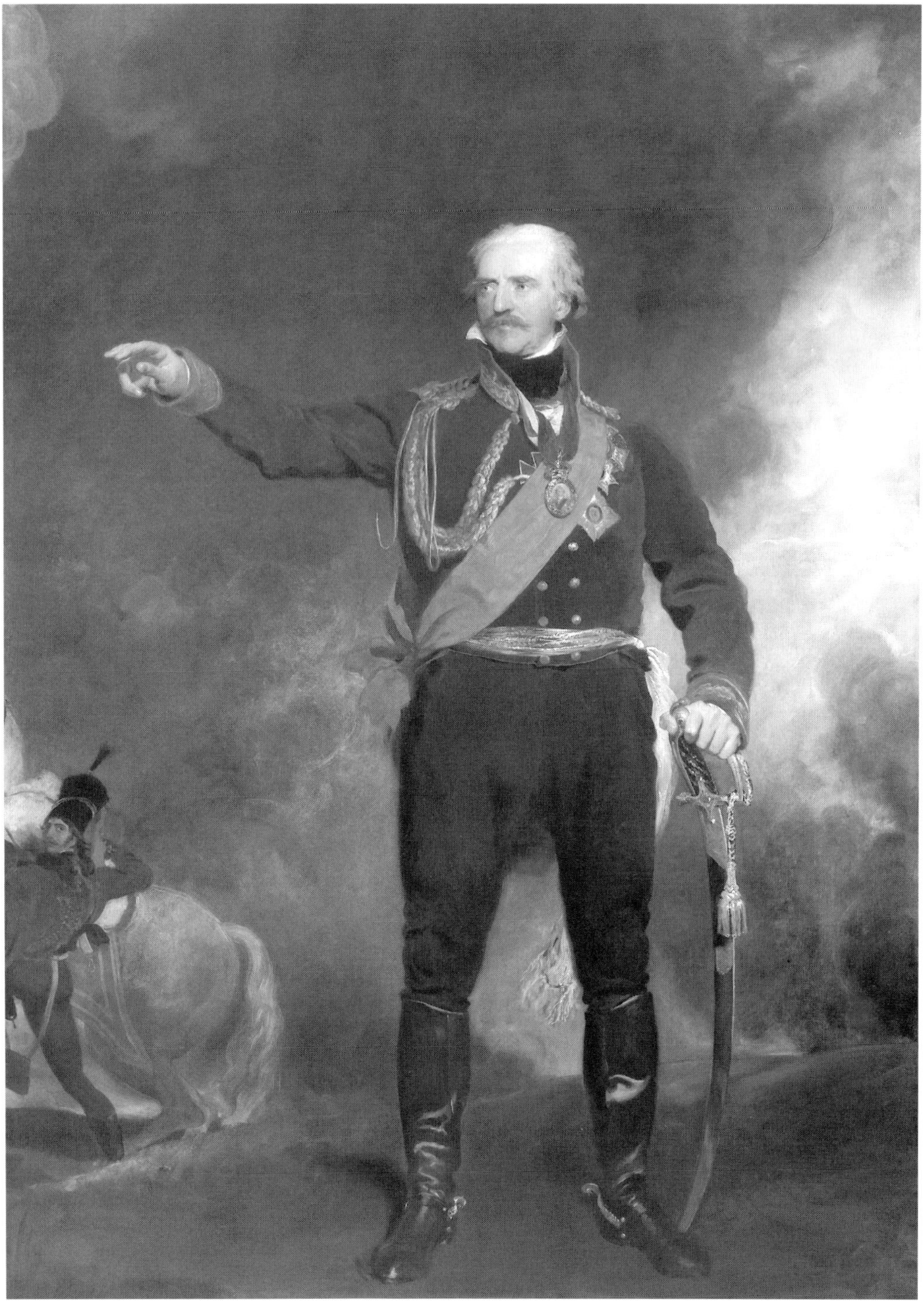

July 1814 for a portrait which was exhibited at the Royal Academy in 1815 (no. 65).[36] Unlike the other full lengths discussed here this one was given away by the Prince to the same Marquess of Londonderry who had helped in the commission in the first place and with whose family it has remained. By this date Lawrence had already developed his own range of 'over-size' canvases the most common being the 9 ft by 6 ft (as always in very round numbers) which he used for Blücher, Platov, the Prussian King and the Russian Emperor and which became the standard full-length size for the Waterloo Chamber. The portrait of the Prince of Wales is of the usual full-length size (8 ft by 5 ft) and that of the Duke of Wellington is of a unique format over 10 ft high and nearly 8 ft wide (318 × 225 cm).

(*opposite*) Figure 52 Thomas Lawrence, *Field-Marshal Gebhardt von Blücher*, 1814, oil on canvas, 270 × 178 cm.

How did Lawrence and George IV plan to display these early Waterloo Chamber full lengths? Nash's 1844 view of the Waterloo Chamber (RC 919785, figure 48) shows three of them in the arrangement they retain to this day, with Platov to the left and Blücher to the right flanking Wellington in the centre. Though it is not possible to determine if they appeared in this way in the 1815 Royal Academy exhibition, the two outer portraits would seem to have been painted with this arrangement in mind, with figures obviously echoing each other's poses. The evidence of Carlton House supports this assumption and also provides interesting insight into the way in which such groups might be read. As we have seen almost all George IV's heroic portrait commissions came in pairs and were so displayed; often these pairs flanked another full length, usually depicting a royal sitter. This triplicate arrangement is a distant development of the altarpiece, where a central enthroned figure is flanked by pairs of saints. In Charles Wild's view of the West Anti Room (RC 922175) at Carlton House Reynolds's Henry Frederick, Duke of Cumberland, 1745–90 (OM 1017) and Hoppner's Duke of Clarence (OM 835) can be seen flanking a more elaborately framed portrait of Louis XV attributed to Greuze (all three paintings damaged in the fire of 8 June 1824, the last one completely destroyed). At St James's Palace Admirals Rodney and Keppel flanked George II (see above). It is just possible that George IV planned to hang his own portrait (Royal Academy 1815, no. 65) between that of Platov and Blücher (or some other pair of heroes or monarchs); its smaller format would then presumably have been offset by a more elaborate frame.

However, the military battlefield character of Lawrence's portrait argues against this suggestion, while the extra-large format and frontal presentation of Wellington makes it impossible to imagine in any other than a central 'altarpiece' position, and affirms his heroic status. Indeed this represents the most striking element of the first campaign of the Waterloo Chamber: the way in which Lawrence portrays the Duke of Wellington not only as a warrior but also as a representative of state. The inspiration comes from one of the highlights of the 'London 1814' celebrations, the Thanksgiving Service at St Paul's Cathedral on 7 July, during which the Duke of Wellington accompanied the Prince Regent and carried the Sword of State. The cathedral appears here in the background with a procession pouring up the steps and the storm clouds of war apparently clearing; the Duke stands within a triumphal arch holding the Sword of State aloft; to the left of the painting appears a baton of command and a paper bearing the name 'George PR' (Prince Regent) and an empty throne. Perhaps the throne is intended to suggest the presence of the Regent and the carpet an honorary platform that Wellington has been raised to by his sovereign, rather as he shared honours in the Thanksgiving Service (or as a Churchill might be invited to join the royal family on the balcony of Buckingham Palace). This interpretation must remain conjectural as there is no precedent in portraiture for a soldier in uniform allowed so dramatic an intervention in matters of state. The equivalent of a state portrait for noblemen would be to show them in the robes of the rank or order of chivalry to which they belong. Such images replicate the effect but do not trump the status of a royal state portrait, just as coronations and other royal occasions contain the necessary ceremonies by which peers formally defer to their sovereign. Wellesley had been created Duke of Wellington on 11 May 1814, weeks before he sat to Lawrence; he could easily have chosen to appear in ducal robes. What Lawrence in fact devises, presumably with George IV's approval, is an astonishing amalgam of military and state portraiture and a striking image of a hero stepping forward to defend throne and church. The nearest precedent might be the ceremonies Napoleon devised for himself.

The Waterloo Chamber and the legacy of Reynolds

It is not just the arrangement of paintings at Carlton House which inspired the inception of the Waterloo Chamber, it is specifically the art and the prestige of Sir Joshua Reynolds. George IV seems to have commissioned Hoppner to paint the full lengths that Reynolds would have painted had he been living and to have turned to Lawrence to keep the same tradition alive into the nineteenth century. The most unequivocal tribute by Lawrence is his 1819 portrait of the supreme allied commander, Charles Philip, Prince Schwarzenberg (1771–1820, OM 912, figure 53), which is directly modelled on Reynolds's Marquess of Granby (figure 49). Lawrence takes Reynolds's dramatic contrast between the casual commander and anxious equerry; the sitter's head is set against a private storm cloud as if some angry god of war has visited the battlefield. Like Reynolds, Lawrence models his general on antique statuary, choosing the most familiar type of heroic action, the Apollo Belvedere (Musei Vaticani, Rome). This statue, along with most of the treasures of the Vatican, had recently been in the news having been taken from Rome by the French in 1798 and restored there in January 1816 by Antonio Canova, supported in this enterprise by the Prince Regent.[37]

The three full lengths exhibited at the Royal Academy in 1815 (OM 886, 910 and 917, figures 51 and 52, and plate 19) all show a similar assemblage of Reynolds-type motifs although no one matches its model as closely (and one suspects deliberately) as does Schwarzenberg. All three show the sitters, like Homer's Zeus, as 'cloud-bearers'; Platov having the light wall of cloud used to set off his dark silhouette; the other two shouldering the customary lowering sky. Platov develops the same fusion of warrior and war-horse which is such a powerful feature of Reynolds's portraits of the Marquess of Granby and Prince of Wales (Lloyd-Webber Collection). Both poses echo those of classical statuary; Platov's recalls the 'Horse Tamers' (Piazza del Quirinale, Rome) and Blücher's the Apollo Belvedere (Musei Vaticani, Rome), though only loosely and in reverse.[38] In the case of the Blücher portrait the motif of an equerry struggling to control a rearing war-horse is relegated to the background. This device has already been recognised in Lawrence's portrait of Schwarzenberg as a means of conveying the power, danger and agitation of war to offset the calm authority by which the hero manages and subdues all threats. This detail also suggests that the Quirinale 'Horse Tamers' is the ultimate source for these un-mounted heroes. It might be argued that in Reynolds's work we see a transition from the characteristic mounted equestrian image of the seventeenth and early eighteenth centuries to the more commonly dismounted warrior of the Romantic period. It might further be argued that the former shows the nobleman controlling his horse by virtue of the authority vested in him by birth and position, while the latter shows the hero matching his horse in physical prowess and heroic vigour. This

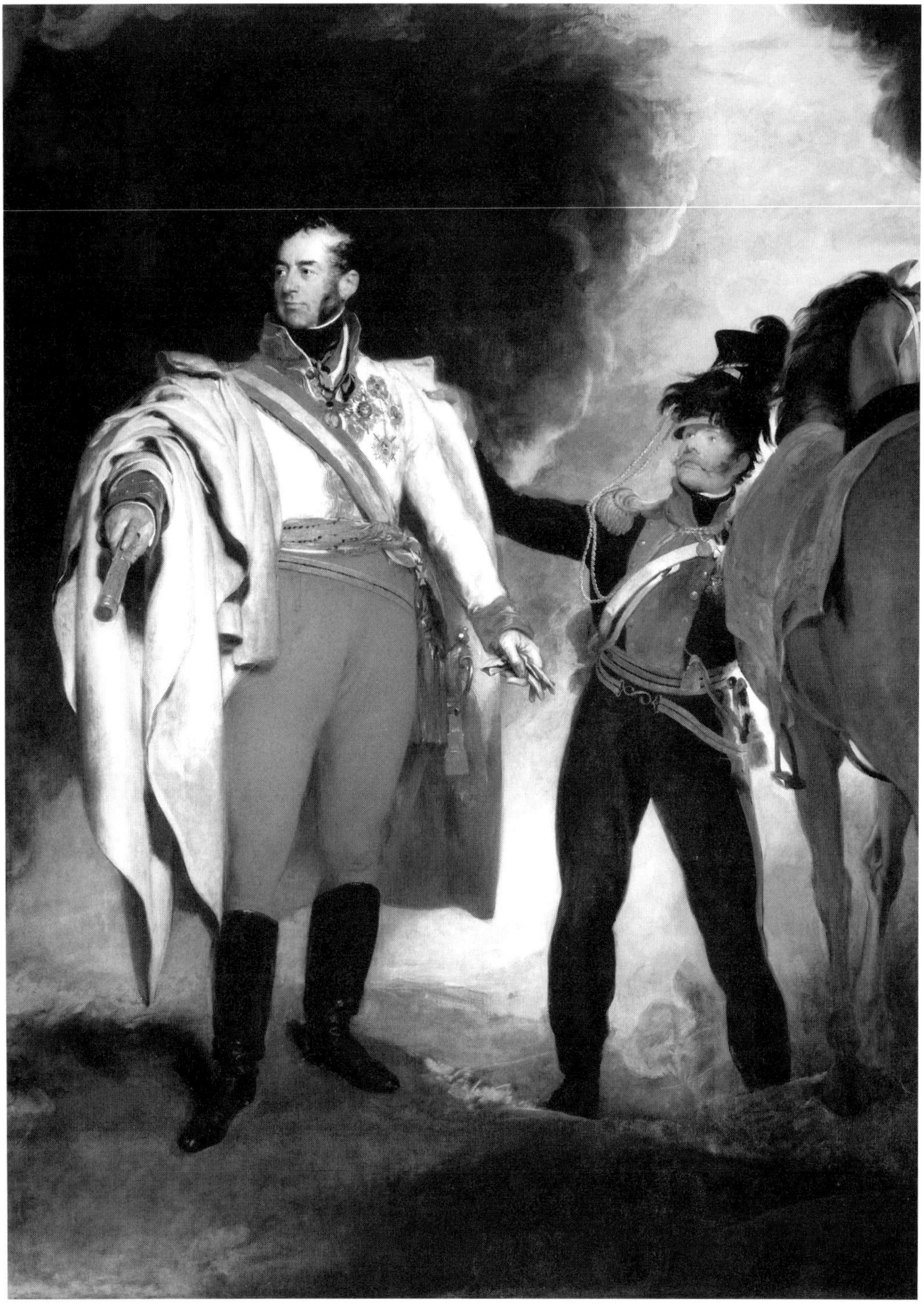

is one way of drawing attention to something which is equally true of Reynolds and Lawrence portraits of heroes: that for all their medals and badges they are represented not simply as holders of positions but as forces of Nature.

What conclusion can be drawn from this exploration of the way in which Reynolds's work was valued and displayed in the quarter century after his death? It is well established that the First President of the Royal Academy remained an inspiration to British artists until well into the Victorian age, though his largely posthumous acquisition of royal favour certainly gives the story something of a twist. What makes the study of this process within one collection of special interest is that comparing so closely like for like allows one to isolate Lawrence's 'unique selling point' in this and other commissions. Setting Blücher beside Granby (figures 52 and 49) reveals the language of Lawrence within the structure of Reynolds. Reynolds's face is broad and sculpted, its details worn away by the process of generalisation as if stone has become weathered; the features in Lawrence's painting are sharp, bright, intricate and asymmetrical; not smoothed off but followed in all their complexity. This effect is acknowledged by artists as different as Benjamin Robert Haydon and Delacroix. On 25 July 1826 Haydon visited Lawrence's studio and recorded his favourable reaction in his Journal: 'I think I can venture to say with truth that he is the only man since Vandyck who has detailed, without destroying, the beauty of a face … That heavy lumbering breadth without detail he has left off, and he deserves his employment.'[39] In 1829 Delacroix devoted an article to Lawrence's portrait of Pius VII (OM 909) finding that Lawrence struck and dazzled his viewers but 'not at the expense of finesse and truth of drawing which in his heads is incomparable'.[40]

(*opposite*) Figure 53 Thomas Lawrence, *Charles Philip, Prince Schwarzenberg*, 1819, oil on canvas, 314.9 × 242.7 cm.

This dazzling precision lies at the heart of the Waterloo Chamber project which is about 'being there'. Palaces in Britain and elsewhere had often included collections of portraits of foreign royalty, usually created remotely (often by generating copies) and sent as ambassadorial gifts. The Waterloo Chamber could thus have been an assemblage of Russian monarchs and generals painted by Russian artists, Germans painted by Germans and so on. In that there would be little wonder, certainly nothing to match the excitement of the London crowds seeing Tzars, strange kings and heroes in the flesh – the crowd that mobbed Lawrence's studio when General Blücher sat, so that only the Bow Street officers could keep them out of the painting room.[41] The unique opportunity of 'London 1814' was that an English artist could be in the presence of these foreign monarchs and celebrities; the unique quality of Lawrence's art was that he could record that sensation so vividly, even if granted the briefest of 'face-time'. In Lady Anne Barnard's words the occasion lay 'in handing down to posterity by such a pencil as yours, the noblest events that the history of the world has to produce ... collecting the countenances as they *now are*'. Lawrence seems to paint the experience not just of seeing a great man but of being seen, of entering into a lively dialogue. This was certainly part of the mythology surrounding the creation of the Waterloo Chamber portrait; Lawrence was said to have given Blücher's expression 'too much spirit about the lower part of the nose', the sitter in reality having a nose which seemed to droop from fatigue and loss of teeth, unless that is Lawrence 'would begin talking of the Duke of Wellington' at which point the truth of Lawrence's ideal spirited nose would show itself.[42]

The final work which Lawrence exhibited at the Royal Academy in 1815 was a portrait of Prince Metternich (no. 76); assuming that this was an early incarnation of the three-quarter length in the Royal Collection (OM 905), it must either have been unfinished or worked up hastily for exhibition. It was presumably substantially altered during the sittings Lawrence obtained with Metternich in Vienna in 1818–19. Whatever Lawrence exhibited in 1815 it is clear that he and George IV had already planned the other important strand of the Waterloo Chamber commission: the series of three-quarter length images of those diplomats who created the fragile new world order at the Congress of Vienna (1 November 1814–18 June 1815) and thereafter. Lawrence missed the Congress of Vienna but made up for it with his brilliant exploitation of the similar opportunity offered by the Congress of Aix-la-Chapelle (October and November 1818) and by following his sitters around the courts of Europe to gain his distinctive *ad vivum* likenesses. Before he could do this however and before the diplomats could re-order Europe another event occurred to alter the composition and meaning of the Waterloo Chamber – a battle fought on the 18 June 1815.

Notes

1 For the heroic portrait see section on 'Heroes' in Martin Postle (ed.), *Joshua Reynolds: The Creation of Celebrity* (London: Tate Publishing, 2005); D.H. Solkin, 'Great Pictures or Great Men? Reynolds, Male Portraiture, and the Power of Art', *Oxford Art Journal*, 9:2 (1986), 42–9; John Bonehill, 'Reynolds' Portrait of Lieutenant-Colonel Banastre Tarleton and the Fashion for War', *British Journal for Eighteenth-Century Studies*, 24:2 (2001), 123–44; Desmond Shawe-Taylor, *The Georgians: Eighteenth-Century Portraiture and*

Society (London: Barrie & Jenkins, 1990); Mark Hallett, 'From out of the Shadows: Sir Joshua Reynolds' *Captain Robert Orme, Visual Culture in Britain*, 5:2 (Winter, 2004), 41–62.

2 H.M. Colvin, *The History of the King's Works*, vol. VI (London: Her Majesty's Stationery Office, 1976), p. 380.

3 W.H. St John Hope, *Windsor Castle: An architectural history, collected and written by command of Their Majesties Queen Victoria, King Edward VII and King George V* (London: Offices of Country Life, 1913), p. 356.

4 The drawings are numbered RL 740041–5; 740042 bears the date.

5 For the financing of George IV's artistic projects see John Morley, *The Making of the Royal Pavilion, Brighton* (London: Philip Wilson for Sotheby Publications, 1984), pp. 25–8.

6 Colvin, *History of the King's Works*, pp. 267–93 (Buckingham Palace); 361–71 (St James's Palace); pp. 373–93 (Windsor Castle).

7 The best description of the Carlton House inventories occurs in Oliver Millar, *Later Georgian Pictures in the Collection of Her Majesty the Queen*, 2 vols (London: Phaidon Press, 1969), pp. l–lii; he also provided the numbers by which they are usually known ('OM'). For this essay I have referred especially to Oliver Millar Inventory Number 45 (RC 1112571), dated 1816 on the title page, and OM Inventory Number 47 (RC 1112591) dated 1819 on the title page. *Carlton House: The Past Glories of George IV's Palace* (London: Queens Gallery, 1991), the exhibition of 1991, provides the most accessible history of the building and its collections, as well as views and ground plans.

8 *Carlton House*, p. 12.

9 Oliver Millar Inventory Number 47 (Carlton House 1819), nos. 15–18.

10 The South Anti Room on the first floor had Van Dyck full lengths of Henry, Prince of Wales (OM 142) and Gaston, Duke of Orleans (Musée Condé, Chantilly) and Beechey's small-scale family portraits (OM 665–70), see Oliver Millar Inventory Number 47 (Carlton House 1819), nos. 19–58 and 65–146.

11 Oliver Millar Inventory Number 47 (Carlton House 1819), no. 64.

12 See Millar, *Later Georgian*, no. 1010; the painting was sent to Sir Thomas Lawrence in 1819 and in 1835 occupied the place currently filled by Lawrence's Charles X (OM 890), where it would have made a group with two magnificent continental heroes, Charles, Archduke of Austria (OM 891) and Charles Philip, Prince Schwarzenberg (OM 912).

13 Joseph Farington, *The Diary of Joseph Farington*, ed. Kenneth Garlick and Angus McIntyre, 16 vols (New Haven and London: Yale University Press for the Paul Mellon Centre for Studies in British Art), XI, p. 3,957 (26 June 1811).

14 Millar, *Later Georgian*, p. 104, no. 1024.

15 A re-enactment of the Battle of the Nile on the Serpentine in Hyde Park was part of the celebration pageant in London on 1 August 1814, see Francis William Blagdon, *An historical memento, representing the different scenes of public rejoicing, which took place the first of August, in St. James's and Hyde Parks, London, in celebration of the Glorious peace of 1814, and of the Centenary of the Accession of the Illustrious House of Brunswick to the Throne of These Kingdoms* (London: Edward Orme, 1814), pp. 53–7.

16 Oliver Millar Inventory Number 47 (Carlton House 1819), nos. 523–4 lists them on the 'Armory Staircase', though each valued at £630 (600 guineas, in comparison to 200 guineas, the value of the Hoppners, nos. 59–60); Oliver Millar Inventory Number 45 (Carlton House 1816), nos. 278–9 lists them in store.

17 Oliver Millar Inventory Number 47 (Carlton House 1819), nos. 59–60.

18 Oliver Millar Inventory Number 47 (Carlton House 1819), nos. 59–60 and 523–4.

19 Oliver Millar Inventory Number 45 (Carlton House 1816), no. 64; Oliver Millar, *The Tudor, Stuart and Early Georgian Pictures in the Collection of Her Majesty the Queen*, 2 vols (London: Phaidon Press, 1963), p. 191, no. 591.

20 Oliver Millar Inventory Number 47 (Carlton House 1819), no. 64.

21 David Mannings, *Sir Joshua Reynolds: A Complete Catalogue of His Paintings*, 2 vols. (New Haven and London: Yale University Press for the Paul Mellon Centre for Studies in British Art, 2009), I, p. 322, no. 1198.

22 *Ibid.*, I, p. 308, no. 1132, dated 1764–67 and p. 322, no. 1199.

23 *Ibid.*, I, p. 216, no. 7199.

24 Farington, *Diary*, XI, p. 3,957 (26 June 1811).

25 A.P. Oppé, *English Drawings, Stuart and Georgian Periods, in the Collection of His Majesty the King at Windsor Castle* (London: Phaidon Press, 1950), no. 647.

26 Oliver Millar Inventory Number 47 (Carlton House 1819), nos. 8–9; the pair was sent to Simpson for cleaning 27 August 1810; Wyatt was paid £153 for enlarging the frames on Lady Day 1811; Millar, *Later Georgian*, p. 103.

27 *Spectator*, no. 422, 1712, quoted in Shawe-Taylor, *Georgians*, p. 84.

28 Jan de Bisschop in 'Paradigmata Graphices Variorum Artificium', c.1672–89 (Hollstein 6; BM 1850,0810.805); see also a print by Paulus Pontius after Rubens, one of 'Twelve Famous Greek and Roman Men', 1638.

29 This pair moved to St James's Palace during the nineteenth century and still hang together there as a pair in the Queen Anne Room.

30 Blücher, Platov, Hardenberg and Metternich sailed from Boulogne on 6 June and arrived in London on the 7th; they departed on 22 June; for the celebration see Blagdon, *An historical memento.*

31 Arthur Aspinall (ed.), *The Letters of King George IV, 1812–1830*, 3 vols (Cambridge: Cambridge University Press, 1938), I, pp. 437–8, letter no. 438.

32 *Ibid.*, I, p. 452, letter no. 451.

33 Farington, *Diary*, XIII, p. 4,533. Stewart became ambassador to Vienna in 1814.

34 A. Cassandra Albinson, Peter Funnell and Marcia Pointon, *Thomas Lawrence: Regency, Power and Brilliance* (New Haven and London: Yale Center for British Art / National Portrait Gallery, in association with Yale University Press, 2010), pp. 217 and 227.

35 For Lawrence's favourable notices at the Royal Academy exhibition of 1815, see Albinson, Funnell and Pointon, *Thomas Lawrence*, p. 233.

36 Farington, *Diary*, XIII, p. 4,548 (6 July 1814), p. 4,563 (23 July 1814), pp. 4,597–8 (24 October 1814) and p. 4,606 (9 November 1814).

37 Francis Haskell and Nicholas Penny, *Taste and the Antique: The Lure of Classical*

Sculpture:1500–1900 (New Haven and London: Yale University Press, 1981), pp. 109–15; the presence of the Apollo and Laocoon in Lawrence's portrait of Pius VII also refers to the Prince Regent's involvement in their restitution.

38 For the identification of the 'Horse Tamers' and their critical history see Haskell and Penny, *Taste and the Antique*, pp. 136–41.

39 Benjamin Robert Haydon, *The Autobiography and Journals of Benjamin Robert Haydon, 1786–1846*, ed. Malcolm Elwin (London: Macdonald, 1950; first published 1853), p. 413; *Journals*, 25 July 1826.

40 'il frappe, il eblouit et non pas aux depens de la finesse et de la verité de son dessin, qui, dans les têtes, est incomparable', *Revue de Paris*, June 1829, pp. 109–13; see also Sebastien Allard and Robert Rosenblum, *Citizens and Kings: Portraits in the Age of Revolution* (London: Royal Academy of Arts, 2007), p. 44 and Albinson, Funnell and Pointon, *Thomas Lawrence*, pp. 238–41.

41 Albinson, Funnell and Pointon, *Thomas Lawrence*, p. 231.

42 Millar, *Later Georgian*, p. 65.

Select bibliography

Published sources

Abbott, Dean Eric, John Betjeman, Kenneth Clark, John Pope-Hennessy, A.L. Rowse and George Zarnecki, *Westminster Abbey* (Annenberg School of Communications: Radnor, PA, 1988; first published 1972).

Adam, William, *The Gem of the Peak; or Matlock Bath and its Vicinity. An Account of Derby; A Tour from Derby to Matlock; Excursions to Chatsworth, Haddon, Monsal Dale etc.* (Derby: John and Charles Mosley, 1857).

Adams, John, *Modern Voyages*, 2 vols (London: G. Kearsley, 1790).

Addison Joseph and Richard Steele, *The Spectator*, 8 vols (London: J. and R. Tonson, 1765).

Adler, K.H., 'Gendering Histories of Home and Homecoming', in K.H. Adler and Carrie Hamilton, *Homes and Homecomings: Gendered Histories of Domesticity and Return* (Chichester: Wiley-Blackwell, 2010).

Albinson, A. Cassandra, Peter Funnell and Marcia Pointon, *Thomas Lawrence: Regency Power and Brilliance* (New Haven and London: Yale Center for British Art / National Portrait Gallery, in association with Yale University Press, 2010).

Allgemeine Deutsche Biographie, 56 vols (Munich: Historische Kommission, Bayerische Akademie der Wissenschaften, 1875–1912).

Almeida, Hermione de and George H. Gilpin, *Indian Renaissance: British Romantic Art and the Prospect of India* (Aldershot and Burlington, VT: Ashgate, 2006).

Ambrose, Miss [E.], *The Life and Memoirs of the Late Miss Ann Catley, the Celebrated Actress: with Biographical Sketches of Sir Francis Blake Delaval, and the Hon. Isabella Pawlet, Daughter to the Earl of Thanet* (London: J. Bird, [1789]).

The Ambulator, or A Pocket Companion in a Tour Round London (London: Scatcherd and Whitaker, 1794).

Anderson, Fred, *The Crucible of War: The Seven Years' War and the Fate of the Empire in British North America, 1754–1766* (London: Faber and Faber, 2000).

The Apollo: or, the Muses Choice: being a Collection of the most Celebrated New

Songs, Sung at Ranelagh, Vauxhall, Marybone-Gardens &c. &c. (London: J. Pridden, [1759]).
Archenholz, Johann Wilhelm von, *A Picture of England: containing a description of the laws, customs, and manners of England* (London: Edward Jeffery, 1789).
Ariès, Philippe, *Centuries of Childhood: Social History of Family Life* (New York: Vintage, 1962).
Arnold, Dana (ed.), *The Georgian Country House: Architecture, Landscape and Society* (Stroud: Sutton, 1998).
Askham, Francis, *The Gay Delavals* (London: Jonathan Cape, 1955).
Asleson, Robyn, *British Paintings at the Huntington* (New Haven: The Huntingdon Library, Art Collections and Botanical Gardens in association with Yale University Press, 2001).
Aspinall, Arthur (ed.), *The Letters of King George IV, 1812–1830*, 3 vols (Cambridge: Cambridge University Press, 1938).
Atwell, Geoffrey, 'Wanstead House', *Essex Review*, 63:250 (April 1954), 67–82.
Aynsley, Jeremy and Charlotte Grant (eds), *Imagined Interiors: Representing the Domestic Interior since the Renaissance* (London: V&A Publications, 2006).
Bachelard, Gaston, *The Poetics of Space: The Classic Look at How We Experience Intimate Places* (New York: Beacon Press, 1994; first published 1958).
Backscheider, Paula R., *Eighteenth-Century Women Poets and Their Poetry: Inventing Agency, Inventing Genre* (Baltimore: Johns Hopkins University Press, 2005).
Baggs, A.P., 'The After-Life of Wanstead', *Georgian Group Journal*, 6 (1996), 131–3.
Bailey, Joanne, 'Reassessing Parenting in Eighteenth-Century England', in Helen Berry and Elizabeth A. Foyster (eds), *The Family in Early Modern England* (Cambridge: Cambridge University Press, 2007).
Baird, Madeleine, *English Landed Society in the Twentieth Century* (London: Routledge, 1989).
Baird, Rosemary, *Mistress of the House: Great Ladies and Grand Houses 1670–1830* (London: Weidenfeld and Nicolson, 2003).
Baker, M., 'The Making of Portrait Busts in the Mid-Eighteenth Century: Roubiliac, Scheemakers and Trinity College, Dublin', *Burlington Magazine*, 137:1,113 (December 1995), 821–31.
Baker, M., 'Ancient and Modern, French and English, War and Peace: The Sculpture in the Duke of Argyll's Gallery at Adderbury', in *Figured in Marble: The Making and Viewing of Eighteenth-Century Sculpture* (London: V&A Publications, 2000).
Baker, M., 'Public Images for Private Spaces? The Place of Sculpture in the Georgian Domestic Interior', *Journal of Design History*, 20:4 (2007), 309–23.
Barczewski, Stephanie, *British Country Houses and Empire, 1700–1945* (forthcoming, Manchester University Press).
Barrell, John, *The Political Theory of Painting from Reynolds to Hazlitt* (New Haven and London: Yale University Press, 1986).
Barrell, John, 'The Public Prospect and the Private View: The Politics of Taste in Eighteenth-Century Britain', in Simon Pugh (ed.), *Reading Landscape: Country-City-Capital* (Manchester: Manchester University Press,

1990).
Barrett, Charlotte (ed.), *The Diary and Letters of Madame d'Arblay*, 6 vols (London: Macmillan & Co., 1904).
Battiscombe, Georgina, *The Spencers of Althorp* (London: Constable, 1984).
Beaglehole, J.C., *The Life of Captain James Cook* (London: Hakluyt Society, 1974).
Beaglehole, J.C. (ed.), *The Journals of Captain James Cook on his Voyages of Discovery. III. The Voyage of the Resolution and Discovery 1776–1780: Part One* (Cambridge: Cambridge University Press for the Hakluyt Society, 1967).
Beckett, J.V., *The Aristocracy in England, 1660–1914* (Oxford: Basil Blackwell, 1986).
Beckett, John, *The Rise and Fall of the Grenvilles: Dukes of Buckingham and Chandos, 1710–1921* (Manchester: Manchester University Press, 1994).
Bending, Stephen, 'Mrs. Montagu's Contemplative Bench: Bluestocking Gardens and Female Retirement,' *Huntington Library Quarterly*, 69:4 (2006), 558–80.
Berger, Harry, 'Fictions of the Pose: Facing the Gaze of Early Modern Portraiture', *Representations*, 46 (Spring 1994), 87–120.
Bermingham, Ann, *Learning to Draw: Studies in the History of a Polite and Useful Art* (New Haven and London: Yale University Press, 2000).
Berry, Helen, 'Women, Consumption and Taste', in Hannah Barker and Elaine Chalus (eds), *Women's History: Britain, 1700–1850, an Introduction* (London: Routledge, 2005).
Berry, Helen and Elizabeth A. Foyster (eds), *The Family in Early Modern England* (Cambridge: Cambridge University Press, 2007).
Bevington, Michael, George Clarke, Jonathan Marsden, et al. (eds), *Stowe: The People and the Place* (Swindon: National Trust, 2011).
Bindman, David, 'Thomas Banks's "Caractacus before Claudius": New Letters to and from Ozias Humphry', *Burlington Magazine*, 142:1,173 (December 2000), 769–73.
Black, Jeremy, *The Grand Tour in the Eighteenth Century* (Stroud: Sutton, 1992).
Blagdon, Francis William, *An historical memento, representing the different scenes of public rejoicing, which took place the first of August, in St. James's and Hyde Parks, London, in celebration of the Glorious peace of 1814, and of the Centenary of the Accession of the Illustrious House of Brunswick to the Throne of These Kingdoms* (London: Edward Orme, 1814).
Blomefield, F., *An Essay towards a topographical history of the county of Norfolk*, vol. III (Lynn and London: W. Whittingham and R. Baldwin, 1769).
Blunt, Alison and Robyn Dowling, *Home* (London: Routledge, 2006).
Boaden, James (ed.), *The private correspondence of David Garrick ... and a new biographical memoir*, 2 vols (London: Henry Colburn and Richard Bentley, 1831–32).
Bold, J. and Reeves, J., *Wilton House and English Palladianism: Some Wiltshire Houses* (London: Her Majesty's Stationery Office, 1988).
Bonehill, John, 'Reynolds' Portrait of Lieutenant-Colonel Banastre Tarleton and the Fashion for War', *British Journal for Eighteenth-Century Studies*, 24:2 (2001), 123–44.

Bonehill, John, 'Laying Siege to the Royal Academy: Wright of Derby's *View of Gibraltar* at Robins's Rooms, Covent Garden, April 1785', *Art History*, 30:4 (2007), 521–44.
Boschung, Dietrich, Henner von Hesberg and Andreas Linfert, *Die antiken Skulpturen in Chatsworth: sowie in Dunham Massey und Withington Hall* (Mainz am Rhein: Philipp von Zabern, 1997).
Bourdieu, Pierre, *The Field of Cultural Production* (Cambridge: Polity Press, 1993).
Bowron, Edgar Peters and Björn Kerber, *Pompeo Batoni: Prince of Painters in Eighteenth-Century Rome* (New Haven and London: Yale University Press, 2007).
Brayley, Edward Wedlake, *The Beauties of England and Wales, Vol. 7, Hertfordshire, Huntingdonshire and Kent* (London: Vernor and Hood, 1808).
Brewer, John, *The Pleasures of the Imagination* (London: HarperCollins, 1997).
Brewer, John and Porter, Roy (eds), *Consumption and the World of Goods* (London and New York: Routledge, 1993).
Britton, John, *The Beauties of Wiltshire*, 2 vols (London: Vernor and Hood, 1801).
Browne, Thomas, *Hydriotaphia, Urn-Burial, or, A Discourse of the Sepulchral Urns Lately Found in Norfolk* (London: Edward Dod, 1658).
Bryant, Julius, *Thomas Banks, 1735–1805: Britain's First Modern Sculptor* (London: Soane Gallery, 2005).
Brydges, Samuel Egerton and Stebbing Shaw (eds), *The Topographer for the Year 1789, containing a variety of original articles, illustrative of the local history and antiquities of England*, 4 vols (London: Robson and Clarke and J. Walker, 1789–91).
'Buckinghamshire', *South Midlands Archaeology*, 26 (1996), 21–3.
The Bull-Finch. Being a choice collection of the newest and most favourite English songs most of which have been sett to music and sung at the public theatres and gardens (London: I. Hinton, [c.1750]).
Burke, John, *A Genealogical and Heraldic History of the Commoners of Great Britain and Ireland*, 4 vols (London: Henry Colburn, 1833–38), www.archive.org/stream/genealogicalhera01burk#page/n27/mode/2up.
Burney, Fanny, *The Early Diaries of Fanny Burney 1768–1778*, ed. Annie Raine Ellis, 2 vols (London: G. Bell & Sons, 1913).
Burney, Fanny, *Cecilia, or Memoirs of an Heiress*, ed. Margaret Anne Doody (Oxford: Oxford University Press, 1999).
Burns, Thea, *The Invention of Pastel* (London: Archetype, 2007).
Byng, John, *An Appeal to the People: Containing, the Genuine and Entire Letter of Admiral Byng* (London: J. Morgan, 1756).
Caldwell, M. John, *Arts and Arms: Literature, Politics and Patriotism during the Seven Years War* (Manchester: Manchester University Press, 2004).
Campbell, Colen, *Vitruvius Britannicus*, 3 vols (London: Colen Campbell and Joseph Smith, 1717–25).
A Candid Review of the Exhibition (being the twelfth) of the Royal Academy, MDCC LXXX. Dedicated to his Majesty. By an Artist (London: H. Reynell for T. Evans, 1780).

Cannadine, David, *The Decline and Fall of the British Aristocracy*, rev. edn (London: Picador, 1992).

A Catalogue of the large and capital museum of Sir Thomas Fluyder, Knt (London, 1769).

Cavendish, W.G.S., 6th Duke of Devonshire, *Handbook of Chatsworth and Hardwick* (London: privately printed, 1845).

Chalus, Elaine, *Elite Women in English Political Life c. 1754–90* (Oxford: Clarendon Press, 2005).

Chambers, William, *A Treatise on Civil Architecture* (London: J. Haberkorn, 1759).

Chamot, Mary, 'English Conversation Pieces', *Country Life*, 67 (8 March 1930), 344–6.

Charlesworth, M.J., 'The Wentworths: Family and Political Rivalry in the English Landscape Garden', *Garden History*, 14:2 (Autumn, 1986), 134–5.

Charlton, John, *Hidden Chains: The Slavery Business and North East England* (Newcastle: Tyne Bridge Publishing, 2008).

Chedzoy, Alan, *Sheridan's Nightingale: The Story of Elizabeth Linley* (London: Allison & Busby, 1997).

Cherry, Deborah and Jennifer Harris, 'Eighteenth-Century Portraiture and the Seventeenth-Century Past: Gainsborough and van Dyck', *Art History*, 5:3 (1982), 287–309.

Christie, Christopher, *The British Country House in the Eighteenth Century* (Manchester: Manchester University Press, 2000).

Christie, Ian R., *Wars and Revolutions: Britain, 1760–1815* (London: Edward Arden, 1982).

Clayton, Timothy, *The English Print 1688–1802* (New Haven and London: Yale University Press for the Paul Mellon Centre for Studies in British Art, 1997).

Clemenson, Heather, *English Country Houses and Landed Estates* (London: Croom Helm, [c.1982]).

Climenson, Emily J. (ed.), *Passages from the Diaries of Mrs Philip Lybbe Powys of Hardwick House, Oxon 1756–1808* (London, New York and Bombay: Longman, Green and Co., 1899).

Cockayne, G.E., *The Complete Peerage of England, Scotland, Ireland, Great Britain and the United Kingdom, Extant, Extinct or Dormant*, 6 vols (Gloucester: Alan Sutton Publishing, 2000).

Cole, R.E.G., *History of the Manor and Township of Doddington: otherwise Doddington-Pigot, in the County of Lincoln, and its Successive Owners, with Pedigrees* (Lincoln: J. Williamson, 1897).

Colley, Linda, *Britons: Forging the Nation 1707–1837* (New Haven and London: Yale University Press, 1992).

Colvin, H.M., *The History of the King's Works*, vol. VI (London: Her Majesty's Stationery Office, 1976).

A companion to the Leasowes, Hagley and Enville; with a Sketch of Fisherwick, the seat of the Right Hon. Earl Donegall (London, 1789).

A Compendious History of Captain Cook's Last Voyage, Performed in the Years 1776, 1777, 1778, 1779, and 1780; in which all the Interesting Transactions are Recorded, particularly those Relative to his Unfortunate Death (London: G. Kearsley, 1784).

A Complete History of the Present War, from its Commencement in 1756, to the End of the Campaign, 2 vols (London: J. Knox, 1764; first published 1761).

Conway, Alison, *Private Interests: Women, Portraiture and the Visual Culture of the English Novel, 1709–1791* (Toronto and London: University of Toronto Press, 2001).

Cook's Log, 26:4 (2003), 12.

Cook's Log, 28:4 (2005), 17.

Coope, Rosalys, 'The "Long Gallery": Its Origins, Development, Use and Decoration', *Architectural History*, 29 (1986), 43–84.

Cornforth, John, 'Stourhead, Wiltshire', *Country Life*, 188 (8 September 1994), 64–7.

Cornforth, John, *The Country Houses of England, 1948–1998* (London: Constable, 1998).

Cornforth, John, *Early Georgian Interiors* (New Haven and London: Yale University Press for the Paul Mellon Centre for Studies in British Art, 2004).

Cotes, Francis, 'Notes on crayon painting', *European Magazine* (February 1797), 84–5.

Coutu, Joan, 'Stowe: A Whig Training Ground', in Patrick Eyres (ed.), 'The Political Temples of Stowe', *New Arcadian Journal*, 43/44 (1997), 66–78.

Darwall, Mary, *Original Poems on Several Occasions. By Miss Whateley* (London: R. and J. Dodsley, 1764).

Davidoff, Leonore and Catherine Hall, *Family Fortunes: Men and Women of the English Middle Class 1780–1850* (London: Routledge, 1992).

De Bolla, Peter, *The Education of the Eye: Painting, Landscape, and Architecture in Eighteenth-Century Britain* (Stanford, CA: Stanford University Press, 2003).

Defoe, Daniel, *Tour thro' the Whole Island of Great Britain*, 3 vols (London: G. Strahan, 1724–27).

Delacroix, Eugene, 'Portrait de Pie VII, de Sir Thomas Lawrence', *Revue de Paris* (June 1829), 109–13.

Delany, Mary, *The Autobiography and Correspondence of Mary Granville, Mrs Delany*, ed. Lady Llanover, 3 vols (London: Richard Bentley, 1861).

De Novellis, Mark, *Pallas Unveil'd: The Life and Art of Lady Dorothy Savile, Countess of Burlington 1699– 1758* (London: Orleans House Gallery, 1999).

A Description of Holkham House in Norfolk with a particular of the pictures, statues, bustoes, and other marbles therein. Published by permission of the Hon. Wenman Coke (Norwich: R. Beatniffe, 1775).

A Description of the House and Gardens at Stourhead, in the County of Wilts, the seat of Sir Richard Hoare Bart with a Catalogue of the Pictures &c (Salisbury and London: J. Easton, 1800).

A Description of the House and Gardens at Stourhead (Bath: Messrs. Barratt and Son, 1818).

Dibdin, Thomas, *Supplement to the Biblioteca Spenceriana: or a descriptive catalogue of the books printed in the fifteenth century in the library of George John Earl Spencer* (London: W. Nicol, 1822).

D'Oench, Ellen G., *The Conversation Piece: Arthur Devis and his Contemporaries*

(New Haven: Yale Center for British Art, 1980).
D'Orléans Aumale, H., *Inventaire de tous les meubles du Cardinal Mazarin. Dressé en 1653, et publié d'après l'original, conserve dans les Archives de Condé* (London: Whittingham and Wilkins, 1861).
Dorment, Richard, *British Painting in the Philadelphia Museum of Art from the Seventeenth through the Nineteenth Century* (Philadelphia: Philadelphia Museum of Art, 1986).
Dossie, Robert, *Handmaid to the Arts* (London: J. Nourse, 1764).
Duckworth, Colin, 'Georgiana Spencer in France: or The Dangers of Reading Rousseau', *Eighteenth-Century Life*, 7:3 (Spring, 1982), 85–91.
Durham, James, *The Collection of Pictures at Raynham Hall, being 3 Annotated Catalogues* (Raynham, Norfolk: James A.C. Durham, 1926).
Durham, Victoria Townshend, *Short Guide Historical and Descriptive to Raynham Hall* (Fakenham, Norfolk: The Lancaster Press, 1951).
Dwyer, Eugene, 'André Thevet and Fulvio Orsini: The Beginnings of the Modern Tradition of Classical Portrait Iconography in France', *Art Bulletin*, 75:3 (September 1993), 467–80.
Edgeworth, Richard Lovell and Maria Edgeworth, *Memoirs of Richard Lovell Edgeworth*, 2 vols (London: R. Hunter, 1820).
Edwards, Ralph, *Early Conversation Pictures from the Middle Ages to about 1730: A Study in Origins* (London: Country Life, 1954).
Egerton, Judy, *British Sporting and Animal Paintings, 1655–1867: A Catalogue* (London: Tate Gallery for the Yale Center for British Art, 1978).
Egerton, Judy, *George Stubbs, Painter: Catalogue Raisonné* (New Haven and London: Yale University Press for the Paul Mellon Centre for Studies in British Art, 2007).
Eidelberg, Martin, 'More about Old Nollekens', *Apollo*, 157:493 (March 2003), 22–6.
Einberg, Elizabeth, *Gainsborough's Giovanna Baccelli* (London: Tate Gallery Publications, 1976).
Einberg, Elizabeth, *Manners and Morals: Hogarth and British Painting 1700–1760* (London: Tate Gallery Publishing, 1987).
Eliasson, Sabrina Norlander, *Portraiture and Social Identity in Eighteenth-Century Rome* (Manchester: Manchester University Press, 2009).
Eliot, Karen, *Dancing Lives: Five Female Dancers from the Ballet d'Action to Merce Cunningham* (Urbana and Chicago: University of Illinois Press, 2007).
Entick, John, *A New Naval History: or, Compleat View of the British Marine* (London: R. Manby, W. Reeve, W. Bizet, P. Davey and J. Scott, 1757).
Entick, John, *The General History of the Late War: Containing it's* [sic] *Rise, Progress, and Event, in Europe, Asia, Africa, and America*, 5 vols (London: Edward Dilly and John Millan, 1763–64).
Eyres, Patrick, 'Fleets, Forests and Follies: Supremacy of the Seas and of the Eye', in Patrick Eyres (ed.), 'Hearts of Oak', *New Arcadian Journal*, 35/36 (1993), 10.
Farington, Joseph, *The Diary of Joseph Farington*, ed, Kenneth Garlick and Angus McIntyre, 16 vols (New Haven and London: Yale Unversity Press for the Paul Mellon Centre for Studies in British Art, 1978–84).

Fawcett, Trevor, *The Rise of English Provincial Art: Artists, Patrons and Institutions outside London, 1800– 1830* (Oxford: Clarendon Press, 1974).
Felton, Samuel, *Miscellanies, on ancient and modern gardening; and on the scenery of nature* (London: printed for the author, 1785).
Flora Triumphans: Wanstead Garden An Heroick Poem most humbly addrest to the Honourable Sir Richard Child (London: William Redmayne, 1712).
Foreman, Amanda, *Georgiana Duchess of Devonshire* (London: HarperCollins, 1998).
Fraser, Antonia, *Love and Louis XIV: The Women in the Life of The Sun King* (London: Weidenfeld and Nicolson, 2006).
Friedman, Joseph, *Spencer House: Chronicle of a Great London Mansion* (London: Zwemmer, 1993).
Friedman, Terry, 'Scheemakers's Monument to the Best of Sons', *Burlington Magazine*, 122:922 (January 1980), 61–7.
Garlick, Kenneth, 'The Earls Spencer, Althorp, England', in Douglas Cooper (ed.), *Great Family Collections* (London: Weidenfeld and Nicolson, 1965).
Garlick, Kenneth, 'A Catalogue of the Pictures at Althorp', *Walpole Society*, 45 (1974–76).
Garlick, Kenneth, *Thomas Lawrence: Complete Edition of the Paintings* (New York: New York University Press, 1989).
Geertz, Clifford, *The Interpretation of Cultures* (London: Hutchinson, 1975; first published 1973).
Gerard, J., *Country House Life: Family and Servants, 1815–1914 (*Oxford: Blackwell, 1994).
Gilpin, William, *A dialogue upon the gardens of the Right Honourable the Lord Viscount Cobham, at Stow in Buckinghamshire* (London: B. Seeley, 1748).
Gilpin, William, *Observations on several parts of the counties of Cambridge, Norfolk, Suffolk and Essex. Also on several parts of North Wales; relative chiefly to Picturesque Beauty* (London: T. Cadell and W. Davies, 1809).
Girouard, Mark, *Life in the English Country House: A Social and Architectural History* (New Haven and London: Yale University Press, 1978).
Glendinning, Victoria, *Vita: The Life of Vita Sackville-West* (New York: Quill, 1983).
Goffinan, Erving, *The Presentation of Self in Everyday Life* (Harmondsworth: Penguin, 1959).
Goodchild, John, 'Matters of Concern: The Life Story of the Third Earl of Effingham', in Melvyn Jones (ed.), *Aspects of Rotherham: Discovering Local History* (Barnsley: Wharncliffe Publishing, 1995).
Goodden, Angelica, *Miss Angel: The Art and World of Angelica Kauffman* (London: Pimlico, 2005).
Gore, St John, 'Prince of Georgian Collectors: The Hoares of Stourhead – I', *Country Life*, 135 (30 January 1964), 210–12.
Gore, St John, 'A Worthy Heir to Greatness: The Hoares of Stourhead – II', *Country Life*, 136 (6 February 1964), 278–80.
Graves, Algernon, *A Century of Loan Exhibitions 1813–1912* (Bath: Kingsmead Reprints, 1970; first published 1915).
Graves, Algernon, *The Royal Academy of Arts: A Complete Dictionary of*

Contributors and Their Work from Its Foundation in 1769 to 1904 (Bath: S.R. Publishers and Kingsmead Reprints, 1970; first published 1905–6).
Green, Richard, '"The Hon. Lady Stanhope and the Countess of Effingham as Diana and her Companion" by Francis Cotes', *National Art-Collections Fund Annual Review* (1988), 106–9.
Griffiths, J., *A Collection of Juvenile Poems, on Various Subjects* (Warwick: J. Sharp, 1784).
Guest, Harriet, *Small Change: Women, Learning, Patriotism, 1750–1810* (Chicago: Chicago University Press, 2000).
Guest, Harriet, *Empire, Barbarism and Civilisation: Captain Cook, William Hodges and the Return to the Pacific* (Cambridge: Cambridge University Press, 2007).
Guest, Ivor, *The Ballet of the Enlightenment: The Establishment of the Ballet d'Action in France, 1770–1793* (London: Dance Books, 1996).
Habakkuk, H.J., 'English Landownership 1680–1740', *Economic History Review*, 5 (1940), 2–17.
Habermas, Jürgen, *The Structural Transformation of the Public Sphere: An Inquiry in a Category of Bourgeois Society*, trans. T. Burger and F. Lawrence (Cambridge: Polity Press, 1992).
Haggerty, George, *Men in Love: Masculinity and Sexuality in the Eighteenth Century* (New York and Chichester: Columbia University Press, 1999).
Hallett, Mark, 'From out of the Shadows: Sir Joshua Reynolds' *Captain Robert Orme*, *Visual Culture in Britain*, 5:2 (Winter, 2004), 41–62.
Hallett, Mark, 'Reading the Walls: Pictorial Dialogue at the British Royal Academy', *Eighteenth-Century Studies*, 37:4 (Summer, 2004), 581–604.
Hallett, Mark, ''A Monument to Intimacy: Joshua Reynolds's *The Marlborough Family*', *Art History*, 31:5 (2008), 691–720.
Hallett, Mark and Christine Riding, *Hogarth* (London: Tate Publishing, 2006).
Harris, Frances, 'Holywell House, St Albans: An Early Work by William Talman?', *Architectural History*, 28 (1985), 32–9.
Harris, Frances, *A Passion for Government: The Life of Sarah, Duchess of Marlborough* (Oxford: Clarendon Press, 1991).
Harris, J., *The Palladian Revival: Lord Burlington, His Villa and Garden at Chiswick* (New Haven and London: Yale University Press, 1994).
Harris, John, *The Artist and the Country House: A History of Country House and Garden View Painting in Britain, 1540–1870* (London: Sotheby Parke Bernet, 1979).
Harris, R., *A Chorus of Grammars: The Correspondence of George Hickes and His Collaborators on the Thesaurus Linguarum Septentrionalium* (Toronto: Pontifical Institute of Mediaeval Studies, 1992).
Harvey, Karen, 'Men Making Home in Eighteenth-Century Britain', in K.H. Adler and Carrie Hamilton, *Homes and Homecomings: Gendered Histories of Domesticity and Return* (Chichester: Wiley-Blackwell, 2010).
Haskell, Francis, 'The British as Collectors', in Gervase Jackson-Stops (ed.), *The Treasure Houses of Britain: Five Hundred Years of Private Patronage and Art Collecting* (New Haven and London: Yale University Press, 1985).
Haskell, Francis and Nicholas Penny, *Taste and the Antique: The Lure of Classical Sculpture: 1500–1900* (New Haven and London: Yale University

Press, 1981).
Haydon, Benjamin Robert, *The Autobiography and Journals of Benjamin Robert Haydon, 1786–1846*, ed. Malcolm Elwin (London: Macdonald, 1950; first published 1853).
Hayes, John, *The Portrait in British Art* (London: National Portrait Gallery, 1991).
Hayes, John, *National Gallery of Art: British Paintings of the Sixteenth through Nineteenth Centuries* (Washington and Cambridge: Cambridge University Press, 1992).
Herrmann, Frank, *The English as Collectors* (London: Norton, 1972).
Herrmann, Luke, *British Landscape Painting of the Eighteenth Century* (London: Faber and Faber, 1973).
History and Antiquities of the County of Norfolk. Vol. IX (Norwich: J. Crouse, 1781).
Hoare, Richard Colt, *The History of Modern Wiltshire*, 6 vols (London: J. Nichols & Son [etc.], 1822–44).
Holman, Peter, *Life after Death: The Viola da Gamba in Britain from Purcell to Dolmetsch* (Woodbridge: The Boydell Press, 2010).
Hope, W.H. St John, *Windsor Castle: An Architectural History, collected and written by command of Their Majesties Queen Victoria, King Edward VII and King George V* (London: Offices of Country Life, 1913).
Hume, Robert D., 'Before the Bard: "Shakespeare" in Early Eighteenth-Century London', *English Literary History*, 64:1 (Spring, 1997), 41–75.
Hussey, Christopher, 'Melton Constable, Norfolk, the Seat of Lord Hastings – I', *Country Life*, 64 (15 September 1928), 364–70.
Hussey, Christopher, 'Melton Constable, Norfolk, the Seat of Lord Hastings – II', *Country Life*, 64 (22 September 1928), 402–9.
Hussey, Christopher, 'Conversation Pieces: Sir Philip Sassoon's Exhibition, March 4th–30th', *Country Life*, 62 (15 February 1930), 263–4.
Hussey, Christopher, 'Stourhead, Wiltshire', *Country Life*, 83 (18 June 1938), 638–42.
Hussey, Christopher, *English Country Houses: Mid Georgian 1760–1800* (London: Antique Collectors' Club, 1956).
Imison, John, *The School of the Arts or an Introduction to Useful Knowledge*, 4th edn (London: J. Murray and S. Highley, 1796).
Ingamells, John, *A Dictionary of British and Irish Travellers in Italy 1701–1800* (New Haven and London: Yale University Press, 1997).
Ingamells, John, *The National Portrait Gallery: Mid Georgian 1760–1790* (London: National Portrait Gallery, 2004).
'Instructions from the High Sheriff, Gentlemen, Clergy, and Freeholders of the COUNTY of BRECON, to the Honourable Thomas Morgan, Esq; their Representative in Parliament' in *The Voice of the People: a Collection of Addresses to His Majesty, and Instructions to Members of Parliament by their Constituents* (London: J. Payne, 1756).
Ireland, John, *A Supplement to Hogarth Illustrated*, 2nd edn (London: G. and W. Nicol, 1804).
Jackson, I., 'Approaches to the History of Readers and Reading in

Eighteenth-century Britain', *Historical Journal*, 47:4 (2004), 1,041–54.
Jackson-Stops, G. and Pipkin, J., *The English Country House: A Grand Tour* (London: The National Trust and Weidenfeld and Nicolson, 1984).
Jackson-Stops, Gervase (ed.), *The Treasure Houses of Britain: Five Hundred Years of Private Patronage and Art Collecting* (New Haven and London: Yale University Press, 1985).
Jackson-Stops, Gervase, Elisabeth B. MacDougall, Gordon J. Schochet and Lena Orlin (eds), *The Fashioning and Functioning of the British Country House* (Washington DC: National Gallery of Art, 1989).
Jacques, D., *A Visit to Goodwood near Chichester, the seat of His Grace the Duke of Richmond, with an Appendix descriptive of an ancient painting* (Chichester and London: D. Jacques, Messers. [*sic*] Lackington, Hughes & Co. and W. Mason, 1822).
Jeffares, Neil, *Dictionary of Pastellists before 1800* (London: Unicorn Press, 2006), www.pastellists.com, accessed 28 May 2012.
Jenkins, Susan, 'Buying Bonaparte', *Apollo*, 172:581 (November 2010), 50–5.
Jervis, S., 'The English Country House Library', in N. Barker (ed.), *Treasures from the Libraries of National Trust Country Houses* (New York: The Royal Oak Foundation and The Grolier Club, 1999).
Jesse, John Heneage, *Memoirs of George Selwyn and His Contemporaries*, 4 vols (London: Richard Bentley, 1843–44).
Jones, Robert, *Literature, Gender and Politics in Britain during the War for America* (Cambridge: Cambridge University Press, 2011).
A Journal of the Campaign on the Coast of France, 1758, 2nd edn (London: J. Townsend, 1758).
Kaufmann, C.M., *Catalogue of Paintings in the Wellington Museum, Apsley House*, rev. Susan Jenkins with contributions by Marjorie E. Wieseman (London: English Heritage in association with Paul Holberton, 2009).
Keeling, Denis F., *Wanstead and Chatsworth: Treasures from Wanstead House Acquired by the 6th Duke of Devonshire* (Wanstead: The Tylney Press in association with The Wanstead Historical Society, 1997).
Kenny, V.C., *The Country House Ethos in English Literature 1688–1750: Themes of Personal Retreat and National Expansion* (Brighton: Harvester, 1984).
Kenworthy-Browne, John, 'A Ducal Patron of Sculpture', *Apollo*, 96:128 (October 1972), 322–31.
Keppel, George Thomas, 6th Earl of Albemarle, *Memoirs of the Marquis of Rockingham and His Contemporaries*, 2 vols (London: Richard Bentley, 1852).
Kimball, Fiske, 'Wanstead House, Essex', *Country Life*, 74 (2 December 1933), 605–7.
Klein, L., *Shaftesbury and the Culture of Politeness: Moral Discourse and Cultural Politeness in Early Eighteenth-century England* (Cambridge: Cambridge University Press, 1994).
Knox, George, 'Antonio Pellegrini and Marco Ricci at Burlington House and Narford Hall', *Burlington Magazine*, 130:1,028 (November 1988), 846–53.
Kriz, K. Dian, '"Stare Cases": Engendering the Public's Two Bodies at the Royal Academy of Arts', in David Solkin (ed.), *Art on The Line: The Royal Academy Exhibitions at Somerset House, 1780–1836* (New Haven and London:

Yale University Press for the Paul Mellon Centre for Studies in British Art and the Courtauld Institute Gallery, 2001).
Laing, Alistair, *In Trust for the Nation: Paintings from National Trust Houses* (London: The National Trust in association with National Gallery Publications, 1995).
Laing, Alistair, *Stourhead: Illustrated List of Pictures and Sculptures* (published online, 2010), www.nationaltrust.org.uk/servlet/file/store5/item629709/version1/w-stourhead-pictures.pdf, accessed 1 May 2012.
Landry, Donna, *The Invention of the Countryside: Hunting, Walking, and Ecology in English Literature, 1671–1831* (Basingstoke and New York: Palgrave Macmillan, 2001).
Langford, Paul, *Public Life and the Propertied Englishman, 1689–1796* (Oxford: Oxford University Press, 1991).
Laurence, Anne, 'Space, Status and Gender in English Topographical Paintings, c.1660–c.1740', *Architectural History*, 46 (2003), 81–94.
Lees-Milne, James, *The Bachelor Duke: William Spencer Cavendish 6th Duke of Devonshire* (London: John Murray, 1990).
Lefebvre, Henri, *The Production of Space*, trans. Donald Nicholson-Smith (Oxford: Blackwell, 1991).
Leppert, Robert, *Music and Image: Domesticity, Ideology and Socio-Cultural Formation in Eighteenth Century England* (Cambridge: Cambridge University Press, 1988).
Lewis, Judith S., *Sacred to Female Patriotism: Gender, Class and Politics in Late Georgian Britain* (New York and London: Routledge, 2003).
Lewis, Judith S., 'When a House is Not a Home: Elite English Women and the Eighteenth-Century Country House', *Journal of British Studies*, 48:2 (April 2009), 336–63.
Liotard, Jean-Étienne, *Traité des principes et des règles de la peinture*, ed. Pierre Cailler (Geneva: Pierre Cailler, 1945, first published 1781).
Lippincott, Louise, *Selling Art in Georgian London: The Rise of Arthur Pond* (New Haven and London: Yale University Press for the Paul Mellon Centre for Studies in British Art, 1983).
Liversidge, M.H., 'An Elusive Minor Master: J.F. Nollekens and the Conversation Piece', *Apollo*, 95:119 (January 1972), 34–41.
Lives of Illustrious British Seamen (Edinburgh, 1764).
Loan Exhibition of English Conversation Pieces in aid of the Royal Northern Hospital at 25 Park Lane, March 4th to 30th (inclusive) 1930 (London: Battley Brothers, 1930).
Loche, Renée and Marcel Roethlisberger, *L'Opera completa di Liotard* (Milan: Rizzoli Editore, 1978).
Lord, John, 'Richard Hayward: An Early and Some Later Commissions', *Church Monuments: Journal of the Church Monuments Society*, 12 (1907), 67–79.
Lubbock, Jules, *The Tyranny of Taste: The Politics of Architecture and Design in Britain 1550–1960* (New Haven and London: Yale University Press for the Paul Mellon Centre for Studies in British Art, 1995).
Mack the elder, M., *The Garden and the City: Retirement and Politics in the Later Poetry of Pope* (Toronto and London: University of Toronto Press, 1969).

Maclean, Gerald, Donna Landry and Joseph P. Ward (eds), *The Country and the City Revisited: England and the Politics of Culture, 1550–1850* (Cambridge: Cambridge University Press, 1999).

Mandler, Peter, *The Fall and Rise of the Stately Home* (New Haven and London: Yale University Press, 1997).

Mannings, David, *Sir Joshua Reynolds: A Complete Catalogue of His Paintings*, 2 vols (New Haven and London: Yale University Press for the Paul Mellon Centre for Studies in British Art, 2000).

Marks, Arthur S., '*Assembly at Wanstead House* by William Hogarth', *Philadelphia Museum of Art Bulletin*, 77:332 (Spring 1981), 3–16.

Martyn, Thomas, *The English Connoisseur: containing an account of whatever is curious in painting, sculpture, &c in the palaces and seats of the nobility and principal gentry of England, both in town and country* (London: L. Davis and C. Reymers, 1766).

The Masterpieces of Nattier (London and Glasgow: Gowans and Gray, 1920).

Maycock, Willoughby, 'Captain Cook: Memorials', *Notes & Queries* 12 S. 8 (26 February 1921).

Maynard, Patrick, 'Portraits as Displays', *Philosophical Studies: An International Journal for Philosophy in the Analytic Tradition*, 135:1 (2007), 111–21.

McCahill, Michael W., 'Peerage Creations and the Changing Character of the British Nobility, 1750–1830', *English Historical Review*, 96 (1981), 259–84.

McKendrick, Neil, John Brewer and J.H. Plumb., *The Birth of a Consumer Society: The Commercialization of Eighteenth-Century England* (London: Europa, 1982).

McPherson, Heather, 'Garrickomania: Art, Celebrity and the Imaging of Garrick', www. folger.edu, accessed 15 June 2012.

Mead Johnson, Edward, *Francis Cotes* (Oxford: Phaidon, 1976).

Millar, Oliver, *Later Georgian Pictures in the Collection of Her Majesty the Queen*, 2 vols (London: Phaidon Press, 1969).

Millar, Oliver, 'Portraiture and the Country House', in Gervase Jackson-Stops (ed.), *The Treasure Houses of Britain: Five Hundred Years of Private Patronage and Art Collecting* (New Haven and London: Yale University Press, 1985).

Mingay, G.E., *English Landed Society in the Eighteenth Century* (London: Routledge and Kegan Paul, 1963).

Mitchell, Charles, 'Zoffany's *Death of Captain Cook*', *Burlington Magazine*, 84:492 (March 1944), 56–63.

Moir, Esther, *The Discovery of Britain: The English Tourists, 1540–1840* (London: Routledge and Kegan Paul, 1964).

Moore, Andrew, *Norfolk and the Grand Tour* (Norwich: Norfolk Museums Service, 1985).

Moore, Andrew, *Dutch and Flemish Painting in Norfolk* (London: Her Majesty's Stationery Office, 1988).

Moore, Andrew (ed.), *Houghton Hall, The Prime Minister, the Empress and the Heritage* (London: Philip Wilson, 1996).

Moore, Andrew and Charlotte Crawley, *Family and Friends: A Regional Survey of British Portraiture* (London: Her Majesty's Stationery Office, 1992).

Morgan, Margery, 'Katherine Read: A Woman Painter in Romney's London',

Transactions of the Romney Society, 4 (1999), 12–17.
Morley, John, *The Making of the Royal Pavilion, Brighton* (London: Philip Wilson for Sotheby Publications, 1984).
Muilman, Paul, *A New and Complete History of Essex*, 6 vols (Chelmsford: M. Hassall, 1769–72).
The Muse's Delight: or, the Songster's Jovial Companion. Being a Collection of Three Hundred of the Most Celebrated New Songs, Sung at Several Societies of Choice Spirits (London, Bristol, Darlington and Salop: J. Pridden, J. Teast, W. Thorne, and J. Eddows and S. Price, 1760).
Myers, R. and M. Harris (eds), *Property of a Gentleman: The Formation, Organisation and Dispersal of the Private Library* (Winchester: St Paul's Bibliographies, 1991).
Myrone, Martin, *Bodybuilding: Reforming Masculinities in British Art 1750–1810* (New Haven and London: Yale University Press, 2005).
Myrone, Martin and Michael Rosenthal (eds), *Gainsborough* (London: Tate Publishing, 2002).
National Portrait Gallery, *The Art of the Picture Frame*, 'British Picture Framemakers, 1630–1950', s.v. 'Peter Babell', www.npg.org.uk/research/conservation/directory-of-british-framemakers/b.php, accessed 20 July 2012.
Noble, C. and Alison Yarrington, '"Like a poet's dreams": The Redisplay of the 6th Duke of Devonshire's Sculpture Gallery at Chatsworth', *Apollo*, 170:570 (November 2009), 46–53.
Nussbaum, Felicity A., *'The brink of all we hate': English Satires on Women 1660–1750* (Lexington, KY: University Press of Kentucky, 1984).
Nussbaum, Felicity, *Rival Queens: Actresses, Performance and the Eighteenth Century British Theater* (Philadelphia: University of Pennsylvania Press, 2010).
Oliver, A. (ed.), *The Journal of Samuel Curwen, Loyalist*, 2 vols (Cambridge, MA: Harvard University Press, 1972).
'On the Present State of America, and General Braddock's Defeat', *The London Magazine; or, Gentleman's Monthly Intelligencer: For April 1756* (London: R. Baldwin, 1756).
Oppé, A.P., *English Drawings, Stuart and Georgian Periods, in the Collection of His Majesty the King at Windsor Castle* (London: Phaidon Press, 1950).
Orr, Clarissa Campbell, 'Countesses and Courtesans', *History Workshop Journal*, 61 (2006), 278–92.
Ousby, Ian, *The Englishman's England: Taste, Travel and the Rise of Tourism* (Cambridge and New York: Cambridge University Press, 1990).
Ovid, *A New Translation of Ovid's Metamorphoses into English Prose* (London: Printed for J. Robinson, [etc.], 1759; first published 1748).
Pagan, H., 'Andreas Fountaine Eques Auratus A.A.A.F. III Vir', *British Numismatic Journal*, 63 (1993), 114–22.
Paget, Julian, *Second to None: Coldstream Guards 1650–2000* (Barnsley: Pen & Sword Books, 2000).
Pallasmaa, Juhani, *The Eyes of the Skin: Architecture and the Senses*, pref. Stephen Holl, 2nd edn (Chichester: Wiley, 2005).
Panofsky, Erwin, *Meaning in the Visual Arts* (New York: Doubleday Anchor

Books, 1955).
Parissien, S., J. Harris and H. Colvin, 'Narford Hall, Norfolk', *Georgian Group Report and Journal* (1987), 49–61.
Parliament of Great Britain, *An Act for Vesting Divers Manors, Lands, and Hereditaments, Part of the Settled Estate of Francis Blake Delaval Esquire, in Trustees, for Raising Money to pay off and Discharge several Debts and Incumbrances; and for other Purposes therein Mentioned* (London, 1756).
'A particular Account of the grand Masquerade-Ball given by the King of Denmark', in *The Ladies' own Memorandum-book; or, Daily Pocket Journal, for the Year 1769. Designed as a Methodical Register of all their Transactions of Business, as well as Amusement* (London: Robinson and Roberts; Newcastle: T. Slack, [1769]).
Pears, lain, *The Discovery of Painting: The Growth of Interest in the Arts in England, 1680–1768* (New Haven and London: Yale University Press for the Paul Mellon Centre for Studies in British Art, 1988).
Penny, Nicholas (ed.), *Reynolds* (London: Tate Publishing, 1985).
Perry, Gill, 'The Spectacle of the Muse: Exhibiting the Actress at the Royal Academy', in David Solkin (ed.), *Art on The Line: The Royal Academy Exhibitions at Somerset House, 1780–1836* (New Haven and London: Yale University Press for the Paul Mellon Centre for Studies in British Art and the Courtauld Institute Gallery, 2001).
Perry, Gill, *Spectacular Flirtations* (New Haven and London: Yale University Press, 2007).
Perry, Gill (ed.), *The First Actresses* (London: National Portrait Gallery, 2011).
Phillips, Winifred V., *Wanstead through the Ages*, 2nd edn (London: Vawser & Wiles, 1949).
Piercy, John William, *An Epistle to the Right Honourable John, Earl of Sandwich, &c. or, the British Hero Displayed. A Poem* (London: J. Rivington and Sons, H. Payne and J. Deighton, 1780).
Pine, L.G., *The New Extinct Peerage, 1884–1971: Containing Extinct, Abeyant, Dormant and Suspended Peerages With Genealogies and Arms* (London: Heraldry Today, 1972).
Pointon, Marcia, *Hanging the Head: Portraiture and Social Formation in Eighteenth-Century England* (New Haven and London: Yale University Press for the Paul Mellon Centre for Studies in British Art, 1993).
Pointon, Marcia, *Strategies for Showing: Women, Possession and Representation in English Visual Culture, 1665–1800* (Oxford: Oxford University Press, 1997).
Pointon, Marcia, 'Portrait! Portrait!! Portrait!!!', in David Solkin (ed.), *Art on The Line: The Royal Academy Exhibitions at Somerset House, 1780–1836* (New Haven and London: Yale University Press for the Paul Mellon Centre for Studies in British Art and the Courtauld Institute Gallery, 2001).
Pointon, Marcia, '"Surrounded with Brilliants": Miniature Portraits in Eighteenth-Century England', *Art Bulletin*, 83:1 (March 2001), 48–71.
Port, M.H., 'West End Palaces: The Aristocratic Town House in London, 1730–1830', *London Journal*, 20:1 (1995), 17–46.
Port, M.H., 'Town House and Country House: Their Interaction', in Dana Arnold (ed.), *The Georgian Country House: Architecture, Landscape and Society*

(Stroud: Sutton, 1998).
Posner, Donald, 'The "Duchesse de Velours" and Her Daughter: A Masterpiece by Nattier and Its Historical Context', *Metropolitan Museum Journal*, 31 (1996), 131–44.
Postle, Martin (ed.), *Joshua Reynolds: The Creation of Celebrity* (London: Tate Publishing, 2005).
Postle, Martin (ed.), *Johan Zoffany RA: Society Observed* (New Haven and London: Yale University Press, 2011).
Praz, Mario, *Conversation Pieces: A Survey of the Informal Group Portrait in Europe and America* (London: Methuen, 1971).
Price, Diana, 'Reconsidering Shakespeare's Monument', *Review of English Studies*, New Series, 48:190 (May 1997), 168–82.
Price, Richard, *British Society 1680–1880: Dynamism, Containment and Change* (Cambridge: Cambridge University Press, 1999).
Proposal for erecting a monument, on Eston-Nab, in Cleveland, in memory of the celebrated navigator, Capt. James Cooke (Stockton: Christopher and Jennett, 1811).
Pullan, Ann, 'Public Goods or Private Interests? The British Institution in the Early Nineteenth Century', in Andrew Hemingway and William Vaughan (eds), *Art in Bourgeois Society, 1790–1850* (Cambridge and New York: Cambridge University Press, 1998).
Raven, James, 'The Representation of Philanthropy and Reading in the Eighteenth-century Library', *Libraries and Culture*, 31:2 (1996), 492–510.
Retford, Kate, 'Reynolds's Portrait of Mrs Theresa Parker: A Case Study in Context', *British Art Journal*, 4:3 (2003), 80–6.
Retford, Kate, 'Sensibility and Genealogy in the Eighteenth-Century Family Portrait: The Collection at Kedleston Hall', *Historical Journal*, 46:3 (2003), 533–60.
Retford, Kate, *The Art of Domestic Life: Family Portraiture in Eighteenth-Century England* (New Haven and London: Yale University Press for the Paul Mellon Centre for Studies in British Art, 2006).
Retford, Kate, 'Patrilineal Portraiture? Gender and Genealogy in the Eighteenth-Century Country House', in John Styles and Amanda Vickery (eds), *Gender, Taste, and Material Culture in Britain and North America, 1700–1830* (New Haven and London: Yale Center for British Art and the Paul Mellon Centre for Studies in British Art, 2006).
Retford, Kate, 'From the Interior to Interiority: The Conversation Piece in Georgian England', *Journal of Design History*, 20:4 (2007), 291–307.
Retford, Kate, 'The Evidence of the Conversation Piece: Thomas Bardwell's *The Broke and Bowes Families* (1740)', *Cultural and Social History*, 7:4 (December 2010), 493–510.
Rhodes, Ebeneezer, *Peak Scenery: or Excursions in Derbyshire Made Chiefly for the Purpose of Picturesque Observation*, 2 vols (London: Longman, Hurst, Rees, Orme, and Brown, and John Murray, 1824).
Ribeiro, Aileen, *The Dress Worn at Masquerade in England, 1730–1790, and Its Relation to Fancy Dress in Portraiture* (New York: Garland, 1984).
Ribeiro, Aileen, *The Art of Dress: Fashion in England and France 1750 to 1820*

(New Haven and London: Yale University Press, 1995).
Richardson, Jonathan, *An Essay on the Theory of Painting*, 2nd edn (London: A Bettesworth, 1725).
Richardson, Jonathan, *Richardsoniana: or, Occasional reflections on the Moral Nature of Man* (London: J. Dodsley, 1776).
Ricoeur, P., *Memory, History, Forgetting*, trans. K. Blamey and D. Pellauer (Chicago and London: University of Chicago Press, 2004).
Rizzo, Betty, *Companions without Vows: Relationships among Eighteenth-Century British Women* (Athens, GA: University of Georgia Press, 1994).
Roberts, William, *Memoirs of the Life and Correspondance of Hannah More*, 2nd edn, 4 vols (London: R.B. Seeley and W. Burnside, 1834).
Robinson, J.M., 'Ancestral Piety', in Donald Garstang (ed.), *The British Face: A View of Portraiture 1625–1850* (London: P.&D. Colnaghi, 1986).
Robinson, John Martin, *Temples of Delight: Stowe Landscape Gardens* (Andover: Pitkin in association with The National Trust, 1994).
Roethlisberger, Marcel and Renée Loche, *Liotard: Catalogue, sources et correspondance*, 2 vols (Doornspijk: Davaco, 2008).
Rojek, Chris, *Celebrity* (London: Reaktion, 2001).
Rosenfeld, Myra Nan, *Largillierre and the Eighteenth-Century Portrait* (Montreal: Montreal Museum of Fine Arts, [c.1982]).
Rosenthal, Angela, 'Kauffman and Portraiture', in Wendy Wassyng Roworth (ed.), *Angelica Kauffman: A Continental Artist in Georgian England* (London: Reaktion Books, 1992).
Rosenthal, Angela, *Angelica Kauffman: Art and Sensibility* (New Haven and London: Yale University Press, 2006).
Rosenthal, Michael, *The Art of Thomas Gainsborough* (New Haven and London: Yale University Press for the Paul Mellon Centre for Studies in British Art, 1999).
Rosenthal, Michael, 'Public Reputation and Image Control in Late Eighteenth-Century Britain', *Visual Culture in Britain*, 7:2 (Winter, 2006), 79–86.
Røstvig, M.S., *The Happy Man: Studies in the Metamorphoses of a Classical Ideal*, 2 vols (Oslo: Norwegian Universities Press, 1954).
Royal Academy of Arts, *Citizens and Kings: Portraits in the Age of Revolution, 1760–1830* (London: Royal Academy of Arts, 2007).
Russell, F., 'A Collection Transformed', *Apollo*, 169:567 (21 June 2009), 48–55.
Russell, Francis, 'The Hanging and Display of Pictures, 1700–1850', in Gervase Jackson-Stops, et al. (eds), *The Fashioning and Functioning of the British Country House* (Washington DC: National Gallery of Art, 1989).
Rybczynski, Witold, *Home: A Short History of an Idea* (London: Penguin Books, 1986).
Sackville-West, Robert, *Knole, Kent* (The National Trust, 2006).
Sackville-West, Robert, *Inheritance* (London: Walker & Company, 2010).
Sackville-West, Vita, *Knole and the Sackvilles* (New York: George H. Doran, 1922).
Salmond, Anne, *The Trial of the Cannibal Dog: Captain Cook in the South Seas* (London: Allen Lane, 2003).

Samwell, David, *The Death of Captain Cook and Other Writings*, ed. Martin Fitzpatrick, Nicholas Thomas and Jennifer Newell (Cardiff: University of Wales Press, 2007).
Sartin, Stephen, 'Arthur Devis: His Life and Art', in John Hayes and Stephen Sartin (eds), *Polite Society by Arthur Devis, 1712–1787* (Preston and London: Harris Museum and Art Gallery, 1983).
Scarisbrick, Diana, 'Gem Connoisseurship: The 4th Earl of Carlisle's Correspondence with Francesco de Ficoroni and Antonio Maria Zanetti', *Burlington Magazine*, 129:1,007 (February 1987), 90–104.
Scott, Jonathan, *The Pleasures of Antiquity: British Collectors of Greece and Rome* (New Haven and London: Yale University Press for the Paul Mellon Centre for Studies in British Art, 2003).
Seward, Anna, *Elegy on Captain Cook. To which is Added, an Ode to the Sun. By Miss Seward* (London: J. Dodsley, 1780).
Shaw, Stebbing, 'A Tour to the West of England, in 1788' (London, 1789), in John Pinkerton, *A General Collection of the best and most interesting Voyages and Travels in all Parts of the World*, 17 vols (London: Longman, Hurst, Rees, and Orme, 1808–14).
Shawe-Taylor, Desmond, *The Georgians: Eighteenth-Century Portraiture and Society* (London: Barrie & Jenkins, 1990).
Shawe-Taylor, Desmond, *The Conversation Piece: Scenes from Fashionable Life* (London: The Royal Collection, 2009).
Simon, Jacob, *The Art of the Picture Frame: Artists, Patrons and the Framing of Portraits in Britain* (London: National Portrait Gallery, 1996).
Sloan, Kim, *A Noble Art: Amateur Artists and Drawing Masters c.1600–1800* (London: British Museum Press, 2000).
Sloman, Susan, *Gainsborough in Bath* (New Haven and London: Yale University Press for the Paul Mellon Centre for Studies in British Art, 2002).
Smailes, Helen, '"Uno sfortunato scultore Scozzese chiamato Campbell": The Correspondence of Thomas Campbell (1791–1858) and His Banking Maecenas, Gilbert Innes of Stow (1751–1831)', *Walpole Society*, 71 (2009), 217–323.
Smart, Alastair, *Allan Ramsay: A Complete Catalogue of his Paintings*, ed. John Ingamells (New Haven and London: Yale University Press for the Paul Mellon Centre for Studies in British Art, 1999).
Smiles, Sam (ed.), *Sir Joshua Reynolds: The Acquisition of Genius* (Bristol: Sansom, 2009).
Smith, Adam, *The Theory of Moral Sentiments*, 2nd edn (London: A. Millar; Edinburgh: A. Kincaid and J. Bell, 1761).
Smith, Bernard, *European Vision and the South Pacific* (New Haven and London: Yale University Press, 1985).
Smith, J.T., *Nollekens and His Times* (London: Century, 1986).
Smollett, Tobias George, *The History of England*, 6 vols (London: R. Scholey, [etc.]; Edinburgh: J. Ballantyne & Co., 1810–11).
Snodin, Michael (ed.), *Rococo: Art and Design in Hogarth's England* (London: Trefoil Books, 1984).

Solkin, D.H., 'Great Pictures or Great Men? Reynolds, Male Portraiture, and the Power of Art', *Oxford Art Journal*, 9:2 (1986), 42–9.
Solkin, David, *Painting for Money: The Visual Arts and the Public Sphere in Eighteenth-Century England* (New Haven and London: Yale University Press for the Paul Mellon Centre for Studies in British Art, 1992).
Speck, W.A., *Stability and Strife: England, 1714–1760* (London: Edward Arnold, 1977).
Spencer, Charles, *The Spencer Family* (London: Viking, 1999).
Stanhope, Philip, 4th Earl of Chesterfield, *Letters of Philip Dormer Fourth Earl of Chesterfield to his Godson and Successor*, ed. the Earl of Carnarvon, 2nd edn (Oxford: Clarendon Press, 1890).
Stanworth, Karen, 'Picturing a Personal History: The Case of Edward Onslow', *Art History*, 16:3 (1993), 408–23.
Stephens, Frederic George and Mary Dorothy George, *A Catalogue of Prints and Drawings in the British Museum: Division I. Personal and Political Satires*, 11 vols (London: Chiswick Press by order of the Trustees of the British Museum, 1870–1954).
Stewart, J. Douglas, *Sir Godfrey Kneller and the English Baroque Portrait* (Oxford: Oxford University Press, 1983).
Stewart, Philip and Jean Vaché (eds), *Collected Writings of Jean-Jacques Rousseau, Julie, or The New Héloïse* (London and Hanover: University Press of New England, 1987).
Stewart, Rachel, *The Town House in Georgian London* (New Haven and London: Yale University Press, 2009).
Stott, Anne, *Hannah More: The First Victorian* (Oxford: Oxford University Press, 2004).
Stourhead, Wiltshire (London: National Trust, 1997).
Stow: the gardens of the Right Honourable the Lord Viscount Cobham (London: B. Seeley, [1751]).
Stowe. A Description of the house and gardens of the most noble & puissant prince, George Grenville-Nugent-Temple Marquis of Buckingham (Buckingham: J. Seeley, 1797).
Straub, Kristina, *Sexual Suspects: Eighteenth Century Players and Sexual Ideology* (Oxford and Princeton: Princeton University Press, 1992).
Strobel, Heidi, 'Royal "Matronage" of Women Artists in the Late Eighteenth Century', *Women's Art Journal* 26:2 (2005–6), 3–9.
Stutchbury, H.E., *Architecture of Colen Campbell* (Cambridge, MA: Harvard University Press, 1967).
Styles, John and Amanda Vickery (eds), *Gender, Taste, and Material Culture in Britain and North America, 1700–1830* (New Haven and London: Yale Center for British Art and the Paul Mellon Centre for Studies in British Art, 2006).
Suzuki, Mihoko, 'Anne Clifford and the Gendering of History', *CLIO: A Journal of Literature, History and Philosophy*, 30:2 (Winter, 2001), 195–229.
Tadmor, Naomi, *Family and Friends in Eighteenth Century England: Household, Kinship, and Patronage* (Cambridge: Cambridge University Press, 2001).
Tague, Ingrid H., *Women of Quality: Accepting and Contesting Ideals of Femininity*

in England, 1690–1760 (Woodbridge: The Boydell Press, 2002).
Tegg, William, *A Sketch of Wanstead Park, and of the House which Formerly Stood there* (London: Tegg, [c.1882]).
Thomas, Nicholas, *Discoveries: The Voyages of Captain Cook* (London: Allen Lane, 2003).
Thompson, F.M.L., *English Landed Society in the Nineteenth Century* (London: Routledge, 1963).
Thomson, James, *The Seasons*, ed. James Sambrook (Oxford and New York: Clarendon Press and Oxford University Press, 1981).
Tilley, Christopher, *A Phenomenonology of Landscape: Places, Paths and Monuments* (Oxford: Berg, 1994).
Tillyard, Stella, 'Paths of Glory: Fame and the Public in Eighteenth-Century London', in Martin Postle (ed.), *Joshua Reynolds: The Creation of Celebrity* (London: Tate Publishing, 2005).
Tinniswood, Adrian, *A History of Country House Visiting: Five Centuries of Tourism and Taste* (Oxford: Basil Blackwell in association with The National Trust, 1989).
Tobin, Beth Fowkes, *Picturing Imperial Power: Colonial Subjects in Eighteenth-century British Painting* (Durham, NC and London: Duke University Press, 1999).
Toynbee, Paget (ed.), 'Horace Walpole's Journals of Visits to Country Seats', *Walpole Society*, 16 (1927–28), 9–80.
Turner Smith, Charlotte, *Celestina: A Novel* (London: T. Cadell, 1791).
Vandervell, Anthony and Charles Coles, *Game and the English Landscape: The Influence of the Chase on Sporting Art and Scenery* (London: Debrett's Peerage, 1980).
Vertue, George, 'Notebooks', *Walpole Society*, 22 (1933–34).
Vickery, Amanda, *The Gentleman's Daughter: Women's Lives in Georgian England* (New Haven and London: Yale University Press, 2003; first published 1998).
Voyage to the Pacific Ocean. Undertaken by command of His Majesty for making discoveries in the Northern Hemisphere. Performed under the Directions of Captains Cook, Clerke, and Gore. In His Majesty's ships the Resolution and Discovery; in the years 1776, 1777, 1778, 1779 and 1780. In Three Volumes. Vol. I and II written by Captain James Cook, F. R. S. Vol. III by Captain James King, L. L. D. and F. R. S. (London: G. Nicol and T. Cadell, 1785).
Walkley, Giles, *Artists' Houses in London: 1764–1914* (Aldershot: Scolar Press, 1994).
Walpole, Horace, *Anecdotes of painting in England; with some account of the principal artists; and incidental notes on other arts; collected by the late Mr. George Vertue; and now digested and published from his original MSS*, 4 vols (Twickenham: printed by Thomas farmer at Strawberry Hill, 1762).
Walpole, Horace, *A Description of the Villa of Mr Horace Walpole at Strawberry Hill near Twickenham* extra- illustrated copy (London: printed by Thomas Kirgate, 1784).
Walpole, Horace, *The Letters of Horace Walpole, Earl of Orford: Including Numerous Letters Now First Published From the Original Manuscripts*, ed. J.

Wright and George Agar-Ellis Dover, 1st Baron Dover, 6 vols (London: Richard Bentley, 1840).
Walpole, Horace, 'Journals of Visits to Country Seats', *Walpole Society*, 16 (1927–28), 9–80.
Walpole, Horace, *Correspondence*, ed. W.S. Lewis, 48 vols (New Haven and London: Yale University Press, 1937–83).
Wanstead House, Essex. Magnificent Furniture, Collection of Fine Paintings and Sculpture, Massive Silver and Gilt Plate, Splendid Library of Choice Books, The Valuable Cellars of Fine-Flavoured Old Wines, Ales, &c., &c. (London: J. Brettell, 1822).
Watelet, Claude Henry, *L'Art du peindre: Poëme* (Paris, 1760).
Waterfield, Giles, 'The Town House as Gallery of Art', *London Journal*, 20:1 (1995), 47–66.
Waterfield, Giles (ed.), *Palaces of Art: Art Galleries in Britain 1790–1990* (London: Dulwich Picture Gallery, 1991).
Waterhouse, E.K., 'The Exhibition of Portraits from Althorp at Messrs. Agnews', *Burlington Magazine*, 89:528 (March 1947), 77.
Waterhouse, Ellis, *Painting in Britain 1530 to 1790*, 4th edn (Harmondsworth: Penguin Books, 1978).
Weatherill, Lorna, *Consumer Behaviour and Material Culture in Britain 1660–1760*, 2nd edn (London and New York: Routledge, 1996).
Webster, Mary, *Johan Zoffany RA, 1733–1810* (New Haven and London: Yale University Press, 2011).
West, Shearer, 'Patronage and Power: The Role of the Portrait in Eighteenth-Century England', in Jeremy Black and Jeremy Gregory (eds), *Culture, Politics and Society in Britain, 1660–1800* (Manchester: Manchester University Press, 1991).
West, Shearer, 'Framing Hegemony: Economics, Luxury and Family Continuity in the Country House Portrait', in Paul Duro (ed.), *The Rhetoric of the Frame: Essays on the Boundaries of the Artwork* (Cambridge: Cambridge University Press, 1996).
West, Susie, 'Studies and Status: Spaces for Books in Seventeenth-century Penshurst Place, Kent', *Transactions of the Cambridge Bibliographical Society*, 22 (2002), 266–92.
Wheeler, Richard, 'Captain Cook's Long Journey to Elysium', *Apollo*, 160:513 (November 2004), 78–81.
Whitley, William T., *Artists and Their Friends in England, 1700–1799*, 2 vols (London and Boston: The Medici Society, 1928).
Williams, Helen Maria, *The Morai. An Ode*, App. 2 in Andrew Kippis, *Narrative of the Voyages Round the World, Performed by Captain James Cook. With an Account of his Life during the previous and intervening periods* (London: J. F. Dove, 1788).
Williams, Raymond, *The Country and the City* (New York: Oxford University Press, 1973).
Wilson, Kathleen, *The Sense of the People: Politics, Culture and Imperialism in England, 1715–1785* (Cambridge: Cambridge University Press, 1998).
Wilson, R. and A. Mackley, *Creating Paradise: The Building of the English*

Country House, 1660–1880 (London: Hambledon and London, 2000).
Wilson, R.E., 'Notes on the Howards of Effingham', in *Transactions of the Historical Society Volume Seven: 1951–1957* (Sheffield: J.W. Northend, 1957).
Wilton, Andrew, *The Swagger Portrait: Grand Manner Portraiture in Britain from Van Dyck to Augustus John, 1630–1930* (London: Tate Gallery, 1992).
Woodbridge, Kenneth, *Landscape and Antiquity: Aspects of English Culture at Stourhead 1718 to 1838* (Oxford: Clarendon Press, 1970).
Woolf, Virginia, *Orlando* (Ware, Hertfordshire: Wordsworth Editions, 2003).
Yarrington, Alison., 'Anglo-Italian Attitudes: Chantrey and Canova', in Cinzia Sicca and Alison Yarrington (eds), *The Lustrous Trade: Material Culture and the History of Sculpture in England and Italy c. 1700–c. 1860* (London: Leicester University Press, 2000).
Yarrington, Alison, 'Turisti britannici a Carrara nella prima metà dell'Ottocento', in Sandra Berresford (ed.), *'Sognando il marmo': Cultura e commercio del marmo tra Carrara, Gran Bretagna e Impero (1820– 1920 circa)* (Pacini Editore, 2009).
Yarrington, Alison, '"Under Italian Skies": The 6th Duke of Devonshire, Canova and the Formation of the Sculpture Gallery at Chatsworth House', *Journal of Anglo-Italian Studies*, 10:1 (2009), 41–62.
Yarrington, Alison, 'Christopher Hewetson: Sculpture, Commerce and Sociability in Rome', in Maria Dolorez Sanchez-Jauregui and Scot Wilcox (eds), *The English Prize: The Capture of the Westmorland. An Episode of the Grand Tour* (New Haven and London: Yale University Press, 2012).
Yarrington, Alison, I.D. Lieberman, A. Potts and M. Baker, 'An Edition of the Ledger of Sir Francis Chantrey, R.A, at the Royal Academy, 1809–1841', *Walpole Society*, 56 (1991–92).
Yorkshire Marriage Registers: West Riding, ed. C.S. James (London: issued to the subscribers by Phillimore & Co., 1914).
Young, Arthur, *A Six Weeks Tour, through the Southern Counties of England and Wales*, 2nd edn (London: W. Strahan, W. Nicoll, 1769).

Newspapers and periodicals

British Gazette and Sunday Monitor.
Daily Journal.
Gazetteer and Daily Advertiser.
General Advertiser and Morning Intelligencer.
General Evening Post.
Grub Street Journal.
Guardian.
Lloyd's Evening Post and British Chronicle.
London Chronicle.
London Evening Post.
Morning Chronicle.
Morning Herald.
Morning Post.
Public Advertiser.
St James's Chronicle.
The Times.
Warwick Times.
Westminster Magazine.
Whitehall Evening Post.
World.

Unpublished sources

Manuscripts

Althorp papers, British Library, London.

Howard, Katherine, Countess of Effingham to Mr Ingram, 18 April 1790, photocopy of an unidentified published source, Papers Relating to the Earl of Effingham, John Goodchild Collection, Wakefield.

Howard, Katherine, Countess of Effingham to Susanna Hussey Delaval, 9 November 1766, Social Letters, Seaton Delaval Manuscripts, Northumberland Archives, Woodhorn Museum, Northumberland.

Howard, Katherine, Countess of Effingham to Susanna Hussey Delaval, 24 May 1768, Social Letters, Seaton Delaval Manuscripts, Northumberland Archives, Woodhorn Museum, Northumberland.

'Inventory of Goods at Donnington House', undated (before 1799), Huntington Library, San Marino, Hastings MS Inventories 3, fo. 28.

'An Inventory of Household Goods and Furniture at Donington Park taken the 9th day of Decemb. 1788', Huntington Library, San Marino, Hastings MS Inventories 3, fo. 8.

'Long vs Phipps: An Inventory of the Household Furniture, Linen, China, Glass, Books, Wines and Effects of the late Sir James Tylney Long Bart deceased at Wanstead House in the County of Essex. Febry 1795', National Archives, C111/215, fo. 21.

Northumberland, Duchess of, 'Diaries', Alnwick Castle, Northumberland, MS 121/4.

'Paintings, Drawings and Prints (the Earl of Dysart) Ham House', c.1820, British Library, London, Additional MS 2817.

Pond, Arthur, 'Account of the Receipts 1734–1750', British Library, London, Additional MS 23724.

'Schedule of Pictures at Stourhead as left by Henry Hoare', c.1785, Wiltshire and Swindon History Centre, Trowbridge Stourhead Archive, T(ST)383/9.

Townshend, George, 4th Viscount Townshend to Lady Ann Townshend, British Library, London, MS Letters (typescript Correspondence) of Ann, Lady Townshend, Blakeney Collection, Additional MS 63110.

Theses and conference papers

Hallett, Mark, 'Pall-Mall Pastoral: Sir Joshua Reynolds, Celebrity and Sensibility', paper presented at the Centre for Eighteenth Century Studies Research Seminar, York (4 December 2007).

Jeffery, Sally, 'The Gardens of Wanstead House', in Katherine Myers (ed.), 'The Gardens of Wanstead: Proceedings of a Study Day held at the Temple, Wanstead Park, Greater London' (25 September 1999).

Lee, Quincy, 'A Catalogue of British Old Master Paintings in the Collection of the Louisiana State University Museum of Art' (MA thesis, Louisiana State University, 2009).

Scobie, Ruth, 'The Many Deaths of Captain Cook: A Study in Metropolitan Mass Culture, 1780–1810' (PhD dissertation, University of York, 2013).
Vibert, Jordan, 'Women, Portraiture and Political Representation, 1765–1787' (PhD dissertation, University of York, 2011).
West, Susie, 'The Development of the Library in Norfolk Country Houses, 1660–1830' (PhD dissertation, University of East Anglia, 2001).

Internet sources

Dukes of Buckingham and Chandos; Stowe, Christie's 15 August – 30 September 1848, Lot 192, www.dukesofbuckingham.org.uk/places/stowe/1848_sale/family_portraits, accessed 8 June 2012.
National Maritime Museum, 'Memorial: M1675', *Maritime Memorials: Commemorating Seafarers and Victims of Maritime Disasters*, www.nmm.ac.uk/memorials, accessed 1 September 2011.
Oxford Dictionary of National Biography, Oxford University Press, 2004; www.oxforddnb.com/
'Thorpe Hall, Middleton Lane', *Leodis: A Photographic Archive of Leeds*, www.leodis.org/display.aspx?resourceIdentifier=200568_34081668, accessed 16 August, 2011.

Index

Page numbers in *italics* refer to illustrations. An 'n.' after a page number indicates the number of the note on that page. 'Pl. refers to the number of a plate in the Plates section. Works of art can be found under artists' names